"You'll be all right — you'll be among friends."
[Bechuanaland will become Botswana when it achieves Independence on September 30]

(Source: *Punch* Magazine, 3 August 1966, page 169)

Very Brave or Very Foolish?
Memoirs of an African Democrat

Quett Ketumile Joni Masire

Edited by Stephen R. Lewis, Jr.

MACMILLAN

Very Brave or Very Foolish?
Memoirs of an African Democrat

© Quett Ketumile Joni Masire 2006
© Illustration and design Macmillan Botswana Publishing Co (Pty) Ltd 2006

All rights reserved. No part of this publication may be reproduced,
stored in a retrieval system, or transmitted in any form
or by any means, electronic, photocopying, recording,
or otherwise, without the prior written permission of the
copyright holder or in accordance with the provisions
of the Copyright Act, 1965.
Any person who does any unauthorised act in relation to this
publication may be liable for criminal prosecution and civil
claims for damages.

First published 2006

06 08 10 09 07
1 3 5 7 9 10 8 6 4 2 0

Published by
Macmillan Botswana Publishing Co (Pty) Ltd
P O Box 1155, Gaborone, Botswana

Typeset in 10 on 12pt Palatino by The Setting Stick
Cover design by Gerry Guy
Cover photo provided by the Department of Information and Broadcasting
Illustrations by Deevine Design

ISBN 10: 99912 404 89
ISBN 13: 978 99912 404 80
WIP 1389.000 (P)

Printed and bound by Pinetown Printers

The publishers have made every effort to trace copyright
materials, but if they have inadvertently overlooked any,
they will be happy to make the necessary arrangements at
the first opportunity.

Contents

List of Illustrations and Maps vi

Editor's Note vii

Prologue – A Reluctant Politician ix

Part I – My Life Before Politics

1. Growing Up 1
2. Teacher, Farmer, Journalist, Husband 13
3. Chief Bathoen II and My Views on Chieftainship 24

Part II – Politics: Creating and Leading a Nation

4. Early Politics and Legco 30
5. Race and Race Relations 42
6. The Botswana Democratic Party 48
7. Creating a Nation 61
8. Selecting the Talent and Leading the Government 83
9. Working with Seretse Khama 103
10. Opposition Parties 110
11. Politics and Elections after 1965 123

Part III – Developing the Nation and Our People

12. Managing Economic Development 146
13. Economic Strategies and Programmes 168
14. Land and Cattle 183
15. Diamonds and Other Minerals 199
16. Economic Opportunities and Disparities 216

Part IV – Dealing with Our Neighbours and Other States

17. Relations with South Africa during Apartheid 246
18. Making Our Way in Southern Africa 274
19. Diplomacy, the Great Powers and the United Nations 297

Part V – Personal Matters

20. Family Man, Farmer and President 317

Postscript 329

Abbreviations 331

Bibliography 334

Index 336

List of Illustrations and Maps

Frontispiece "You'll be all right-you'll be among friends."
              From *Punch*, 1966

Map of Botswana showing land use at independence 41

Tsholetsa Domkrag (BDP symbol) 51

Photos—Early Life and Family and Early Politics .... following 102

Map of Botswana transport network 151

Map of Botswana showing rainfall distribution 178

Map of Botswana land use, 2000 186

Photos—Late Politics .... following 198

Photo—One Man One Beast statue at University of Botswana 224

Map showing SADC member countries, 2004 280

Editor's Note

For four decades, Botswana has been one of the developing world's great success stories. Its combined record of economic growth, political vitality, avoidance of corruption, and democratic development is arguably unmatched in the developing world, despite beginnings in 1966 that could only be described as desperate. How the people of Botswana achieved all they have is a story that has not been told.

Quett Ketumile Joni Masire was one of the founders of the nation and framers of its constitution. He was the principal architect of its economic development as minister of finance and development planning. From the founding of the Bechuanaland Democratic Party in 1962, he was the close partner of Sir Seretse Khama, Botswana's first president. Following Sir Seretse's death in 1980, he served as president until 1998, when he retired from office and handed over to his vice-president, Festus Mogae. He contested seven national elections. Though he lost his own seat in Parliament in 1969, he led the Botswana Democratic Party to four national victories as its secretary and chief organiser, and three more as president.

When Sir Ketumile, as he became known after his Knighthood in 1992, retired from the presidency on 31 March 1998, I was privileged to speak on behalf of his friends at the dinner in his honour. Later that week I asked if he was planning to write his memoirs. He said: "I will if you will help me." I readily agreed. For several years, his new responsibilities in relation to the Rwanda genocide inquiry and the Inter-Congolese dialogue, and mine as a college president, prevented us from beginning. We were finally able to start in September 2002. Over the succeeding three-and-a-half years we met for four extended sessions in Botswana and a half dozen times in Europe or the US.

As Sir Ketumile and I discussed the project, we agreed that it would focus largely on the why and how of Botswana's political and economic development. Since none of Botswana's founding citizens left a memoir, it was important that Sir Ketumile set down his recollections of why he and his colleagues had made the choices they did. He said that in doing so he would not avoid difficult or controversial subjects, failures or disappointments. We outlined a series of major issues, and I also asked long time friends and colleagues what they most wanted to learn from his memoirs. This combination of topics guided us during some 65 hours of recorded conversations. I transcribed and edited them, producing drafts for Sir Ketumile to edit and correct.

The taped conversations were supplemented by countless hours of informal discussion before and during the drafting and editing process, research in the Botswana National Archives, whose staff was most helpful, and information from many secondary sources. After Sir Ketumile had reviewed and I had redrafted several times, four of his colleagues, Dr Gaositwe Chiepe, Archie Mogwe, Elijah Legwaila, and Mogolori Modisi, and his daughter, Mmasekgoa Masire-Mwamba read complete drafts and offered helpful suggestions or corrections. Gilbert Motsemme and others in the Office of the Former President in Gaborone assisted us at every stage. Janet Hermans worked with us in Gaborone to check facts, dates and names, offer editorial comments on several drafts, and select photographs. The Information Department generously assisted by providing many of the photos reproduced here. My wife, Judith Frost Lewis, read multiple drafts, and her detailed suggestions greatly improved the clarity.

A grant from the Carnegie Corporation of New York helped defray the costs of bringing Sir Ketumile and me together. The Botswana Institute for Development Policy Analysis administered the grant and provided me with office facilities when I visited Gaborone. A sabbatical grant and professional development funds from Carleton College were invaluable to my participation. The Bemis Company and its chairman, John Roe, generously provided me with office space in Minneapolis. I am grateful for the support of these organisations.

I first worked with Sir Ketumile in 1975 as economic consultant to his ministry, and from 1975 to 1987 I spent nearly half my time in Botswana. My family and I lived in Botswana twice, the second time for the first two years of his presidency. I was afforded a rare privilege and unique opportunity both during those years and again as I have helped him prepare this memoir. Over the past 30 years I have developed an appreciation and admiration for the way Botswana conducted its political and economic affairs. I also have great affection for Botswana and its citizens and have formed many close friendships there. I did not come to this project as a neutral observer and analyst. However, I hope that my 40 years as a consultant to several governments and assignments in a number of developing countries in Asia and Africa have brought a comparative perspective to the questions Sir Ketumile addressed in his memoir.

Sir Ketumile carefully read every draft; if errors have crept into the account, they should be seen as my responsibility as editor.

Stephen R. Lewis, Jr.

Minnesota, USA

April 2006

Prologue

A Reluctant Politician

In 1961 I attended a public meeting in Lobatse of the recently formed Bechuanaland People's Party (BPP). I was a journalist and editor of the monthly newspaper, *Naledi ya Botswana*. I had been interested in public affairs for some years, and I was curious about the new political party. At the end of the meeting I thought, "If these are the kinds of people who are going to lead our country, we are in trouble." So, when the late Seretse Khama called a group of us together in November of that year to propose the formation of a new party, the Bechuanaland Democratic Party (BDP), I decided that if I could be of any use to the nation, then I needed to participate in politics. But, I did not think of politics as a career, or something I would do forever—I have always been a farmer at heart.

From 1966 to 1980, I served as vice-president of Botswana, and when President Seretse Khama died in 1980, I was ready to go back to farming. However, I agreed to serve as president, since that was what my colleagues in the BDP and other Batswana wanted. In the early 1990s, having led the party to re-election in 1984 and 1989, I was again ready to retire. Regrettably, conflicts within the BDP leadership had greatly weakened the party and its ability to govern effectively. So, I stayed on as president until we could arrange for a smooth constitutional transition of leadership. On 31 March 1998, I retired as president, and the next morning my successor, Festus Mogae, was sworn in as Botswana's third president. I returned to private life for the first time in 37 years.

Over those years, Botswana was transformed. We had been a British protectorate since 1885, and we were among the poorest countries in the world. We were surrounded by racist minority regimes in Namibia, Zimbabwe and South Africa. The vast majority of our citizens who had wage employment worked not in Botswana but in South Africa in mines, factories or on farms. Tribal chiefs ruled almost all aspects of our people's lives, from when and where we could plant our crops to where we could build our homes and whether our children would be educated. There were no government schools of any kind, and fewer than eight kilometres of paved road—in a country larger than France and Belgium combined. Our administrative capital was located in South Africa in the British Imperial Reserve in Mafeking. Economic experts thought there would never be a time when Botswana would be off the international dole. Many people expected Botswana to be absorbed into South Africa, and many feared it would be. Seretse Khama and I often reminded our colleagues that when we asked for independence, everyone told us that we were "either very brave, or very foolish". That judgment is the origin of the title of these memoirs.

By the time I retired in 1998, our circumstances had changed dramatically. The World Bank calculated that Botswana achieved the highest growth rate of real income per capita of any country in the world from 1965 to 1999. Transparency International rated Botswana as having the lowest level of corruption in Africa, lower than all but one developing country, and lower than many European countries. We held multi-party elections in 1965 and 1969, and then every five years, most recently in October 2004. There have always been highly vocal opposition parties, and a vigorous independent press has developed. Botswana has achieved a reputation for principled positions and leadership in regional affairs, especially during the long struggle to liberate southern Africa from colonialism and racist white minority regimes. By 1998, all the countries that surrounded us had been transformed into independent states with democratic systems of government.

Major challenges remain, though their nature has changed. The nation suffers from one of the worst epidemics of HIV/AIDS of any country in the world. It threatens to destroy the decades of investment in our people, and the economic and human costs of combating the disease continue to mount. President Mogae is to be justly praised for his work in combating the disease. A political and economic crisis in Zimbabwe led to a new wave of refugees, both political and economic. Nearly 40 years of a rapidly expanding economy have created expectations for continued progress that almost certainly cannot be matched by future economic performance. These challenges are for the current generation of political leaders to address, and they will test the institutions and policies my colleagues and I established as we built the country and raised up the nation.

In the pages that follow, I have set out my recollections from my years as an active politician: how my colleagues and I saw our country and our options, how and why we made choices, and how we dealt with our neighbours. Politics involves people and personalities, and understanding events requires understanding the people who were participants. I have mentioned many individuals, but I have not always named those who were involved, nor have I said everything that some readers or historians might have wished. I have been guided by two aspects of our Tswana culture. One concept in Tswana law and custom is that of a "lie"; this is not something that is untrue, but it involves telling something one ought not to tell, especially if it might hurt someone. The person telling the lie might or might not be punished in the *kgotla*, but the society would look askance. The second practice in our culture is one of sometimes reporting the facts without attributing the behaviour to an individual. When asked if the story was about a particular person, the response would be: "*Mma seikubeng pina ga e go reye.*" The equivalent in English might be: "If the shoe fits, wear it."

This is not meant to be a comprehensive account or definitive history. But, I hope the present generation of Batswana will learn something of the history of our country, and how we built a new nation on the foundation of important traditions and practices in indigenous Tswana culture. Perhaps others outside Botswana will be interested in how and why we made the choices we did in political and economic policies, the new institutions of society, and how we played our role in regional and international affairs.

Chapter 1
Growing Up

I was born on 23 July 1925, the first child of Joni Masire and his wife, Gabaipone, who was of the Kgopo family. My parents named me Quett Ketumile Joni Masire. I think Masire is a good name, because it means "the protector". It is shortened from "*Masira pheho ya borwa*" (the protector against the cold from the south whose chill gets into the marrow of one's bones). As was common in our family in those days I had several names. Ketumile means "I am well known" and it was the given name of one of my mother's uncles. Quett is a shortened form of Marquette, after the 17th century French missionary and explorer, Father Jacques Marquette. This was given by another uncle, my mother's elder brother Tom Kgopo, who had an avid interest in French history and called himself "Valois" Kgopo. Joni was the given name of my father. Most of my life I was known to my friends and colleagues as Quett, and that is how I have introduced myself to others.

My parents lived in the Motebejana ward, a sub-division of the Ngwaketse tribal area, on the southern side of Kanye, where my father was the headman, as his father had been before him. A headman is a traditional leader—a sub-chief—at the ward level within a tribe. The position is hereditary; it would have come to me had I wished it. The headman could be removed by the *kgosi* (chief), but there would have to be some good reason to do so, and it seldom happened except in the case of serious disputes. The headman undertook the functions of the chief within the ward, allocating land, presiding at *kgotla* (our traditional meeting place), settling disputes and rendering judgments in civil and criminal cases.

Our ward, Goo-Motebejana, was named after my great-grandfather, who had been part of the Bahurutshe people on the South African side of the border near the present town of Motswedi. My ancestors, the Batebejana, had first been of the Bahurutshe tribe and later the Baphiring. They migrated from South Africa and came under the rule of Bangwaketse chiefs early in the 19th century. The ancestors of my chief, Bathoen II, had invited them to move to Kanye. Their family totem was the *phiri* (hyena) as a reminder of the difficult times during the migration to the Kanye area. My mother's family, the Kgopos, were direct descendants of Chief Moleta (c.1770-1790), the father of Makaba II (c.1790-1824), though they were not considered royalty. Their family totem was the *kwena* (crocodile). We became members of the Ngwaketse tribe of Botswana by virtue of our settlement there.

In the traditional hierarchy of tribes among the Batswana, the Bahurutshe were the most senior. Although they live today almost exclusively in South Africa, some are found in Botswana at Manyana, Gabane, Mmankgodi, Tonota and Makaleng. The Bahurutshe are followed in seniority by the Bakwena, the Bangwato, the Batawana, and the Bangwaketse, in that order. We Batswana tend to follow our bloodlines back in our genealogy. I used to tease the late president, Sir Seretse Khama, by telling him that despite the fact that he was a chief, he was a Mongwato, and I, having ancestors who were Bahurutshe, was therefore senior to him!

My parents were people of modest means, ploughing land and rearing some cattle. My father, Joni, was also responsible for the day-to-day running of the Rowland Brothers and Peat Trading Store in Kanye, owned by Richard Rowland, one of the more prosperous traders in the Protectorate. Only whites, Asians and coloureds (as people of mixed racial heritage were known in southern Africa), could obtain trading licenses from the colonial government. My father established his *moraka* (cattle post) at Moshaneng, and it was one of his favourite places when he was not at Rowland's store. His lands were at Tlapaneng, some 23 kilometres south of Moshaneng.

My parents were living in the compound of the Kgopo family when I was born. Three years later, my father built his house for our family in the Motebejana ward. I was followed in the family by two sisters (Gabalengwe and Morufhi) and three brothers (Basimane, also called David, Basimanyana, also called Peter, and Bontlohile).

In typical Tswana society, families would have three homes, one in the village within a ward, another at the *masimo* (lands area) where cultivation of crops took place, and a third at the *moraka* (cattle post) where cattle were kept. In this respect I was from a typical Tswana family. The extent of the three-home system can be seen in the 1971 Census: Of the 140,000 dwellings enumerated, only 98,000 were occupied; 42,000 or nearly 30%, were vacant. In *masimo*, more than 40% were vacant.

Virtually all households with able-bodied adults participated in growing crops for subsistence in the years before independence. Most households in the Protectorate also owned some cattle. Many of those who did not own cattle participated in the practice of *mafisa*, whereby they looked after the cattle owned by others.

Young boys would be at the cattle post from the time they were eight or nine until they were old enough to go to the mines in South Africa. Their task would be to look after the cattle, and, after the ploughing season, to keep the cattle from moving to the lands areas and grazing on the new crops. Men and women would move from the village to *masimo* when the chief had decided it was time to plough and plant. They would generally stay there until after crops were harvested in the winter, two or three months after the end of the rainy season. As a child growing up, I was part of these economic and cultural traditions.

When I was young, my siblings and I stayed with my maternal grandmother whenever my parents were away at the lands. In the village, we took our turns at household chores, and in the evening sat with my parents or my grandmother who told us stories, sang us songs, or held quizzes or riddle competitions. There were no radios or recorded music then, and we were left to our own devices to provide amusement. Often we would be told *dinaane*, a Tswana form of Aesop's Fables, which could be in a story form or in the form of conundrums, such as: "It is slashed but no mark is left", which would be water. Or there were riddles: "I planted it here but it came out there", which is an echo. These activities conveyed ideas and were ways of sharpening one's mind. On Sunday we went to Sunday school, followed by a main service, and our family was very regular in attendance at the London Missionary Society (LMS) church in Kanye.

From the age of eight until I was thirteen and a half years old, I grew up largely at the cattle post. Life at the cattle post was somewhat like the law of the jungle, or the survival of the fittest. The older boys protected the younger ones while at the same time expecting each young boy to pull his own weight. We enjoyed bringing someone's bull to fight another's bull, and for their amusement the older boys would encourage the younger boys to fight. One of them would say: "So-and-so has been saying nasty things about you and swearing at you, so why don't you swear at him, or even fight him—or are you afraid to do so?" And a fight would ensue. Some of the fights would start between boys just to prove who was the stronger. Sometimes the fight would be physical, and sometimes it would be by using the lash made of *moretlwa* (a bush that made strong lashes) in a game of *nxabi*. In *nxabi*, a thorn branch would be placed between the two boys, and they would exchange lashes at each other around the thorns until the weaker one gave in. It's said I was good at that game—I would just say I never ran away from anyone or gave in.

At the *moraka* the younger boys looked after the small stock (sheep and goats), and the older ones looked after cattle. At six or seven in the morning we would let the cattle out of the *kraal*, and we would collect the cows for a first milking at eight or nine. If water was a problem, we would take them to water. In the evening we would bring all the stock back to the kraal and milk the cows again. For the evening meal we would eat *logala* (porridge cooked with milk), and then we would sit around the campfire telling stories and talking until bed time.

My brothers and I had a good many adventures when we were at the cattle post together, some of which could have ended in disaster. Once my brother Basimane and I lost our bull so we went from herd to herd to look for it. It was late in the day when we started back to the cattle post. Basimane was following me, and we were talking. In the middle of our conversation, we saw a kudu. I took a shot at it with my rifle, but I missed it. As we walked further on, I suddenly landed right on top of a black mamba in the path. I was very frightened, and fortunately so was the snake. I was jumping and dancing and trying to keep myself suspended in the air! I eventually got past the snake without being bitten, and it disappeared into the bush.

On another occasion we were collecting cows for *re phokisa* (grazing the cattle before milking in the morning), and we found a trail where something had been dragging an animal. We found a python in a pile of rocks; it had just killed and swallowed a young duiker. I shot the python and killed it, and we took it home and skinned it. For the whole day, we dared not touch any utensils, since my mother had a strong aversion to touching snakes. Some months after I had killed the python, I came upon a black mamba that had swallowed a small hare. I knew that if I shot at the mamba and missed I'd lose my life; but I shot it and killed it. The independent life at the cattle post was often exciting for a boy growing up!

Early Influences
My father was not formally educated, but he was literate and could sustain a conversation in English. He became the headman in our ward after his father,

Masire-a-Sealetsa, passed away. He attended to his headman duties during weekends, afternoons and evenings. I used to sit at the *kgotla* listening to him deciding cases and giving advice to those who came to consult him, and I wondered if I would ever be that wise. He was slightly taller than average, light complexioned like his mother, and many people thought him a very handsome fellow. He was a delightful person to be with; always full of jokes irrespective of the society he interacted with. He also would be busy with his hands, since he was a jack-of-all-trades: carpenter, tailor, farmer. He had a well-developed sense of humour, and I suspect that is one of the traits I may have inherited from him. He had a good deal of drive and was an optimistic person, and he saw people as the individuals they are. I have been described as having the same traits as my father. If this is true, I would say it is just a gift of God; a case of like father, like son.

My mother's given name was Gabaipone. I was the first-born child, and since mothers and fathers are ordinarily known by pre-fixing Mma or Rra to their first-born's name, she was commonly known as Mma-Ketumile, or Mma-Quett. My mother had eight siblings—Keosele, Keafiwa, Seagiso, Nkgopolang, Tom, Keoditse, Bantsejang, and Mokome. Keosele died young, but the others lived to adulthood and raised families. All had primary education, and the eldest three went for post-primary education to Tiger Kloof in South Africa, where I later attended school. All except Keosele, Keafiwa, and my mother held clerical or teaching posts.

My mother is said to have been very lively as a girl, and was well liked as well as being the most outspoken in her family. I recall her as very sociable, a real live wire, and very hard working, whether at our village home in Kanye or at *masimo* at Tlapaneng. She had a strong work ethic, and perhaps she passed that along to me. In those days a child was expected to relieve his or her parents of some of their chores, and my mother, and no less my father, loaded a lot of the family chores on me. I was proud to shoulder some of those responsibilities for them. As a strict disciplinarian with many "don'ts", my mother would not tolerate seeing me with my hands in my pockets, which was a taboo for her. She did not spare the rod, but she could be scolding a child one minute and talking tenderly to the same child the next. She loved to sing hymns or to hum them while she was working, and she was a very good singer. She could talk about me openly as a clever boy, but she did not have a good word for me as a singer and wondered why I was in the school choir!

My grandfather, Masire-a-Sealetsa, was an important influence on me as a young boy. He was one of those who had taken Chief Bathoen II to task in the 1930s. In 1934, the resident commissioner, Colonel (later Sir) Charles Rey, had introduced two proclamations. The proclamations established tribal councils to assist *dikgosi* (chiefs) in administration; made the selection of chiefs subject to approval of the British government; and amended the customary legal tradition to provide, among other things, for keeping proper records of decisions in customary courts. However, the proclamations were seen by the chiefs as infringements on their rights. Tshekedi Khama, regent of the Bangwato and the uncle of Seretse Khama, and Chief Bathoen II, who was then a relatively new chief, took the resident commissioner to court, and the case was ultimately decided in favour of the resident commissioner.

My grandfather and his friends took the position that most provisions of the new proclamations, especially the establishment of tribal councils and keeping judicial records, were good ones. They had the effect of limiting the sometimes arbitrary powers of the chiefs and providing an element of democracy and regularity in tribal affairs. As a group they were called "The Petitioners", and they said: "What ho, let it be done!" to the proposed reforms. This, of course, put my grandfather in direct conflict with Chief Bathoen II. Subsequent reforms, under other resident commissioners less confrontational than Charles Rey, were actually approved by Tshekedi and Bathoen during the 1940s and 1950s.

My grandfather was a great one for naming his children by all J's. My father was Joni, and his brothers were Jameson, Justice, Jan, Jerome, Jacob and Joshua. He named me "Jupiter", but only a few people other than my grandfather used that nickname of mine.

Another influence on my thinking came from two of my father's uncles, Montshusi Batsui from Moshaneng and Gasennelwe Moswene from Motlhabang. Late in the 19th century, they farmed as other Batswana did, growing sorghum and rearing cattle. When tobacco arrived on the scene, they each decided to raise it, and they did so using hand irrigation. They produced leaf tobacco (*maswaswana*) and rolled tobacco (*togwa*), a leaf tied into a sausage shape. They would trade a small *togwa* for a goat, and a larger one for a head of cattle. They heeded the American advice: "Go west, young man." They took the tobacco into the Kgalakgadi to trade and came back with animals to build up their herds of cattle. With these cattle, they bought ox wagons and then additional teams of oxen. They carried merchandise from Mafeking throughout Botswana, starting in the south and working farther north over time. They reached as far as Bulawayo, where unfortunately their oxen died in the 1896-97 outbreak of Rinderpest. They were old men by the time I was growing up, and one lived to an age of 110 or 112. I saw in them examples of what one could do if one tried to diversify away from the traditional activities.

It was unthinkable when I was young that children could be left on their own when their parents were at the lands. There had to be an adult present, so my siblings and I stayed with our grandmother at Goora-Kgopo along with her other grandchildren. She almost ran a boarding facility. Once our mothers came back from the lands we would disperse back to our respective homes. Life with my grandmother was great—we created no problems for her, and she gave us no trouble. She was a disciplinarian, though not extravagantly so. However, if you saw a look of disapproval on her face, you knew what the right thing to do was!

My grandmother's life was exemplary in many ways. As the Kgopo family were descendants of Moleta, father of Chief Makaba the Great, half the village of Kokong were people on whom the Kgopos could call if they needed them to serve. There were other people in the village who did not have such a relationship, but whom my grandmother nonetheless felt obliged to help, so she ran a kind of social security system. Sometimes people would come to her home and say they had nothing to eat, and she would give them *mabele* (sorghum) to stamp for themselves at their homes. My brother would sometimes ask me: "How are we related to these people?" But it was simply accepted in those days that sometimes one had distant relatives who were in unfortunate circumstances and whom one looked after. My grandmother was very sympathetic—although in another sense, I suspect, she wanted everyone to remember who she was in society!

I learned from my grandmother that a person of her status, related to a royal family, not only deserved to be respected but also should behave in a manner that deserved respect. It was clear to me as I grew up that respect was a two-way street—it was something that must be deserved. Or perhaps I should say: Respect must be earned; it is not something that one should expect willy-nilly. In fact, I have often thought the problem with some chiefs and politicians is that they do not behave as they should, and therefore they do not deserve to be respected, even though they demand it of people.

Our culture has many practices that reflect the concept of *Botsadi*, courtesy and respect for one's elders. This includes how we attach prefixes to names that connect an older relative with a younger person. Since our eldest daughter is Gaone, I am known as Rra-Gaone, and my wife as Mma-Gaone; or even more respectfully, Rragwe-Gaone and Mmagwe-Gaone. The element of respect is very strong in Tswana culture, and it may explain why our political process has developed differently from that in some other countries. However, to be respectful does not mean to be subservient.

Education

I began school when I was thirteen and a half. My mother had felt strongly that I should go to school much earlier, and I suspect that my father also wanted me to go to school, but only at a ripe old age! Eventually it became a common view that I should go to school, especially as my Kgopo cousins, who were of the same age, were already far advanced in school. The Kgopos were a relatively educated family. It became a kind of social issue—it was not fair that I was not at school when my cousins were. Although my father had resisted my going to school, once I did I set the example, so he had no problem in sending my younger brothers and sisters.

My first school was the Rachele Primary School in Kanye, where I advanced quickly. When I was very young almost every man went to the mines in Johannesburg when he turned 18, so I had anticipated that I also would be a miner. There were boys in my class who were 20 or 21, many of whom later dropped out and went to Johannesburg to the mines. We also had men who had already been to the mines and who came back to begin primary school at the age of 21 or even older. They were not of any different social class, but going to the mines was something many just did in those days.

Because of my age and the fact that I did not give in easily, when I was told I was wrong in school I wanted to be shown where and why I was wrong. Perhaps one could say I was difficult and argumentative from a very early age, and the trait persisted! I pressed my teachers, particularly my uncle, Mr Kgopo Kgopo, with whom I frequently would argue in class. He would get so annoyed with me that he would leave the classroom and walk around the garden to cool off. He said I was trying to show off that I knew more than he did, but that was not the case. I just wanted to get to the root of the matter so that I could understand things better. Uncle Kgopo Kgopo and Mr William Tjamzashe, who taught me in Standard 6, were among the teachers I remember from those days. Our teachers were qualified by having a three-year teacher-training course after they had passed Standard 6 (primary school). Most students in the early standards were girls, but in the upper grades it was mainly boys who remained. Since independence that pattern has changed, there are now more girls than boys in both primary and secondary schools.

After I was in school, I started to think, well, one could do something better than being a miner. I applied myself seriously and managed to complete seven years of primary school in five years. I topped the class at the end of primary school and was awarded a government bursary (scholarship) to go to Tiger Kloof Institute in South Africa, since there were then no secondary schools in the Protectorate. I thought I should study agriculture and be a farmer, as that seemed the best way to earn a living in Bechuanaland.

My father did not see things the same way I did. My aunt and two of my uncles had gone to Tiger Kloof to do post-primary studies. Two had become teachers and one had become a civil servant and ultimately a district commissioner. My father said I should do what they had done, and either be a teacher or a clerk; or else I should take a building course. He was never keen on my taking a course in agriculture. I had a paternal uncle who had gone to Tsolo Agricultural School in the Transkei, and another distant relative had done a course in agriculture; but neither of them had anything to show for it. So, my father thought I would be just like them if I studied agriculture. But I thought perhaps he was not taking account of the different nature of the raw material!

Because of my record of achievement in primary school, my government scholarship was not only to do JC (Junior Certificate, the end of junior secondary school) and Matric (secondary school graduation) at Tiger Kloof. It also provided that I could go to Fort Hare University in the Cape Province, where I planned to do a BSc degree in Agriculture. I travelled by train in 1944 from Lobatse to Tiger Kloof Institute, a school run by the London Missionary Society seven miles south of Vryburg in the Northern Cape. Its former students had included Seretse Khama, my own Chief Bathoen II, and such future educational and political leaders as Gaositwe Chiepe and Archie Mogwe. My contemporaries at the school included Bias Mookodi, Moutlakgola Nwako and Motsamai Mpho, whom I also encountered in later life as well.

Family Responsibilities

Unfortunately, my mother died in 1944 while I was doing Form I. She loved her children, and we all loved her dearly, and we were all deeply saddened when she passed away. Two years later, my father died, and it became clear that I could not go all the way in school. Chief Bathoen had visited Tiger

Kloof to tell me how seriously ill my father was. He talked with me in very fond terms, I would say, though we later developed serious differences and mistrust that persisted through the remainder of our lives.

The loss of my parents by the time I was only 21 was profound in three ways. First, it was traumatic to lose first one and then the other parent at such a young age. Second, my father had been both harsh and loving, so he played both a father's role in firm guidance and a mother's role of consoling and comforting. This meant that, after my mother died, we still had the kind of support, discipline, love, and comfort that children need, despite the fact that we had lost our loving mother. My father was also a friend, and we deeply mourned his death. Third, as the first born in the family, I felt the burden of sheer responsibility for five younger siblings.

After the death of my father, I had to grapple with what to do with the family and our modest property. All members of the family from both the maternal and paternal sides looked to me to exercise my responsibility as the oldest son. They more or less said I should forget about further education.

There were three points to the case that my maternal and paternal uncles made that I should not to go back to school. First, and this was the most important to my paternal uncles, was for me to take the headmanship of our ward, following my father and grandfather. Second, and this was most important to my maternal uncles, was to look after my father's family. Third, and this was important to all, was to look after my father's property—his cattle and his right to cultivate on tribal land. My father was not a rich man, but he had enough to sustain us, so it would be unfortunate if it were to be lost.

The least attractive option of all to me was to be a headman. I thought it was a job my uncles could do. In fact, both Uncle Jacob and Uncle Bethel, my father's brothers, served as headmen, as later did my Uncle Frank; and now my brother, Basimane, is the headman of Motebejana ward. It was much more important to me to have an education than even to be a chief of the Bangwaketse; and to be a headman was not at all what I wished for myself. Chief Bathoen was helpful in executing my plans. The word of the chief was all that mattered at that time. If he had sided with my relatives, it would have been difficult for me to go to school, as I would have had to become a headman.

I decided I could delegate some of the responsibilities to my uncles to look after the property, the *kgotla* and my siblings, and I could keep an eye on all of them from school. I felt that while my brothers and sisters didn't need babysitting, they did need some way to make sure their future was secured. I sent my sister Gabalengwe to St. Joseph's at Kgale, south of Gaborone, and later my brother Basimane to St. Joseph's and then to Zimbabwe, and my sister Morufhi to the home craft school in Mochudi. With arrangements made, I decided there was no reason I should not go to school myself, so I went back to do Form IV.

I was bent on going the whole distance in school to graduate with a BSc in Agriculture. However, while I was doing Form IV, my brothers and sisters who were staying with other members of the family became unhappy with their arrangements. At the relatives' homes, they were subject to different types of discipline, and also they did not have the choices of foods they were used to having. For example, in our home there had always been milk to drink, and both mealie (maize) meal and sorghum porridge, as well as meat two or three times a week. I had to take their unhappiness into account, and therefore I decided to change the arrangements. I consulted the Department of Education to see if a different course of study would prejudice my scholarship. While they regretted that I couldn't go the whole way to a university degree, they thought a change could be made, since they understood my circumstances. So, I added a two-year teacher-training course and combined the first year of that course with Form V to save a full year.

Because of my attention to the details of how our lands were managed, I acquired a nickname in the family: *Molemi* (the farmer). I was demanding as the manager, and, given what today would be called my work ethic, it was virtually a punishment to work with me. My brothers objected to the ways I was doing things at *masimo* as head of the family. I had a simple way of resolving it. I told my brothers: "I know that anywhere you go you will have to work hard, whether under a South African farmer or under me. So, feel free to go; but if you stay here, you will do it my way." People complained to my maternal grandmother that I was being too hard on my siblings, and she raised the issue with me. I said to my grandmother: "There are just two choices, Granny. Either I come and see you and we talk about things other than this one subject, or I won't come at all." That seemed to settle it, since she wanted me to visit her. Over time my siblings came to regard me as a sort of a father figure. Even now my brothers and sisters won't let me stand up to get a cup of water. If I were a chief, I would even say I was revered!

Tiger Kloof

I liked my teachers at Tiger Kloof, and they made a big impression on me; and for whatever reason, they liked me too. They became my role models, and I didn't want to do anything to disappoint them. Later in life when I was talking with one of my farm managers, he asked why I was being so hard on him. I told him that sometimes when you are reprimanded it can be a better compliment than if you are complimented directly. I told him of a time I topped the class at Tiger Kloof. However, I was given very low marks according to the teacher's expectation of me. He did not say a word to the class, but afterward he scolded me for not having done better. It flattered my ego that he thought I could have done better, even though I was first in the class. One wants to live up to, or better yet to exceed, the expectations others have of one.

At Tiger Kloof I was good at all subjects except music and Afrikaans, and I had a particular interest in and aptitude for mathematics. I once asked my Afrikaans teacher: "Why should we be bothered with learning Afrikaans?" He replied: "You don't like it because you find it difficult." I told him: "I don't do well in Afrikaans because I hate it, and when I go back to Botswana I will have nothing to do with it." But later when we were dealing with the Afrikaners in the South African government, it was handy to know more than a bit of Afrikaans. From Sub-A to Form III, I always topped my class—

not in all subjects, but on average I would come out first. Only once, in Form III, was I topped by Bias Mookodi, who was later best man at my wedding and both a senior civil servant and an ambassador.

I found out many years later that I suffer badly from dyslexia. When I read, my mind transposes letters or words on a page. I discovered my own problem when our son, Mpho, was tested after he was having difficulties in school. I had always been a slow reader, but I had concluded it was because I had started school late and had thrice jumped a grade in school. In addition to difficulty reading to myself, my dyslexia is very evident when I am reading a speech in public; even though I read it slowly, I often stumble and mix up the words.

However, nature sometimes compensates for a disability or weakness, so when I read a book or a poem and find something that has a good idea, I will remember the quotation. I like to keep good expressions or phrases in mind, and somehow those stay with me. I frequently use quotations I've remembered in conversation or when I am addressing a meeting. I am fortunate to have the same ability to recall specific numbers, whether I have read or heard them. This was very useful in my years in finance, as well as in my farming ventures.

I was involved in a variety of activities at Tiger Kloof in addition to my studies: debate, beekeeping, gardening, preaching at local churches on Sundays, and serving as a prefect, including head prefect in my final year. I was not a good athlete, but I played football and ran the 220 and 440 yard sprints for my house (Moffat House), and served as the sports secretary of the school. I also developed my writing skills by contributing articles to the school magazine.

I have always enjoyed doing things with my hands. While I was doing my JC, we had an hour of woodwork each week, and I made all sorts of things—people, airplanes, and other items. I joined the beekeeping club, and I made beehives. I tended the hives and made pocket money from honey while I was at school, though one day I was stung by a swarm of bees. I suppose beekeeping was an early example of my inclination to create a business in something related to agriculture. I liked precision instruments, too. Growing up I inherited a pellet gun from my uncle, but the spring was weak. I had to be able to shoot a bird right in the head to kill it, so I became a good marksman, which was sometimes very handy. I actually disliked hunting, because it was so time consuming—taking a gun and being lost in the bush and turning up hours later with nothing.

Since there were so few white people in Kanye, I had little contact with whites while I was growing up until I was at school at Tiger Kloof. There our contact with white people was principally with our teachers. When we wanted to be naughty we called the teachers *"baas"* (boss in Afrikaans), to which they vociferously objected, since they were all English-speaking liberals who objected to the way Afrikaners treated Africans. Of course, we followed the political developments in South Africa with great interest and then with real alarm when the Nationalists took power. Their separate development (apartheid) education policy had three elements. One was separate education for whites and blacks, the second was different curricula for whites and blacks, and the third was a prohibition on natives from the neighbouring countries going to school in South Africa. Where they allowed exceptions, the so-called extraterritorial students would have to pay full economic cost. For these reasons, South Africa was no longer a serious option after the National Party came to power; we had to develop more educational opportunities in Bechuanaland.

In South Africa we suffered the indignities to which all black people were subjected. As a member of the Young Christian Association, I was one of the volunteers who went to the neighbouring farms to preach on Sundays. One day when I went to Kuruman, I placed my belongings in the cloakroom at the train station in Vryberg. When I came back to claim my baggage, I spoke in English, and it offended the Afrikaner official who was on duty. Fortunately, I was with Joel Morake, one of my village mates, who intervened and said in Afrikaans: "*My baas* (my boss), this is a spoiled chap from the Protectorate; what he should be saying is, would you please, *my baas*, give me back my things?" We did what we needed to survive in that society. But it also taught us what we did not want to have in Botswana, and that was a very important lesson for our future. When we went to preach in the farms, the African farm workers told us about the atrocities they endured when we were not there. Some student preachers were arrested and beaten for trespassing on farmers' land, though fortunately I was never abused. Paul Tsatsi, a friend and schoolmate, was once beaten badly by whites for alleged trespassing. He was left for dead, but luckily he recovered from the ordeal and survived.

During my early years I had experiences of just how bad whites could be, but I also had experiences where whites treated me very well. When I came back to Kanye to teach, there were only about five or six whites, including the district commissioner (DC), traders and a policeman, I interacted with government officials, and a DC named Dennis Atkins almost adopted me as a member of his family. We had a very good agricultural extension officer named Hubo Going, with whom I related as I would have with any friend. My more intense interaction with whites began when I was elected to the Legislative Council (Legco) in 1961 after I had reached my mid-thirties.

World War II started when I was first in primary school, and it ended as I finished my JC in 1945. We received news of the world at primary school on a regular basis, but we did not have any radios nor did we follow the news closely. At Tiger Kloof, we had food shortages as a result of the war. We were given a talk every Wednesday on "the world food and material situation", so that we wouldn't strike over the food at the school! Near the end of the war, Mr A. J. Haile, the principal at Tiger Kloof, used to invite two or three of the students to listen to the news on the radio in his office. It was the first time I had listened to a radio. It was a special privilege, and it provided us with a chance to talk about the war and its effects.

There was no distinction at Tiger Kloof between royal or non-royal students, nor did I feel any tribal consciousness or allegiances. We students tumbled in from all over southern Africa. Regrettably, there were very few who finished their studies at that time. For example, when Archie Mogwe,

Gaositwe Chiepe and Sedumedi Rantshado did Forms IV and V in 1942 and 1943, they were the only three students in those forms from the whole of southern Africa—as far north as Nyasaland and the Rhodesias—and all of them came from Bechuanaland. Even a few years later, when I did Form IV, there were only eight of us, two girls, Tsholofelo Kgosidintsi and Neo Raditladi, and six boys: Felix Mokate, Abram Mokgatlhe, Bias Mookodi, Donald Phala, Joe Seboni, and I. We were also the first group of students to do mathematics at Tiger Kloof. By contrast, Seepapitso Senior Secondary School, which I started as a junior secondary school in 1950, now has an enrolment of about 1200 in Forms IV and V. And these days we have tens of thousands of students in Botswana alone who are doing Forms IV and V.

The big political news in South Africa while I was at school was the battle between the Afrikaners and the English speakers. The Afrikaners were led by Dr D. F. Malan, whose National Party won their first election in 1948, defeating General Jan Smuts and the United Party.

I had a debate with a fellow student, William Letlhaku, on the consequences of a Nationalist victory. I expressed the view that we extra-territorial students would all be sent back into our own countries for education. Also, since the curriculum for whites and blacks would become different and unequal, this would be a disincentive to black students from outside South Africa to seek places there. And, this was what happened. William Letlhaku could only see the apparent advantage to South African blacks from having access to the places vacated by the extra-territorial students, not the dangers from unequal and inferior education. To point out his error, I think I used a Setswana phrase, *Kori e bonye mae lorapo ga e lo bone* (the bird sees the eggs that are the bait, but not the snare).

We all talked about the 1948 marriage of Seretse Khama, the heir to the throne of Bangwato, to Ruth Williams, an English woman. We were all of like minds: Yes, Seretse was married to this lady out of his love for her; but why bother them? We all thought, though without any evidence, that the British government's effort to keep Seretse out of the country and to prevent him from becoming a chief was simply the result of South African influence. The records now show, of course, that our suspicion was correct.

I completed the final year at Tiger Kloof and received my Teaching Certificate, having scored a high pass in the "Cape National Primary Higher 2" examination. Chief Bathoen thought I should come back home to Kanye to start a junior secondary school with the sponsorship of the tribe. I was to become the only qualified secondary school teacher in Ngwaketse territory, since Archie Mogwe and Ben Thema, who were also from Ngwaketse, were teaching in South Africa.

By January 1950, I had secured a responsible position as a teacher. I was the head of a family responsible for five younger siblings and for managing the family's property—the land and cattle my father had accumulated. Our family was reconciled to the idea that I would not to be the headman in our ward. I had been exposed to many exciting ideas, and to a variety of formative experiences at Tiger Kloof and by travelling in South Africa. I was ready to begin a new stage of my life as teacher and farmer.

Chapter 2
Teacher, Farmer, Journalist, Husband

After leaving Tiger Kloof at the end of 1949, I spent the next dozen years working as a teacher and head of a school, a farmer of crops and cattle, and a journalist; and I became involved in tribal affairs in Kanye. As a journalist, I travelled throughout Botswana and frequently to Johannesburg and other parts of South Africa. And, I married and started to raise a family.

Teacher

The Bangwaketse Tribal School Committee decided to establish a secondary school in Kanye. Their decision was influenced by the 1948 election of the National Party in South Africa and the reduced prospects there for education of blacks. Chief Bathoen II was the committee's chairman, and a local missionary, The Reverend John Shaw of the London Missionary Society, was its secretary. All schools in the Protectorate were either tribal or church schools; there were no government-supported schools then, or, indeed, until just before we achieved independence. The colonial government in Bechuanaland took no responsibility for schools at any level. It only provided bursaries to send some Africans to secondary schools, and a very few to university, outside the country.

In January 1950, I was appointed acting headmaster of the new Kanye Junior Secondary School, and I taught its first students. My salary of £102 per annum was a princely sum at the time, but it was basically at a primary teacher's level. Archie Mogwe was also a qualified teacher and a matriculate, and he had balked at the salaries in the Protectorate. He went to teach in South Africa, where his initial salary was £168 per year; he returned as an education officer in the 1950s. Three others from Tiger Kloof had gone to Southern Rhodesia for the same financial reasons. The Reverend Aubrey Lewis had asked me to teach in one of the LMS mission schools in Kuruman or Mafeking, but I returned to the new school in Kanye and remained there through the end of 1955.

No budget had been established for the new school except for one teacher's salary, and there had been no provision for classrooms. I found some space at the King George Memorial Hall, but we were overcrowded the whole time. We were, in effect, treated as if we were just another primary school, especially after Chief Bathoen and the school committee moved both the Standard 6 and the teacher training students to the same facility. In 1951, I was joined in teaching by Rre Montshiwagae and in 1952 by Mr George O. Manchwe, one of my former teachers at Tiger Kloof. He was also appointed headmaster, but after a short time he became ill. He was unable to fulfil his duties and finally resigned, so I became head of the school again. Mr Manchwe as he was not replaced and we were short of teaching staff. In 1954, Bias Mookodi, a former classmate from Tiger Kloof who had been able to complete a degree at Fort Hare University, joined us as headmaster. At the same time, we were finally provided a new location at one of the former primary schools where the Seepapitso Senior Secondary School is now located.

Bias Mookodi and I worked together to come up with a scheme for a school feeding programme. We had found that many of the children walked a long distance to school and had not had anything to eat at home before they left. They were unlikely to have a good meal at mid-day after classes ended, and they wandered off and did not study their lessons. So, we proposed that a simple meal mainly of *dikgobe*, a mixture of beans with either maize or sorghum, be served at the school for lunch. We convinced the chief that this would work, and it was adopted. Nutrition and attentiveness improved, as did study habits, since the students stayed at the school in the afternoons to study. We made good use of this precedent for a school feeding programme in the 1960s, when we established drought relief programmes throughout the country. It remains part of our programmes to this day.

I was active in local tribal affairs, and, as secretary of the Bangwaketse Teachers' Association, I organised speakers for the group. I also served as chairman of the Bangwaketse School Sports Association, setting up matches with schools from other places nearby. The school's enrolment had grown from twelve in 1950 to more than sixty students in three classes in 1955, but staff and facilities had not increased. Further, without consulting anyone, including the school committee, Chief Bathoen decided that year to reorganise affairs at the school. By that time, I had developed my farming to the extent that I realised that as a part-time farmer I would not be successful. So, I resigned effective in December 1955. The chief told me I would still be functioning as a teacher who was conducting adult education classes, because what I would be doing as a farmer would have an effect on other people through example and demonstration.

A Farmer First

Farming has been part of my life since my earliest memories, and it was my main livelihood in the 1950s and 1960s. I have always experimented in agriculture, and I continue to do so to this day. I remained an active farmer for all my years in politics, and I took many lessons from farming into my political life. If it had not been for my success as a farmer, I might not have been able to participate as fully in our political life before I became a minister and started to draw a regular salary from government.

At the time I was growing up, farming was the only means to a livelihood that was available to black people in Bechuanaland. I had an instinct that improved methods could be found, and my spirit was kindled by a resident commissioner who had visited Tiger Kloof. He had given a short talk on the agricultural prospects in Botswana, and he related the results they had obtained from government experimental plots.

While I was a teacher, I would visit the government experimental plots at Lobatse, Gaborone, and Mahalapye on Saturdays and Sundays and look at their records. I also visited progressive farmers such as Mr Bertie Adams, who was just outside Lobatse at Hildevale. He was a grain and cattle farmer with farms in both Lobatse and Ghanzi, and he was later in the Legislative Council and a member of Parliament. He was quite fatherly and treated me as he might a young white boy who was interested in his systems; but, of course, I suspect it also flattered his ego that someone was interested in what he was doing. Mrs Adams reared chickens and sold chickens and eggs to the Lobatse hotel, and this gave me ideas of commercial farming ventures beyond crops and cattle that I pursued later. I also visited other people who were farming well such as Rre Tau Manthe, a successful and energetic older man whose lands were at Mmopane in the Mogodishane area. Mr Norman Matthews, who was a district commissioner, said "Tau Manthe couldn't be a Motswana, he must be a Chinese!" I thought this showed the stereotypical views held by some of the colonial servants.

When I visited Mahalapye to see what was being done there, Mr Russell England, who had retired from his position as director of agriculture but was still very active, treated me like his godson and provided advice. Mr Wandie, an agricultural officer who ran the experimental station where the Cumberland Hotel now stands in Lobatse, also gave me advice. I once asked Mr Wandie if I could bring seeds for a certain crop into the country. He said: "You know, you are wrong to have asked me, because if I tell you I don't know, then you have asked and you didn't get an answer. If I say no, you have even a bigger problem. But, if you had just gone ahead and brought it in, then people would not know what to say to you, and they might say nothing." It was a good lesson: When dealing with officials who would either not know the answer or would find it difficult to take a decision, there could be an advantage of acting as if one did not know the rules.

I visited experimental farms and collected the reports the resident commissioner had referred to, and they demonstrated that if one did things properly, then one would be properly rewarded. In one of my earliest innovations, I collected kraal manure, and put it in a heap by my lands while the crops were in the fields. Mr Hubo Going, an enterprising agricultural officer in Kanye, often brought people to my lands from as far a field as Mahalapye, Ramotswa, and the Kweneng, just to show them the heaps of manure I had collected. Some people took pity on me. "Poor fellow," they said, "if only he had taken advice when he came from school, he would have known that bringing kraal manure to his lands only attracts weeds to them."

I was the first person in Ngwaketse to use kraal manure on my fields. At first, I was able to get it free from my neighbours just for taking it away, since they saw no value in it. Later they realised it had value, and they sold it to me. From my experiments I discovered that the best time to manure was in the autumn immediately after harvest, or in early spring; or if one had fallow lands, the best time was before the end of the last summer rains. I ploughed the manure underneath and then worked it into the soil; I could then reap a crop that was influenced by the manure in the coming season. Breaking up the soil also permitted it to retain moisture during the dry winter and to absorb the rains more effectively in the summer. If one manured at the ploughing time in November or December, one didn't really benefit that year, but rather in the following year and on down the line.

The farming system I developed had many elements beyond just the use of kraal manure. First of all, I de-bushed my lands, since I wanted to use mechanical tools such as planters and cultivators, and it was necessary to have cleared space for the equipment to operate. Second, using a planter, or what the Americans call a seed drill, the plant population of a given space could be controlled. In the broadcast system of sowing traditionally used in Botswana, the plants were either too close and crowded or had more space than they could make use of. Also, if I used a row planter, I could cultivate and weed mechanically, whereas if I broadcast seeds, then I could only cultivate or weed by hand.

There were many different elements to the improved system that I adopted. I learned in part by reading and observation and in part by trial and error. My father, who was a good farmer, used to produce three tons of grain with traditional methods. Using the methods I developed, on the same lands and with only the addition of spaces between the areas that I had de-bushed, I was able to produce 100 tons.

Until I acquired additional lands, which I had to request from my chief, I could not operate a multi-field system. To do the latter I had to have enough land to cultivate during the ploughing season, and I needed spare land to prepare for the next season. Because ploughed soil both soaks more moisture and retains more moisture than unploughed land, if the fields were prepared before the rains came, then I could produce a crop even in a very dry year. And, of course, the earlier I planted, the longer my crop would spend on the field when photosynthesis was at the maximum with direct rays to the leaves, so the growth of the plants and of the heads of corn would be the greatest.

There had to be enough rain not only for the crop but to water the oxen as well. Sometimes water would be so scarce that we were obliged to go 20 kilometres from Tlapaneng to Moshaneng, or 22 kilometres to Mmamokhasi, to provide water for oxen. I came to realise that if we watered the oxen by day, we could plough by night. The ploughed portion was dark while unploughed land was light, so it was possible to see well enough to plough at night. Night ploughing also conserved moisture in the soil. This was another means by which I could get a crop when others who used conventional methods did not. I was encouraged in all these experiments by Mr R. C. Pitso, the agricultural demonstrator in whose "parish" my lands were located.

After my new techniques became successful, people no longer thought I was badly advised. Instead, they concluded I must be doing something other than what they could see to produce the results I was achieving. In simple terms, people in the village thought it was witchcraft. Rre Wapoloko in the village remarked to my Uncle Jacob: "You know, in life you would think people are friends, but when it comes to the real secrets of life, not even their best friends will be told the secrets of their success." My uncle said: "Why do you say that?" He replied: "You are so close to your brother's son, but he makes sure he doesn't tell even you his secret." My uncle dismissed it, and said: "Quett's secrets are open secrets. You all can see what he does." And Rre Wapoloko laughed, and said: "Do you think we are fools to believe what you are saying? We know he has a secret, and he won't even tell it to you!"

My landlord's wife, Mma-Tshegofatso, came to see me one day. She said "Your father (actually just a man who was an elder to me) has sent me to see you to ask you if you could please help us. We know it is difficult for you to part with some of these secrets, and if you don't want to, we will understand. But, could you please, for a price, share your charms with us?" I was so embarrassed because she had concluded I might not be willing to share what she believed was my secret. So I said to her: "Honestly, there is nothing other than what you see me do." And, as I had feared, she replied in a disappointed tone: "We were just hoping; but we accept it is hard for you to part with these secrets of yours." How embarrassing it was for me!

It was not just that people had a belief in magical powers; some thought my methods were simply symbolic. Rre Kesupile Seralanyane had been my father's friend, and he knew I used phosphate fertiliser. He begged me to give him some, so I gave him a bag of super phosphate. When the crop was up he came to me and said, in a secretive voice: "Man, I did it. I went to all the fields and put a little in each corner, and the crop is better!" He thought his field was doing well because the fertiliser worked as *morurelo* (a charm) when placed around the ploughed fields! The truth was that by coincidence it was a year when the rains had been good.

We are all social creatures, and we want to go by what the herd approves. Many people have new ideas, but they do not like the social sanctions that come from trying something different. In fact, they can only make a breakthrough if they ignore those sanctions. If one wants to be viewed as a good boy, one doesn't touch the new ideas. But I was always something of a rebel, willing to try the new ideas. I have always been a believer in rational thinking and analysis of problems, and I researched and reached logical solutions. One can imagine how the success I had in farming added to the other problems I was having with my chief and with others cast in the traditional mould, as I explain in the next chapter.

On the other hand, one should not easily throw away ideas only because they are traditional or are tribal taboos. When I was growing up, we were told never to stand by the centre pole in a rondavel during a rainstorm—it was a traditional taboo. Of course, when I went to school I learned how, and why, lightning would strike the highest point in an area—such as the centre pole in a rondavel.

I raised both sorghum and maize, and the mix of the two depended on the weather each year. The wetter the year, the better the yield with maize; the dryer the year, the better the yield with sorghum. Occasionally I grew green manure, nitrogen-fixing plants like legumes that I ploughed into the soil. Sometimes there was enough moisture so I could plant beans; some would be harvested and some would be ploughed under. I've grown cotton and other crops as well, and in 1973 I had a harvest of 6,000 bags of unshelled peanuts.

I have been farming with improved methods since 1950, and because of the system I developed to farm in our very dry country, I have managed to get a crop in every year except three. The first was a year that was so bad even I did not plant much, and in the latter two I planted three times; each time there was enough moisture to rot the seeds, but not enough to germinate them. I got a crop in every other year, though sometimes I did not recover all my expenses. But in most years, no matter whether the year was good or bad, my take-home income was about the same. In a dry year, there were lower yields, less labour employed, and higher prices, and the reverse in a wet year.

In my farming, I first of all concentrated on the lands, almost to the point of neglecting the cattle my father had left. I did this first, because I had to give my undivided attention to developing one thing. Also, when I was in arable farming, I could sell sorghum for between £1 Shs10 and £2 for a 90kg bag, while the cost to purchase a one-year old beast, either a heifer or a *tolley* (a steer), was £15. However, if I were to barter sorghum for cattle, I could purchase a beast for two bags of sorghum, the exchange rate in those days. Therefore, my marketing strategy was to produce sorghum, then buy cattle by bartering with sorghum, and then to convert the cattle into money. This was three to five times better than selling sorghum for money directly and either buying or raising the cattle from scratch. When I purchased my farms in Ghanzi after independence, I used this barter method to stock them.

Once I became a politician, I concentrated more on cattle, since rearing cattle was more amenable to remote control management than arable agriculture. At the time I moved into cattle, a Danish veterinarian by the name of Dr Jansen was recruited to start artificial insemination (AI) at the Ramatlabama Research Station. However, people at the time were very sceptical about what they called Jansen's "artificial cows". I suspect I was the first chap in Botswana to do AI. Initially I sent 100 heifers to him, but as other people became interested, each year an individual could bring fewer and fewer head of cattle to the AI stations, which had limited capacity. So, I sent my herdsman, Bantu Motlogelwa, to be trained at Ramatlabama so we could do our own insemination. I started buying semen preserved with liquid nitrogen, and we did the insemination at the Logora cattle post 40km southwest of Kanye. When I later started farming in Ghanzi, I employed two inseminators, Ralph Molefe and Pheranyane Mahalelo. In addition, the government had AI stations, and sometimes their grass would be wiped out by veld fires. With no grazing for cattle at the station, they could not operate and would look around for someone who could hire their AI teams for the season. So, I was able to add capacity by hiring excess inseminators from government stations.

The risks in farming are not only from drought or disease. Farming is a physically demanding occupation, and there were two occasions when I had close shaves with ox-wagons. The first was at Gamolefhe where the road made a curve around a tree. We were carrying a load of *matlhaku* (branches); the load shifted, and the wagon almost crushed me against the tree. On the second occasion a similar thing happened, but that time I fell between the rear ox and the front wheel of the wagon. I spun and rolled away, and just escaped with my life. I still remember the incident as if it happened yesterday. The ox was named Dutchman, and I can see in my mind's eye the colour of his hide, *phatshwe* (black and white), and the shape of his horns!

In my approach to farming I have always had a curiosity about what other people were trying to do, and I possessed a willingness to borrow good ideas from others. I learned very early that "a fool's experience is a wise man's lesson", and I took the message seriously. I saw the need to try things and to experiment with them on one's own farm. I knew that farming involved a series of calculated risks. I also believed one should take advantage of the potential available from resources that others are neglecting. Later I often used these same approaches in politics and in government. The early leaders of the Democratic Party, who were also farmers, shared many of these same attitudes of mind as we tried to build a new nation.

Journalist

While I was a teacher, there was no newspaper in the Protectorate other than the South African papers. There had been a paper, called *Naledi ya Botswana*, which I understood had been subsidised by the colonial government, but it had gone out of circulation. During the 1950s, we could see politics developing in a number of countries like Ghana, where Dr Kwame Nkrumah was pressing for independence. We were worried about the impact of the National Party government in South Africa and its policies of apartheid. We were also concerned that we might one day be dumped by the British. If we were not ready to take care of ourselves and build a nation, we were fearful that we might simply fall back into the old tribal entities. Given the political climate of the times, a number of us felt there was a need to circulate ideas in the Protectorate.

So in 1955, three of us—M. L. A. Kgasa, Aaron Gare, and I—came together and decided we should start a paper. Mr Kgasa had been one of my teachers at Tiger Kloof, and Mr Gare was a schoolmate, and they had both come back to Ngwaketse. We wrote to the *Bantu World* in South Africa, which was part of the Argus Group, and to the *Bulawayo Chronicle* in Southern Rhodesia, to see if they would print a paper for us. However, their price quotations were at a level that we could not afford, so we gave up.

Three years later, the *Bantu World* people must have found in their files that there were these three people in Bechuanaland who had been interested in a newspaper. So two gentlemen, Messrs. D. S. Harrison, and Henry Dumbrell, the latter a former director of education in Bechuanaland, descended on me in Kanye with a proposition. They asked if they produced a monthly paper that had common features for the three High Commission Territories (Basutoland, Bechuanaland, and Swaziland); would I be willing to be the kingpin for the Bechuanaland supplement? It turned out that Basutoland already had some papers, so it ended up that the *African Echo*, as it was called, was produced for Bechuanaland and Swaziland. They included the new *Naledi ya Botswana* for us as an insert, and a similar one for Swaziland. I became the Bechuanaland director, and, there was a director from Swaziland (someone from the royal Dlamini family, of course). Every month I took the train to Johannesburg for a meeting with other directors. I also took a journalism course from Transafrica Correspondence College in South Africa.

While I worked as a journalist, I was on the school committee and the tribal council, and I was farming. Those other meetings were only single-day meetings, since no subsistence allowance was paid at that time to encourage longer meetings! I had plenty of time for journalism, since the intensive time for farming was from November to early January. And, I had a very conscientious brother, Basimane, who would look after the balance of operations.

I was the Argus Group's representative in Bechuanaland and the Northern Cape Province, which included places such as Kuruman, and I appointed stringers all over that area. I travelled around by donkey back, horseback, motorbike, on foot, by rail, and by getting a lift with someone. If I knew someone who was a school inspector, I would hitch a lift with him, which is how I first went to Ghanzi and the Chobe. I travelled around the whole country and made friends and cultivated people all over. Some were school teachers, some later became chiefs but were at the time in the civil service, and some later became MPs. I looked for leading personalities—some, like Mr Tsheko Tsheko from Ngamiland, I had never met before but I had read about from reports of the African Advisory Council meetings. In some cases, I would visit a place where I knew no one and would stay for a few days, chatting with people and talent spotting. As a way of recruiting people, it worked well.

The stringers fulfilled two functions: They collected news and wrote stories, and they also were responsible for distribution of the papers in their areas. They were cost effective, since they retained a portion of the proceeds from the papers we sent them. They also received a modest fee for each article that was published. The articles came to me for editing, and I then sent them on to Johannesburg.

We thought of the paper mainly as a conveyer of ideas, but that pill had to be coated with some news. The stories covered whatever in the area might be newsworthy—whether it was a *kgotla* meeting that reached a decision, a lion eating someone's cattle, a dispute about some matter, or a visit by the resident commissioner. We also encouraged people to write opinion pieces, and among those who did so were B.C. Thema, Mout Nwako, Festus Mogae, and Louis Nchindo. The latter two were still students at the time, but we encouraged them to write. I recall one of Mr Nchindo's pieces concerned the use of the waters of the Okavango, and one of Mr Mogae's advocated considering everyone within the boundaries of Bechuanaland to be a citizen of a future Botswana. Mr Nwako would write harder stuff, criticising government policies. Most of the stringers used a pseudonym—Mr Nwako's was "Tribesman"—to avoid identification and victimisation from the colonial government against teachers or civil servants.

The whole enterprise was driven by three factors. First, we felt there was a need for a newspaper. Second, the Johannesburg people had taken an interest in publishing it. Third, we were becoming more politically aware as a people, so there was a market for the paper. The readership was mostly teachers. Sometimes I was disappointed to find that the papers were used in the toilets, and the explanation would be that those were the papers that could not be sold! I learned much later that the paper had received a subsidy from the Protectorate government, but none of us who were writing for the paper knew anything about that at the time. I'm sure the interest of the Johannesburg people and the subsidy the paper received might have been another of the bright ideas of Mr Peter Fawcus, the resident commissioner from 1959 to 1965, who believed in moving things along in Bechuanaland.

I have seen reports that we were called to Mafeking to be scolded about opinions in some of the articles, but I have no recollection of any such meeting. I might have been talked to by the DC in Kanye, as I had been about conflicts I was having with Chief Bathoen, but more "by-the-way". However, I certainly thought the Mafeking crowd had an eye on us as possible trouble makers during those years.

The paper was published monthly from 1958 to 1962, just after the formation of the Bechuanaland Democratic Party. Our principal motivation was not financial—the money only covered our costs plus a bit extra—but our motive was to gather and to spread ideas about what was going on. The stringers largely ended up in the Democratic Party when it was formed—in fact, you might say we just transferred them! I moved almost directly from editing for the *African Echo* to editing and publishing the party newspaper, *Therisanyo/Consultation*. One of the side benefits of my involvement in *Naledi ya Botswana* was that the Democratic Party started out with a trained and experienced journalist and editor for its paper.

Husband

My marriage is the old story of a boy met a girl. My sister Gabalengwe studied at Tiger Kloof, and she became friends with a young woman named Gladys Olebile Molefi, who was also training to be a school teacher. She was the granddaughter of Rre Andrew Saane, a local chief at Modimola near Mafeking. Her father had studied at Fort Cox in South Africa and had trained as a policeman, and her mother was a primary school teacher. After she finished at Tiger Kloof in 1953 and had begun teaching in Mafeking, she came to Kanye for a holiday to visit my sister. When I met her I thought she was a very good girl, and so I started courting her. After a number of months of that, I paid a visit to Mafeking to meet her family, and after dinner I proposed to her. My family then sent a delegation, headed by my maternal uncle, Mr Koodibetse Kgopo, to meet her family and introduce themselves, though to start with they did so under the pretext that they were on a horse buying expedition! We set a wedding date for December 1957, and the church posted the marriage banns.

In November, shortly before the wedding, I made a trip to Mafeking to restock fertilisers for the planting season, and I also picked up a mercuric chloride fungicide known by the trade name Agrison G.N. At the time there was no indication of the dangers of this product to humans, and no warnings were issued when I purchased it. In packing to come back to Kanye, the fungicide was placed in a suitcase with my pyjamas, and it leaked onto them. Of course, when I wore the pyjamas I absorbed the mercury chloride into my system, and it went to work. I was feeling lethargic, so I spent more time in bed—wearing the same pyjamas. Soon my kidneys started to fail, and my brother Basimane took me to the Seventh Day Adventist Hospital (which we called "*Sabata*") in Kanye. It took some time for the doctors to diagnose the problem. Once they had done so, they discovered that the only known antidote was supposed to have been administered within a day or two of the initial exposure; otherwise death was likely. As my long-time colleague Mr Kedikilwe would have said, the Lord nearly found another assignment for me!

My friends D. M. Mokaila and Seepapitso Gaseitsiwe, Chief Bathoen's son, made an emergency trip from Kanye to Mafeking, 100 km away, to find a pharmacist on 16 December, a South African public holiday. Chief Bathoen insisted there be two vehicles, so in case one broke down on the dirt roads the other would be able to bring the medicine. (At the time I was not yet the chief's political rival but just a naughty boy who differed with him in *kgotla*.) I received injections of the antidote, but I was very sick. The doctors told me at one point there was only a five percent chance that I would recover; and if I lived, it would be years before I was completely well. In fact, pre-death counselling of my family had already begun.

I began to recover a bit, but my feet would get very cold, and I would have to get out of bed and walk to aid the circulation. Dr Hay, my physician, advised that we should go ahead with the marriage, since it might be many months before I would really be well. He told me I might look healthy, but I was seriously ill, and my body would only slowly regenerate itself. His second piece of advice was that we be married in the hospital. I put the proposition to Gladys and to our families, and they agreed to the change. We were advised to keep things to the barest minimum to keep the activity and excitement of the occasion down.

Our wedding took place in the hospital ward on 2 January 1958, with our families and the doctors and nursing sisters present, and with Mr Bias Mookodi, my schoolmate and fellow teacher, as best man. I managed to leave my bed for a while to talk with guests and to have a photograph taken. But following doctors' orders, it was a much more subdued occasion than weddings usually are. Fortunately, I recovered my strength much sooner than the doctors had predicted, and I was able to leave the hospital and resume my activities after several weeks. However, we never had a traditional honeymoon.

My kidneys are still weak, though they have not deteriorated further. In 1964, after I had entered politics, I had to go to hospital with a very serious setback. I was flown to Johannesburg in a private plane so that I could be treated in the Baragwanath hospital there. I had total renal failure, and all I wished for was that I could come out and help Seretse Khama win our first elections, and then I could die peacefully. I have to watch my diet carefully from time to time. Over the years I have learned to anticipate the signs of when I might be heading for trouble; then I can take steps to head off the problem.

After our first child, Gaone, was born, Gladys became known to all as Mma-Gaone, as is our custom among Batswana. I'm a troublesome fellow, and Mma-Gaone has endured a great deal. I have a tendency to go all out once I believe in something. For instance, one time early in our marriage while I was in *kgotla* I learned that some of my cattle were scheduled to be sold and slaughtered at the abattoir at Lobatse, but there was no one to look out for them. A lorry was going the 44 km to Lobatse from Kanye, so I just jumped on the lorry and went to Lobatse; there was no way to contact Mma-Gaone. The next day I came back, and I found a very distressed wife. She was wondering what kind of a marriage she had entered into with me. We sat down and I said to her: "I can look after myself, and it is my responsibility to provide for my family. Even if I were confined to a bed, I could write articles and send them to papers in order to earn a living. But for you and the children we hope to have I should do more than sit with you day in and day out. *Monna ga jewe matlhoe se kgomo.*" (Figuratively: A wife will not have a livelihood by merely admiring her husband all day.)

And so I think we developed an understanding. Mma-Gaone has said she knew before we were married that it would be different from an ordinary life in Botswana at that time, where the husband would go off to work at the lands or the cattle post and would be back at a specific time. She knew I had aspirations for our country, and she has always supported me. She has also looked after both me and the children; when anything was bought for me, whether it was socks or suits, she took that as her responsibility.

After I became involved in politics, Mma-Gaone's life became even more complicated. She learned how to fulfil the role of the wife of the secretary-general of the party, the deputy prime minister, then of the vice-president; and then she became the First Lady. She also raised our six children and looked after all of our needs. When I travelled, she and I usually would not know when I would return home. Of course, in these days of mobile phones I can easily be in contact with her, and vice versa. Now if I am off to a meeting in the Congo or the UK we are in touch much more easily than was possible even a few years ago when she was in Kanye and I was in Lobatse or Gaborone. She has been an indispensable partner, and I was very lucky to have married the woman I did.

Chapter 3
Chief Bathoen II and my Views on Chieftainship

All my experiences before politics—as a student, teacher, farmer and journalist—influenced how I thought about what Botswana should become. Before I became involved in elective politics in 1961, I had also dealt with my chief, Bathoen II. He was often referred to as "B2", and many of us used that nickname for him throughout his life. I had seen how Chief Bathoen controlled so much of the lives of those living under his rule. From my experiences in dealing with my chief, it was not surprising that I was especially concerned about eliminating the autocratic rule of the chiefs without tampering with their ceremonial role.

My relationship with Chief Bathoen went back to my early days. To begin with, I had little to do with him, but I was very close to his wife, Mohumagadi Mmafane. For some reason Mma-Seepapitso, as she was known, had been very fond of me when I was a boy. During my sojourn at Tiger Kloof in South Africa, Chief Bathoen decided to divorce Mma-Seepapitso at about the time I started to interact with him. When I was in Form III, B2 had visited me at Tiger Kloof, and he was very fatherly. But soon after I returned home, we began to differ, since I was generally willing to take a risk to try new things. Many people had new ideas, but most did not like the social sanctions—from the chief and other traditionalists—that would come from treading new ground. However, I was not one of those.

The tradition in my tribe was that we started the *kgotla* meeting at four o'clock in the morning; therefore, no one had an excuse for not going to the *kgotla*! Starting in 1950, I went to the *kgotla* to participate. B2 thought I put wrong ideas into people's heads, and he would say: "*Nna hatshe, Quett, o tla itaya batho tsebe.*" (Literally: Quett, you are disturbing people's ears.) But what he meant was: Quett, you are misleading people. And so began the friction between us.

While I was teaching, the chief would sometimes visit my class. He considered himself an authority in Setswana, and during a Setswana class he would correct something I had said with an example. I would say: "Of course, *kgosi* is right; but what he is quoting is called an exception to the rule. It doesn't prove the rule." I don't think he was amused. In addition, he didn't know any Biology or Mathematics, so he didn't approve of teaching those subjects, and he couldn't stand a disagreement about it. He would just speak up from the back of the room: "I don't know why useless subjects like Mathematics and Biology are taught in school, because they hardly come up in real life."

After I left teaching in 1955, I was made a member of the school committee where we continued to have encounters. For example, as the number of schools expanded, he named them East School, West School, and so on. Mr M. L. A. Kgasa came up with a motion in the committee that we should name the schools after our heroes—past characters that played a role in our tribe. The chief took exception and raised a fuss. He said he was the one who named projects, such as the King George Memorial project. We said we didn't want to take away the chief's prerogative, but when he had run out of ideas and started using East School and West School, then something must be done! He disagreed and said: "No, on matters like this the *kgotla* has to be consulted first." But we knew he would not consult the *kgotla* on a matter like that. So, we left it for six months, and then I asked for a progress report at a school committee meeting. That peeved him, but he really had no way out. So, he said: "Let's see what ideas you have." We chose names such as Kgosikobo Chelenyane, the first qualified teacher in Kanye, and Makaba, one of our well-known chiefs, and they were adopted.

The district commissioner, Mr Thomas Moore, who also was on the school committee, became concerned that we were doing things that disturbed the chief. One day, as he saw me riding by on my tractor, he called me into his office. He said: "We thought fellows such as you and Mr Kgasa who miss meetings should be relieved of your duties on the school committee." I said I could only remember missing two meetings, once when my sister was ill and I had to take her to see a doctor, and one other time when I was ill. On the latter occasion, I had asked for someone to come to fetch me. He responded quickly: "There you are, there you are! Do you expect every member of the committee to be fetched to the meetings?"

"Well," I said to him, "perhaps it is a matter of relative importance. Some of us come 20 or 30 kilometres from our lands to attend these meetings because we think they are important. However, if the authorities think fetching someone a kilometre away is too expensive, then perhaps we are wrong in attaching such importance to these meetings." He said: "You educated people!" and turned away. But then he remembered I did not have all that much education, so he added: "At least people with some education—really at times you embarrass the chief. For example, why did you pursue the matter of re-naming schools when you realised the chief did not want to do it? In any case, your tractor must not be used as a taxi."

This was a good example of the relationship of the DCs to the chiefs. One of the principal tenets of the British system of indirect rule was that the colonial government should rule the people through their chiefs. Therefore, making the chief uncomfortable made the DC, as representative of the colonial government, uncomfortable. The DCs needed to reinforce the powers of the chief if their method of controlling, or ruling, the people was to succeed.

Another source of friction with Chief Bathoen and other elders was the idea of drift fences, since it disturbed traditional ways of doing things. Under our traditional system of farming, when the ears on the sorghum started to emerge around day five of the crop, the cattle would try to move from the unfenced cattle posts to the lands to feed on the fresh shoots. Boys and girls were required to keep them away so the cattle wouldn't eat the crop. I proposed the introduction of drift fencing to separate the lands from the cattle posts. These were not fully fenced fields, but long fences erected to keep the different land uses separate. Using the fences would release the boys from being herd-boys, and the girls from being guards on the lands' side, and they would be able to go to school. People have asked where I got the idea of drift fencing, but I don't recall how it came to me. It was just something I thought was an obvious thing to do. At the time, I didn't think of fencing completely, though that idea came later on. Because of my ideas on fencing, I was nicknamed *Rra-terata* (the father of fences—after the Afrikaans word for fencing wire: *draad*).

After reforms adopted in the 1950s had created elected tribal councils, I was selected at *kgotla* to be on the Ngwaketse Tribal Council and its executive committee. Mr Ntau Mogobe and I were also appointed by Bathoen to new posts that gave us the power to represent the chief in agricultural matters, including allotment of arable land and the introduction of new methods. In August 1956, not long after my appointment, Chief Bathoen created a new grain control board with himself as chairman and members drawn from the white and Asian grain traders. I naturally objected to the lack of producers on the board. But my ideas were seen to be too revolutionary, and not long afterward, following another confrontation, the chief removed my power to represent him in agricultural matters.

We came to harder blows over cattle sales and the allocation of tribal land. Chief Bathoen had established a cattle marketing scheme to improve prices for producers. It was a good idea, but it was run poorly; the person he chose to run it was making a mess of it. For example, cattle were trekked 38 km from Mmathethe to Kanye and then a further 44 km to Lobatse. This created a dog-leg in the route that could have been avoided; the cattle would have maintained better condition on their way to the abattoir by going 37 km directly from Mmathethe to Lobatse. Mr Herbert Kgaane moved a motion in tribal council that the cattle should go directly from Mmathethe to Lobatse. B2 became very angry at this challenge to his authority and criticism of his scheme; so the matter was dropped, and we kept quiet.

While we took cover at that time, I felt it was a good idea, and we included it in the agenda on a later meeting. I had a friend named Motsalore Lotshwao, who became very agitated as we moved toward this item, and he shot up and said: "I think there is a mistake that this item is on the agenda, since we discussed it the other day." I said: "Yes, but what you are forgetting is that when we discussed it, the chief became angry, and we discontinued." And the chief became angry again! I said "*Kgosi*, when you become angry, we naturally keep quiet; but it is not because we agree with you, but rather because we respect you. And then, when we think you are in a good mood, we reintroduce the subject." Chief Bathoen just said: "*Ehe, Rra*", which meant that he was giving in; and the route was changed.

However, the chief was still to punish me for this impudence. It came about in this way: I had brought my cattle to Kanye to have them registered for slaughter at the abattoir at Lobatse, and they were refused by the chief's cattle scheme manager on the basis that the quota had been filled. So they had to go back to the cattle post, 37 km and two days travel away. The following week I brought them again, and again I was told the quota was full. I decided I would graze them gradually toward Lobatse, so that mine would be taken with other cattle as part of the next quota. However, the following week my cattle were once again not included as part of the quota. I decided to give up and sold them to Ben Steinberg's younger brother. Later Russell England saw me in the Pakistan Trading Store in Lobatse and asked: "What happened to the quota for your cattle, Quett?" But he and others knew I had already sold them, a fact that would upset the chief.

The chief was really angry that I had sold the cattle outside his marketing scheme! He also didn't think I had been properly punished for disagreeing with him, but he wouldn't talk to me directly. He chose to attack at *kgotla*— at a time when we were talking about manganese mining at Kgwakgwe. The chief announced that he had agreed to let a certain man undertake the mining, and that the fellow had already bought some equipment. Rre Morewagole Solomon spoke up to say that the manganese mine was like our big ox. We should auction it as we would any valuable ox; the highest bidder should mine at Kgwakgwe. The chief took exception to this challenge, and he gave Rre Solomon a hiding. He included me in his tongue-lashing, and he spoke of his disdain for: "what some of you people think—like *Morwa Masire a re sola dikgomo a di neela Maburu* (the son of Masire who sold his cattle to the Boers)."

At the end of the meeting I went to see Chief Bathoen with my friend Mr Kgasa, and I said: "*Kgosi*, I don't know if you have had the full explanation of what happened to my cattle, but if you knew it, you would understand that I should be the one who should be suing the tribe." B2 replied: "Well, I suppose the day might come when one could sue a tribe!" However, I believe he could not imagine such a thing at the time.

I think Chief Bathoen was also disappointed that I was succeeding without any advice from him as my *kgosi*. A number of other people, like Morewagole Solomon and Pitso Kedakubile, had started seeking advice from the Department of Agriculture. Some also visited my lands to see what I was doing with the system of farming I had developed. So, much as some felt there was witchcraft involved that would explain my success, some thought otherwise. Others such as Rre Tshwene Tshweu at Ranaka tried my methods, and the new ideas worked for them as well. The chief appeared to be envious of the influence I was having on other farmers in his tribe.

In addition, some of the traditionalists who farmed near me were jealous, and this feeling increased in 1956, since I had purchased a new Fordson tractor, the first new tractor in Kanye. B2 had a tractor, but it was second hand. By that time I had been allocated some additional land at Ditojana, outside the Motebajana ward. Someone at the *kgotla* said I might take over the whole country, and others said I was ploughing lands beyond those that had been allocated to me. Among those complaining was Chief Bathoen's brother, Mookami Gaseitsiwe. I was called to the *kgotla*, and the chief's brother said: "We understand you have gone beyond the land that was allocated to you." I asked: "Who said this, *Monna Kgosi*?" and he replied: "*Ke batho*" (just people). So I asked: "What made them say these things?" Of course, he didn't have an answer since he had no facts.

To settle the matter, a group of men were sent out to investigate. They found I had ploughed the lands I had been allocated in about ten pieces, leaving rows of trees in between the fields to avoid wind erosion on the sandy soil. (One shouldn't plough a long stretch on such soil, but rather find a line of trees that could make a good wind break.) I had ten hectares here and ten there, and the men had never seen an African plough this much land. They went back to *kgotla* and said: "He has ploughed all over!" The chief asked me: "Is it true you have done this?" And I said: "Not quite; I have certainly ploughed more with the tractor than I could have with oxen, but it is nothing to write home about." I sketched the outline of my lands on a piece of paper to show the chief the layout. A gentleman called Rre Molwakapelo said: "*Mothaka yo! Oa ba a re lefatshe le le kana kana le ka phuthelwa ka pampiri?*" (This fellow! Does he think this huge piece of land can be wrapped in a piece of paper?)

The chief asked: "How much land do you want?" I said: "As much land as I can plough with a tractor for the whole of the ploughing season." Chief Bathoen asked: "Couldn't you give me a direct answer? You have a reputation for evading questions. If a person says he drinks two cups of tea, then I know he drinks two cups of tea." I responded that I had bought a new tractor, and as I was using it for the first time, I did not know how much I could plough. By the following year, I could tell him exactly how much land I could plough. Mookami Gaseitsiwe didn't like to have the matter dropped, and as he was the chief's brother, he said he would send someone to show me what I could retain and what I should lose. Indeed, that is what he did. Some of my land was taken away to reduce my capacity to farm. I thought it was quite unfair, since the land had not been used by anyone else before it had been allocated to me. I thought long and hard about what I should do. People like Mr Jerry Germond, who was divisional commissioner (South) thought it was devilish for the tribal administration to have treated me that way. He advised me to take them to court; but I thought this would not bring me anything.

Then I remembered that the chief's brother had his eye on a piece of land that had been cleared during World War II to produce more food. After the war it was not being farmed, and Mookami wanted to use it. By custom, when you were allocated land by the tribe, you paid no rent for it. So I offered instead to hire that particular piece of land from the tribe and to pay rent. One day Mookami rang me. He liked to call people by their English names, and as I have said, my grandfather's nickname for me had been Jupiter, a name the chief's brother liked. When he phoned he said: "Jupi, how many lands do you say we took away from you?" I told him, and then he asked: "Have any people begun ploughing on those lands?" I told him yes, on one of them. He said "Well *Monna*, let's leave that one, but give you back all the others." My plan worked, when I offered to rent the one piece Mookami wanted to use without paying rent, I was given back the others that had been taken from me.

I did manage to avoid one conflict over the chief's prerogatives. In Tswana society, the chief had always been able to call on a *mephato*, an age regiment, to provide free labour for any purpose he chose, whether it was to build a public amenity or even to build a house for the chief himself. The chief would allocate the responsibility to the *mephato* to do a task. The senior-most person in that *mephato* would be given the details of what was required of them, and then he would pass the instructions down the line.

My *mephato* had been formed while I was at Tiger Kloof. Chief Bathoen named it *Malatlhamokgwa*, which means "those who don't respect custom"—and some think we were well named; perhaps he was prescient in his choice! The head of the *mephato* always communicated with me through Rre Segolobe Setlhatlhane, who lived in the Tsopye ward, next to mine. I was teaching and farming; I was 25 years old; and I knew there was an opportunity cost of giving away my labour for free. Therefore, I never attended a single meeting, and I would pay someone to do the work. I had to be quiet about buying my way out, since Chief Bathoen would wish for nothing better than to know I refused to serve, and therefore I would deserve punishment. So, I always made sure the arrangement was settled between me and my *mephato*, and it never went further than that.

By the late 1950s when the new constitutional proposals for the Protectorate had been adopted, Chief Bathoen was the longest-ruling chief in the Protectorate. He had become chief in 1928 and had been involved in the politics of the Protectorate for over 30 years. Time after time he had frustrated me and my fellow tribesmen in our daily lives. He tried to control us and our commercial activities and to prevent individuals from innovating unless he personally approved. All these experiences had a profound effect on how I saw the future of the country. If Batswana were to really experience freedom to develop their own potential, I felt we had to find ways of democratising the society at the local level as well as the national level.

Chapter 4
Early Politics and Legco

I became involved in national politics in 1961 following promulgation of a new constitutional arrangement for the Protectorate. I was elected first to the Ngwaketse Tribal Council and then to the newly created African Council. The African Council then elected me and seven others as members of the new Legislative Council (Legco).

During the three years and five months from Legco's first meeting in June 1961 to its final meeting in November 1964, we fundamentally changed the legislative basis of Bechuanaland at all levels. In a different forum, we developed a constitution which led us to full national elections and internal self-rule in March 1965. We then built new institutions of government and established new political and legislative processes, and we achieved our independence on 30 September 1966. I don't believe any of us in Legco thought seriously in June 1961 that we would become completely independent in just over five years.

Political Developments before 1961

I was not a participant in national politics prior to 1961, but I will set out some history as background for the task we faced.

The British had declared Bechuanaland a Protectorate in 1885. Cecil John Rhodes wanted to control Bechuanaland, but fortunately his ambitions were dashed after the so-called Jameson Raid of 1895 exposed the imperialist aims of Rhodes and his British South Africa Company. Otherwise Bechuanaland might have gone the way of Southern and Northern Rhodesia and become a colony rather than a protectorate. As a protectorate, overall administration was left to the British government through a resident commissioner located in Mafeking in the Cape Province. Subsequent administrations in the Protectorate followed the British system of indirect rule: Chiefs would retain the law of their people in all civil and most criminal matters. As in classic indirect rule, the district commissioner ruled all Africans through the chiefs, and they governed non-Africans directly under statute and common law. While eight paramount chiefs were from distinct tribal groups, in fact each paramount chief governed not only his own tribesmen but all Africans living within particular geographic areas. This led to many disputes of chiefs with other tribesmen under their authority. Despite our democratic reforms and history, these tribal differences are still a source of ill will in modern Botswana.

The colonial government had established an African Advisory Council in 1919 and a European Advisory Council in 1920, though there were very few white people in the Protectorate at the time. In 1951, a Joint Advisory Council (JAC) was created with eight members from each of the two councils and four "official" (i.e. colonial civil service) members. Those of us outside the governing circles read accounts of the meetings of these councils, and we later reported on them in *Naledi ya Botswana*. Beginning in 1956, the colonial administration called on the JAC to debate not only general questions of policy but also the detailed provisions of proposed legislation for the Protectorate. For the first time black and white representatives worked together with officials of the colonial government to seek consensus about policies. However, the JAC was not a legislative body; it was only advisory to the colonial administration.

In 1956, Seretse Khama and his uncle, Tshekedi Khama, agreed between themselves and with the British government that both would renounce any claims on the chieftainship of the Bangwato—a matter that had been in dispute since Seretse's marriage to Ruth Williams in 1948. This cleared the way for proposals to create elected tribal councils to advise chiefs—a development Tshekedi Khama had fought against bitterly in the 1930s when he was regent during Seretse's minority. Tshekedi Khama served as the first secretary to the Ngwato Tribal Council.

The next development at the level of the entire Protectorate came in 1958. The JAC established a constitutional committee with four European members and four African members, including Seretse Khama and Chief Bathoen. Tshekedi Khama had also been appointed, but he died before the committee met. The new high commissioner in South Africa, Sir John Maud, who had the formal responsibility for governing the Protectorate, wanted the constitutional proposals to be drafted by a South African professor who had done the same for Basutoland. However, Peter Fawcus, the new resident commissioner, and his officials differed strongly; they wanted the leaders in Bechuanaland to work with one another in the Tswana tradition of consultation. In seeking and finding consensus, he hoped they would build trust in one another. Alan Tilbury, the legal secretary, provided the committee with examples of transitional constitutions from other British dependencies, and he served as legal draftsman and advisor to the committee. In October 1960, the JAC accepted the committee's proposals for a Legislative Council (Legco) and an Executive Council (Exco). The latter included four of the "unofficial" (i.e. elected), members from Legco, two white and two black. The new constitution was then promulgated by the British government and took effect in 1961.

Chief Bathoen, Russell England and Tshekedi Khama had been advocating for a legislative council for a number of years. Those of us in the country who were outside the African Advisory Council or the European Advisory Council were only learning things through the minutes when they were made available. And, as everyone knows, what is in the minutes is not always reflective of the nature of the conversation. In developing the 1961 constitution, Peter Fawcus did a great deal of consultation, much of it with individuals and in separate groups. His book, *Botswana: The Road to Independence*, refers to the 1961 constitution as having been the result of a unanimous recommendation of the Joint Advisory Council. He noted that Prime Minister Harold Macmillan had remarked that it was the first time he had ever seen a legislative body being unanimous about something! But, in my view, the 1961 constitution was effectively designed and imposed by Peter Fawcus.

The Beginnings at Legco
The African Council was constituted by a series of elections throughout the country. We elected people from each ward, and they represented their ward in the tribal council. The tribal council elected people to the African Council, which in turn served as an electoral college to elect members to Legco. Africans

elected eight to Legco: Seretse Khama, Chief Bathoen, Goareng Mosinyi, Archelus Tsoebebe, Tsheko Tsheko, Leetile Raditladi, Letlole Mosielele, and me. Eight Europeans were elected by the white community. The government appointed two Europeans, Russell England and David Morgan; two Africans, Dr Modiri Molema and Joe Gugushe; and Mr A. E. Chand from Lobatse, to represent the small Asian community, who were mostly traders.

The government appointed Seretse Khama and Chief Bathoen to the Executive Council (Exco), and I attended as an alternate whenever either of them was not able to be present. I was in Exco for a stretch when Seretse Khama was ill and for another when Chief Bathoen was in the United States for a month on a leadership programme. Russell England and David Morgan were the Europeans on Exco, with Jimmy Haskins as their alternate.

My first real meeting with Seretse Khama, with whom I soon formed a close partnership, was at the first gathering of members of the African Council. When the African Council met for the first time in 1961, the order of business had been established in the agenda set out by Peter Fawcus and delivered to each of us in advance. It provided for the African Council to meet and then to immediately constitute itself as an electoral college to select those who should be members of the Legco. When I received the agenda, I wrote to Peter Fawcus to say we had all been living in our tribal territories, not knowing who was who; consequently it would be difficult to be saddled with the responsibility to select the appropriate people on the very first day we met. I proposed that the elections be held at the end of the session, so that we would have a chance to find out about one another.

But the stage had been set; Peter Fawcus didn't change the agenda. In fact, he did not even respond to my letter. However, after we had all arrived in Lobatse, he postponed the first meeting of the council for several days. The postponement gave us the time to interact and become acquainted as we lived together. So, we were better able to make judgments once the council actually began meeting, and we became the electoral college.

In many ways it was a very clever thing for him to have done. He apparently saw my point, and he found a way of accommodating the substance of my proposal without rearranging the agenda. The agenda would doubtless have been set up in consultation with many other officials. I suppose he did not want to be seen by his critics to be giving in to a cheeky young fellow from Kanye! I, too, was keen that it be done not because Quett Masire had suggested it, but because it was the right thing to do. It was obvious to me that he was accommodating the suggestion, so I made it a point not to claim any credit for it to anyone else. It was an example of the way in which Peter Fawcus accomplished things by accommodation and indirection rather than by confrontation.

The first time I had met Peter Fawcus was on his visit to Kanye in 1959 to attend an agricultural show; I served as the interpreter for his speech. The next time I met him was at the African Council. I had not previously formed any impression of him, but right away both he and his wife Isabel, later Lady Fawcus, were very kind to me. When I fell ill with renal failure in September 1964, they made a plane available to fly me to Johannesburg. When I was discharged, I was hoping I might be provided a flight back, too. I sent a message to David Finlay, who was then Fawcus' private secretary, to say I was to be discharged, but he indicated I needed to make my own way back. The Bechuanaland Protectorate government did not spend money needlessly! When I returned, both Peter and Isabel greeted me warmly.

Much of what was accomplished over the short time between 1961 and 1966 came about through a partnership that was established quite quickly between Seretse and me on the one hand, and Peter Fawcus and Alan Tilbury on the other. Seretse and I shared a sense of direction for the evolution from Protectorate to statehood, and I believe it tallied with that of Peter Fawcus and Alan Tilbury. We all had a sense of a common agenda; we were on the same wavelength, and the relationship seemed completely natural. We saw several objectives: To build a unified nation; to come to terms with traditions such as the chieftainship as we laid the basis for a modern state; to create a society that was non-racial and non-tribal; and to achieve independence.

The level of trust among the four of us was substantial. Seretse and I never really talked about whether or how far we could trust Peter Fawcus and Alan Tilbury. I suppose it was because our objectives were so compatible—indeed, identical. Peter Fawcus once commented that the fact that we were all looking toward independence made it possible for us to be friends. We simply worked on the basis that, if we had a problem, we just needed to figure out how to solve it and to move on. I think they counted on me to help solve problems because all three of them knew that if I differed with them, I would not hesitate to say so. One could say I acted as a litmus test for their ideas.

Our luck in Botswana has not only been discovering diamonds, but also that we have discovered people. One piece of luck was in having Alan Tilbury as an excellent lawyer before and for three years after independence. And we were especially fortunate to have had Peter Fawcus; he was the right man at the right time. If he had served Bechuanaland earlier, he would have rubbed some people the wrong way, and he would have been frustrated by the resistance of some people to change. If he had come later, he might have found the damage already done, and things would not have developed in the democratic and practical way they did. We found in him a man more accommodating than any we had ever met, and a man who did not accommodate or condescend because he thought we were lesser mortals. He was a liberal and a democrat not because of circumstances that pushed him into the position, but because he believed in those values. Peter Fawcus also argued our case and promoted our interests continually, both with the high commissioner in South Africa and with the authorities in the UK. He must have been a nuisance to the British authorities, since he was always pressing them to do more for Bechuanaland financially and to move more quickly on issues than they seemed willing to do. He was very anxious to get things going, and I am sure he felt frustrated by the slow pace of the British government.

Of course, we as a people were becoming more politically awakened—Mr Leetile Raditladi's Federal Party and the Bechuanaland People's Party had been established by the time Legco began in 1961. Peter Fawcus was not dealing with unleavened dough. Like some of us, he realised the way we were could not go on forever, and if we were to become independent, we had to anticipate such a development.

Isabel Fawcus was much like her husband in terms of attitude. One of her contributions was to provide the social connections among individuals, African and European. Her teas and parties and her social skills brought us all together. Peter Fawcus' official position may have constrained him from performing as much of that role as he might have wished, but she was not constrained in that way. Governments are composed of people who have to interact and understand one another, whether they agree or disagree. A level of social contact and a degree of personal familiarity is very important. At the time of Legco, we were almost all, whether African or European, coming together for the very first time. Isabel Fawcus' successful efforts to help us get to know one another as individuals were very important in helping us to work together more effectively in Legco and later in Parliament.

I came to know Peter Fawcus through my own extensive contact, but I also saw him through the eyes of Seretse Khama, Quill Hermans and Bob Edwards. Quill Hermans was a young South African who had joined the Protectorate service in Mafeking in the early 1960s, and Bob Edwards was a young American lawyer who was sent out for two years by the Ford Foundation to work with the Bechuanaland government. After Quill and Bob had arrived to work in Mafeking, they had an office together. Peter Fawcus said he used to walk down to their rondavel to talk with them, both to get new ideas and to have his own sense of urgency confirmed. I doubt this practice endeared him to some of the other senior colonial officials. They would have felt it was most improper for such a senior man as Peter Fawcus to go directly to such junior officers without going through their supervisors.

Working in Legco
The Legislative Council met in Lobatse, though the capital was still officially in Mafeking. We held our sessions in the High Court chambers, and Peter Fawcus had caused a residence next to the court to be converted into a guest facility with catering service, initially for members of the African Council and later for Legco. It was the location for many informal discussions, which we all knew were important in actually accomplishing our objectives.

In Legco, the government would bring its business; members asked questions of government; and there were arrangements for private members' motions (i.e. those not brought by government) as well. It was very clear from the beginning that Legco was a precursor to self-government and independence. The questions were how long it would take, and what the path would be like.

At the first meeting of Legco, Mr Richard Barlas, who later became Clerk to the House of Commons in London, spent time with all members of Legco. He had prepared the first Standing Orders, or rules of procedure; they had become law by virtue of their inclusion in the Order in Council in the UK establishing the new constitutional arrangements. Our sessions with Mr Barlas were very useful and interesting. He explained in detail the purposes of particular provisions and how they related to the functioning of the democratic process. The Standing Orders were subject to amendment by Legco if we considered it necessary. I would say all of us were intrigued by these new procedures and their purposes. It was exciting to see how they could be used in formulating the legislation that would achieve our objectives.

We had always followed procedures and systematic practices in our traditional *kgotla*, but the complexities and the reasons behind these new formal and elaborate procedures fascinated all of us. Batswana have always been very oriented to processes, and this gave us a new arena in which to work with process. In many ways, we were just changing the nomenclature. We were aware that procedures were different in different bodies, and people later came to understand that the High Court, the cabinet, and the Parliament each would have its own appropriate procedures. Of course this was true in the *kgotla*, as well, since procedures were different if the *kgotla* was functioning as a judicial body, or consulting with the chief, or acting as part of the tribal administration.

In the course of Legco's relatively short history, we developed and adopted a whole series of laws. Some were amendments to or substantially replaced former proclamations; some were entirely new and dealt with subjects on which laws in the Protectorate had never been established. Peter Fawcus said it well in his book: "It fell to Bechuanaland's Legislative Council to enact the laws and create the institutions that were needed to turn the country into a modern state in as short a time as possible."

As part of our educative and consultative approach, all proposed legislation was published in the *Government Gazette* and distributed widely in the country. We allowed two weeks between publication and any action by Legco. This went beyond the time specified by the Standing Orders used by the British Parliament, but we felt it was important for us to be as widely consultative as possible. In just over three years, we dealt with everything from town and country planning and building regulations to a new Companies Act, a comprehensive employment law, and legislation regulating electricity and urban water supplies. For the most part, the details are not of great interest—the important point was that for the first time we as citizens were drafting and adopting a wide range of laws that would govern us. It was a new experience for all of us, and it was a responsibility we took very seriously.

Between the adoption of the new constitutional arrangements and the first meeting of Legco, Peter Fawcus decided to add what he called "an embryonic ministerial form of government". The senior officials responsible for a substantive area, such as finance, were designated as "members" for those areas. At the first meeting of Exco, an "unofficial" ("an inelegant designation", as Peter Fawcus remarked) from Exco (Seretse Khama, Chief Bathoen, Russell England or David Morgan) was "associated" with each member. The members were required to consult with the associated unofficials on proposed policies and to keep them briefed on the affairs in that area. In effect, the four unofficial members of Exco became members of a cabinet, with broader political responsibilities. Civil servants at all levels started to get experience working with and discussing political issues, as well as those of a more administrative nature. It was all part of the learning process, both for us politicians and for the civil service.

We took another step in 1962 to involve the representatives in Legco in the governing process. We established advisory committees falling within the portfolio responsibilities of the members of Exco, such as natural resources, or the livestock industry. Each committee had other officials as well as several elected members of Legco. This system gave us useful practice in creating legislation before we had to take over the responsibility for government ourselves.

When we came to self-rule with an elected Legislative Assembly, therefore, we were not just a bunch of fellows from the bush. We had learned how to ask questions and move motions and get information from those in administration who were responsible for different areas of government. Several of us had made trips abroad to get experience with other parliaments. Because of the Executive Council and the member system, a number of us had the experience of what it would be like to be a member of cabinet. I had gained my experience playing the role of "spare wheel" when either Bathoen or Seretse was absent.

I knew most of the African members of Legco from my work as editor of *Naledi ya Botswana*. I knew Bertie Adams from visiting his farms, and Jimmy Haskins from my days of journalism and travelling up north with the publishers of *African Echo* and *Naledi ya Botswana*. I knew Russell England, since as an auctioneer he used to sell some of my best cattle, and also Abas Chand, the merchant from Lobatse who represented the Asian community. I did not know any of the officials from the Mafeking crowd, except for the few I had met briefly when Peter Fawcus visited Kanye.

If one goes through the instances of recorded votes in Legco, or if one looks at the debates themselves, one sees there were seldom divisions of whites versus blacks, traditionalists versus modernists, northern versus southern, or the like. We all pitched in as individuals. I remember one particular occasion after the BDP had been formed; there was a heated debate with Goareng Mosinyi and Seretse Khama on opposite sides, despite both being founding members of the party. Mr Mosinyi was strongly opposed to taking away the chief's prerogative to distribute stray cattle in any way he pleased, and Seretse argued that we should remove the chief's powers. Dr Alfred Merriweather, head of the Scottish Livingstone Hospital, leaned over to me and asked: "Does Mosinyi still belong to your party?" In another debate, I was complaining about the lack of government facilities and services in Hukunsi, Lokgwabe, Lehututu, Tshane and some other places well outside Ngwaketse, from where I had been elected. Russell England asked another member: "What's wrong with Quett this time?" But there was nothing wrong with me. We all felt we had to take a national view, not a parochial one.

Strongly encouraged and supported by Peter Fawcus, we also went abroad to learn the art of government. Among our trips were two visits to the Commonwealth Parliamentary Association—Seretse and David Morgan went one year, and Jimmy Haskins and I went the next. We learned a great deal and became better friends as well. Actually, observing how friendly David Morgan and Seretse Khama were with one another, and how friendly Jimmy and I were, James Batten, the assistant secretary of the Commonwealth Parliamentary Association came up to ask me: "Are all of you in Botswana like this?" Indeed, we all worked together toward a common goal of an independent, united, non-racial, modern country.

At the first meeting of Legco in June 1961, Peter Fawcus delivered an opening address about our purposes. He said, among other things, that there were three priorities for improving the economic situation of the country: (1) livestock and agricultural improvement; (2) mineral development and associated industries; (3) diversification of the economy through the establishment of other industries. These priorities stayed with us for the next 40 years, though each generation of leadership in politics or the civil service seems to think it has discovered them. In some cases we were very successful, and in others we did not do as well as we had hoped.

Seretse Khama set the tone for our subsequent activities and approaches during those first days of Legco when he said: "I think it has been quite openly demonstrated that practically any constitutional change which is reasonable in this country can be obtained just by asking. It is now for the people of the African areas to demonstrate that they can control those modern machines of government to the benefit not only of themselves but of the country as a whole." During one debate, he spoke to those who were attracted to the slogans of the opposition politicians like Mr Philip Matante of the People's Party: "There are other factors that have to be taken into consideration which perhaps mean a little more than just to be able to shout 'we are free'."

We were conscious from the beginning that we were the first legislative body in Botswana, and people would be watching both what we did and how we did it. Racial discrimination, by practice though not by law, was the rule in the townships. Mindful of how our actions might be seen if we were to address one aspect of discrimination without looking at others, I noted in one debate: "As a body of law makers, it must be evident to us that what we intend is one thing, and the interpretation that will be given to the law is quite another thing, and people are going to live by their interpretation, not by our intention." We were all conscious that we were under close scrutiny, and we had to behave properly.

We also were aware that we were creating not only legislation but also traditions for the future. We needed to consider not just how things would be seen, but also how they would outlast us. Would our laws stand the test of time? During a 1962 debate on a Livestock Advisory Committee report, an argument was put forth that seemed to be based on the well-known views of particular members of the council. So I asked: "…are we sure that the same people will be here? Are we not going to be confronted with all these things which we did because we did not work on principle but on personalities, because we are going to make such and such an enactment which is only suitable while so and so is here, but when he is out it is no longer suitable?" Russell England responded in kind: "The hon. Mr Masire has hit the nail on the head. One knows the composition of this House today, Sir, one does not know what it may be even a few years hence…"

The Site for a New Capital
In September 1961, Legco considered a White Paper prepared by government on the location of a new capital for Bechuanaland. The seat of government was in the Imperial Reserve in Mafeking, and we had long held the dubious distinction of being the only country in the world with a capital

outside its own borders. Of course, this situation was made worse by the apartheid policies of the South African government, which made it acutely uncomfortable for Africans to travel to our own capital. In fact, the leading political figure in the nation could not even visit his own capital city, since Seretse Khama, following his marriage to Ruth Williams, had been declared a Prohibited Immigrant in South Africa!

The White Paper considered a number of locations and recommended Gaborone for several reasons. It was located on the line of rail (we had no paved roads except for a few kilometres in Lobatse). There was a potential site for a dam on the Notwane River to provide adequate water. It would be located on Crown land, so no tribe could be seen to be either losing land or, perhaps more important, claiming it owned the capital. And, it was close to a number of tribes in the south-east, such as the people from Thamaga, Tlokweng, Ramotswa, and Gabane. These tribes were not endowed with large tracts of land like other Batswana, so they could perhaps find jobs and markets if the capital were located nearby.

As the debate in Legco opened, Jimmy Haskins, who was from Francistown, proposed a motion that Legco establish its own committee to study the issue of location rather than rely on the White Paper. There was a lively debate, which quickly raised the issue of north versus south as an issue relevant to the decision. I told the council: "I would like to strike a note of warning that we must try to aspire to the unity and oneness of this country and not be tempted to split it into political regions such as North and South. I think we must not think in terms of any geographical lines of demarcation when we come to think of this country. We must solely think of the development which will help the country in its entirety." Jimmy Haskins withdrew his motion.

Of course, other sites were suggested as alternatives to Gaborone. There were motions for Lobatse, since it was already the home of the High Court, Mahalapye, based on its centrality in the country, and Francistown, on the basis that a larger number of whites, the most economically active citizens, lived in the north. All were either withdrawn or defeated. Chief Bathoen commented that he had initially favoured Lobatse but had changed his mind when he read the White Paper. Seretse Khama joined in the general affirmation of the recommendation for Gaborone, and in a subsequent vote the choice was made. In retrospect, it seemed to be such an obvious decision, but at the time there were arguments for other choices, and they were fully aired. The potential for further development mentioned by those talking in favour of Gaborone was to me the most interesting part of the debate. But even in my wildest dreams I never thought it would develop into the size it is today.

Localisation

Localisation of the civil service, i.e. replacing expatriates with citizens, was a major issue for Legco. A central question was: Who should be considered a local? After South Africa withdrew from the Commonwealth in 1961 and established itself as a Republic, we saw the need to define citizenship more precisely, since many residents of Bechuanaland also held South African citizenship. In the May 1962 session, we adopted legislation allowing such persons twelve months' grace period to decide in which country they would determine and declare their citizenship—an issue that would be important in the next round of elections. If they opted for their citizenship in the UK and colonies, then they would be eligible to vote; otherwise they would not.

The vast majority (over 85%) of senior civil servants, and even of secondary school teachers, were expatriates—primarily whites in the civil service, and mainly Africans from other countries in the teaching service. Therefore, localisation of the civil service and the teacher corps was vital. An early government statement in Legco on the subject of localisation emphasised one point: "Every officer in the service must understand he has a vital duty either to train others or to be trained by others. Indeed training is the key to the success of a very large part of our localisation plan." We explicitly decided to separate race from the issue of localisation. We defined a local as one who was born in Bechuanaland or who had one parent born in Bechuanaland and who came to live here before the age of 18. We also wanted to make it clear in legislation that there would be no discrimination among locals in any way, including terms of service, e.g. wages or pensions—an issue that had been raised for many years by the Bechuanaland African Civil Servants Association.

We considered and approved a White Paper on Localisation at the November 1964 session. During the debate, I signalled why our priority for education spending in the near term would need to move toward secondary and tertiary levels: The deficit of people educated to those standards of achievement was a major cause of the low levels of localisation in the civil service. In the past, I noted during the debate, when people "of ability tried to apply for bursaries to go and study elsewhere, they were given a typical analysis of how many people could be passed through primary schools with the money they would need [in a bursary] to further their education. This was due to the lopsided thinking of [the colonial] government. We must consider the facts as they exist now. We must ensure that the efficiency of the government must be maintained when we take over the administration of the country." To do so, we needed to train people with advanced skills.

Seretse Khama chimed in with another concern: People were expecting too much after self-rule and independence. "I feel I should state that during my travels in Africa and perhaps elsewhere I have been a little disturbed by the attitudes adopted by the civil servants in emerging countries, not only civil servants but even politicians, too. So much is expected of self-government, so much is expected of independence and nearly all of it is selfish, and is without tradition and any sense of service to one's country. It would be unfortunate if here we also thought that self-government next year meant the upgrading of everybody and higher wages. It would be equally unfortunate if the politicians in this country all hope to become ministers, that there will be no back-benchers and that they are all going to have wonderful motor-cars and consequently live like lords and kings."

We thought three points were important. First, we had to retain an efficient administration so we could implement development programmes and deliver services. Second, we needed to ensure training of citizens so we could localise the service. And third, we wanted to be sure people who sought positions in the civil service or politics should not expect more than their share of the nation's wealth—a point that led to our developing an Incomes Policy after independence. Maintaining the balance among these three issues continued to be a challenge for the entire time I was in politics.

When we promoted people who were not terribly able in the name of localisation, I was often disappointed. I even had people say to me: "Of course he's not good—but you should promote him anyway; what do you think democracy means?" I couldn't disagree more, since I believe that in a democracy positions should be secured on merit.

Livestock and the Abattoir

The livestock industry was the backbone of our economy in the 1960s, as it had been for generations. Prices and marketing of cattle were important issues economically, socially and politically for virtually all Batswana. Starting in the 1940s, the Colonial Development Corporation (now the CDC) made a series of investments in the livestock industry and in an export abattoir. In the 1950s, Cyril Hurvitz, a South African entrepreneur, took over management of the abattoir through ECCO, the Export Canning Company. The earlier negotiations with the Protectorate government had resulted in an export monopoly for the abattoir operators. The result was that the abattoir and canning facility in Lobatse had a monopoly on exports of beef and live cattle, with the consequent ability to set the prices paid to Botswana producers.

In April 1963, I moved a motion in Legco that there be an investigation of the operation of the abattoir and development of recommendations to deal with management, the relationship between the abattoir and ECCO (i.e. Hurvitz), control of the abattoir by producers, and the possibility of a statutory corporation to take it over. The motion was in effect a demand for government control and a criticism of both CDC and Hurvitz, as well as of the colonial government for having gone along with the agreement. During the course of the debate, an amendment was offered to water down my statement that "the producers are not receiving a fair price for their cattle." I responded: "We do not need to hide the truth in circumlocutions statements and get engaged in calling a spade an agricultural instrument. We must just call it a spade." *Hansard* recorded that the amendment was subsequently "negatived".

Seretse Khama strongly supported my proposal in Exco, and it was clear, too, that we had the support of Peter Fawcus. In August 1964, the report on the livestock industry was presented to Legco. It proposed the creation of a statutory corporation, buying out the CDC and Hurvitz, and returning any profits of the abattoir to the producers. While it took some time to implement the recommendations, the Botswana Meat Commission (BMC), which is ultimately responsible to the president of Botswana, was established in 1966. It became the largest and most modern abattoir in Africa, some have said in the Southern Hemisphere. It maintained standards that permit Botswana to export the highest quality beef to Europe and other markets. Given the political, economic and social importance of the livestock industry in the 1960s, and the fact that many members of the BDP leadership were in Legco, our initiative doubtless did us some good in our recruitment to the party before the elections, as well as in the election results themselves.

We dealt in Legco with a number of other critical issues: The annual budgets and a five year development plan, the reform of local government institutions in relation to the chiefs, the relationship between traditional law and statute or common law, and aspects of our relationship with South Africa and Southern Rhodesia. As Legco continued meeting, a new constitution looking forward to self-government was also being drafted during 1963. Seretse, Mout Nwako, and I from the BDP were members of the Constitutional Conference in Lobatse. The conference resulted in a White Paper with proposals that were presented to Legco in November. We were very conscious that we were creating the new institutions, procedures, practices and traditions that would form the basis for our independence as a nation. It was an exciting time for all of us.

While we were forming the Botswana Democratic Party and framing our platform and our programme, we were aware of events in other countries, especially in Africa. We also knew the positions being taken by the People's Party on a variety of issues. Having observed these developments, we concluded that running to extremes really didn't pay, and we thought moderation would be a virtue for us. If our goal was independence, and we didn't need to fight in order to get it, what would be the point of picking a fight? On the other hand, we didn't think it would be right to sit around and wait for someone to hand it to us. We meant to cling to the golden mean.

Map of Botswana at independence, showing tribal reserves, State land and freehold land

Chapter 5
Race and Race Relations

The racial conflicts in neighbouring countries have always had an impact on Botswana and on our own race relations. Differences in economic status and legal rights based on race had been part of our existence for decades. As I grew up and entered adult life, I had plenty of experiences to know just how bad whites could be, but I also had experiences where some whites treated me very well. When I met the right people, I knew it.

An example of the negative side may show the nature of the Protectorate in the 1950s. Once I had developed my new methods of cultivating sorghum and had become a large producer, I needed to move my crops to the market, and Lobatse was the nearest railhead. I had sold some corn to Kahn and Kahn, the big grain merchants in Johannesburg, and it needed to be consigned to Vryburg Milling, so I booked two rail trucks (box cars). As I couldn't bring all of the grain in one day, I asked for a place to temporarily store a number of loads that could fill a truck. The Station Master in Lobatse, a Mr Wallace, asked me whose sorghum it was, and I said it was mine. This peeved him, as I don't think he could imagine a black farmer producing that much grain. He thought I was loading for a white farmer, not for myself. So, he decided I was cheeky and said there were no trucks to be had, and he refused me.

I groaned and moaned, and Russell England appeared out of the blue and asked me: "Why are you so morose, Quett?" So I told him the story. He turned to Wallace and said: "Aren't there trucks out of which I've just off-loaded my petrol drums?" Russell England was a big man, and a member of the European Advisory Council, and when he spoke, the earth trembled! Mr Wallace said "Yes, Mr England, but an Indian has booked it already." And England said: "Yes man, but these poor fellows are struggling, and you ought to help them."

Mr Wallace felt I had put him on the spot by complaining to Russell England and that Mr England was rapping him over the knuckles. He said I could have the trucks, but he gave me a quotation for the trucks that was four times the normal rate. When I pointed this out, he said the normal rate was not for a boogie (a large truck) but for a short truck. I replied that would explain why it should double, not why it should quadruple in price. Mr Wallace said: "But you'll take two days." I explained that the first day I had to hire people to clean the trucks, since they were dirty, and the next day I would load the sorghum. And, I pointed out, there was an Indian from the Pakistan Trading Store in Lobatse who had done the same thing that I proposed, but he had not been charged any extra. Then Mr Wallace just switched off and wouldn't talk with me anymore.

So I went to complain to the district commissioner, Mr C. C. McClaren. Instead of thinking of ways to help, he picked up the phone. "Mr Wallace," he said, "There's a man here in my office." I could hear Wallace ask: "What?" The DC said, carefully: "There is a Native here. He says you have refused to listen to him and then have overcharged him." Mr Wallace explained about the long truck and the short truck, to which I said: "It is fine to double, but not to quadruple, the rate," and I told him about the Indian trader who was charged less than I was. The DC was trying to salvage Wallace, not to support my position, because he said: "Isn't a railway day twelve hours, so if you took more than twelve hours, then the charge would be for two days?"

I decided there was nothing further to do in Lobatse, so I took it up with the system manager in Kimberley. Somewhat to my surprise, he decided in my favour but said I would have to pursue it with a formal written complaint. Since it was already the ploughing season, I thought instead of wasting my time with Mr Wallace, I should get to ploughing, so I dropped the issue. This is one of the many examples I could give of petty but continued harassment where I, or my fellow black citizens, were frustrated by whites in positions of authority. It was the practices of whites, not just the laws prohibiting Africans from owning freehold land or holding trading licences that kept blacks from developing enterprises in Bechuanaland.

However, there were always some whites in southern Africa who rose above the societies in which they lived. While I was vice-president and minister of finance and development planning, I had purchased a farm in Ghanzi in western Botswana. One Saturday I took my men to Gobabis, over the border in Namibia, to purchase supplies and equipment. We spread out to make our purchases, and when we came back to the truck we discovered more cash was needed to complete our shopping. I went into the Standard Bank and went to a teller who, of course, was white, and asked if I could see the manager. I received a quizzical look, especially because I was a black man dressed for farming, but I was taken to the manager's office. I explained the situation to him and said I would be happy to pay for a trunk call to Standard Bank in Gaborone so he could ascertain that I had a sufficient balance for him to honour my check. He picked up the phone and asked to have the call booked—there was no direct dialling in those days.

After he had booked the call, we chatted, and he asked me about my farm. After a while he asked me how it was that I farmed in Ghanzi but banked in Gaborone; and I told him that I worked in Gaborone. He asked me: "What do you do in Gaborone?" So, I told him. He immediately picked up the phone and cancelled the call, and then he took me to the teller to ask her to cash the check. This was a small bank in a small town, everyone in the bank knew that the long distance call to clear the check had not gone through, and I received puzzled looks from the white staff at the bank. It was good to see that a man could simply do the right thing, despite all the customs to the contrary.

Race Relations at Legco
When the Legislative Council was formed in 1961 as the first legislative body in the Protectorate, the membership included ten whites, ten blacks and one Asian, plus various officials of the Protectorate government. While whites were far less than one percent of the population, and there were even fewer Asians, there was little public complaint about the fact that blacks and whites had equal representation, and similarly no complaint about Mr Chand, the

Asian representative. Equally, when we became more democratic and each person had an equal vote under the constitution developed in 1963, there was no complaint that we had become more democratic. We were matter-of-fact and pragmatic in our approach to race relations as on all other issues; and by we, I mean almost all the political leadership, both black and white. However, some members of the opposition, particularly Mr Matante and others in the BPP, were not committed to non-racialism as we were in the Democratic Party.

In Legco, the white members behaved very properly, though people like Hendrik van Gass, an Afrikaner farmer from the Tuli Block, would sometimes say things that we black people would find outrageous. But even Mr Van Gass had his good moments. At one point, he argued that because education was expensive, it should be aimed first at helping Batswana become better producers of cattle. The economy should grow, he argued, before it was asked to support further education. However, during a debate on education and localisation he also added: "I thought the majority of us in the room here were willing to pay higher taxes to back up this localisation plan." After Mr Van Gass passed away, I told the council: "I must say I did not always see things in the same way as Mr Van Gass, but I have always enjoyed him and liked him because of his frankness and tenacity in fighting issues to the end. I should say he was above all true to himself, and I am sure there will be a loss which we will all feel in this House."

It helped that whites were such a small minority in Botswana and did not see any chance of surviving apart from the rest of us. They realised that if they could find a reasonable home in one of the political parties, they would be better off. When Peter Fawcus announced in July 1962 that he would be putting forth some proposals to further advance constitutional development, Mr George Sim responded in Legco: "We can assure Mr Matante that he does not have to institute boycotts nor does he have to waste his party's political funds travelling to New York to achieve an African majority in the Legislative Council. All hon. Members of this council who represent the people, and who are in touch with public opinion are fully aware and understand the aspirations of the people and the implications involved. Both African and European members of this council are prepared to act in concord to assure a steady progress and a peaceful solution of the Territory towards political emancipation and independence."

There were many such instances where the European members were very forward looking. But sometimes in private, you would find someone like David Morgan, who was very liberal in public, would talk very badly after a few drinks had loosened his tongue.

Before Legco, there had been the European Advisory Council and the African Advisory Council and the Joint Advisory Council. In the latter body there was conversation about some issues, but generally people were just clapping one another on the back. In Legco, we were having proper debates that were open and honest, and we were passing legislation and were all asking questions of government, as anyone could see from reading the *Hansard*.

In Legco's first meeting, a number of African members of Legco used the word apartheid to refer to various aspects of how Africans were treated in Bechuanaland. The whites were shocked; some even said we should not use that word in council. But, they quickly came to understand, since it was the early 1960s, at the same time that South African blacks started to be very vocal. We had an interesting debate on race relations; everybody let loose, and the remarks were very candid. The whites in particular had thought all was well until the debate started, and then they realised that all was not well. The whites must have initially thought racial discrimination was an issue that pertained only to South Africa; but when the specifics were pointed out in Legco, it became very real to them.

Legco moved to make Bechuanaland non-racial both in policy and in practice, even though some inclinations to the contrary were being harboured here and there. While there were not many laws on the books in Bechuanaland that specified race, in practice much of what was going on in South Africa was also going on in Bechuanaland. A number of people thought we should do something that would demonstrate that racism would not be tolerated, so in 1962 Legco established a Select Committee on Racial Discrimination.

The select committee sat for nearly a year. The African members included Seretse Khama, A. M. Tsoebebe, Tsheko Tsheko and me, all founding members of the BDP. We took written and oral evidence around the country from people of all backgrounds, including the trade unions, traders, farmers and members of the People's Party. We identified 25 instances of racial discrimination of a statutory nature (such as specific references in laws to African, or Native, or European) and seven of a financial nature. It was easy to deal with the matters of legislation, and in the August 1964 meeting of Legco, we amended all legislation (e.g. by abolishing the African Acquisition of Land Proclamation) to eliminate all such discrimination. There was still an issue of whether we should adopt legislation that defined and outlawed racial discrimination and provided penalties for discriminatory behaviour. We had a lively debate, with both whites and blacks on both sides of the question of whether such legislation was necessary.

In the end, the kind of pragmatism reflected in so much of our formative years prevailed. The chief secretary to the government, Mr Arthur Douglas, commented in the debate that, on the one hand the committee felt it was necessary to have legislation, but on the other hand they did not want to suggest that "there was a serious and alarming situation in Bechuanaland". We thought in fact that it was so encouraging that the time would come when one could, by fairly simple means, knock the rest of it away. The proposal was made to adopt a law, but to delay bringing it into force unless specific circumstances warranted; its coming into force would have to be approved by Legco (or its successor). Further, if the law was not brought into force by 31 December 1967, it would lapse. "A measure of this kind should be there for all to read and all to know," Douglas said. The law would serve "primarily as a deterrent, something which exists, serving as a warning to those who need a warning, serving as a reassurance to those who need reassurance, serving a purpose simply by being there for all to read". In the end, this was the path we followed. In fact, it was never necessary to bring the law into force, and it lapsed at the end of 1967.

In the aftermath of passing the Race Relations Act, a number of people throughout the territory sought to bring cases against whites for discriminatory practices or for abusive and insulting language. For example, some servants who had been scolded by their white bosses tried to get them punished for treating them racially. Some of the white bosses were quite interesting—and amusing, too. They would defend themselves by saying: "I didn't say that, I said Mister So-and-so." Well, one knew very well an employer would never address a servant as "Mister", especially in the heat of anger. There was one famous instance of a white man by the name of Mr Nethering, nicknamed Jambo, who ran Jambo Electrical Shop in Lobatse. He was accused of calling someone a *Kaffir*—a demeaning word for blacks often used by white South Africans. Jambo said "No, I didn't call him a *Kaffir*, I called him a baboon! He was going to grab a live wire that would have electrocuted him, and I had to call him something that would shock him so he wouldn't electrocute himself." There was a fellow who needed some shock treatment! Needless to say, Jambo won the day.

On the crucial matter of race, we knew we were dealing with ingrained attitudes. It is very difficult, and it takes a long time, to change attitudes. We tried to be sure that the changes would take place over time, since it is impossible for legislation and punishment to change attitudes.

On the other hand, Mr Matante, the leader of the BPP, was of a different view; he was primarily a Pan Africanist Congress (PAC) man, and he did not believe in non-racialism. He mainly preached South African politics, addressing the question that was not raised, which was what to do in South Africa. He did not answer the question that was raised, which was: How could we make Botswana successful after independence? We in the BDP felt that if Botswana was successful in matters related to race relations, then there was a better chance of South Africa becoming successful.

When we got to the Lobatse constitutional talks, some people were expecting there might be a demand for some kind of qualified suffrage based on race. However, we in the leadership just worked on the assumption that it would not be a serious issue. Rather than have a fight the whites would lose in the end, David Morgan decided to pre-empt the debate, and he proposed universal suffrage. It simply was accepted without any discussion.

We also took advantage of opportunities to educate other Batswana whenever they presented themselves. For example, just before independence, while the Legislative Assembly was meeting in Lobatse, I was travelling to a meeting with Moleleki Mokama, who later was the first Motswana to be attorney general. He asked me: "When are you really going to show everybody that you folks are running the country?" I said: "Come along, Moleleki, what do you mean, aren't we delivering the goods?" He said: "No, there are some of these whites you should get rid of." I told him I thought such a move could undermine confidence. He said: "Not the good ones, I mean the bad ones." I said to him: "If we are precipitous in sending out the bad ones, the good ones would not know when it might happen to them. While we might be happy to see the bad ones go, we must not make it appear as if we are starting a witch hunt." By the time we got to Lobatse, I think I had convinced Mr Mokama.

Defending Non-racial Principles

Given the dominance of white minority regimes in Zimbabwe until 1980, and in Namibia and South Africa until 1989 and 1994 respectively, racial issues and racial tensions continued to occasionally spill over into Botswana, and we had to deal with them. During the war in Rhodesia, tensions were high in Francistown. I went there and had the DC announce a meeting for everyone in the town hall. I spoke in English, and Mr Richard Mannathoko, the permanent secretary of local government and lands, translated it into Setswana. I made the point of addressing the Francistown community as a whole, not just the whites, although they were clearly the problem at the time. I talked in the strongest possible terms about the importance of being a non-racial state. The exhortation seemed to have worked, as the incidents of racist behaviour decreased.

Another time I went to Ghanzi where some of the white farmers were talking in glowing terms about the Smith regime in Rhodesia and how good it was for the whites there. I reminded them that there was a war going on in Rhodesia. We certainly wouldn't stop them from sympathising with the whites there, but I told them they should be very careful not to disturb the peace here in Botswana.

Our approach right from the beginning was to define the most difficult and contentious issues, such as race, discuss them broadly with people, come to conclusions as quickly as possible, and then implement the means to resolve them. By being forthright in our principles, and by living those principles day-to-day, we tried to help foster genuine non-racialism on the part of the vast majority of our people of all races.

We knew from our own history and from the unfortunate experience of some other African countries how divisive tribal differences could be. Our experience with South Africa showed that a country based on racial differences was something we had to avoid. Therefore, a unified nation was one of our principal objectives as we thought about the future of Botswana in the early 1960s. The late president frequently talked of the need to put aside anything that would divide us. Both in policy and in practice we strove to have a non-racial and non-tribal society.

Chapter 6
The Botswana Democratic Party

As I tell the story of the Botswana Democratic Party, it is important to state a principle that the founders and other leaders took as an article of faith: *The party only matters to the extent that it can meet the needs of the nation; otherwise there is no need for it. If it ceases to meet the needs of the country, then it should cease to exist.*

I have mentioned my concerns about the Botswana People's Party. Those concerns were shared by others, and there were informal conversations about forming a new party among those of us who were meeting in Legco and in the African Council. Then one afternoon in November 1961, Seretse called all of the African members of Legco to a meeting in the dormitories in Lobatse. He started by commenting that we were going through a period of decolonisation; our fathers had asked for British protection, but the British were bound to leave us one day. So, we needed to start working together to form a new political organisation and figure out how we were going to run our own affairs. His statement was received with acclamation; in a way, since he was the natural leader in the council, everyone had been wondering when he was going to say what he said! At that point no one really differed; even Mr Leetile Raditladi, who was leader of his own Federal Party, said: "I throw in my lot." We resolved to create a party that was later named the Bechuanaland Democratic Party.

Serious business had still to be done, so a few of us—Mout Nwako, Tsheko Tsheko, M. A. Maribe, A. M. Tsoebebe, Goareng Mosinyi, and I—were elected to come up with a constitution for the party. Seretse did a first draft, and we next met in Hens Memorial Hall in Mahalapye to knock it into shape. We had planned to have a final meeting in Mochudi, but Mr Mmusi Pilane, then regent of the Bakgatla, apparently influenced by some people, either other chiefs or the opposition, denied us the right to meet in Bakgatla territory. On 28 February 1962, 200-300 people from all over the country met under a *morula* tree in Gaborone, near where Orapa House, the diamond sorting building, now stands. Seretse Khama was elected president of the party, and I was elected general secretary, with Archelaus Tsoebebe as vice-president (later chairman), Ben Steinberg as treasurer, Amos Dambe as vice-secretary, and Mout Nwako as deputy treasurer.

Seretse and I worked together very closely from that time onward. We met every Wednesday starting early in 1962. Seretse attended an Exco meeting nearly every Wednesday in Lobatse, and I would go to Lobatse to have lunch with him. When there was no Exco meeting, I would go to his home in Serowe. Seretse and I were extremely candid and honest with each other. If I differed with him, he would reconsider his position. From the beginning, there was simply a fund of trust between us and a great deal of give and take as we discussed issues.

We put out a short document in 1962 that was intended to outline, in broad-brush terms, the direction in which we were moving as a party. This statement on "Aims and Objectives" evolved and later crystallised into our

"Four National Principles". The statement not only indicated our direction, but also when carefully read, one sees the kinds of things about which we were concerned. We proposed establishing non-racialism, one united nation, fundamental human rights, reformed and democratic local government, and so forth, since these were all missing in Bechuanaland. We also realised they were missing as well in a number of other countries that had preceded us into independence. We knew what we wanted; and from observing other countries, we knew what we wanted to avoid.

We learned from experience and by trial and error as we built the party. No one came with a dogma to be followed. We shared stories, and we learned from each other and from the people we consulted. The party grew organically, and it was very encouraging to see it happen. This was the fundamental difference between us as a party and the People's Party and its subsequent mutations. They fed their followers with slogans and dogmas picked up from elsewhere. They thought they could just tell people any cock and bull story, and the people would accept it. Our experience was that ordinary people wanted to be given reasons. We did our best to show them why we were thinking and acting the way we were.

As we prepared for moving to self-rule and then independence, our biggest fear was that we would lack unity, and that each tribe might think of itself as a separate entity. We feared if we went the way of some other states, we would be in for serious trouble. This is why we laid emphasis on finding all the things that would unite us, and trying to avoid all the things that would divide us. Our Four Principles—Democracy, Development, Unity and Self-Reliance—addressed the things that really worried us during the formative years before independence. We knew we needed both to adhere to our principles, and to fight against anything that would threaten them.

As we built the party, all eight African members of the Legco who were in the party moved around the country addressing meetings. It was very useful, because we spoke with one voice; we said the same thing to all the people, all the time. It would be erroneous to pretend everyone in the party saw these things—non-racialism, opposition to tribalism, reduction of the arbitrary power of the chiefs, and commitment to a real democracy—in the same way. People in the BDP subscribed to the party's principles, of course, but one never knew whether the person had had held those views all along or had become convinced, perhaps even reluctantly.

There were difficult issues in the beginning, the role of chieftainship being a major one on which we did not have unity of views in the party. In 1962, Seretse, Mout Nwako and I had sustained debate during a trip from Maitengwe to Francistown. Seretse was against chieftainship as being divisive, since one was taught that one must lay one's life down for the chief. "Where would be the nation," he would ask, "if the chief is against the principles that favour the nation?" Having been a chief himself, Seretse was not enthusiastic about being a chief, and he did not see why others did not see things the same way. Mr Nwako was all for putting the chiefs down as soon as possible. I held the chieftainship flag, which some would think very ironic. I said: "Look, much as I agree with you, I think we must recognise that the source of authority in a community is the chief. You must talk to people in their own language. The chiefs must not be tampered with—nor must they be promoted to be anything more than what they are."

Our fundamental objective was to make sure that when we took over as an elected government, our authority would be recognised the same way as the British authority was recognised by all the tribes, if not more so. The chiefs must come to know that too; but, I thought: Why should we spell out to them how they would lose their authority if we did not need to?

Sometimes Seretse would talk of the chiefs who were then incumbents, and he would go through the list from tribe to tribe and ask: "What would we lose if these individuals were no longer in positions of responsibility?" He made a convincing case. Some were just inefficient; some were not well endowed intellectually; some drank so excessively that even if they were the brightest of men, their intellect was so soaked in alcohol that it had lost its usefulness. One could see there were few chiefs who would be missed if they were no longer chiefs. We felt a new generation coming after us would not place the premium on chieftainship that our generation had, and it was an institution that was sure to die.

I thought the chieftainship would resolve itself as we went along; the lustre of the clan would wear off, and people would recognise that ministers are senior to chiefs. But when I became vice-president and went to my village, people didn't know how to address me. One man referred to me as *Molaodi* (district commissioner). Someone started to correct him, but I said: "Don't—he has given me the highest respect he knows of!" It was clear to us that we had to do a massive job of education if people were to understand the nature of the representative democratic government we espoused.

One man who is often not given enough credit for the building of the party is Archelaus Tsoebebe. Mr Tsoebebe had been a moving spirit in the formation of the Botswana People's Party, and he was responsible for getting Professor K. T. Motsete to head it. But Tsoebebe made a mistake when he sent Professor Motsete to try to recruit me to the People's Party. If he had come himself, he might have succeeded, but Professor Motsete was unpersuasive. Mr Tsoebebe dropped the People's Party like a hot potato when he realised they were going off at a tangent, and he became one of us from the beginning of the BDP. He was very good at listening to people around the country, and he'd come to me to say: "This is what people are saying, so get ready to address these issues." Because of his very active participation he was elected the first vice-president, and later chairman, of the party.

One sometimes hears reference to Tsoebebe as having been "left wing", but that is a mis-reading. He often questioned things the colonial government was doing, and at that time to be critical was often thought of as being anti-government, and anything that was anti-government was perceived as being left wing! But, when one looks through the *Hansard* for Legco, the Legislative Assembly and Parliament, one will see that Tsoebebe was not saying anything different from what any of us in the party said.

Others who were major contributors in building the party included Mout Nwako, Ben Steinberg, Tsheko Tsheko, Edison Masisi, Motlatsi Segokgo,

Amos Dambe, Englishman Kgabo, and Goareng Mosinyi. (Mr Mosinyi was a nephew of Khama the Great, Seretse's grandfather, and on occasion would show he had not abandoned his roots as a royalist.)

We had limitations as we recruited for the party. For example, teachers couldn't engage in party politics. They could, however, attend meetings, ask questions, and ensure that their questions elicited answers that people needed to know. After the meetings, we could all sit down and talk and plan together. There was a different problem with civil servants; many were not too certain of what was happening, so they neither supported nor opposed us. I remember going to one of them and saying: "Look, some of us are not lawyers, let alone constitutional lawyers, could you help us with this drafting?" But he said: "No, I won't come to help you, I'm a civil servant." However, there were a few who did help.

As we were recruiting, we added members one, or two, or a few at a time. We would just put it on the table: "Brother, here we are. Very few of us have any education, and we are supposed to be the leading lights. You are as answerable as we are or anybody else is. What help are you willing to give us, especially in the form of ideas? What is your view of the future of this country, and how should we move to be sure that the vision you have of the country is realised?"

Symbols and Slogans

The nickname for the party, *Domkrag*, was given to us as the result of a remark by Mr Matante of the People's Party that was meant to ridicule us. *Domkrag* is an Afrikaans word for the screw jack used for lifting an ox-wagon—to change a wheel or pull it from the mud. *Domkrag* literally means "stupid power". Mr Matante said: "Those fellows are just stupid power—*Domkrag*," making fun of the word "democratic" in our party's name. But, it was appealing to us, since we knew it was an object that everybody in the country recognised, and they knew what function it performed. *Domkrag* is used to lift up (*tsholetsa*) an ox-wagon; and we were going to lift up this country! So, our slogan became: "*Tsholetsa! Domkrag.*"

There is a story that the word is just a corruption of the word democratic, and there were even some in the party who suggested that we should use a perversion of it, such as *Demo-krag*, but the rest of us said: "No, no, no, let's use something everyone understands." I think Mr Matante never forgave himself for giving us a nickname we came to like so much; and the screw jack even became the party symbol.

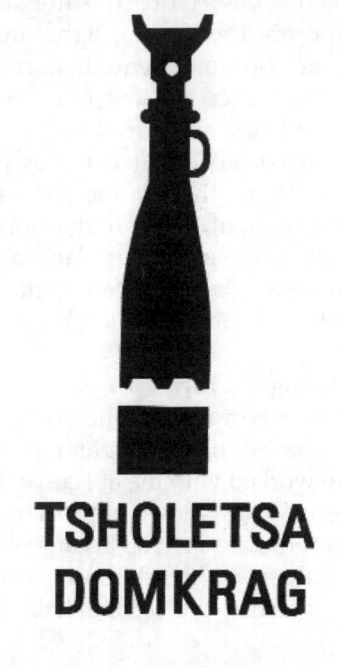

TSHOLETSA DOMKRAG

Once when I was campaigning in Lobatse, an elderly man stopped me and said: "You know, my son, I believe in you because you are not a hydraulic jack, which is unreliable. If you go under the vehicle with a hydraulic jack, you never know if you are going to get out of it alive. But the screw jack is the reliable one!"

The country used a voting counter, a square piece of hardboard, for elections. Later we changed to circles, since a circle is much more difficult to duplicate. Each party needed a colour for its election counters, and we selected red because it was from our party flag. The idea for our colours—Black, Red, and White—came from Lady Khama. They represented progress, from darkness through difficulties into light. The party anthem, which was composed by one of our early organisers in the north of the country, Maruti Joseph Anderson, is based on that theme as well.

Therisanyo/Consultation, our party newspaper, was one of the projects I undertook as secretary-general. It started at the same time as the party and we published it monthly and sent it all over the country to places that later became constituencies. The object was to spread our message by all the means we could muster. We would run stories that talked about our objectives for the country, and our members would respond to things that Mr Matante and company were saying in favour of the People's Party and against *Domkrag*. The opposition had nothing comparable in the beginning. Their party paper was called *Puo-Pha* (straight talk), and the first issue came out after independence. It was also very irregular, and was likely to be published as one issue, and only during an election year.

We had no way of judging the overall usefulness of *Therisanyo*, but we believed it helped to spread the message. We took it that it was like the effect of the meetings we held around the country. Before we were organised for elections, and before constituencies were organised, we would ask ourselves: "Who are the leading lights in Maun who would be sympathetic to our cause?" We would send them copies to distribute; and we did that all over the country. Later we sent bundles of papers to each party organiser in each constituency, and after 1965, we sent them to members of Parliament.

Therisanyo/Consultation was published as long as I did it as a one-man band. Then others in the party thought I was too busy with other things—vice-president, leader of the House, secretary-general of the party, minister in charge of development planning—and so they set up a board to oversee the magazine. Unfortunately, that was the end of it. It came to be routinely published only in an election year.

Building the Party

When we organised the party, we all were volunteers for our first eight months. Starting in September 1962, I had a staff of one, Bennett Keaiketse, who worked with me at Kanye. The following year I acquired a driver, Kgosi Thebe Moses. As we approached the elections, we were joined by Pulafela Sebotho, who in 1965 became our candidate for the Ngwaketse-Kgalakgadi constituency. In addition to Mr Sebotho, three other organisers were employed in the second half of 1964 to help with electioneering: Messrs

Kgabo, Dambe and Segokgo. All three ran and were elected to the Legislative Assembly. We recruited K. P. Morake in 1965 to be the executive secretary to manage the office while I was running around the country, and we organised constituencies as the need arose. MPs, ministers, the deputy prime minister and the prime minister became the party's itinerant officers as they toured the country and coordinated their activities with the secretary-general.

The process we adopted for the organisation of the party was very close to that followed by the British Labour Party. I went to the UK for a time to observe the Labour Party, and we followed many of the lessons we learned there. We didn't make changes in the party constitution, but we did adopt some different procedures, such as the method of conducting primary elections. To start with, of course, we had to organise the local committees with the first national elections in view. Later, the constituency executive was elected in the constituency meeting of all party members in the area after each party congress.

In the party congress there was representation of each constituency: the women's wing, the youth wing, and so forth. The national congress chose the central committee of the party on the basis of secret ballots. The officers of the party and a number of others elected at the congress formed part of the executive. We started with an annual congress, but we changed to meeting every other year and alternated meetings of the congress with meetings of the Executive Council, which included representatives or officers of the various groups, plus the members of Parliament.

At the beginning, I took the lead in recruiting people. I was young and energetic, and I also knew a good many more people throughout the country than most if not all of our members, due to my work on *Naledi ya Botswana*. The others, especially Seretse, trusted my judgment. Occasionally, but only occasionally, he and I differed. For example, some years after B2 had resigned as chief, Seretse thought it would be good if we were to bring Bathoen into our party, and he attempted to recruit him. I differed with Seretse, though I did not do anything to stop him. After elections in 1969, Bathoen wanted Seretse to form a "Government of National Unity" and include him. Seretse told B2 all the circumstances under which one might require such a national unity government—such as a war, or the need to form a coalition to reach a majority in Parliament—and he pointed out that none of these applied. Since our party had won the elections decisively, Seretse asked: "How would I explain the need for a coalition to our party supporters?" B2 said he'd think over their conversation, but he never came back to Seretse.

When we started the process of nominating those who would stand for elections, what was most helpful to us was the general understanding that there was not something for nothing. People knew things happened because there was a reason. You didn't give people positions in the party or the government because they were your cousins. You didn't kid yourself by coming up with a candidate for election who was not going to serve the purpose you wanted to achieve. So we inculcated the concept that a vote is like a spear: Make sure that the spear is used to serve you well, not to point it against yourself.

In selecting candidates for elections, the local party committee came up with a series of names on which they would vote. The local election was a preliminary device to help the central committee decide who should stand for election. The local committee's votes were placed in sealed envelopes and sent to the central committee, who opened the envelopes and counted the ballots. They then put the ballots back in the envelopes and placed them in a safe. Any candidate could come to the office to see how he or she was voted for or voted against. We hardly ever changed the decisions of the local constituency, primarily because we wanted to be seen to be honouring their decisions. Also, if we decided on a person for whom the local constituents would not vote, then we would lose both the person we wanted and the seat we should be occupying in Parliament. On the other hand, the local committees knew they should not choose a buffoon, since there was the possibility that the central committee would not accept him.

When we did overturn a constituency decision it was for good reason. In 1989, Mr Calvin Batsile had won the constituency in Kanye by one vote; he was almost tied with Mr Mogwe, so we felt it was not decisive. Since Mr Mogwe was the more experienced, we chose him. In one case, the popular candidate was hobnobbing with someone we knew was a South African agent. The locals could not have known that fact, but we knew because of reliable reports from the Special Branch and other sources. Once in Shoshong, the votes were almost equal, but one candidate was a woman and the other was a man. Representation of women in Parliament was so low we felt we should take the woman, and we did. It had been difficult to bring enough women into Parliament, and we were sure she would win the election. With single-member constituencies, the overwhelming consideration for us was to win the constituency. Parties in countries with proportional representation could more easily increase the representation of women by including them in the national party list.

Confidence needed to be instilled; we knew it was not plucked from trees. So, our moves in the constitutional discussions, our arguments in Legco, selections of party candidates for the elections, and so forth, were all made with that in mind. We wanted to instil confidence in our leadership. Our political choices were important not only for the party but also for the nation. We felt justice must not only be done but be seen to be done. When we had opportunities, we seized them. For example, we felt that Colin Blackbeard, who was white, could be elected to Parliament by a constituency that was almost 100% black, and he was. It was also important to include him in cabinet, since whites were not otherwise represented, and we wished them to feel fully included.

Over time, the local committees wanted to take the sole responsibility for selecting candidates without involving the central committee in any way. After I left office, the central committee yielded to pressure, and the new arrangement is that every member of the party who has paid dues is eligible to vote for the nominee of the party. They call it *bulela ditswe* (open and let them come out). While this "open primary" has some merit, I personally feel the central committee has abdicated its responsibility for leading the party and for ensuring a balanced national list of candidates.

Between elections, the party office assumed a variety of functions that in the early years were performed by volunteers alone. The office kept members informed, looked after membership recruitment, and followed the activities of MPs and local councillors. All elected members needed to hold good meetings in their constituencies, provide reliable information about problems, and give feedback on government policies. It was very important that the party leadership be well informed about what was going on around the country. When we saw problems arising, we would consider them and decide what to do. If an issue in Ghanzi might best be addressed by the talents of a member from Francistown, we would detail that person to go and sort things out.

The executive secretary of the party needed to understand the issues facing the nation and the party, and he or she also needed to be well informed about what was going on in terms of both legislation and policy. We involved the executive secretary in the parliamentary caucus, as we wanted the executive secretary to be available when matters relevant to the party were being discussed. K. P. Morake, Patrick Balopi and Clara Olsen all moved from positions as executive secretary of the party to candidates for Parliament, and Mr Morake and Mr Balopi became ministers of government as well.

Financing the Party

In the earliest days of the party, we each paid our own way in doing the organising. We took a decision that each of us would bear our own burden and pay for our own participation, travelling, or whatever we did for the party. If we met in Francistown at a hotel, each one paid for his or her own room. We had our own kind of *mephato*—regimental free labour! Every thebe we collected went to the party's coffers and could not be spent until we had sufficient funds to run the party on a sustainable basis. At the beginning, the organisational problems fell on one person—me, as secretary-general. From December 1961 to September 1962, I wasn't given a thebe, or a penny, to organise. I paid for the postage on every letter I posted for the party. I was carrying out the major responsibilities for travel, letters, and so forth and it was my pocket and my family's that were being used for most of the expenses. Mma-Gaone's salary as a teacher was supporting the party!

We worked it that way until we met in Mahalapye in September 1962. I remember that meeting well, since I had been planning to read a telegram of congratulations from the Swedish Socialist Party. When I began to speak, I apologised for the fact that I had left the telegram in my other jacket. Seretse interrupted me: "What, Quett, you have two jackets?" The meeting roared with laughter. After the Mahalapye meeting, some of Seretse's friends gave us a bit of money, which, together with what we had saved, enabled us to buy two four-wheel drive vehicles that lasted us over four years. Later we bought a third from Dr Williams, a veterinary officer, and then another second-hand vehicle from Bias Mookodi. By the time we were campaigning for the first elections, we had a "fleet" of four vehicles to travel on dirt roads throughout a country larger than France! By 1965, we had proved ourselves in Legco and the policies we were supporting were popular. Some people in the private sector, such as Mr Makgalemela of Shoshong, decided that we would be good for the country, and they began to provide financial support by paying monthly contributions.

We wanted to be sure there was a minimum chance of any embezzlement of party funds, so we decided that all money should come to one place, the central treasury office, from where it would be disbursed by the treasurer of the party. Later on, we decided that a certain proportion of the money would go back to the branch or the constituency in which it had been raised, but first it had to come into the main fund to be properly accounted for.

In the early 1960s, someone from Pretoria who claimed to be from the American embassy offered financial support for the party. The late president was approached, but he refused the offer and told me about it afterwards. Later, when Mout Nwako was minister of state in the Office of the President, he was approached by the South African foreign minister who offered to help finance the party. Mr Nwako seemed excited by the prospect, but we told him this would be a very bad idea; the South Africans would start dictating terms and would say they had us in their pocket.

We raised money in the early days by having fetes and concerts in the main constituencies. Ben Steinberg was a very dynamic treasurer; I don't think anyone did more for the party than he did. He came up with innovative ideas for funding. For example, we would sign people up, and they would pay a discounted fee for future years of membership. We also raised money for particular projects, such as building Tsholetsa House, the party headquarters. We gave each constituency a target for the amount of money it should raise for that project. Mr Nwako was appointed to be chief fundraiser, and he worked very hard until the building was completed. He was assisted by others such as Mr Sham Khan, every member of Parliament, every mayor, and every district council chairman. We all raised funds and we had to dip our hands into our own pockets, too. We each signed a stop order in favour of the party for a direct transfer from our bank accounts each month, and my stop order still stands to this day.

When we obtained a plot of land for the party headquarters, we applied like any other organisation would do, and we were given an allocation. However, we were running around raising money, and we did not register it properly to receive the title deed. The title deed eventually was delivered, but the plot was not in the name of the party but in the name of someone who was working for the Gaborone Town Council. So, of course, we had to apply again, and the party was allocated the plot on which Tsholetsa House now stands, adjacent to the mall and the government enclave in Gaborone.

The 1965 Elections
When we were campaigning for the first time for elections in 1965, we took the following saying seriously: "The essence of a democracy is an informed public." Therefore, we in *Domkrag* treated our campaign as an opportunity for education. We felt people should vote with the full knowledge of the consequences of their vote, and also of what the representatives they elected were expected to do and were capable of doing. That approach was widely accepted in the party and among the candidates for election. However, the approach has changed a little over time as the party has won more elections. Today we seem to do more education relating to why *Domkrag* is doing a

better job for the people, rather than educating the people more broadly about the country and its problems and possible solutions.

Our message in 1965 was very basic: We Batswana were going to take over responsibility for running our country. We were going to do it on the basis of parties. Any group of people with ideas for policies and programmes could form a party. When the elections came about, the people would elect from those groups, or parties, that had a convincing programme and that had proposed candidates in different constituencies. The party that won the majority of seats in the Parliament would be the one that would run the country. To run the country, there would be different ministries, headed by political ministers, and so on and so forth. We were starting from scratch. We had no history of elections, no country-wide government other than the colonial administration, no history of political parties, no authority other than the traditional ones of the chiefs and those of the colonial government.

There was not a village in the country we did not visit in the mid-1960s, regardless of the size or location. The real crunch was between 1962 and 1965, when we were talking to the uninitiated. Until September 1962, the burden fell largely on me, single-handedly, and then help came from some others. I also took the lead in talent spotting around the country, though sometimes after a Legco meeting we would take other members of Legco as we travelled around.

The overriding consideration in the politics of that time was the question of what would happen after the withdrawal of Her Majesty's Protection. Would we go back into tribal entities, or go forward to build a united nation? Of course, the latter was by far the most favourable option, so we built around that. We had to ensure that we did not encourage tribalism but rather encouraged nation building. That was why in the draft constitution the party was called "The Bechuanaland National Democratic Party". It was very important to declare publicly that this was not a local party, but a national party. For the nation to survive it had to be democratic; it had to be united; it had to be developed; and it had to be self-reliant. That's where our four principles came from.

The whole process became organic, and we picked up a lot from our meetings around the country. As we compared our experiences, we realised how much common sense prevailed in the country. For example, Mr Kgabo had addressed a meeting at Takatokwane, and there were as usual questions and comments. Someone asked: "What can you do immediately to convince us that all the things you have said about the future of the country will come true?" Before Mr Kgabo could answer, someone stood up from the crowd and said: "If you had been listening carefully, you would have heard him say that some of the things will not benefit us now, but perhaps tomorrow, or the year after, and some will only benefit our children but not ourselves."

At about the same time, I addressed a meeting at Kang, and someone asked: "Since you talk about the grandeur of running our own country, why can't you be giving us pots of meat and mealie meal." Someone at the meeting immediately stood up and said: "Now look, this gentleman is talking to us as people, not as dogs to be attracted by mealie meal and pieces of meat." We found that ordinary people, the so-called man in the street, had a fund of common sense. Most people didn't expect things to just happen—they knew there had to be causal relationships that could be seen and understood.

While we in *Domkrag* were going to every village, Mr Matante and others in the opposition stuck primarily to places along the line of rail in their campaigning. They also preached a story that might have been relevant to South Africa, but not to Botswana. For example, we had experienced racial discrimination in Botswana, but it was not at the level and scope practiced in South Africa and Rhodesia. It was not a policy, it was just something that was done but not agreed upon to be done. So, we talked about eliminating racial discrimination as a part of our programme, but we did not make a central theme of it; discrimination was not what touched most people's lives.

Domkrag had an educative approach, while the opposition had a critical approach, particularly concerning things that in fact did not happen in Botswana. I remember lying with renal failure in the Baragwanath Hospital in South Africa in October 1964, and reading the Johannesburg *Star*. The paper commented on the forthcoming elections in Bechuanaland, saying if there was plenty of rain and no drought, Seretse might win, but if there was a drought, Matante would win, because he promised people things, even though he knew he could not deliver. Yes, there was a drought, but yes, Seretse won! It proved *The Star* was wrong, and it demonstrated the fund of common sense of Batswana.

The difference in approach can also be seen in the way *Domkrag* and the opposition saw their election losses. When we lost an election, we felt it was because we had not been successful in explaining the issues and the choices to the people, or we had not campaigned hard enough. When the opposition, principally the People's Party and later the BNF, lost, they claimed vociferously that the BDP had cheated and rigged the vote. In the first meeting of the Legislative Assembly in 1965, Seretse responded to the BPP: "The hon. Mr Matante, the leader of the opposition reminds me of that section of the boxing fraternity, where the manager of a boxer shouted: 'We was robbed' when the boxer lost the fight. He is doing exactly that, and the people who normally shout 'We was robbed' are those people who tend to employ boxers of dubious character, and their integrity as managers is questionable."

Domkrag swept the boards in the first round of countrywide elections in March 1965. We captured 81% of the votes and 28 of 31 seats in the new Legislative Assembly, with the BPP winning the other three. We then won the local council elections in June 1966. In those first local elections, we were really babysitting all the councillors, since they were far less experienced than those who ran for Parliament. We organised the primary elections for local councils under the same system of selection we used for parliamentary elections, and then afterwards we took the winners around to introduce them to all the voters in their wards.

Following the 1965 elections, we held about 150 meetings all over the country to introduce ministers of our new government. We wanted to help people understand that the powers of the Protectorate authority previously held by a foreign government now resided in our own people, with the exception of finance and foreign affairs. We had problems and concepts that were new to us—even the nomenclature of the government was new. We needed to talk about a prime minister and a deputy prime minister and cabinet ministers, all of which were new concepts and titles. There were still district commissioners and chiefs, but they now had different functions from those they exercised under the colonial system. Indirect rule had given way to direct rule by the people's own government.

To start with, we trotted around as a pack! We wanted to make sure we were all saying exactly the same things; even though the specific examples people used might be different, the principles would be the same. Before elections, of course, we had travelled as members of Legco who were also members of *Domkrag*, carrying the message of our objectives. During internal self-government, we explained that we were still working with the colonial government. We were having *Puso ya naalano* (a period of handing over), so we wouldn't be required to change things in too much of a hurry but would learn as we went along. We explained the function of each ministry, and what the policy of the ministry and of the government would be about education or whatever its area of responsibility. Our effort was all part of trying to ensure that the electorate was as fully informed about what was going on as was humanly possible. Since most people did not have radios, nor were there newspapers, we had to carry the full message directly to the people in meetings in villages throughout the country.

Some questions we received were very uninformed such as: "You say you can run the country; can you make cloth?" Or: "If you can run the country, can you fly an airplane like the whites?" Others were more well-informed, such as: "There has been a director of education, and you say you have a minister of education; will that be a minister in the district or in the whole country?" There was quite a range, and often we were pleased when someone from the crowd volunteered to help explain. It was a massive educational effort.

We translated the constitution into Setswana, and we would read articles from it at meetings and discuss them. We especially wanted to make sure we mentioned the chiefs at all the meetings, as we knew there would be confusion between the role of chiefs and the role of government. We explained that government would be dealing with matters through various ministries; these would be headed by political leaders who would be ministers of government. We said in the past our government had been run from Mafeking, but the government would now be run from Gaborone. We explained that ministers would be sharing responsibilities previously handled by the chiefs and the colonial administration. It was really great fun talking about these changes, explaining them, and seeing people start to understand. They could see that, while there were similarities, there would be a different system of government from what there was in the past. And, they began to understand that government would be in the hands of those who showed ability and were then elected, not those who ruled because of a birthright.

The way we looked at politics at the beginning was like a football team wanting to field its best players in order to win the match. In this case, the match was service to Botswana, and we were all geared up. As in football, substitutes and reserves would be called upon. Even if one had to give up an office in order to give it to someone better suited for it, we would do it.

In many respects, the development of the Botswana Democratic Party was inseparable from the emergence of an independent Botswana. The people who founded and built the party were the same as those who were leaders in Legco, the Constitutional Conference, the Legislative Assembly, and the government that took Botswana to independence. The practices we established in the early years all carried over; they guided our actions through nine national elections and two successions in the presidency.

Aims and Objectives of the Bechuanaland Democratic Party 1962

Objectives:
- At all times to promote the welfare of the people of Bechuanaland in accordance with the Principles of the Party;
- To attain one man, one vote and an African majority in the Legislative Council by the next elections;
- To attain full internal self-government based on a proper ministerial system by the following elections; and
- To attain an economically viable form of financial and other assistance.

Attendant Principles:
- To protect fundamental human rights and to tolerate no forms of discrimination on the grounds of race, colour or creed;
- To recognise that Bechuanaland is the home of African Tribal and non-tribal communities together with minority communities of other races, all of which form one nation, and that all of these communities are entitled to enjoy their own religion, language and way of life, and have a stake in the economic progress and good government of the country, which must nevertheless be essentially the government of the majority community;
- To tolerate no interference in the affairs of Bechuanaland from the outside;
- To improve tribal administration in Bechuanaland by the formation in all tribes of executive committees elected by and responsible to tribal councils; by the substitution of constitutional rule for the exercise of arbitrary powers by *dikosi*, and by the introduction of proper elections to the tribal councils;
- To develop the economy and natural resources of Bechuanaland energetically and to provide equal opportunities to all who are prepared to work for the good of Bechuanaland;
- To encourage the development of cooperative societies;
- To raise the prosperity and standard of living of all people in Bechuanaland;
- To intensify education and improve health services;
- To staff the civil service of Bechuanaland from the people of the territory, except where suitable candidates are not available, and to take energetic steps to fit the young men and women of Bechuanaland, both within and out of the service, for appointment in all grades of the service;
- To strengthen labour and the trade union movements, so that no man may be exploited by his employer, but that all may work to foster the economic strength of the country;
- To encourage all people of Bechuanaland to live together in harmony; and
- To support the spirit and the letter of the United Nations Charter.

Chapter 7
Creating a Nation

Of our four principles—democracy, development, unity and self-reliance—democracy and unity involved primarily political, legal, constitutional matters and new institutions. The task of creating a new legal and constitutional framework and new democratic institutions for an independent Botswana fell to several groups. The African Council (1961-64), of which Seretse was the *de facto* leader and on which I and many BDP founders and leaders served, debated on such issues as local government and the relationship between customary law and statute law. Legco (1961-64) and later the Legislative Assembly (1965-66) had strong *Domkrag* majorities. We enacted laws to help unify the peoples of Botswana—those from different tribes as well as whites and Asians. We established democratic local government, began to re-define the role of the chiefs, dealt with access to tribal land by all citizens, and began the process of transferring mineral rights from individual tribes to the national government.

At the constitutional level, Peter Fawcus had told the Legislative Council in July 1962 that he would be presenting proposals for consultation with "representatives of the political parties, and of the chiefs and other interests and communities" regarding "further constitutional advance". This led to the July 1963 Constitutional Conference in Lobatse, at which Seretse, Mout Nwako and I represented the BDP. The conference led to a White Paper on a self-rule constitution that was presented first to Legco in November 1963 and then to the British authorities. The new constitution was formally enacted in 1964. A population census that year was followed by a Delimitation Commission to define the boundaries for legislative districts.

Our first elections were held in March 1965. The BDP became the responsible government during self-rule, and during 1965-66 the Legislative Assembly passed a wide range of new laws. During that same time, a small committee—Alan Tilbury, Arthur Douglas (the government secretary), and I—prepared amendments to the self-rule constitution. The amended constitution was approved by the Legislative Assembly and presented to the British in London in February 1966 at a final constitutional meeting, which Seretse and I attended. These steps all led to independence on 30 September 1966.

Our task in that short time was in many ways monumental. Almost every aspect of life had to be changed. At the beginning of Legco in 1961, the average Motswana saw the chief as the sole authority for almost all the affairs that affected his or her daily life—access to land, any matter of civil or criminal law, local developments such as public works, education—the lot. The only other authority derived from the colonial government, and that mainly affected whites or our small urban populations, mostly in Francistown and Lobatse. Colonial authority was exercised by the local DC, to whom all other government officials, from police to agricultural officers, reported. The DCs were seen by everyone to be persons of enormous authority—even the chief listened when the DC spoke. While there had been a rapid increase in the funds available for development starting in the mid-

1950s, the total size of development funding was very small, and few government projects touched the average person. The colonial authorities were also responsible for foreign affairs and immigration, and citizens were hardly involved at all.

In establishing a democratic state, we needed to create new and democratic forms of authority that would substitute for old autocratic ones at every level and for virtually every function in society. We needed to move carefully in making changes, so that the average person retained the security that came from knowing the source of order and authority. We had to achieve the objective of having people identify themselves as Batswana—not as Bangwato or Bakalanga or Bangwaketse or white or Asian. We confronted hostile white attitudes towards rule by a black majority, especially with Rhodesia and South Africa on our borders. Many people in the Protectorate—including chiefs, most whites and many colonial officials—were not in favour of democratic changes. None of us, of course, had any experience of an elected government, either as voters or as leaders. Seretse and I and other leaders of the BDP, as well as Peter Fawcus, Alan Tilbury and the younger enthusiasts in the colonial service all felt we needed to address these issues urgently. It was an exciting time and a great challenge.

The Role of the *Kgotla* in Tswana Culture

In order to understand the proposals we made for new democratic institutions at both local and national levels, one must understand the consultative traditions of Batswana. The *kgotla* had always been the focal point for the whole community. It was a place where people were called for announcements by the chief. It was a place where the chief would discuss affairs related to the tribe, as well as a place for making laws and for addressing administrative requirements. It was also a consultative council—the chief might say he was considering something, and he wondered what the people thought of it and what their views were. The people were provided the opportunity to opine. It was rare for the chief to call people merely to pronounce things. Consultation did not prejudice his prerogative of making a decision that was contrary to the views of the majority if he chose. However, he would have consulted before doing so.

The *kgotla* was also the place where people's needs for justice could be met. Whether it was getting married, or divorcing, or children seeking to settle a misunderstanding between themselves and their parents, or resolving a dispute about inheritance, or a dispute about land—if an issue was troublesome, people would say: "We will meet at the chief's place." The *kgotla* system began at a *lwapeng* (family ward), and if unresolved then it would go to a ward *kgotla*, and then to the chief's *kgotla*. And, if you tried to jump that order, you would be told to go back and follow the correct order. At the ward, they might say: "This seems to be a family matter—could you go back and talk about it?" So you would follow the matter up the chain.

The *kgotla* fulfilled various functions: It could be a court of law, a Parliament, or an administrative body. There were different procedures depending on the particular function that was being carried out—just as there would be different rules of procedure for legislative, judicial and executive arms of government in an independent democratic country. The colonial authorities always used the *kgotla* when they wanted to address the people regarding matters of government policy. The *kgotla* dealt with criminal matters such as theft, as well as civil matters such as inheritance. If you accused someone in your family, it would begin in *lwapeng*; if it was someone in another family but in your ward, you would start in the ward *kgotla*.

While I was a journalist, I owned a business in Kanye for a short time. When I got into politics, I couldn't manage the business, so I sold it to John Makwa. We agreed he would pay me in instalments, and the first was paid on time, as was the second. The third payment was not made, and the fourth was not coming when due. I went to see Mr Makwa and said: "If you keep missing the instalments, you will have another big bill, and you will be unable to pay." He claimed he had paid me the third instalment, and he asked me: "Where are your receipts?" I told him he knew we had nothing on paper; if there had been receipts, he would have had records of the first and second payments, which he did not.

We agreed to differ, and as was the custom when one had a dispute, we went to the *kgotla* and asked Mookami Gaseitsiwe, the chief's brother, to be the arbiter. I presented my case, and Mr Makwa made his rebuttal. Mookami asked who would be Makwa's witness, he said: "My wife." And he asked me who my witness would be, and I replied: "Mr Makwa's wife." That was a bit of a surprise, and the chief's brother asked me why I had chosen Mr Makwa's wife. I told him: "His stories are made up, and his wife will not be able to repeat them." So, Mr Makwa said: "Let me go and fetch my wife," and I said: "If he goes, I go, too." When Mokgami asked why, I said: "Because otherwise he will influence Mrs Makwa's account." Rre Mmakgongwana, a driver for the chief's brother, fetched Mrs Makwa; when she was asked the very first question, she was unable to tell the story as Mr Makwa had told it. Mr Makwa just laughed it off; he knew he had tried a trick that didn't work. Then he paid me without complaining. Our traditional process worked well. It was the least expensive form of litigation, and it provided quick decisions that were generally regarded by the whole tribe as just and fair ones.

Local Government Reform and Customary Law

As we approached the task of introducing democracy at the local level to substitute for traditional rule, we each came with our own experiences and sense of what needed to change. I had experienced many skirmishes with my chief because I was inclined to challenge irrational decisions. I had suffered from B2's arbitrary actions on a number of occasions. We each knew of many others, such as the case of a man from Mmathethe in Ngwaketse, who worked in Johannesburg, and who wanted a place where he could start a business. Every Christmas holiday, he came to Botswana to seek an allocation of land from his chief, and after every Christmas holiday he went back disappointed that he was not allocated land, and no good reason was ever given. Many of us had had similar experiences that led us to conclude that democracy needed to be instituted at the local as well as the national level.

In 1963, the African Council established a committee on local government to which Chiefs Bathoen, Mokgosi and Linchwe, and three other members, A. M. Tsoebebe, K. T. Motsete and Motlatsi Segokgo, were elected. The committee reported in 1964, and it was agreed that their report would form the basis of legislation that would be prepared by government. Based on the report, a White Paper, "Local Government in the Bechuanaland Protectorate", was approved by Legco. The report was groundbreaking in many respects, since it proposed elected councils with non-racial criteria for voters. Any resident of the area governed by the council (i.e. not just members of the tribe in the tribal reserve) would henceforth be eligible to stand for, and vote in, local elections. Chiefs would be the ex-officio chairmen of the councils, providing what the report called "a strong tribal element" to each local council. Further, the report proposed that any citizen could be a member of a tribe for purposes of land allocation. This addressed an issue we had raised in Legco the previous year: By past tradition, a Motswana could only receive a land allocation from his chief in his own tribal territory, while whites or Asians were free to move about the country in search of economic opportunities.

The report also recommended uniform salaries and other terms of service for local government employees. This eventually led to the Unified Local Government Service, as well as Unified Teaching Service and a similar nursing service under the Nurses and Midwives Act. These reforms meant the wealthier councils, such as the Ngwato region (which became Central District), or the town councils, would not have a monopoly on the employment of the most talented people. It also meant employees of a council need not come from the geographic, or ethnic, area defined by the council's jurisdiction. On one critical matter, the committee was in general agreement that mineral rights should be transferred from tribes to central government.

These proposed reforms were fundamental to many of our objectives, and they had been developed by a broadly representative group, including chiefs. They removed the arbitrary power of chiefs by democratising a number of local government functions; removed the district commissioner from the position of pre-eminence in administration of policy; established rights for all citizens in all tribal areas; and eliminated racial discrimination in local elections. Those changes took local government out of the province of Tswana law and custom. While the legislation bringing all these changes into effect was not formally proposed until self-rule or even after independence, the fundamental approach was settled in 1963 and 1964 in the African Council and with the publication of the White Paper. July 1966 was set as the date when the new district councils would come into effect, with elections held prior to that date. After independence, we changed the timing of local elections so that they would correspond with elections for the National Assembly.

In 1963, the African Council began consideration of a uniform Penal Code for the country, one that would apply to all residents of Botswana regardless of race, tribe or creed. Members of the Standing Committee of the African Council met regularly with the Law Reform Committee of Legco to develop a Penal Code. Alan Tilbury was the key person in the Law Reform Committee. He played a major role in developing the uniform penal code, as he had done in so many other pieces of legislation.

The reforms to local government did nothing to reduce the role of chiefs in matters of customary law or, at that time, in the allocation of land. The African Council's approach to customary law was of great importance to our transition to independence and to our social cohesion as a nation. We agreed within the council that we should permit the two systems of civil law to function in parallel—Tswana customary law on the one hand and statute law with its Roman-Dutch common law tradition on the other. People would be free to choose under which of these two legal systems they might choose to bring a matter. This meant the ordinary Motswana in the village would be able to continue to regard most matters of daily life—marriage, inheritance, contract disputes, ownership of cattle, complaints against other persons—in the same way after independence as before. There would be no need to find a trained lawyer, to go to a distant court, or to deal with a strange body of law or a strange language. It also meant the chiefs, and the sub-authorities under the chiefs, would continue to serve the judicial function as they had for generations.

After independence, the BDP governments continued these parallel systems of law. As we became urbanised, we established *kgotlas* in the new cities. These *kgotlas* are designated as "customary courts", since they don't provide all the other functions of the traditional *kgotla*. They were organised by the Ministry of Local Government, in consultation with the people of the area; it would be inappropriate to simply install someone as a headman in a customary court if the people had not been consulted and were not in agreement. There were eventually three customary courts in Gaborone, at Bontleng, Gaborone West, and Broadhurst. Each was established as the volume of cases grew and the need for a *kgotla* in a new and growing area became obvious. If you were originally from Maun and had a dispute with a family member who was also in Gaborone, you would take up the matter in Gaborone, not back at your *kgotla* in Maun.

The language in customary courts, or the *kgotla* serving as a court, is the language of the local area. If one of the parties does not speak the local language (for example, a Mosarwa in a case in Serowe), a translator is provided. In the urban customary courts, the language is Setswana, and translators are provided if necessary.

We in government thought it would be good to codify Tswana customary law, since over time minor differences had arisen between different parts of the country governed by different chiefs. For example, if a chief was not very knowledgeable or very able, then a person would get a decision different from that of a chief who knew the law well and was a good judge. After independence, we invited Professor Simon Roberts, a lawyer and anthropologist from the School of Oriental and African Studies in London, to try to unify customary law. However, it proved to be very difficult due to the intricacies of the regional differences in customs and practices.

To provide a degree of uniformity in interpretation and to ensure there was not an arbitrary element in decision-making, we established a system of appeals from decisions of customary courts. In the appeals court for customary law, the judge sits with local assessors who understand the local conditions. The High Court in Lobatse makes a final determination if there is a further appeal. After 40 years of independence, it is estimated that more than three-quarters of all civil and minor criminal matters in Botswana are still adjudicated in customary courts. Ordinary citizens and the whole nation feel they have been very well served by this arrangement. On the basis that "justice delayed is justice denied", people have a preference for bringing a case under customary law, since the process moves more quickly than the common law system.

Another matter that had to be cleared away concerned local government taxes. Prior to the establishment of the 1961 constitution, income tax was not paid by Africans, and African and graded taxes were not paid by Europeans or Asians. There were different rate structures in the taxes, as well as different thresholds of income at which one would be subject to tax. We needed to integrate the two taxes and agree on the distribution of the revenue between central and local governments. We eventually adopted a Graduated Personal Tax (GPT) applicable to all taxpayers regardless of race. It supported local councils, and central government supplemented these revenues with direct grants.

We merged the GPT and the income tax in the 1970s and provided the lion's share of council revenues by direct grants from the central government. I was minister of finance and development planning during most of these fundamental changes in the approach to taxation. As with any tax, there were issues of the cost of collection in relation to the revenue gained, especially at the lower rates. I felt strongly, and I still do, that everyone should be liable for tax, even if it is somewhat inefficient in terms of cost of collection. Paying tax gives everyone a stake in the system of government.

While Legco was discussing the income tax, there were some complaints from white members that the tax was racially discriminatory, which indeed it was. During the debate I said: "While we are discussing and adjusting discriminatory laws, we shall [need to] continue to pay taxes and run the country." Mr Wharren, a white member, made it clear that he agreed on the need to pay taxes in support of our development efforts. He remarked: "This Bill should have been called the Flogging of the Willing Horse Bill."

Two other matters concerning the prerogatives of the chiefs, *matimela* and *mephato*, needed to be addressed as part of the transition toward democracy at the local level.

In our tradition, *matimela* (stray cattle) were sent to the chief who would dispose of them as he wished. A motion was made in the African Council that *matimela* should go to the local councils for distribution, and this led to heated debates. Mr Segokgo, a member from Tlokweng, the extremely small tribal area between Gaborone and the South African border, was one of those in the middle of the debate. Following one session, I had hitched a ride back to Kanye with Chief Bathoen, who joked: "That Segokgo, how can he talk of stray cattle? How can cattle get lost on that small farm of his?" Eventually we abolished the practice of *matimela* going to the chief, and they are now disposed of by the district council.

Another dispute with the chiefs arose over *mephato* (regimental labour). Under that system, people in an age regiment could be directed by the chief to do certain jobs without any compensation. The chiefs wished to maintain this power, and again there was heated debate. One of Chief Linchwe's people, Rre Dihatlho Seame, raised the issue in *kgotla* in Mochudi. He told the tribe that the new BDP government was proposing to prohibit people from serving their chief. I intervened to say that his interpretation was not correct: "Just as your uncle cannot force you to do work for him or give him *masori* (what is due to an uncle from his nephew), all the new law does is to prevent the chief from forcing you to work. Nothing in the law prevents you from serving your chief if you wish to do so." Such distinctions were very important for us.

The work begun in the African Council and Legco, continued by the Legislative Assembly during self-rule, and completed by Parliament after independence achieved a complete restructuring of local government. We established democratic non-racial institutions at the local level and reformed the financing and the staffing of local authorities. We laid the basis for the transfer of mineral rights to the nation as a whole, and we created a uniform, non-racial penal code throughout the country. We retained customary law as the legal system by which the vast majority of citizens would still govern their day-to-day lives.

Constitutional Reforms

During the latter half of 1963, the issues of democracy at the national level and the role of the chiefs in that democracy were also being settled. In April 1963, Peter Fawcus invited various groups in the country to nominate representatives to a conference in July 1963 to consider proposals for the next stage of constitutional development. Five groups were invited to nominate three persons each: the political parties (the BDP and what were by then two factions of the BPP), the European members of Legco, and the chiefs. Mr Abas Chand represented the Asian community. Peter Fawcus was in the chair; Arthur Douglas, the government secretary, and Alan Tilbury, the legal secretary, sat with the group as official advisors.

Seretse Khama, Mout Nwako and I represented the BDP; Chiefs Bathoen II, Mokgosi III and Linchwe II represented the chiefs, David Morgan, Jimmy Haskins and C. J. Mynhardt were chosen by the Europeans. One faction of the BPP was led by Motsamai Mpho, who had started his political career as a member of the ANC in South Africa. The other faction included Philip Matante, who preached the gospel of the PAC in South Africa, and Professor K. T. Motsete. We in the BDP felt the BPP was over represented, and we would occasionally be a bit naughty if they raised a point in opposition to one of our proposals. We made much of the fact that we were at a disadvantage in terms of numbers!

Before the constitutional conference began, all the delegates received copies of constitutions from recently independent Commonwealth countries.

These gave us good background on what was being tried elsewhere. We in *Domkrag* expected that the colonial government would come up with their own proposals, and we decided we should not be in a reactive position; we wanted to have our own clearly defined ideas on each issue. So, eight members of *Domkrag*—Seretse, Mout Nwako, Englishman Kgabo, Motlatsi Segokgo, Tsheko Tsheko, Amos Dambe, Letlhole Mosielele and I—drafted our own proposals on how to address each of the relevant areas of a constitution. We developed not only the proposals but also the arguments to support each one.

The opposition parties were not well prepared in the constitutional conference. None of them had been elected to the African Council or Legco, so they had no legislative experience, nor did they have a lawyer among them. It did not seem they had read the papers carefully, and they did not make substantial proposals. The whites seemed to have decided it would be preferable to play a minor part in a political system that was likely to lead to a responsible government than to seek a larger formal role in a constitutional setup that was likely to produce a bad government. Further, the whites did not act in a coordinated way or as if they were a political party. Notwithstanding the problems with the opposition parties, the rest of the group worked together as a team to discuss and negotiate the arrangements. The government representatives seemed almost to be waiting to take their cue from the BDP leadership concerning what the constitutional talks should do.

The conference decided early on that since the self-rule constitution would be in force for a short time, we should make that constitution applicable to a republic, other than the changes needed to replace British authority during self-rule by an independent national authority. During self-rule, for example, the prime minister would become head of government, but the colonial government would retain responsibility for foreign affairs and finance. It was agreed during the conference and confirmed by Legco that the constitution we constructed would lead to elections in 1965, and that the government elected in 1965 would lead us to independence. However, after the 1965 elections, both the chiefs and Mr Matante wanted new elections before we went to independence. The chiefs wanted to renegotiate the provisions for chieftainship, while Mr Matante thought he might improve his position if we postponed things and held another constitutional convention and further elections.

Our constitution included a Bill of Rights. A list of individual rights in a constitution was popular in new constitutions in Africa. However, it was also a good idea for substantive reasons. We in the BDP were conscious of the trend toward one-party states elsewhere. We felt that if rights such as free speech and freedom of association were protected, then a one-party state would not be possible, even though Botswana's constitution did not specify that we would be a multi-party country.

During the constitutional talks, the leadership from *Domkrag* always started with Botswana and its context. We looked carefully at the constitutional provisions of other countries, but we did not include things simply because they were included someplace else unless they had a relevance to Botswana.

We were not interested in importing ideologies from other places such as were being introduced in some other African states. We in the BDP prided ourselves on the fact that we did not have any "isms" in Botswana.

Of course, the constitution had to provide for legislative, executive and judicial powers, as well as for provisions governing citizenship, financial responsibility, amending the constitution itself, presidential succession, and rules by which the National Assembly would conduct its business. It was very helpful that by July 1963 some of us already had benefited from two years of experience in the Legislative Council and the Executive Council. We could think of concrete examples related to the more abstract concepts that go into a constitution.

We decided that the president should be elected in a constituency and would be the presidential candidate who had the support of the majority of elected MPs. After independence, we concluded that since the president is the leader of the whole nation, that provision should be amended. The president should not have to handle constituency matters in Parliament, nor did we want other constituencies to feel jealous of the one represented by the president.

We concluded that the president should be the leader of the government as well as head of state. We also felt it would be very difficult to govern if there were to be a situation where the president was from one party and the majority in Parliament was from another. One might be able to run an industrialised country like France that way, but we didn't think it would work in a new country. That is why the constitution specifies the leader of the majority party in Parliament will be the leader of the country. Candidates for Parliament must indicate who they will support to be president if they are elected to Parliament. Therefore, once one knows which party has won a majority in Parliament, one automatically knows who will be president. We were very conscious in choosing the system we did, and we felt the arrangement would minimise unnecessary friction between the president and Parliament.

While I was president, a Norwegian visitor to Botswana asked me where my constituency was, and I told him: "My constituency is Parliament." This was true literally, since Parliament elected the president. But I explained it was also true politically: The president must pay attention to the constituents in Parliament in the same way a member paid attention to those in his or her constituency. Each must lead, and each must help people form opinions on important issues. But ultimately each was voted in or voted out by his or her constituency.

As a part of the package of constitutional changes in the 1990s when we laid down specific procedures and protocols for presidential succession, we introduced a limit of two terms for a president. I must confess, eager as I was to leave, I was not completely happy with the two-term limit. However, I went along with it. There were arguments on both sides, of course. On the one hand, an incumbent had an edge for re-election even if he or she was not very able; and even one term would be too long for a poor president. On the other hand, if we had a very able person, why should that person not serve a longer term? If we had had such a limitation at the beginning, Seretse would have had to stand down before the 1974 elections, and the nation would have been deprived of his excellent leadership for the rest of that decade.

The constitution recognised the need for "collective responsibility" in the cabinet—i.e. whenever a decision is made in cabinet, all ministers agree to abide by the decision and not to dispute it in public, regardless of differences expressed during the debate. This necessitated a substantial effort to discuss issues fully in cabinet. Collective responsibility in cabinet also implied that, in order to have good substantive discussion and debate in Parliament, we needed to have a strong and articulate opposition and good government party back-benchers. Otherwise, debate in Parliament would not bring out arguments against or alternatives to proposals from government. What should not be forgotten, however, is that cabinet is an advisory body. The president could listen to cabinet's advice and then do what he or she thought was best for the country, just as would a chief after a *kgotla* meeting.

While the constitutional conference had agreed on a definitive number of constituencies, it was left to the Delimitation Commission (an independent commission established in the constitution and chaired by a judge) to establish the boundaries of each parliamentary constituency. Only the High Court can overrule a decision of the Delimitation Commission, and government had no power to amend its decisions. We did not know all the facts about the size and location of the population when we were drafting the constitution. Every Tom, Dick and Harry had the right to make representations to the Delimitation Commission as it went around the country gathering evidence about how constituencies should be defined. The views of all people, regardless of politics or party, were taken into account, and *Domkrag* made its views known, but it did so just like any other citizen or group of citizens.

In order for the Delimitation Commission to function, we needed to know how many people we had in the country and where they lived. The 1964 Census was the responsibility of the colonial government, with almost no input or interference from the political parties or even the chiefs. It was treated as an administrative matter. However, we in *Domkrag* did express our strong insistence that there be no identification of individuals by tribe or race. We felt that tribal or racial identification would be abused by some who would infer dominance from numbers, or that a group like the whites should not be simply counted as a small minority.

When people have asked me how many people we have on a racial basis or a tribal basis, I've always responded with complete truthfulness: "I don't know." We wanted all people to think of themselves as Batswana, and we didn't want people to be counted by race or tribe. As a result, nobody really knew how many people constituted his or her tribe. There were and are no statistics. Further, given our history of migrations and intermarriages in past centuries and in the time since independence, no tribe in Botswana has been "pure". Mma-Gaone and I are from different tribes, for example, and our children have married people from outside Ngwaketse.

Because of the need to make sure there were sufficient seats to accommodate a government majority and an opposition, and still leave enough backbench seats to be a healthy democracy, there has been a progressive enlargement of the Parliament in the years since independence. The enlargement has also been influenced by population migration and densities in different areas. Consideration has also been given to which areas could conveniently and sensibly be lumped together as a constituency and which would not be amenable to that kind of treatment. For example the geographic size of some areas, like Maun and Chobe, or the Northern and Southern Kgalagkadi, was so large that it seemed impossible for one member of Parliament to adequately service the district. But, if we separated them, then the population in some areas would be so small that it would be substantially over-represented. A balance was always called for, and the Delimitation Commission has had to make the judgments.

The constitution also provided for four specially elected MPs. This idea arose because we knew voters were voters, and one could not count on the electoral process producing the most able people to run the country. So, whether it was our party or Mr Matante's party who won, we felt they should be given the opportunity to find the people who would be most effective to serve in a cabinet.

We also felt that the majority party, whichever it might be, should have a working majority, and we wanted to avoid a hung Parliament. Further, if the majority was too narrow, we might have what we used to call "the village football player's mentality". If a player is very important to a small team, he is likely to say, "I don't have proper shoes", so shoes will be bought, or "I need a cup of tea", so tea will be brewed. We did not want a majority party to be held to ransom by one or two individuals in the party, or for anyone to play the role as a spoiler.

The concept of the specially elected members was not a controversial one in the constitutional talks. These were not people who were simply to be appointed by the president; rather, Parliament constitutes itself into an electoral college, and it elects the specially elected members. Of course, specially elected members are not elected until after a president is elected by the constituency-elected MPs.

A number of provisions in the constitution are "entrenched" provisions; amendment of such provisions requires a two-thirds majority in Parliament in two separate votes taken at least three months apart. While some of these provisions were expected by the British, we in the constitutional conference agreed the constitution should be difficult to change. We in *Domkrag* never thought of Botswana as having a single party, or being a single party state. So, we felt that whatever we did, it should be guided by how the constitutional provision would affect either a bad government or a good government. We needed to create a situation in which, if a bad government succeeded us, it should be denied any excuse to act inappropriately.

Seretse said to me once: "But surely, Quett, you know we wouldn't abuse this provision." I said: "Yes, Sir, but we must set it down properly. We don't want to give a future government any excuse to misbehave." This principle and approach lay behind the way we drafted the various provisions in the constitution. It also carried over to our behaviour when we were in office. We would sometimes say amongst ourselves: "We don't intend to lose any elections, but just in case we find ourselves in the opposition, we would want to have set an example of how a government should behave toward the opposition"—or toward the press.

The constitution provides for an independent attorney general with powers to bring criminal charges independent of the government or any other authority. We thought the chief legal advisor to the government should not be in a position of trying to please the president or the government as he tendered advice. This was a very important issue: We wanted to be sure there was accountability, and such accountability should not be encumbered by someone trying to guess what advice was wanted. The advice should be honest and professional. The attorney general can only be removed from office for reasons of inability to perform or for misbehaviour, and even then only by recommendation of a special judicial tribunal.

The Chiefs
Some history is needed in order to understand our purpose and method of dealing with chieftainship. When the British granted protection to the amalgam of tribes that became Bechuanaland, there were two groups of tribes. In one group, each had a definable territorial area and all tribes within that area recognised one chief as paramount, though there might also be a number of other chiefs in the area under him. There were eight such tribal entities in Bechuanaland, and the areas governed in this way were called tribal reserves. For another group of tribesmen, several tribes lived within a definable area of Crown lands or freehold land, but each had its own chief, and none was recognised as paramount.

Of the eight tribal areas in the first group, the Ngwato area, which became Central District, had one large tribe. It was ruled for many years by Seretse's grandfather, Khama the Great, who was an able administrator. A number of small tribes coming from all over—from Mathathane, or Bokaa, or the Bakalaka from the north—came under Khama of the Bangwato. The Bakalanga were split in two, some under Khama, and some in the Tati Concession in the north-east.

At Protection in 1885, the eight tribes with paramount chiefs varied from the viable entities to the questionable. The Bangwato were the most viable; the Bakwena, the Bangwaketse and the Batawana were truly coherent; and then the Batlokwa, the Balete, and the Barolong were more questionable, with the Bakgatla standing somewhere in between. If one looked at the Bangwato, one would see among them the Bahurutshe in Tonota, the Babirwa in the Bobonong area, Batswapong, the Bakaa in Tswapong, and so forth. Chief Khama III had put them into one cohesive whole, while recognising the smaller tribes. He encouraged marriage of his relatives to royals from those tribes so that the others would feel a part of the larger whole. Similar things happened in other areas that had a paramount chief. During the colonial era, the district commissioner dealt with all tribes in the area through the paramount chief.

The other groups of tribes did not have a viable tribal administration over a whole geographic area, so each of the chiefs in these areas was ruled directly from Mafeking through a DC. In Ghanzi District, for example, you had

Nojane, Kule, Makunda, Kanagasi, Karakubisi, and Ghanzi (the latter also being a township). Each had its own chief, though they were all in Ghanzi District. The DC for Ghanzi would deal with each chief separately, but the DC for Serowe would deal only with the paramount chief in Serowe, who would in turn deal with the chiefs under him in Bobirwa, Tonota, and so forth.

There were four territories where there were no paramount chiefs: Ghanzi, Kgalakgadi, Chobe and the Tati Concession. In the Protectorate era, the first three areas were Crown land, and the latter was freehold land owned by the Tati Company. After independence, the BDP government tribalised the Crown land in Ghanzi, Kgalakgadi, and Chobe, and we also purchased land from the Tati Company and then tribalised it. We did so to ensure that citizens in all four areas had access to communally held tribal land as did those in the other eight geographic areas. I address the fundamental importance of tribal land in Chapter 14.

In addition to all these tribes, there were Basarwa from many different clans. They were scattered in almost every part of the country. Just as smaller tribes were often part of a larger group, the Basarwa were a part of tribal areas in which they lived. Some Basarwa were more settled, some worked for other Batswana, and others, especially in the Kgalagkadi, lived a more traditional life of hunting and gathering.

In the colonial period, the British had governed through indirect rule; that is, they governed the people through the chiefs. The DCs worked with the chiefs and were responsible for all government offices in the district. But after independence, the people would be ruled directly by their own elected government, and there would be no reason to govern people indirectly through the chiefs. That change would mean, necessarily, that the chiefs, and the DCs, would lose some of their authority.

When local government reforms were beginning in the 1950s, it was fortunate that the chiefs' reactions, including Chief Bathoen's, were predicated on their assumption that the new arrangements would just transform a Joint Advisory Council of whites and Africans into a Legislative Council, and an African Advisory Council into an African Council. I believe they went along because they were unrealistic—they didn't envisage elections taking place, and they didn't envisage other people holding office above them. The chiefs had ruled autocratically for decades, and they had been dominant during the years of the African Advisory Council. During the Legislative Council, while Seretse Khama and Chief Bathoen were serving on the Executive Council, the chiefs, and B2 in particular, persisted in thinking that it would be the chiefs sharing the spoils, since they all viewed Seretse Khama as a chief.

Therefore, one of the biggest issues we faced in the constitutional conference was how to deal with the chiefs. We decided chiefs should not hold both their traditional positions and also elected seats in Parliament. We also decided chiefs should not have automatic seats in the National Assembly, nor should a chief serve as a minister or as president, so long as he remained a chief. The example of Nigeria, where a major role for chiefs had led to extreme divisiveness, was fresh in our minds.

The House of Chiefs

Once we had developed our general approach to chiefs and their role in both national and local government, we had to be sure that both constitutionally and legally we achieved our goal. Seretse was anxious that we should not leave open any loopholes for the chiefs in the legislation that affected the chieftainship.

The House of Chiefs was always a somewhat contentious issue. The initial proposal from the chiefs was that they be a Senate. Then Chief Bathoen proposed that the House of Chiefs should be like the House of Lords, a second chamber with power to block legislation that went to Parliament. The conference countered by making the House of Chiefs advisory to the Parliament on matters related to customary law. One substantive reason was that with such a small Parliament it was likely that no one in Parliament would be expert on customary law. The House of Chiefs could perform an important function in tendering advice on such matters. In the initial drafts, it was called the Council of Chiefs. It was not until the final talks in London that it was agreed that the functions of the legislature would include consultation with the House of Chiefs on certain matters. This met the view of Chief Bathoen and some others that the House of Chiefs should be part of the legislative branch of government.

The constitution specified that the eight chiefs who had for decades been recognised as paramount chiefs were to be members of the House of Chiefs. This reflected the reality of how the Protectorate had been organised and ruled by the British; it was, in effect, the status quo. The tribes outside the areas ruled by the paramount chiefs were to choose four representatives from among the chiefs in Chobe, North East, Ghanzi, and Kgalakgadi. The words "principal tribes" have sometimes been used by people to describe the eight entities whose chiefs sit in the House of Chiefs by constitutional provision, even though those words are not in the constitution. The connotation, of course, was that there are minor tribes—those whose chief is not specified by the constitution to be in the House of Chiefs. This has proven to be a divisive point, and one that has produced tensions and hard feelings.

At the time of the constitutional conference, our biggest fear was lack of national unity. Having eight chiefs with rights to representation (simply by being chiefs) was already eight too many if we were to be successful in unifying all Batswana. However, we reached a compromise position in order to bring the chiefs along, and as a result we achieved a constitution that was unanimously accepted.

In our discussions of chieftainship in the 1960s, Seretse would point out that there could be no permanent role for un-elected rulers in a democratic country. "If we are really going to be democratic, people should look to their elected MPs and cabinet. So where does the chief come in under a democratic set-up? There is a ceremonial role, of course, but of how much value is that in our daily lives?" Unfortunately, the issue of chieftainship has not disappeared with time as Seretse and I had hoped it would.

The constitutional talks had been completed and the proposals unanimously approved by Legco, and the Local Government Committee

Report also had been finalised and accepted. However, Chief Bathoen and the other traditionalists then realised what would happen to their powers, and they reacted with utter disappointment, feeling they had been cheated. On 14 April 1964, Chiefs Bathoen and Linchwe met with Peter Fawcus and Alan Tilbury at the chiefs' request. Peter Fawcus did not mince words with them as he reviewed all the arguments that had been considered in the constitutional talks. He has given an extensive account of the meeting in his book *Botswana: The Road to Independence.*

During the meeting, the chiefs asked many questions, but Peter Fawcus and Alan Tilbury held their ground and defended the constitutional proposals. They explained again why a democratic system required surrendering some traditional powers of chiefs who were, after all, unelected leaders. I think the chiefs went away smarting under their collars as they correctly saw some of their powers were being taken away from them and transferred to elected politicians. Since there had been unanimity in both the Constitutional Conference and at Legco, both of which included chiefs, it was virtually impossible for them to appeal to anyone in the British government, either the high commissioner's office in South Africa or in London, to propose any major change.

Shortly before we went to the UK for the final constitutional talks in 1966, I was touring the country up north, and Seretse was away. Jimmy Allison, the permanent secretary to the prime minister, called and pleaded with me to return to Gaborone. The House of Chiefs, meeting in Lobatse, was trying to wreck the progress on constitutional matters. Tsheko Tsheko, who was minister of local government, and I went to their meeting and were able to put out some of the fires. However, the House of Chiefs did pass a "no confidence" vote in the new constitution that included the House of Chiefs.

Then as Seretse and I were getting ready to leave for London, Julian Tennant, a very good DC in Kanye, reported that the chiefs, led by Chiefs Mokgosi, Bathoen and Linchwe, were planning to sabotage the London talks, to which Chief Bathoen had been invited. They hoped to cast doubt on the fundamental basis of the constitution by promoting the impression that the political parties in Botswana were anti-authority. Of course, that meant against the authority of the chiefs! They planned to liken the elected politicians in Botswana to the banned ANC in South Africa, who were against the authorities there. I believe they thought they would gain sympathy in the British government and among the whites in Botswana.

The late president heard about their efforts and made a pre-emptive strike. He called the chiefs to Gaborone early in the week in which the House of Chiefs was due to sit, and he and I met with them. Seretse told the chiefs we were coming close to D-Day, and he asked: "So, could we hear the views of your tribes on the draft constitution?" He knew, of course, that none of them had consulted their tribesmen. One by one, they told us they had not consulted their tribes. Seretse then asked if we could know why they had not. Almost all of them said it was because they had not fully understood the constitution. Seretse asked to whom they had made their lack of understanding known, and they responded that they had not talked with anyone. B2 then suggested they consult their people and report back in two days. Seretse inquired as to how they could consult if they did not understand? And how could they do so at such short notice, when all along they had failed to consult with their tribes? It was obvious they were caught completely unprepared.

They wanted to break for tea, and I said to Seretse: "These fellows want to be unnecessarily difficult." Seretse said: "Let them sweat a little." We adjourned the meeting and then invited them for a drink in the evening. At drinks, Seretse said he would be glad for the chiefs to call meetings, and he would be glad to send his ministers to explain to the people how the new constitutional proposals were going to work! The chiefs seemed grateful that Seretse had saved them from the embarrassment of being told publicly they had not consulted their tribes on a matter of great importance. I went to a meeting in Mochudi, Ben Thema went to Kanye, and other ministers went to meetings in other villages to explain the constitution. Following these meetings, we did not have further problems, since the chiefs found little support among the people for their views. However, if we did not continue to have problems with the chiefs, it was not because they did not want to cause problems.

We had tried to set the minds of the chiefs in the right directions during the African Council and the Legislative Council. We wanted them to understand the meaning of self-government and to feel a part of the whole process. We did not want them going off on their own to find allies who might destroy the national unity we were seeking to build. Much later, when Nelson Mandela came to talk with us during South Africa's constitutional discussions, we urged him to deal with the Bantustan leaders and give them their due as we had done with the chiefs in Botswana. We told him: "Look, these leaders are not what you want in the new South Africa. However, they have gone through the motions, they have registered the electors, they have had elections, they have universities, they have parliaments, and it has been an educational process. It is also important that you have them on your side of the table during the discussions with the government; you should not drive them into the hands of the National Party and its supporters." It seemed that he took the advice based on our experience.

Of course, in dealing with the chiefs, our position was greatly helped by the fact that Seretse Khama could have been the chief of the largest tribe in Bechuanaland. Instead, he had taken himself away from competition for the chieftainship and had joined elective politics. In December 1965, the chiefs went to Peter Fawcus to complain about Seretse's attitude toward them. Peter Fawcus later wrote that the chiefs had "believed and hoped that the position of Seretse Khama as chief by tradition would enable him to understand the need for gradual transformation of traditional customs and ways". In fact, Seretse was a real democrat; but some of the chiefs did not realise that, and they just thought they had been tricked in the process. I daresay what went unsaid was Seretse in effect saying to the others: "If I can give this up, why can't you do so as well?"

Taking Proposals to the People

After political parties were formed, two venues for public meetings developed. When the parties began to canvass issues—promoting ideas of a particular nature—they did so at a "Freedom Square", i.e. any place where political rallies are held. If I wanted to hold a political meeting, I would let the police know I was doing so. There was only a need for permission if there was a potential conflict in time and place between political parties, which was really only an issue in urban areas. However, if government were hawking around an administrative policy, it would do so at the *kgotla*, since from time immemorial the *kgotla* in each village had been where leaders consulted the people.

If a chief did not like the policies that were being advanced by government, he might try to keep government officials or ministers from doing their duty, but government would ultimately be successful. As vice-president or later as president, when I wanted to address a meeting in *kgotla* to discuss a proposed policy, I would simply ask the DC in the area to announce I was addressing a *kgotla* at a particular time and that the chief be so informed.

The issue of addressing meetings was particularly sensitive in 1965 and 1966, since Chief Bathoen in particular was so fundamentally opposed to the reforms we were promoting. Once when I was travelling out of the office, my assistant Pulafela Sobotho made the mistake of writing to ask B2 for permission to hold a meeting at the village of Ranaka in Ngwaketse. Having asked, we could not hold the meeting until Chief Bathoen had granted permission, which he did not do—though he did not refuse, either. So, I went to the *kgotla* in Kanye and put the matter as delicately as I could, saying we had long hoped to hold a meeting at Ranaka, but I believed permission had not been given by the chief to do so. Chief Bathoen grilled me, as if he were just one of the old men at the *kgotla*. He developed the argument by asking first: "Why do you want to go to Ranaka?" I responded that we wanted to address people. "What do you want to tell them?" I said we wanted to tell them about the new political developments. "What are all these political parties about? And why is it you go to Ranaka to talk to people but you don't talk to us here in Kanye?" I said: "I didn't know you wanted me to talk with you at the *kgotla*." He then said: "Well, tell us what you will."

I addressed the *kgotla* as I would have done at a Freedom Square, and when I finished I said: "When I end a political meeting I always ask for questions." The old men in attendance were a bit bamboozled by this approach and didn't know what to say, so Chief Bathoen took over. "How would you proceed if you ask for permission and the chief denies you?" I replied: "We take it the chief would not refuse permission without a good reason, so the chief must have a good reason, and therefore I would be grateful if the chief would give us his reasons." The chief didn't respond but instead asked: "What if you want permission, but the government is going to hold a meeting there?" I told him we would yield to government, of course. Then Chief Bathoen said "The other day Matante was marching against government at Lobatse." I asked him: "Can you liken us to a fellow like Matante?" The whole *kgotla* laughed. The issues were important, and things could often be tense, but the verbal sparring was a great deal of fun.

Puso ya naalano **(Self-Rule)**
In April 1965, the first elected Legislative Assembly met, with Seretse Khama as prime minister in charge of the internal affairs of the nation. We called self-rule *Puso ya naalano* (the period of handing-over). *Naalano* is from the reciprocal verb *naalana*, meaning exchange or hand-over. We and South Africa each had a *Puso ya naalano*. It was valuable for both countries to have had an extended time for a deliberate take-over in order to establish the institutions and the practices of governing a new nation.

In May 1965, shortly after elections were held and the new government established, Peter Fawcus left the country to give the newly elected government, with Seretse Khama as prime minister, a clear field of operation. He knew if he remained, some people would look to him and not to Seretse and the BDP government when there were difficulties or controversy. Mr Arthur Douglas, the chief secretary, was thought to be Peter's choice to succeed him as Queen's commissioner, but Arthur Douglas was more distant, and his attitude was very different from that of Peter Fawcus. Seretse made it clear to the British authorities that he did not want to have Arthur Douglas as Queen's commissioner. Sir Hugh Norman-Walker was then appointed, but he did not seem to be really interested in the affairs of the country and simply did the necessary formalities.

During the self-rule period of 18 months, we had many learning experiences as we gradually moved into control. For example, Hugh Norman-Walker chose not to come to cabinet meetings, which he would have chaired as the senior figure in government. Therefore, Seretse chaired the meetings of cabinet from the start. We also had to develop procedures for conducting business as a government and as a cabinet, and to establish working relationships with the permanent secretaries who ran each ministry on a day-to-day basis. We had to establish Standing Orders for the conduct of business in the Legislative Assembly, which we modelled on those of Legco. When we assumed full responsibility for the country on 30 September 1966, we had been practicing and increasing the level of understanding and responsibility, bit by bit, for over five years, including our time at Legco and that of self-rule.

A very great deal was accomplished between the end of March 1965 and the end of September 1966. We repealed the whole African Administration Act, which had governed our daily lives, and replaced it with legislation that introduced Local Councils and other organs of democratic local government. If this change had been tried too early, I believe the chiefs would have been a problem. Had it been tried too late, the game would have been over. We dealt with many other matters during self-rule. I discuss the questions of economic and financial planning and our relationships with the liberation movements in southern Africa in later chapters. Here I mention three other issues that deserve special mention.

Learning to Govern
We needed to develop our own traditions both for the interface between civil servants and politicians and for doing business as politicians in the National

Assembly. The traditions and procedures we developed came from the honest pursuit of what we thought was good for Botswana. We were not going to discard any existing process or procedure until and unless we had the opportunity to determine whether it was good or bad. We did not have to create an administration from scratch. We didn't want to reject whatever we found in the British administration just because it was British. We certainly did not swallow whole every aspect of the way they did things, but we needed to observe it and see how it worked. I think we were lucky, because the British left us an honourable tradition to emulate. Given the meagre financial resources with which the colonial authorities had been provided, it was as near perfect as possible. An especially valuable legacy was an efficient and corruption-free civil service.

During self-rule, I learned how to be the leader of the House, managing the government business in the Legislative Assembly. I worked closely with Alan Tilbury, the attorney general. If I thought during debate that it would be necessary to propose an amendment to legislation, I would call for a recess, and he and I would work on the appropriate wording of an amendment. If I felt something else needed to be done, I would talk to him about it. We would find a way of solving the problem, and then I would introduce it. I used to argue with Alan Tilbury sometimes, of course. Once when we were having a disagreement, I said to him: "It is bound to be done this way, otherwise it would be repugnant to justice." He just laughed, since this was a phrase he often used with me to make a point.

Famine and Drought Relief
Around the time of independence, we suffered from a severe drought and famine. One-third of all our cattle died, and virtually all crops failed. As we had already become the government for internal rule, we were responsible for the famine relief programmes. We were fortunate that resources were made available from external donors. I went to the World Food Programme to seek assistance, and as we faced periodic droughts, it became almost an annual pilgrimage. Once we had met the critical family needs, we added schools throughout the country, based on the success of the school-feeding programme Bias Mookodi and I had developed in Kanye.

We ran the drought-relief programme just the way we did finances in the consolidated fund. Even though we had a number of external donors and volunteer agencies, all resources came into the government, and we decided how they should be spent. It was not the external agencies that decided where things would go; their role was to give us a helping hand as we administered the programme. We felt it would be a formula for confusion, and even disaster, if we did not have a central administration to coordinate everything through our own famine relief unit. At the same time, we knew we needed more hands than we could provide on our own. Our experience in coordinating the activities of many donors was instructive later on. Once the British ceased to be our only financial supporter, we were able to manage multiple donors who provided both finance and technical assistance personnel.

During the period of famine relief, we went beyond simply handing out food and introduced a number of self-help projects. At least three factors interplayed in our discussion of self-help projects in the 1960s. First, if people were starving, we needed to find food for them. Second, if people got food from elsewhere, it was a disincentive for them to produce food for themselves. Of course, there were variants within that latter issue, such as whether food relief should be withdrawn during the ploughing season. People might develop inertia and not go to plough because they were living on the handouts. A third issue was whether people should work for their food if it was a gift to the country from donor agencies.

There was also a big debate about the benefits of self-help projects—for example, when a school was being built and some people didn't want to work, should their children be allowed to attend that school? Opinion was divided, with some feeling that yes, they should be allowed, since the children were not the parents—a view held by the late president. And others said no, citing the scriptures that even the good God had said: "I am a jealous God who will visit the iniquities of the parents on the children even unto the third generation," and I held that view! Much as I was usually in sympathy with Seretse, I felt people would ask themselves: "Why should I work on the projects when my children can get the benefit anyway?"

In practice, there was a blending of self-help projects with food for work projects. This gave rise to yet another problem. When people worked on self-help projects they were donating their labour. They were not obliged to come on time nor obliged to do a certain amount per day. Some developed attitudes to work that were not conducive to productivity. In Parliament I commented that a woman who carried a few stones in a plate on her head once or twice a day who then demanded full rations would be abusing the idea of food for work.

There was a good deal of disagreement within *Domkrag* about this issue, but it was on the question of how we should do it. The opposition was simply negative; they said we just should not have self-help projects. If food was donated from countries abroad, people should not be required to work for it. We in *Domkrag*, however, looked at it differently; especially the fact that if people thought they could get food for nothing it undermined production. There was no opportunity cost to their time and effort if there was drought, since they could not plant or cultivate or harvest. Therefore, it was appropriate for people to be expected to work for their food.

Symbols of a New Nation
We had to decide on those things that would represent Botswana, both to ourselves and to the world. When it came to the choice of national symbols—flag, coat of arms, national anthem, and the currency—some in *Domkrag* thought the choice should be made within the party. But Seretse was very clear that it should be a national decision. He did not want to have such symbols changed if a different party came into power. We put the questions to the nation and invited people to make submissions. Professor K. T. Motsete, a founder of the People's Party, who held a degree in music from London,

proposed two compositions for the National Anthem: *"Fatshe leno la Rona"* (This Land of Ours) and *"Botswana, Fatshe le Lentle"* (Botswana, a Beautiful Country). There was a contest at which these and other compositions were performed. Motsete's compositions finished first and second, and *Fatshe leno la Rona* was chosen.

The flag was a design proposed by George Winstanley, one of the colonial officials who was PS in agriculture. The black band in the centre represented the African majority, and the two narrower white stripes stood for the white minority and our commitment to non-racialism. The blue at the top and bottom represented the sky and rain, reflecting our national motto, *Pula* (rain). For the coat of arms, Bridget Winstanley, George's wife, proposed a design based on ideas from Isabel Fawcus and Sheila England. Our coat of arms includes symbols of sorghum, cattle, the wheels of industry, livestock, wildlife, and water—things we either owned or wished to! The final design for the coat of arms received a slight input from me. Part of the design included three cogged wheels, symbolising the industry we one day hoped to have. But in the original design the wheels were touching. I pointed out that if they were constructed in that way, they would be completely fused and would never be able to move!

When it came to naming the currency in 1976, we put that to the nation as well. *Pula* (rain) was an easy choice for the currency, and the decimal coins were called *thebe* (shield), though a proposal was made by some that the coins be called *marothodi* (drops of rain).

Development of Civic Institutions

At the time of independence, there was recognition that there were many desirable things to be done, but government was short of funds and other resources to accomplish them. Where government couldn't do things, people were encouraged to do them on a self-help basis. This was how adult education, the national library, the Botswana Society, the national museum, and even the national stadium, where we celebrated our independence, came about. Once when we were leaving the new stadium I heard a woman say that if we had achieved nothing else by our independence than the national stadium, it would have been worth it! English medium primary schools, and later Maru a Pula Secondary School, in which Archie Mogwe and others played a leading role, and many other institutions were started by voluntary efforts. We now have a whole range of NGOs, from the Red Cross and Girl Guides through schools, environmental and women's organisations; but in the beginning, except for the churches, there were virtually none.

Those of us who held senior positions in government, whether in politics or the civil service, took it upon ourselves to be sure these kinds of organisations, which today would be called part of civil society, were started, and that they included both locals and expatriates. For example, there was a private club called the Gaborone Club that catered almost entirely to expatriates and local whites in its membership. A group of good-spirited men and women, largely from the civil service, established the Notwane Club, a place for tennis and other sporting activities. It had been conceived by people when government was still in Mafeking; after the move to Gaborone they encouraged locals to join, and it was a great success. Also, people wanted more access to secondary education, since at that time there were only one government, four tribal and two church secondary schools in the whole country. So, many of us took up the challenge and volunteered to teach classes in the evenings at the Capital Continuation Classes in Gaborone.

Independence

On 29 September 1966 we gathered near midnight in the national stadium that had been built with private subscriptions. We watched the British Union Jack lowered for the last time and the new Botswana flag raised for the first time. Seretse Khama was sworn in the next day as the nation's first president. My main concern for the events was that, as deputy prime minister and the new vice-president, I would have to dance with Princess Marina, who represented Queen Elizabeth at the independence celebrations—and I was not a dancer!

We had achieved our independence. Now the real work of building the country and developing its people would begin.

Chapter 8
Selecting the Talent and Leading the Government

The BDP government was the first elected government in Bechuanaland. We had to learn how to use the institutions of government—cabinet, Parliament, the House of Chiefs and the civil service. We needed to select those who would hold positions of major responsibility in government. Seretse as prime minister and then president had the responsibility for 15 years, and he often consulted me about his choices. From 1980 to 1998, the responsibility was mine. How and why we made our choices were important elements of the successes and failures we had as a government from 1965 to 1998.

Working with Cabinet and Parliament

According to the constitution of Botswana, the president is the leader of the executive arm of government. He delegates responsibility to ministers whom he has selected and then works with them to achieve coherence and implementation of overall policy. Those the president appoints deserve to be respected, but the president doesn't have to accept everything they say just because they are respected. The president knows he has to act in accordance with their advice as much as possible, but he must take the final responsibility. The president cannot say: "Because Minister So-and-so advised me, the responsibility for the decision was his."

When there were differences between me and my cabinet ministers, we discussed them in cabinet and in party caucus until the differences were settled. I apparently managed this system so smoothly that I was even asked on a few occasions whether I knew I had the authority to disagree! The party caucuses were used to ensure that the party members fully understood the policies and were behind them. And, many of the caucus discussions were held to be sure *Domkrag* back-benchers were not taken for granted. Members were given the opportunity to be in the know, so they would be supportive of whatever Minister A or Minister B or the president was proposing.

The president can either sign, or not sign, any law Parliament approves. I never refused to sign any Bill, because in my view there was never a good reason to refuse to do so and there was no need to force the issue just to make a point about my authority. The constitution also requires the government to refer certain Bills to the House of Chiefs. We once referred a Bill that proposed changing responsibility for a matter having to do with chiefs from the president to the minister of local government. Because they wanted to deal with the president directly, the House of Chiefs refused to discuss it. Parliament went ahead and passed it because government had met the constitutional obligation of referring the Bill to the House of Chiefs. The chiefs sent me a petition saying because they hadn't discussed the Bill, I shouldn't sign it. I told them if I thought they had reasonable grounds for not discussing it, I wouldn't sign the Bill, and I was obliged to tell the nation why I did not. But, since I did not think the chiefs had a good reason, I owed it to the nation to sign it.

In the end, it is the president who must decide, and there were a few occasions when the late president or I decided against the advice of cabinet. One instance involved whether or not to have a resident mission in Botswana for the People's Republic of China. The majority of cabinet was opposed to it at the time. We had nothing against the Chinese, but we were concerned that the South Africans might increase their military or clandestine actions against us because of their intelligence activities directed at the Chinese. The South Africans would not believe it was not the Chinese interest in Botswana per se that led them to desire an embassy here, but because they wanted to spy on South Africa. However, Seretse felt very strongly that it was the right thing to do, and so we did it.

Every decision is a calculated risk. To the best of my ability I took others on board, but I did not abdicate my responsibility. Ultimately, the cabinet ministers were only my advisors. They did have the power to make trouble for me as president, of course. If Parliament wanted to vote against the president, it had that right. One cannot rule by fear, nor can one rule by not making decisions simply because the decisions may be detrimental to one's own person.

During my time in office, there were times when cabinet was going in a direction with which I disagreed, and I had to become active in the discussion. One tries to avoid a collision, and I'd found that if one sensed the vote was going the wrong way, the meeting should be adjourned. Then one could talk to the people who might realise the error of their ways, or who might become convinced it made sense to do it the way one wanted. I did not want cabinet to feel that there was no use advising me, and that in any event I was going to make up my own mind regardless of their advice. If disagreement ultimately occurred, people should understand that it was done with reluctance, not because of defiance.

In the late 1980s, we faced an issue of whether we should swap Debswana's stockpile of diamonds for shares in De Beers. Cabinet definitely was against the share deal, and in this they were influenced by one of our diplomats. Cabinet knew, of course, that I was in favour, and I used my persuasive power to try to change people's minds. I pointed out that we had a window of opportunity to invest some of our assets that would otherwise be at risk of being wasted on poor projects. I felt we should not turn it down just because De Beers was a South African company.

Another case where I differed with cabinet, and even with my vice-president, was on the issue of assistance to small citizen-owned building contractors during the serious slump in the building industry in the early 1990s. The large companies could sustain the downturn, but the smaller, newer contractors did not have the capacity. I felt the negative effect of seeing so many citizens who had taken a risk fail because of general business conditions would not be good for the development of Batswana entrepreneurs. And so I decided that the small contractors needed to be given government assistance.

Whether the first diamond-cutting factory should be in Molepolole or Serowe was another issue on which there were serious differences. That was an issue that nearly split cabinet, and I had to nurse it very carefully. My view was that Molepolole already had the advantages of being near Gaborone, and it derived benefits from all of the jobs and purchasing power that came from that proximity. Therefore, I felt it would be better to locate the factory in Serowe. I also thought that, to the extent the decision could be seen as mine rather than as a victory by one faction and a defeat for the other, it would do less damage to the working of cabinet and the party.

Selecting One's Colleagues

There may be nothing more important for the president of Botswana or the leader of any country, or even of any organisation, than the selection of the people who will hold the senior positions of responsibility. A general is only as good as his lieutenants. In the 1970s, a representative of one of our donor agencies paid Botswana a nice compliment. He remarked that Botswana was perhaps the only country in the world where the 20 most able people held the 20 most important jobs. To the extent that this was true for both ministers and permanent secretaries, it was not by accident.

In the early days, the late president and I built the team that would first carry the country into independence and then develop the nation and its people. We made bets on individuals, and there were surprises in both directions—some whom we thought would be wonderful failed, and some about whom we were concerned turned out to be very successful. And, of course, there was the mix of the intellectual and the emotional strengths. Some were very bright but couldn't do the job because they would not make the commitment, or they couldn't control their emotions. Some overcame intellectual deficiencies by strong character, persistence, maturity and good judgment.

In selecting people for cabinet, Seretse and I made our principal consideration the issue of merit, and merit in an all-embracing manner. The dimensions that constituted ability of people as ministers were and are quite varied: efficiency and decisiveness, attitude towards life, how they handled people, temperament, training, and so forth. We looked at individuals and their multiple talents: their ability to run ministries, to speak effectively about policy, to think clearly, to sell policies both in Parliament and in public, to address meetings, to relate well to people of different backgrounds. We also wanted to know whether they had a constituency of their own, as it was important to know they were truly independent persons.

Of course, no one had these important dimensions in equal measure, so each person had to be weighed on his or her own. Also, each had to be weighed in relation to the other people who were going to be in the cabinet, which as a composite whole had to have all these dimensions. There were many factors to be taken into account, and the complex relationships made it impossible to come up with a formula that easily judged performance. Further, over time the training and background of those engaged in public life changed, so the context for judging each person changed as well.

For example, it was absolutely essential to have people in cabinet who could speak English, and in the early years there were two members of Parliament whose English was deficient. They hardly ever spoke in

Parliament, but their work with their constituencies was excellent. Because of their lack of proficient English, parliamentary questions and even motions were drafted for them by their constituents. We could not put them in the cabinet, which one might say was a pity; but otherwise they were very able people who were extremely valuable to the party, the country, and their constituents. On the other hand, we had someone with a university degree who was made an assistant minister, but he made serious blunders in the House and was clearly a howler and had to be dropped. It was obvious that the question of academic qualifications could sometimes be irrelevant, especially in politics.

Some of the risks we took in making appointments in both cabinet and the civil service paid off, but one could not say they had not been risks at the time of our decisions. We sometimes made mistakes of judgment in keeping a person in a job too long, or having expectations that were unrealistic. But some young people, such as Baledzi Gaolathe, rose to the challenge and performed very well indeed for a long time. In 1980 the Customs Union Commission met in Botswana, and Baledzi, who was then our permanent secretary for finance, chaired the meeting as was customary for the host country. At a reception for delegates that evening, the Afrikaner who was head of the South African delegation remarked to one of our officials: "Mr Gaolathe is so able he would be a permanent secretary in any country of the world." Our official asked: "Even South Africa?" The South African smiled and replied: "For him we might have to make an exception."

The late president did not consult as widely on ministerial appointments as I later did when I became president. When Seretse and I discussed ministers, the one person on whom we disagreed most was Mout Nwako. Mr Nwako rubbed many Batswana the wrong way; Batswana are polite and humble people, and he was not that type. But I said: "Sir, you have always told me you are glad when I agree with you, because you know you have my honest opinion and that I would tell you if I disagreed. The other person who will disagree with you openly is Nwako. When he does so, this means you also know there may be other people who would disagree with you. So, if you throw him out, how will you know about other views which may be against yours?" Seretse apparently agreed with my argument, since he included Mr Nwako in all of his cabinets.

When making ministerial appointments, I consulted widely, even outside the cabinet. I would ask people what their cabinet would look like if they were making the choices. As I asked people to serve, I had to be careful about the effects of each appointment. For example, in 1994, one minister wanted to be appointed as minister responsible for presidential affairs—the civil service, police, the army, and so forth. Since I planned to make him minister of foreign affairs, I made the appointment of the presidential affairs minister before talking to him about the Foreign Affairs Ministry. Then there would be no way he could ask me to go back to the person who had already been appointed. In another case, a woman would have preferred finance and development planning, yet she did very well after I appointed her in health. Both performed superbly in the ministries to which they were initially reluctant to go.

In London someone once asked me what we do about appointing people from various geographic areas, and I said: "We look at people, not areas, when making appointments." We did not seek strict geographic balance for its own sake. For example, at one time we had two ministers from the little village of Tonota, and none from the big village of Mochudi. However, we wanted to pay attention to people who felt they had been discriminated against and should be represented. And, of course, the whites and other minorities needed to know that we would not visit their iniquities upon their second and third generations! One should not force the issue, but all else being equal, one should balance things. When I selected Peter Mmusi to be vice-president, I did not give consideration to the fact that he and I were both from the south of the country. In fact, it was almost a good thing to have Mr Mmusi, just to show that geographic balance was not necessary, since, of course, he was a good person for the job.

One of the most important characteristics of working together in government was that from the very beginning we had a collective responsibility for decisions, and we took teamwork seriously. This was true of ministers as well as senior officials. No one made claims that something was being done because of him or her, or that things would not have gone wrong if he or she had been listened to. We sometimes discussed things in our regular Wednesday morning cabinet meetings well past the lunch hour; and when we had concluded the discussion, it was decided. We all took the responsibility for whatever decision we had made.

Our approach came about somewhat naturally. It was obvious that if we met at cabinet as mature individuals, we were bound to have differences. At the end of the day, one person, after taking all into account, would decide. That decision would be the outcome of a process, not just a brainwave of one person. Even when he or she who had the last word said that last word, others would have the satisfaction of knowing that their views had been taken into account, even if another view prevailed. This approach started at the top. If Seretse or I as president had not been committed to thorough consultation within the cabinet, then the inclination of the ministers to be team players would have been undermined.

I was often asked about the nature of my advice to the late president, and I felt I should never comment. A willingness to keep one's views between oneself and one's boss is one of the most difficult, but most important, aspects of being a vice-president, or even a cabinet minister. It is also true of former presidents. One of the things that has been difficult for me since retirement is that I have not wanted to offer unsolicited advice to my successor. On a very few occasions, I thought the issue was so vital to the nation that I felt I should just tell President Mogae my views. Sometimes I have been blamed for some of his decisions when people disagreed with them. People have said: "He must have consulted you; what did you say?" That really put me on the spot, so I have just laughed it away.

There were, of course, instances when ministers did not agree with one another. In the days of my vice-presidency, some would come to me to resolve differences, but I would say: "I'm only a minister like you, except I act

when the president is away. It is better if you try to solve the problem first."
I would tell them that in school whenever I had a problem with maths, I
would try explaining it to someone else. In the process of explaining where I
had a problem, I would discover the answer. So I would say to the ministers:
"If you define the problem carefully so that you say exactly what is
presenting the problem between you, you can generally find the solution.
The two of you should sit down and talk about all the areas about which you
agree. When you come to the area in which you disagree, then you will
figure out how to settle it." A big part of achieving a sense of teamwork is to
have the people on the team sort out their problems for themselves.

Changing the Cabinet
While I was vice-president I often had a tussle with the late president when
he wanted to snatch someone from Parliament to be a minister. I would tell
him that the strength of the party depends on both the front and the
backbenches. The party would die if we didn't have good people in the
backbench to criticise the government in the name of the party. The danger of
creating too many ministries, for example, is that the backbenches are starved
of good people. I didn't want the number of the opposition back-benchers to
outweigh that of the government backbench. The concerns of the man in the
street, not those in office, must be represented not just by opposition, but also
by the government party's own backbench. So, when we shuffled the cabinet
over the years, we were not just worrying about the quality of the cabinet but
also the effect on what the party was saying by the questions and motions and
comments of its back-benchers. We might have a strong cabinet but we risked
losing the elections if we removed the outspoken and articulate critics within
the party; people might never hear the party say things the average person
could share. It is a good thing that President Mogae increased the size of
Parliament after he increased the size of the cabinet. He needed to have
articulate back-benchers talking like the ordinary citizen.

A number of people have been both in and out of cabinet over the years.
The decision on whether to include or exclude someone has to do with the
abilities of the individual, of course. But the decision is also affected by the mix
of people and skills in cabinet, as well as the representation from different parts
of the country and the balance of the front and back benches. One looks at the
pool of people who have the potential to be ministers, and decides accordingly.
There should be no stigma about being cycled out of the cabinet.

I also kept people in cabinet but changed their portfolio responsibilities.
After the 1984 elections, I switched Mr Mogwe from foreign affairs to minerals,
and Dr Chiepe from minerals to foreign affairs. I did so for a number of
reasons. First, I thought Dr Chiepe would be very good in foreign affairs. With
her dignity and calm demeanour she would be very effective in dealing with
the South Africans, especially their outspoken Foreign Minster Pik Botha.
Second, Mr Mogwe's colleagues had begun to think he was drifting away
from Botswana, and that he was seeing himself more as an international
politician. In the 1979 elections, people like Mr Nwako wanted Mr Mogwe to
fight an election and lose, so he would be brought down to Mother Earth and

be dropped from the cabinet. But Mr Mogwe and Joe Legwaila were at that time playing a crucial role as brokers between ZANU and ZAPU in Zimbabwe, as well as between the Patriotic Front and the British. Because of the crucial role he was playing in the interests both of Zimbabwe and of the relations between Zimbabwe and Botswana, I kept Mr Mogwe in the cabinet and in foreign affairs. But in 1984, by appointing him in minerals I was bringing him home after he had done a sterling job in foreign affairs.

Selecting Vice-Presidents

Under the constitution, it was the responsibility of the president to appoint a vice-president, and during my time as president, I made three appointments. My vice-presidents were very loyal, but sometimes a little too aloof from me, and did not always communicate with me in the open ways that would have been most valuable. The late president always knew that if I differed with him I would tell him so, as politely as possible. And, if I thought things were drifting the wrong way, I would be pre-emptive, and we would sit down and have a serious exchange. But once he had made up his mind, I supported him completely.

As I was thinking about my appointments of the vice-president, I would sound out a few people, but without giving them the impression that I would necessarily take their advice. I essentially said: "We are without a vice-president, who do you think would be best qualified?" We would then discuss it, and after they had expressed their views, I just left the matter there. Each, of course, would have been disappointed if I did not appoint his or her preferred candidate. Mout Nwako, of course, and David Magang were very candid about wanting to be appointed. But someone like Dr Chiepe was a true diplomat, and you didn't easily find out her real feelings about these things. Dr Chiepe had a very successful career as a civil servant and as a diplomat, and she was a very able minister, and I thought about her very seriously as a vice-president. She truly had the ability as well as the personality that would have kept the herd together.

Lenyeletse Seretse was my first vice-president. I had worked with him as my assistant minister in finance, and I knew him fairly well. I made the choice because, first, he was as good as any of the other choices from the cabinet in terms of all around ability and was a very agreeable fellow. Also, the nation was grieving for Seretse, and Lenyaletse was a cousin of Seretse's. We had to do things in such a way that the Bangwato didn't feel that everything was taken away from them at Seretse's passing.

When Lenyeletse Seretse died in 1983, I felt the moment of national mourning of Seretse Khama's death had passed. I also thought it would be wrong to give the impression that the country belongs to north and south, and that every time one or the other, president or vice-president, must be from each area. So, I selected Peter Mmusi. This, of course, disappointed my colleague Mr Nwako, since he thought he was the natural successor. But, the decision to ignore north and south worked, and people didn't make any hullabaloo about it. I'm glad I did it, and I think people like President Mogae later appreciated that I did it that way, since he was free to select Ian Khama as his vice-president without too much complaint that both were from the north. We had established that the vice-president could come from anywhere. We settled another issue during my presidency: Some people thought Seretse was the president for 14 years because he was a chief. But I had no claim to be a chief, and everyone knew it, and I served as president for 18 years.

When I selected Peter Mmusi as vice-president in 1983, he was the one of all my colleagues in cabinet I knew best and trusted the most. He had been my assistant minister in finance, and he had been very open with me. He tendered what advice he thought I needed, and our relationship was much like that between Seretse and me. Peter Mmusi knew he was advising me, and he would leave it to me to make a decision. He also had been a very successful negotiator as commissioner of labour, and his human relations were very good.

I succeeded Seretse Khama as president in July 1980, shortly after the 1979 elections, so I had a full four years until the next elections. There were spoilers who opposed my being president, and they persisted through the 1984 elections. In that year, Peter Mmusi, who was then vice-president, was contesting a Gaborone seat against Kenneth Koma. Mr Mmusi won the election, but someone had hidden the ballot box at the Tshiamo polling station, and the lost box meant there had to be a by-election. I strongly believe that those conducting the elections failed Mr Mmusi. Had that box not been lost, I believe there would have been no question that he would have won. But, the lost box meant there had to be a by-election. I campaigned for Peter Mmusi in the by-election, and I said that if people did not vote for him, they would break my backbone. Mr Nwako was incensed; he said people asked him if I meant that he and other ministers except for Mr Mmusi were just scarecrows and not important to me. Of course, when you have a by-election, people no longer vote for a party, especially if the party has already won, but just for an individual. And they may even want to cast a vote to remind government that there is an opposition! As a result, Peter Mmusi lost the by-election to Dr Kenneth Koma.

I had to replace Peter Mmusi as vice-president in 1992 after he had resigned. I thought of the team I had and of my own plans to retire soon. Some of the most obvious candidates were openly ambitious for the presidency. My concern was: Why were they so keen to become president and what was it that they wanted to do? If one is too keen, you never know if the person will want to leave at the end of his term. In addition, serious factions had developed within *Domkrag*. I knew it could be very bad for both the party and the country if a vice-president was visibly from one of the two factions.

Festus Mogae had joined government after the 1989 elections when I appointed him minister of finance and development planning. He showed no inclination to seek the presidency at that time, and he was not known to be associated with either faction. I wasn't even sure whether he would accept the vice-presidency; and that, in my view, helped make him the best candidate. I had no problem choosing him, since intellectually he qualified as one of the brightest amongst us. Nationally, there was no reason he shouldn't do well, and internationally I was sure he would perform superbly. And he has done so.

Leader of the House
When I was deputy prime minister during self-rule and vice-president from 1966 to 1980, I also served as leader of the House. The role of the leader of the House was to manage government business in Parliament. If anything went wrong, I had to make a decision and get us out of the mess. For example, once a Bill was on the floor, I might find that the language needed to be rephrased to accomplish what we wanted. Or, if the opposition made a motion that could not be implemented, I would want to revise the motion so that if it passed, we wouldn't lose out. Sometimes we needed to use a variety of tactics, such as moving for an adjournment if I felt we might be defeated. A skilful legal advisor could help achieve our objectives, and the livelier the opposition, the more I needed the use of those skills. I particularly enjoyed the years of working with Alan Tilbury.

Being leader of the House was one job, and being party whip was another, and I combined both roles before I became president. The leader and the whip had to decide: Were we going to have a free vote, so that members could vote their conscience alone? Or would we have one line whip, or two, when more party discipline was enforced? These were matters of judgment one had to exercise, sometimes at short notice. A case like abortion, for example, was a difficult one—should mothers whose lives are in danger have the right to have an abortion? That is a matter of conscience, and so one can't, or one shouldn't, try to force people to vote one way or the other; one could only try to persuade them to one's view. On the other hand, had the question of whether to exchange Debswana's stockpile of diamonds for shares in De Beers come to Parliament, I would have asked all *Domkrag* members to vote for it.

Although I was doing the two jobs myself, I got the job done. I tried to discourage the use of the whip as much as possible, since we had to play two roles in our agenda. First, we had to make sure the government survived without being discredited, so we needed to secure majority votes. Second, we also had to nurse the people in the party who were criticising the party, so it would not be seen as a bunch of "yes-men". We needed a lively backbench on the government side, people to speak and to vote their conscience.

After I became president, the role of leading the House was done largely through the party caucus. We would identify issues, and then identify who would best handle each one. It was a "diffused whip" system. It worked in part because we had the benefit of discussion in caucus to show the dangers of doing it this way, or the benefits of doing it that way.

Choosing "Mr Speaker"
The speaker of the National Assembly is nominated by the president in consultation with the leader of the opposition. The speaker must be someone

who has a sense of fairness and balance, who has a good feeling for when one side has debated enough, and when the other side should also be heard. He or she should know when to rule someone Out of Order, and not wait until members are clamouring for the speaker to make a ruling. When Mr Speaker says "Order, Order," all members must be prepared to click their heels and obey. If the speaker has to adjudicate, everyone must respect him. In the selection of Mr Speaker, our choices were between someone from within the House or from outside. If we chose from among us, we would reduce our numbers by one, since the speaker could not take sides. So, we opted for a person not in Parliament who was visibly independent, but who was sympathetically disposed to the broad objectives for which we stood.

When we began Legco, Peter Fawcus was in the chair, but in 1963 he decided he should relinquish it, and he asked Dr Alfred Merriweather to be his replacement. He had consulted Seretse first, so Dr Merriweather was, in fact, Seretse's choice to be speaker. We elected Dr Merriweather as the speaker of the Legislative Assembly during self-rule and then as speaker of the National Assembly at independence. His personal qualities, including primarily his integrity, made him an excellent choice, and the fact that he was both a medical doctor and a *moruti* (a pastor of the church) added to his stature. When Dr Merriweather stepped down in 1968, we asked The Reverend Albert Lock, since our experience with a *moruti* had been a good one, and Rev. Lock was also an excellent Mr Speaker.

Jimmy Haskins, the next Mr Speaker, had been a good minister, and this was an appropriate post for him. He was fair-minded, and he was seen to be independent. In addition, he had not been a strong constituency man for the party, so we were not foregoing talent in that area.

I had a great problem when we made Mr Nwako the next Mr Speaker, not because he was unsuited but because of Mr Nwako himself. He felt he should have been president, and if not president, then at least vice-president, and if not vice-president, then at least a minister. Mr Nwako became a reluctant speaker because he thought I had demoted him from being a minister by nominating him as Mr Speaker. During Mr Nwako's first term as speaker, Mr Masisi was made the deputy speaker, and he got to know the Standing Orders better than Mr Nwako. I felt Mr Nwako was not doing the best he could as a speaker, and many people felt Mr Masisi was performing better than his boss. It was touch and go as to whether we would retain him as speaker. Mr Nwako himself came to know that the BDP members were having their doubts about him as speaker, since we discussed the speakership in caucus. Nonetheless, he felt that having been moved from minister to speaker, he did not want to be demoted further. We decided we would stay with him, because we did not want to leave him a bitter man. The proviso was that I would talk with him to tell him he had let us down, and I emphasised that it was not a question of his ability, but of his attitude. Fortunately his attitude did change, and he began to enjoy being Mr Speaker and to perform to everyone's satisfaction.

At the time of his second election as speaker, Mout flirted with the opposition to support him. In that Parliament, the opposition held 13 seats and *Domkrag* 31, and he was prepared to have an open contest if *Domkrag* and I did not nominate him. I had always consulted the opposition, and fortunately they agreed. Later Kenneth Koma would say he didn't favour Mr Nwako but would have favoured someone from his own party; but it was typical of Mr Koma to say one thing in private and then say another in public.

I have made frequent mention of Mr Nwako in these memoirs in part because he was one who was with me from the time I edited *Naledi ya Botswana* to my retirement from politics. He was also the only person besides the late president on whom I could count to always state his honest opinion. Sometimes he would stand alone against the whole cabinet, and at the end he would say: "Though defeated, I am not vanquished!"

Other Major Appointments

In making other key appointments, such as attorney general, permanent secretary to the president (PSP), or the chief justice, I felt I should talk with people who knew the individuals. I would ask: How do they operate? Do they know what they are expected to do? Do they have the ability and the personality to do the job? I followed the same approach when thinking about moving someone out of a job.

I did not consult as much about permanent secretaries (PSs) or the PSP as I did in appointment of ministers. The PSP is a very personal appointment, so my consultation was much more selective. The PSP has a complicated role, since he is the head of the civil service and secretary to the cabinet as well as the president's right hand man, and he must run the office and manage the president's time and energy. The PSP also provides a link between the political and the administrative arms of government. This was not a structure we set out to invent, but one we found in place in the position of government secretary in the colonial administration, and we felt it worked. Many things that emanate from the civil service the PSP can deal with, since he knows what the political arm would like to see done, and vice versa.

Managing the president's time and making sure he is prepared are also extremely important. After I became president, I said to the people in my office: "I am like a boxer. When I am in the ring, I can do the job. But you have to be sure I am ready in the same way a boxer's managers tape his hands, put on his gloves, scout the opponent and explain the opponent's strengths and weakness, and so forth." I told them they had to do the same thing to get me ready, whether for meetings or speeches or public occasions or visits abroad.

When I became president, Phil Steenkamp was PSP. I replaced him not because I myself was unhappy with his performance, but because people were making very frivolous and unfair accusations against him. They were exploiting the fact that he was a white, naturalised Motswana, and he did not shrink from taking unpopular decisions. While Phil Steenkamp was an excellent and loyal administrator, he became somewhat of a liability to me in political terms. One has to pick one's battles.

Festus Mogae followed Phil Steenkamp as PSP. I had worked with Mr Mogae in finance, and I thought he was eminently suited for the job. He had spent four years at the IMF; during that time I invited him to meet with me when I was travelling, and at our meeting he agreed to come back to run my office. When he returned, I first appointed him governor of the Bank of Botswana, and he then became PSP in January 1982. Obviously, I had to settle on Festus Mogae before talking with Phil Steenkamp so I would have continuity of support in my office.

There was a big difference between how the two men worked. Every morning and evening Steenkamp would go through a few things of which he wanted to inform me, or on which he wanted my view or a decision. Mr Mogae, on the other hand, kept to himself, and I had to show I needed him before he would appear; he didn't consult others—even me, his boss. Elijah Legwaila succeeded Festus Mogae, and while I might not see him in the morning, every evening we made sure we would meet to talk things over before each of us made his way home.

I appointed Elijah Legwaila PSP in 1989 after I made Festus Mogae minister of finance and development planning. I had had the experience of working with Mr Legwaila while he was deputy attorney general. It was very important to have a trusted colleague who would be honest in both criticism and support, and Elijah Legwaila provided both. I also thought it was useful to have a lawyer in the Office of the President or to have a PSP who was a lawyer, as had been the case with Phil Steenkamp. This was not to take over the role of the attorney general, but rather to give one early warning on when or whether one needed detailed advice from the attorney general.

The president has the responsibility for appointing the attorney general. Our first attorney general, Alan Tilbury, was a good lawyer, a good colleague, and honest in his opinions. I worked closely with him in finalising the constitution, converting it from one appropriate to internal self-government to full independence. When he left Botswana in 1969, the appointment of Moleleki Mokama as attorney general was virtually assured. He was the only Motswana who was properly qualified and had some experience, and at the time we were under a great deal of pressure to have a citizen as attorney general. One thing I enjoyed about Moleleki Mokama was the very strong views he had on things. We could differ, and he made his case, but he knew that at the end of the day it would be my decision to take. He accepted that, and we got on well. Regrettably, Mr Mokama on occasion could be like some other civil servants who would not take action to implement decisions with which they disagreed. The appointment of Phandu Skelemani as successor to Mokama after the latter became chief justice was also obvious, since he was the senior deputy, and his only senior as a lawyer in the public service was Legwaila, who was already PSP.

The president appoints the chief justice, and while I was in office the attorney general would look at possible candidates and bring several to meet me and a few other people. We were always looking for quality; we would look at how the person had handled cases in the past, and so forth. It was many years before we had citizen lawyers who were senior enough to become chief justice, and Moleleki Mokama was the first to hold the office. The choice of Julian Nganunu to be chief justice as Mr Mokama's successor was relatively easy, since I thought he was among the brightest of our local lawyers. I always preferred to take the initiative to seek out the talent, so I approached Nganunu to see if he would like to be a candidate; and he agreed.

Permanent Secretaries
In building our own civil service, we followed the British model of a strong permanent civil service. The Americans and the Canadians do it differently, and they have many layers in government filled by political appointees. We concluded there was virtue in the independence of the civil service that would allow them to serve whichever was the government of the day. That proposition was generally accepted, though sometimes there has been criticism that civil servants are more influential than they should be in setting policy.

The permanent secretary is the top civil servant in each ministry, and as such he or she plays a central role. The PS is the connection between political decisions and the administration and is responsible for the execution of decisions by the civil service. The PS must ensure that the minister is well served in two ways. First, the minister must receive good analysis and advice on pros and cons of different alternatives. Second, the PS must make sure decisions made at the political level are carried out by the civil service.

In appointing a permanent secretary, we looked at people who were in that particular ministry, as well as people across government. Especially in the early years, we tried to look at older people in the civil service as well as the bright young people coming along who were not yet senior in terms of years of service. We would review things from time to time to see if there would be any benefits from changing the PSs, and who might be involved. There might be no need to change, and while sometimes we thought a change might be desirable, we did not see the personnel available to effect that change; so people might be left in place despite dissatisfaction with their performance.

I avoided consulting ministers on who they would like as their PS, since they would all have wanted the brightest stars in the firmament. While I would ideally have liked to think of providing complimentary strengths and compatible styles between a minister and the permanent secretary, we were limited by the pool of talent. And, the circumstances changed over time. A PS who would have been a very good administrator of the system in place might not have been the right person to oversee a major change, or a major negotiation, or a very important project that needed to be developed and implemented. The late president tended to appoint a PS and just send him to the ministry, whereas I would always tell the minister about my choice after I had made up my mind but before the appointment was announced.

Some ministers were headstrong, but so long as they allowed their officials to do their work and advise them properly, the country was well served. Of course, ministers had their pet projects and their own ideas that were not necessarily shared by the rest of us. But these differences were discussed through extensive consultations, and often ministers were disabused of their ideas. I remember Mr Kgabo once commenting that he had wanted to take a particular action, but the attorney general's Chambers pointed out that he would be wrong in the law. Mr Kgabo laughed and said: "Poor Kgabo, I thought I could do this thing, only to find out that I cannot!" The sense of limits imposed by a strong civil service was very important in restraining ministers from overstepping their legitimate authority. It was also important for a minister to be willing to work to implement the policy agreed, even if he or she was not in agreement before the decision. Someone like Dan Kwelagobe, for example, would move heaven and earth to get a policy implemented, even though he hated to read the files beforehand and might not have agreed personally with the decision taken.

The Processes of Consultation

In the early days when both our population and the government were smaller, we all knew one another, and some junior staff were also involved in a weekly briefing of the minister, sometimes even the briefing of the president. This produced good training for the youngsters. It also gave the senior officers and ministers a practical assessment of how well the juniors were doing and whether or not they were learning and maturing. Of course, consultation was an important part of our Tswana heritage; and by our nature both Seretse and I were inclined to consult people before reaching a decision.

Another very useful purpose was served by holding briefings that involved a number of people. When each person, however junior or senior, had a say, then the president or the minister had a better sense of the lay of the land, the complexity of the arguments, and the differences of opinion. One then was better able to make up one's own mind than if one was fed a distilled version of the story. The one good outcome of the Landell-Mills case that I discuss in Chapter 9 was the establishment of the principle that a minister could talk with junior officers without necessarily going though the permanent secretary or department head. The minister should be able to contact a junior officer dealing with an aspect of policy in order to better inform himself. However, such talks should never undermine the ultimate authority of the senior officer over the junior; and decisions should only be taken by the minister after discussion with the PS.

The practice of providing ministers and the president with the full range of opinion and recommendations, and not just a single recommendation, had other advantages. Occasionally, the minister or the president would be put into a situation where there were no officials present. This often happened in international forums or negotiations. The more one knew of the alternative arguments and positions, and the more thoroughly one had been briefed, the stronger was one's negotiating position with the other parties. The essence of decision making in a democracy is that you get from people the collective wisdom, not just wisdom according to seniority. This is one example of the benefits of openness and accountability at all levels of government, and it served Botswana well throughout my time in politics, from Legco onwards.

While I was in finance, my officials and I strongly believed in the principle of the informed public, and we convinced the late president to adopt the idea of educating the cabinet. He became very good at making the point that the meetings were for education, and the practice caught on. Seretse felt free to ask questions if he did not know the answers, and that emboldened others to ask questions, too.

The Economic Committee of Cabinet (ECC) grew up over time, and it served the purpose of producing an informed government throughout the senior levels. The idea began when we had posed questions to Peter Fawcus—why did such and such happen, or why did things work the way they did? We started with Peter Fawcus, as the Queen's commissioner, meeting with the prime minister, the deputy prime minister, and the key ministers; and then we added the planners to the process. The ECC eventually came to include the cabinet, all permanent secretaries, the governor of the Bank of Botswana, and the heads of the Police and the Botswana Defence Force, especially when discussing the development plans, budgets, and similar matters.

Part of what led to the creation of the ECC was my worry that cabinet might make a decision, and the president could agree or overrule them, without having full knowledge of the consequences. It was one thing for Quill Hermans or Peter Landell-Mills or others in my ministry to have very bright ideas; but if the cabinet and the president were not brought along to understand the reasoning, then they might say yes or no without knowing why they were saying it. So, in ECC, officials had the opportunity to present the full range of arguments behind their recommendations.

Another mechanism for broad consultation was provided by the appointment of presidential commissions. Commissions were usually appointed after a thorough discussion within cabinet and a conclusion that the issue would benefit from a complete investigation involving a number of people. The minister responsible for that portfolio subject would have been part of the decision, so he or she would not be undercut by the use of a commission.

We used presidential commissions for a number of different purposes—sometimes to address a matter that was under dispute, sometimes when we thought an issue needed thorough airing and investigation, as well as widespread participation and consultation. Over the years, presidents have appointed several commissions on tribal land, including the tribal grazing land policy and land allocation. Other subjects included urban land policy, education, the structure of local government, incomes policy, civil service salary structure and levels, and economic opportunities.

Under most circumstances a commission had broad representation of interested groups, ensuring wide consultation on important issues before they were addressed by government. Members included elected politicians, ordinary citizens, civil servants, and other experts. Commissions often took evidence around the country, held meetings in *kgotlas*, accepted written submissions, and then would deliberate and subsequently write a report. When the subject was one of public policy, such reports resulted in a government paper. Government addressed the issues and conclusions of the commission's report, and often made clear why some were rejected. It then proposed legislation or regulations or new policies. Our experiences with the Select Committee on Racial Discrimination in Legco and the Local Government Committee in the African Council had provided good models for the subsequent use of commissions. When appropriate, the government would respond using the normal processes: consultation between ministries, circulating a cabinet memorandum, a final decision by cabinet, and, if necessary, legislation in Parliament.

As president, one could affect the process in a number of ways. After consultation, the president selected the person to chair the commission as well as the commission members. The president could also frame the terms of reference for the commission and help define the nature of the questions to be addressed. The report of the commission was delivered to the president, who decided on its disposition. The device of the presidential commission provided an additional mechanism both for taking new initiatives and for ensuring that consultation went beyond the elected politicians and the persons or groups who might have a direct interest in the outcome.

The Civil Service

As we made the transition to independence, there were some who felt those who served with the colonial administration should be told that independence was the end of their road. There were some who felt we should not even pay pensions to those who had served the colonial government. However, we in the leadership felt we needed consistency as well as equity. These people had loyally served the country during colonial times; it was by accident that the authority was foreign, not local. After independence we might change the government ourselves, and we wanted to have sound precedents that Botswana would meet its commitments. If a government of the People's Party were to throw out the laws or other obligations adopted by a government of the Democratic Party, how would other countries view Botswana?

In the early years, virtually all permanent secretaries and other senior officials were holdovers from the colonial government. Only a few among them had taken citizenship. Some of the colonial officers, such as Mike Williams, the DC in Molepolole, were so good that we hoped they would apply for citizenship. However, we did not take the initiative to encourage such people, since we did not want to be seen to be giving signals of who might be favoured. Some officials stayed to be certain that they would get their retirement entitlements. And some officials were such that, while we did not push them out, as soon as we could find someone to replace them, we let them leave. Those who applied for and were granted citizenship fitted in very well, though sometimes they were judged harshly when they expressed their opinions. David Finlay, on the other hand, was virtually regarded as a black man wearing a white skin.

The vast majority of higher-level civil service posts, those that required university education, were held by expatriates in the early years. Only one of the 38 most senior posts in the colonial service in 1965 was held by a

Motswana. The late president decided we needed to talent spot and that promotions should be made according to merit, not necessarily on the basis of whose number in the register came first. There was transparency, in that he told people who lagged behind that they were being passed over for people who were better able to do the job. We wanted to get an impression of who might be good, and then give people an opportunity to prove themselves. If they were bright and talented, they were given the opportunity to move quickly. This was true both for the youngsters and for some who had not been promoted in the colonial service because of their lack of formal education. Mr J. J. Tebape had many years of experience in junior positions, and we chose him to head the Directorate of Personnel as the first local in the job. He was very successful and as efficient as anyone who has been in the job since then.

The group of Batswana we sent abroad for training just before independence was a talented lot. I was part of a committee that selected these students to go abroad, and we found some very able people. Virtually all of them came back to some form of public service. In fact, in his later years, Seretse used to ask: "When shall we have the Mpuchanes and Tibones and Mogaes again?"

In those years when we were very short of trained personnel, and technical assistance people came only for a period of few years, it was very difficult when a valued person left us, especially when he or she was a citizen. Therefore, on some personnel issues I found myself a bit emotional. For instance, when Festus Mogae went to the IMF, or Quill Hermans went to the World Bank, or when Julian Nganunu went into the private sector from his position as a permanent secretary, I was quite upset with them. I even appealed to the late president to try to get some of them to change their minds. But Seretse was of the view that we should not try to keep people against their will. I talked with a number before they left, but they had made up their minds. In some cases politics played a role. Charles Tibone resigned from the civil service after many years as one of our very effective permanent secretaries. He had crossed some people who then undertook a lobbying campaign against him, and I think he was falsely accused of a number of things. It was unfortunate for the country that we lost his service in government, for I consider him an able person. I was pleased when he stood for elections in 2004 and was included in cabinet after he won his seat.

Despite our shortage of trained people, we did have one great advantage over many African countries. Because of our openness, able people were not exiled for their political views, as happened in many other countries. People like Klaas Motshidisi, commissioner of labour, and Mike Molefhane, who headed the Botswana Development Corporation, to name but two, were well known to have links to the opposition parties. But as long as they were professional in their jobs, there was no reason for us to deprive the country of their skills just because of their politics.

Developments over Time
The young people we promoted early such as Baledzi Gaolathe, Charles Tibone, Sam Mpuchane, or Lebang Mpotokwane were very successful bets.

For many years we had Quill Hermans and Peter Landell-Mills in the Ministry of Finance and Development Planning, and with them was a team of young officers, very energetic and enthusiastic, many from the British Overseas Development Institute or other donors. They were very dedicated and hard working, and they pushed new ideas and proposed new projects and convinced us politicians to consider them. We also had a core of very experienced colonial officers, and we benefited from many senior expatriate administrators and technicians who had proved themselves elsewhere and served us under technical assistance agreements.

Over the course of our development, however, I believe our capacity for execution of projects has deteriorated, or at least has become much more uneven. We have become more complex as an economy, larger as a government, more demanding as a nation, and therefore more difficult to manage. Despite increased professional qualifications, the quality of the staff work has also declined in many departments of government. Some of this may be inevitable with the growth that has been compounding rapidly for 40 years. Also, the public service had a virtual monopoly on talent in our early years, but over time more and more able young people have gone into the private sectors instead of working in government.

After Elijah Legwaila became PSP, he and I talked a good deal about the promotion and selection process. We felt that in the later years we had not done as good a job in the personnel process as we should have. In theory we had the scoring system in personnel evaluations, but we suspected a lot of dishonesty. In some cases, we thought that if a senior officer wanted to get rid of people, he or she would give the juniors good marks so they would be promoted to somewhere else! When we were a smaller government, people who had to make decisions on personnel had direct personal experience of who was who and of their quality. As we grew, we developed evaluation systems that were, of course, a good idea, but supervisors did not want to confront their subordinates who were not performing. Another factor was that the senior civil servants became less likely to give their juniors access to department heads, permanent secretaries or ministers. As a result, a senior officer would have less direct knowledge of the abilities of the junior officers.

Our implementation capacity has always been a constraint on the pace of development, but the nature of the implementation problem has changed. At the beginning, we had experienced civil servants at the top, though not enough of them, and we were very thin at the middle levels as well. As the experienced officers either emigrated or retired, they were replaced by people who had not necessarily come up through as rigorous a process to gain necessary skills and experience before being given progressively larger responsibilities. We had once dealt with wine of old vintage, and later we had wine that came from the press the day before! People of lower executive ability were promoted into positions of responsibility they should not have held. As the civil service expanded rapidly, people continued to rise rapidly even though not as quickly as in the early years. Therefore, we now have a larger body of officials, but not a more effective one. We have adopted many schemes such as Work Improvement Teams (WITS) and Organisation and

Method Reviews to address efficiency in the public service, but we certainly have not solved the problem.

Civil Service as an Obstacle

I suppose all governments have a large difference between official policies and those actually implemented. The civil service has a very large role to play in implementation, and its officials have the capacity to facilitate or to frustrate the policies that have been agreed at the political level. For example, we had decided in the 1960s that we should have an Economic Committee of Cabinet, but officials in the Office of the President simply dragged their feet, because they did not like the idea. They did not circulate a draft cabinet memorandum under the pretext that it had been lost. Then, after they had been provided with another copy, they did not circulate it for comment. There was a long delay, and only by being very persistent were we able to establish the Economic Committee of Cabinet. It was a clear case—cabinet had made a decision, and the implementation was deliberately thwarted by some in the civil service.

In another case, the Ministry for Home Affairs made decisions about residence permits through the Immigration Department, and it made decisions about work permits through the Labour Department. Cabinet had approved policies in the 1980s that would give longer-term arrangements for residence and work permits for legitimate foreign investors. However, by the time I left office those policies had not been implemented by the civil servants. These were matters where officials had their own view of what the policy of government should be, and they proved to have the ability to frustrate those policies that did not conform to their view.

When government opened up farms on state land at Pandamantenga along the Nata-Kazungula road, we said the land could not be used to graze cattle, since there were many other ranching projects throughout the country. It turned out, however, that opportunities for arable farming at Pandamantenga were more limited than we had first thought. The land appeared to be a good location for dairy herds, and, at the time, we were still importing our dairy products from neighbouring countries. One might have had a 500-hectare farm for crops, and if the farmer was imaginative, he might have planted half a hectare of *stower* (fodder) for stall-feeding of oxen or dairy cattle. However, officials in the Ministry of Agriculture simply said "no cattle of any kind", even though it was clear our initial decision had been based on beef cattle ranching, not dairy cattle. So, we lost opportunities for dairy production in an area where there would have been lots of grain and roughage to support it.

After I retired and began growing vegetables, I experienced another example of the effects of inaction. I applied for a place in Kanye to put up a stand where I could sell my vegetables. I got neither a yes nor a no, but was told that the decision would be deferred indefinitely. I was told to contact the relevant authority if I was not satisfied with the decision—but there was no decision! If they had said no, at least I would know where to go to appeal the decision. Even when I wrote to the minister, I failed to get a yes or no answer.

Since independence, we have been busy putting in new bureaucracies instead of streamlining them. We often acknowledged that bureaucracy was holding things back, but we continued to adopt legislation that added to the roadblocks. Two problems have contributed to inhibiting development and initiative of individuals. First, we have accepted many suggestions from other countries, visiting experts, and international bodies. We have adopted legislation similar in complexity to that of more industrialised countries and then added regulations and more civil servants to administer those regulations. Second there was the inclination of officials to not make a decision. They would neither say yes or no, since then they could not be accused of making an error in judgment. As our bureaucracy has grown, and legislation and regulations have increased, the possibility for delay and inaction has increased. Several commissions and many consultancy reports have recognised the need to eliminate regulations that stifle initiative; unfortunately, we have not yet found the will to do so.

Teamwork

Our overall record as a government led by *Domkrag* over my 37 years in politics would, I think, be regarded as successful. We built and sustained a multi-party democracy; the vast majority of our people enjoyed improved health, education, and increased incomes and employment opportunities; and we managed our way through a dangerous security situation created by our neighbours.

After her retirement, Dr Chiepe was asked to what she attributed Botswana's successes. She said, simply: "Teamwork." I think her succinct reply summed up our approach very well. The times we were most successful were when we worked together, both as politicians and with civil servants. Our success could not have been achieved had we not found able people, convinced them to enter politics or the public service, and encouraged and enabled them to work productively with one another. Our failures came at those times when we lost the commitment to teamwork, consultation, consensus and cooperation.

Early life and family

Senior Prefect Masire with fellow prefects at Tiger Kloof (L-R): Edison Masisi, Aaron Gare, Gogowa Kgomanyane.

As sports convenor (far left) with the Rugby Club at Tiger Kloof.

Wedding day, January 1959 (L-R): Bias Mookodi, Peter Mmusi, Aaron Gare; Gladys and I are seated.

Driving my tractor at mosimo.

Cattle farm in Ghanzi.

Throughout my life, visits to the farm have always meant hard work.

Standing on a stack of groundnut bags after a good harvest.

A Basarwa delegation from Ghanzi. I was always ready to meet with citizens for consultation about any issue.

Our farmhouse in Ghanzi.

At Maradu Ostrich Farm near Lobatse, one of my ventures in diversification.

With my sons (L-R): Mpho, Moabi, Mmetla.

Family portrait, 1985 (L-R): Mpho, Moabi, Mmetla, Mmasekgoa, Tshidi, and Gaone standing behind MmaGaone and me.

Education has always been important for both of us as former teachers. Our daughter Gaone was the first to graduate.

Sharing a joke with our daughter Mmasekgoa. I'm told my boisterous laugh is readily recognised by friends and family.

With our youngest daughter, Matshediso, looking at a BDP farewell programme.

Early politics

I set aside an office at our home in Kanye where I could attend to a variety of matters.

MmaGaone smiles as Seretse and I clasp hands in victory.

Celebrating after the first elections in 1965.

With some of the 35 members of the first National Assembly, 1965.

Constitutional talks at Lancaster House in London, 1966, with the Bechuanaland delegation on the right.

Seretse addressing a political meeting in the early days. Even though the weather was extremely hot, it was important that we reach out to all our people.

A 1968 meeting with Harry Oppenheimer of De Beers (seated second from left), Jimmy Haskins (standing centre), Seretse and me.

Signing a World Bank loan in 1971; Chief Linchwe II, Botswana's Ambassador to the US, on my right.

Greeting Ruth Khama, Daniel Kwelagobe, and Seretse at a BDP rally.

Seretse and I at a victory rally after the 1979 elections.

Seretse forcefully making a point at the same rally.

Reviewing a Guard of Honour with Haile Selassie before an OAU meeting in Addis Ababa.

Chapter 9
Working with Seretse Khama

I have never had the occasion to share with anyone else the kind of relationship I had with the late president, Sir Seretse Khama. Seretse Khama was my boss, but I did not hesitate to differ with him as respectfully as I could. He didn't think I was telling him my opinions because I thought little of him or doubted his judgment. Sometimes Seretse would say to me: "Well, Quett, now that you have said it, I feel relieved, since we may both be wrong, but at least there are two of us who feel the same way. And, I know if you differed with me you would not hesitate to tell me. If it were not so, your advice would not be worth it, since you would be anticipating what you thought I wanted to hear."

Though I'm a difficult and strong-willed person, and I was often troublesome to deal with, the late president and I worked very well together. And if we did not agree, which was seldom, once I had expressed my opinion, we just left for it him to take a decision. We both knew that, once I had had my say, it was his prerogative to do what he thought was right. I mentioned one example in the last chapter, where we differed over a resident mission for the People's Republic of China. At the time of independence, I tried to prevail on Seretse to let six months or a year pass before we plunged into it. The nation was literally on the verge of starvation, and we didn't know if the British would still help us if we took over as scheduled. But he disagreed and sent me to England to negotiate the final independence settlement. I knew all the arguments as to why it should be done in September 1966 and not later, and I presented them to the British as forcefully as I could!

Seretse was a democrat through and through. He was a marvellous person in that he was able to see people as they were as individuals. Much as he had been born a chief, he was liberal and democratic in his attitudes. He shared with me and other leaders of *Domkrag* the view that the nation resides in the people, and not in any individual. We agreed that we needed to move people from thinking about their tribes as their separate communities to thinking about the whole nation as their community. We both believed that in any society there needed to be a balance between the interests of individuals and those of the larger community. Both Seretse and I believed individuals should be given the freedom to come up with the best they were capable of.

While Seretse and I were of one view on many important issues, we came to the same conclusion from different starting points. I may not have started as a liberal in a philosophical sense, but I had suffered from decisions of my chief, and I had seen other people who suffered as a result of tradition or authority being used as a pretext to keep them down. In a few cases, people were so frustrated they even left the country. So, we lost what development those people could have effected for the nation, and we lost the individuals as well. The freedom people were likely to enjoy if they threw in their lot with the Democratic Party was viewed as an enabling environment for everyone's development. We did not find it hard to sell this view to our colleagues at the time the Botswana Democratic Party was formed, especially since we all wanted to form a united nation.

It was hard to tell whether all those in the party in the early days agreed with Seretse and me on the matter of non-racialism, for example, or whether they were just trying to please us. We in the leadership took non-racialism as one of those objectives to hold very close to our hearts. Other people may have just felt: Well, if that is what has been decided, that is what we will do. Of course, we were very much influenced by the situation in South Africa. We saw what it meant to be racialistic, and we knew we didn't want a society like that. Indeed, we thought if our non-racialism worked, it would help to prove apartheid was wrong and thus help achieve change in South Africa.

It has been said that the late president handled foreign relations, while I handled the domestic management of the economy and the party. In fact, we were jointly involved both inside and outside. I represented him abroad on many occasions, and, therefore, I had to know the details of what was going on. I also had strong views on a number of issues related to our international and regional relationships, and these were considered as we decided on policy. On domestic management issues, while I took the lead, I made sure he was as fully briefed as possible on the details. Since he was the person to make the final decision, I did not want him to make any decision in the absence of the full knowledge of what had gone into the recommendation and what had gone before.

Seretse was not particularly interested in most details, so to be sure he was informed we established the habit of Thursday briefings of the president by each ministry, with people from the Ministry of Finance present. Even though his officials thought these meetings were a bother to him, they took place regularly. Overall, we were fortunate in that his permanent secretaries did not want to come between us, which was extremely important. I don't remember finding that his officials had done anything inappropriate that would interfere with our close working relationship. Of course, they were fellow human beings, and they had their preferences, but they were always very professional. This was extremely important in ensuring that the government functioned smoothly even on those occasions when Seretse was taken seriously ill.

Throughout the time we worked together, Seretse and I saw eye to eye on virtually all of the important international issues—refugees, relations with South Africa, and how to deal with SWAPO, the ANC and other liberation movements in southern Africa. We agreed as well on the questions of domestic strategy, economic policy, and our approach to the party and to domestic politics. Some would say our relationship looked too perfect. However, we both knew how important it was not only that we work very well together but also that we be seen to be doing so. I was really treated as a member of his family from the beginning, and there was always a room ready for me when I went to Serowe to see him. The two of us were close all the way, for nearly 20 years.

During the 1963 constitutional talks at Lobatse, I served as a kind of kingpin in drafting because I was secretary-general of the party. In the talks themselves, Seretse and I developed a strategy: I would make the most extreme demands to see the extent to which they would be accommodated by the other parties in the conference. If my proposals were accepted, well and good; but if they were not, he would be the accommodating one. He would step in and say: "I think I understand what this fellow Quett is saying, but perhaps it would be better if we put it this way." This was true, for example, on the question of whether we should have a bicameral legislature, with the House of Chiefs like the House of Lords in the UK. We felt that if I took a strong position first, then the compromises would be close to what we really preferred. This turned out to be the case.

In 1966, when I was in England representing the BDP government at the final talks on post-independence financial arrangements, the British periodically had to call Seretse in Botswana to say: "Please come, your deputy prime minister is really being impossible." Then Seretse and I would strategise, and he would seem to be mitigating the venom I was seen to be spitting! The big issue in London at that juncture was the financial deal regarding the support we would receive after independence. Much as the British did us a great deal of good, sometimes they were tough, such as when they opposed supporting local councils (if I remember well, the sum was £156,000). They said: "What? Do you expect us to look after your government and also look after subordinate local authorities?" This was a very serious issue for us, since the development of democratic local government structures to replace the autocratic chiefs was a major part of our programme.

Seretse had a wonderful sense of humour. He was well known for the quips that he delivered with perfect timing. He had been on a trip to Singapore when Idi Amin deposed President Obote in Uganda. Seretse returned to Gaborone, and, as I greeted him as usual at the bottom of the stairs to the plane, he asked: "What, no coup, Quett?" One of the most famous of Seretse's quips was to the white leader, Russell England, who would sometimes identify what he thought was a major problem or sticking point in a debate by saying: "Ah, there's the nigger in the woodpile!" England seemed completely unaware of how offensive this remark was. When England asked Seretse what he proposed to call the official residence of the president of Botswana after independence, Seretse said dryly: "I'm thinking of calling it 'The Woodpile'."

The late president honoured all the decisions we took in cabinet whenever, as a result of either illness or international travel, he was absent. The only exception was a minor one having to do with awarding Botswana Honours to a particular individual: We had decided to do so, and Seretse reversed it. That he did not otherwise second-guess what we had done was, of course, good for the stability of the government and also for the self-confidence of the cabinet. We knew we had his trust to act in the interest of Botswana as a whole.

Seretse was plagued by ill health for many years. His health issues predated self-rule and were very serious—he was diabetic and he also had a pacemaker for his heart. Over the years there were numerous incidents when his health was of great concern. Once I was in Nojane in western Botswana, and I heard on the radio that he had fallen ill at his cattle post in Nata and had been taken to Bulawayo. This was before any roads were paved, and for three days I rushed nearly 800 kilometres over dirt roads from Nojane to Ghanzi, through Maun and Francistown to Bulawayo to be with him. Fortunately, by the time I arrived his health was better than had been reported; but there was often grave concern.

President and Husband
Seretse and I were extremely close politically and professionally, and also as friends, but Lady Khama was his partner in every sense. He was a husband to her and father to their children as well as the president. Lady Khama was almost always with Seretse as he travelled to campaign, attend party meetings, or make state visits abroad. She was a determined person who had endured the years when they were exiled by the British, and she cared for her husband as he faced attacks of ill health. While in a sense we competed for his time and attention, there were only a very few occasions when Lady Khama and I had problems. During self-rule, I had been invited to a party at their home, and I failed to go because I was handling a delicate matter related to the chiefs. Lady Khama was reported to have said that in other countries when a prime minister invites his deputy prime minister, he must come. I felt it was rather unfair of her, since her remarks were made without the full knowledge of my assignment from Seretse.

Toward the end of Seretse's life, I was addressing a meeting in Molepolole, and halfway through my speech I received a message that the president was delirious and needed to be flown to Johannesburg. This was a shock, since there had been no prior notice that Seretse was unwell. I ended the meeting and rushed to Gaborone to make arrangements to get him into a plane. After he had recovered, I was with both of them, and I told Lady Khama that such a situation regarding the health of the president of the nation should never be allowed to develop again. I said that those of us responsible for the government needed to know when he was in ill health. She disagreed and told me in other countries only members of the household would know things as personal as the state of the president's health. To support her argument, she cited the case of Juan and Eva Peron in Argentina! Fortunately, Seretse gently said to her: "Come along, be serious."

After Lady Khama's death in 2002, I was asked to speak at her funeral. In my address, I told the mourners that I knew her to be a warm and genuine person, a concerned and supportive woman, a dedicated and effective servant of the people, a caring mother, a devoted wife and a gracious human being. She persevered in the midst of the injustices meted out on them by the British authorities. I told of a trip when we found ourselves and our three-ton truck caught in a dust storm, literally buried overnight in sand at Serule. I had taken ill, and Seretse and Lady Khama both climbed into the back of the truck and told me I should sit in the cab with the driver. We travelled through sand tracks for a long way—all the way from Bobonong to Sefophe,

Mogapinyana to Serowe. That was one of the times when I recognised the determination of Lady Khama's character; she was a power to reckon with. I also spoke of the many times she accompanied her husband on the campaign trail and on countrywide tours. Although, of course, she did not sit in on our meetings, her ideas were an inspiration to us. She was a fine person as wife, mother and First Lady. I meant all of it, and I tried to express it as best I could. I believe the family was happy with my comments at her funeral.

Our Most Difficult Moment
The most serious disagreement Seretse and I had in all our years of working together occurred just after independence. It was related to economics and finance, but it also involved our transition from colonial traditions to a modern state and my relationship with Lady Khama.

We had embraced with both arms people like Peter Landell-Mills, a young and energetic British economic planner. I have mentioned that Peter Fawcus would be energised by the optimism of Quill Hermans and Bob Edwards and their conviction that things could be done; they recognised the need for action and were ready to help us solve the problems. I had similar feelings about Peter, Quill and Bob, and others who came later. This energy on the part of younger officers was at the crux of a conflict with Alf Beeby, the financial secretary. When he learned I was talking directly with the young economists, especially Peter Landell-Mills, Alf Beeby felt his authority was being undermined.

Beeby went to Seretse and suggested I was being corrupted by the ideas of these young economists. More importantly for him, I was circumventing the authority of the financial secretary by speaking directly with them. He seemed especially upset that Peter Landell-Mills was advising me during our financial negotiations with the British regarding the post-independence arrangements. Because these young civil servants were responsible to the financial secretary, Beeby felt that I as vice-president and as a politician should have contacted his subordinates only through him. Beeby proposed to dismiss Peter from the service and send him home. I was aware of Alf Beeby's concern and his actions, and though he could have talked with me, he did not do so. Therefore, I decided to allow the matter to take its course. It was a civil service matter, and there were procedures for disciplining officials, as well as procedures for Peter Landell-Mills to appeal if he felt unjustly punished.

However, before the case was settled, Beeby had surreptitiously informed Seretse about the situation without my knowledge. He had told Seretse there were only two ways to solve the problem: Either the young officials left the service, or he, Beeby, would leave. One day I went to State House to discuss some matter with the late president, and at the end of the conversation I said to him: "There may be trouble brewing in my ministry." I saw this was not a surprise to him as he did not ask for details but said: "Well, Quett, I would rather lose those chaps than lose Beeby." I knew that Beeby's resignation would have meant the loss of Sammy Assails, the assistant financial secretary, too. I apparently took on such a troubled look that Seretse asked: "Quett, have you lost a relative or something?" I said to him: "Do you mean this is the way we are going to run the country? It only takes two chaps like Beeby and Assails to come and frighten you, and you take an action like this?" To me, Beeby was altogether wrong to issue threats to Seretse instead of allowing the matter to be settled on its merits through the regular channels.

Seretse was very disappointed by my reaction; and I went further to say it might not only be the young economists he would lose if this was the choice he was going to make. While I did not say it in so many words, it was clear I would resign as well if he were to persist in backing Beeby. I was very upset and left quickly and rather unceremoniously in a very, very gloomy mood. Lady Khama must have been sitting in the next room; I apparently went past her without knowing she was there or acknowledging her as I left. I wasn't seeing much, given my state of mind. I later came to understand she told Seretse I had nearly pushed her aside, and that unless I was reprimanded and gave her an apology, she would make trouble.

Seretse tried to mollify me, and even took me to Zambia on a trip, which he normally did not do when he travelled abroad. Our relationship became very tense during this time as I was not prepared to talk with him about anything. Alan Tilbury was asked to talk with me, and so was Archie Mogwe, who was then second in command in Seretse's office.

Finally, I decided this was not a way to proceed. I went to Seretse, and we talked. He told me the situation and said I should apologise to Lady Khama. I said: "I think it's very wrong in principle to apologise if you do not think you are wrong. If I thought I had done anything to wrong her, I would apologise immediately, not because it is Lady Khama, but I would do it for anybody I felt I had wronged." However, during the conversation I realised how serious the issue had become for him. So, in order to solve the problem for Seretse, I gave in. I said: "I will apologise if it is necessary to put this behind us." And, I did make my apology.

That was the most tense moment in our relationship. When it was past, we both must have said: "Never again," since we never had another serious difference.

To finish the story, Peter Landell-Mills appealed his dismissal and won his case on appeal. He was re-assigned to the Ministry of Local Government and Lands for a time, and then joined Quill Hermans and me in a new Ministry of Development Planning. Alf Beeby left Botswana and retired to Natal in South Africa. I became minister of finance, and we merged finance with development planning to form a single ministry.

1980

In June 1980, I was on a visit to China when I received a message recalling me to Gaborone. Seretse had been taken to England for treatment, but was flown back after medical treatment there had failed. I learned on my return to Botswana that he was dying. He passed away at 4:45am on 13 July 1980. It fell to me to make the announcement to the nation, which I did with great sorrow early that Sunday morning. I said: "I believe that you will face this time of great sadness and loss with the dignity and calm that our great president always displayed in his own lifetime during times of difficulty. We may also remember that we, above all men and women, have been privileged, in that we have had the opportunity to live with, work with and know so great a man as Sir Seretse Khama. We give thanks for the years we have been allowed to have him as our president, fellow citizen and friend."

In later remarks, I spoke about some important aspects of his legacy. "The Republic of Botswana has been fortunate that at the time of its greatest need it could call on a man of the stature of Seretse Khama to be its first president. We would have wished for the continued leadership of Seretse Khama for many more years, but we can take comfort, and he can take pride, in the fact that the foundations of this country and this nation are well laid and that if we who follow him can continue his task in a rational and constructive way that the future of Botswana is well assured."

I had lost both my great friend and the political collaborator who was closer to me than anybody before or since. I think we were a good team. Our close cooperation on all aspects of politics and government for 20 years was, I believe, an important factor in achieving the success we had as a new country.

Chapter 10
Opposition Parties

In a democratic system, parties that are in opposition to the government of the day have an important role to play. If opposition parties are strong and full of ideas, they sharpen the wits of the governing party and keep it on its toes. If the opposition parties are weak or lacking in ideas about alternative policies, they weaken both the country and the ruling party. While I would not attempt a history of Botswana's opposition parties, I want to try to give the flavour of the issues and some of the principal personalities involved, especially in the years shortly before and just after independence. I have also included some specific examples from more recent years to illustrate some of the tactics used by some in the opposition, in particular some in the Botswana National Front (BNF).

Leetile Raditladi was the first to start a political party, called the Federal Party, in 1959. It never went beyond a small number of people, including a few whites. It was largely in the Mahalapye area and existed more in name than in fact. He made an effort to recruit me into it, and if the party had been really alive, I would have been willing to join. But the party had no substance, and the approach was no more than: "We wish to recruit you."

The Botswana People's Party (BPP) was much more active. It was founded in 1961, and the leaders moved heaven and earth to get the attention of Batswana. A number of its founders had been active in politics in South Africa with the ANC or the PAC. Some of us just didn't look at the BPP as a serious party, since they did not seem to be addressing the country's real challenges.

The BPP leadership went to Ghana to get Dr Kwame Nkrumah's approval, and I think his attention went to their heads. Philip Matante came back in flowing West African robes. We in Botswana had no such robes, and the late president mocked Mr Matante's robes as his "maternity cloaks". Mr Matante and his People's Party were also hobnobbing with the ZAPU folks from Zimbabwe, and they were making hats from pelts of springhares, mimicking the traditional hats worn by the ZAPU people. In addressing our 1963 conference in Francistown Seretse jokingly said: "*Ya rona ipuso re tla e bona re sa e rwalela negatla ya bo ntole.*" (We shall get our independence without having to wear the tails of springhares.)

The BPP was also ineffectively organised. One of its founders, Professor K. T. Motsete, who had been at Tiger Kloof with my uncle Luke Modisi, came all the way to Kanye on the advice of Archelaus Tsoebebe that they should get me into the BPP. Professor Motsete stayed the night, but he left the next day without even asking me to join!

As a journalist I covered a BPP meeting in Lobatse in 1961, and that was the point at which I made the decision that I would never join them. To start with, they were talking about foreign politics, not local politics. What they were saying may have been of relevance to South Africa, but it was not relevant to Botswana and our conditions. Secondly, they were ignorant.

Apart from Professor Motsete, they didn't seem to know whether David Livingstone was a trader or a missionary, to say nothing of their lack of general knowledge of the world. Mr Fish Keitseng, one of the ANC people who had joined the BPP, once let off a howler in Lobatse. He was arguing that whites should not have farms in Botswana, because "we don't have farms in London." Ben Thema was so amused that he shouted out: "*Lontone motse ga se lefatshe!*" (London is a city, it is not a country!) Professor Motsete was, of course, a well-educated man, but he left everything to the party hotheads. We thought our country would be truly lost if it got into their hands.

The effect of the People's Party was to demonstrate that if we did not stand up to do something, we would have a party of that kind leading the country. And by we, I mean all the people who came together to form the Democratic Party: Seretse Khama, Mout Nwako, Archelaus Tsoebebe—who left the BPP when he saw how irrelevant it was to Botswana's problems—and all the rest. In a way, I suppose, one could say that the BPP recruiting effort was successful; but they recruited me into the Democratic Party, not the People's Party.

After 1962 we were two lively parties—the Democratic Party and the People's Party. Then the People's Party split, which was inevitable, as its leadership had come from South African politics and reflected the divergent views there. Mr Motsamai Mpho had been secretary of the ANC branch in Roodepoort before he had been arrested and deported to Bechuanaland. Mr Philip Matante was an adherent to the African nationalist philosophy of the PAC, which was opposed to the non-racialism of the ANC. With such fundamental differences over philosophy they divided, and by the time we came to constitutional talks in 1963 they were actually three parties, though formally the Matante/Motsete wing was part of the same delegation. Mr Matante was actually opposed to the Constitutional Conference, and his faction probably would have boycotted it. However, since Mr Mpho and his delegation would have stayed, Mr Matante could not afford to be left out, so he participated.

During self-rule, Mr Matante was leader of the opposition in the Legislative Assembly, having been elected with two others from the BPP in 1965. Because of his position, he went with us to Lancaster House in London for the final constitutional talks in 1966. A Motswana named Philip Sechele was working for a London law firm at that time. Mr Matante assumed he was a lawyer, and he said he wanted to delay constitutional talks with the British until he had held discussions with Mr Sechele. However, Matante then found out that Philip Sechele was a doorman, not a lawyer, at the firm. Having caused a first delay, Mr Matante then returned to propose that, since there had been inadequate consultation, there should be a new constitutional conference. It should be comprised of all political parties, the Protectorate government, the UK government, and the chiefs, and it should consult throughout Bechuanaland. Then general elections would be held prior to independence. The rest of the delegates said that in light of the consultation that had taken place and the unanimous agreement both in the constitutional conference and in Legco, and subsequently by the Legislative Assembly, there was no validity in his contention of inadequate consultation. Mr Matante then walked out of the talks. The British took this in their stride, and he was simply declared absent for the final meetings.

We in *Domkrag* made an effort to reach out to the other countries in Africa from the beginning. However, the opposition parties caught the ear of the Pan-African movement before we did. In 1965 I paid a courtesy call on the secretary-general of the OAU, Mr Dialo Telli, during a meeting in Accra. Despite everything I told him about our approach, he said we in the Democratic Party were frustrating what he called "nationalist movements" in Bechuanaland. He took what they said as gospel truth, and what I said as simply wrong. President Nkrumah just ignored the BDP delegation and paid no attention to us. But, I did have the occasion to meet a few people, such as Leopold Senghor from Senegal, who I found had great respect for Seretse, President Tubman from Liberia, as well as Julius Nyerere, Kenneth Kaunda, and a number of others. Prior to the 1965 elections, when I was visiting Addis, I met Philip Kgosana, a man considered by the South African government to be a troublesome fellow. I explained to Mr Kgosana that the Democratic Party was the strongest party in Botswana, but unfortunately the other parties had given the world the impression that their party was the main party in the country. Mr Kgosana said to me: "It is not the Pan-Africanists outside Botswana who are going to vote, it is the Batswana who are going to vote, and so long as you can endear yourselves to Batswana, you are going to win." And we did.

Our position on the liberation movements in southern Africa, as a party and as a government, was based on this same sentiment: It is the people of the country themselves who should choose their leaders. We did not feel it would be right or proper for anyone outside a country, whether Botswana or the UN or anyone else, to decide who would be the legitimate representatives of their people. Some have suggested that our position was influenced by the hostility we had felt from the Pan-Africanists in the early days. But it was really the matter of principle, not the recollection of how we had been treated. We believed that our fundamentally democratic principles extended to our relations with other peoples and their governments or representatives, and we felt we should not be interfering. The different liberation movements, such as the ANC or PAC or Black Consciousness in South Africa, or ZAPU or ZANU in Zimbabwe, had different approaches to liberating their respective countries; but it was not for us to choose which of them was appropriate. We gave recognition to the efforts of each one to solve their country's problems, not to the legitimacy of any one organisation.

The biggest weakness of the opposition parties in Botswana has been that they haven't had any coherent policy to put forward. They existed to oppose the Democratic Party, and they did not say: "This is what we would do." Where they did make an effort, they merely came up with preposterous ideas, and their policies resembled a jumble sale. They would say, for instance, that agriculture was failing because there was no programme of irrigation, without saying from whence the water would come. They would promise to do this or that for people, without explaining where they would get the resources necessary to do it. They talked of using the waters of the Okavango as if it were just a pond to be pumped. We, on the other hand, had done a feasibility study that showed what the consequences would be if we did pump the water to the east.

If one reads the *Hansard* over the years, one can see how many of the interventions by members of the opposition, especially when Mr Matante was in the House, were simply sloganeering or off-hand comments. Mr Matante frequently called those of us in *Domkrag* stooges, or puppets of the colonialists, or referred to us as a neo-colonialist government, rather than making substantive contributions to the debate. The opposition MPs were at their worst when they tried to move a motion of "no confidence" in the government.

In the first session of the newly elected Legislative Assembly, Mr Matante moved the motion of no confidence and argued that the 1965 elections had been unfair and rigged and the people were given instructions by their chiefs on how to vote. Seretse commented: "I am quite certain that he sincerely believes all that he thinks is correct, partly because he is so misinformed, and secondly because he is so ignorant of the politics of Bechuanaland and is inclined to think that he can get inspiration from outside the country rather than by dealing with the actual problems of Bechuanaland." As part of government's response I added: "An opposition is necessary to point out to government whenever government goes wrong, that it is wrong. But when the opposition tends to be frivolous and speaks more for the entertainment of the Gallery than to correct or give counsel to the government, then it becomes dangerous."

We debated the Transitional Plan for Economic and Social Development in Parliament in 1966. It was very ambitious and made many difficult choices about priorities. The opposition offered practically no contributions to the debate; they only asked that we declare whether we were a socialist or a capitalist government. My response was: "We want to develop this country, and we do not care whether we are called capitalists or socialists or whatever he [Mr Matante] will; but what interests us most is to see Botswana developed." The following March, after the budget speech, the opposition walked out of the National Assembly and did not participate in the debate on the budget. This was at a time when money was scarce, and when choices about priorities were hard ones. Their disinterest showed they were not serious about governing.

The opposition promised things, and some people were taken in, since not everyone had a rational approach. The opposition appealed to those who like to hear good things but did not care to know how those good things would come about. The American political writer William Buckley criticised liberals in the United States by saying that they are in favour of "pleasant thoughts", not realism; and I think one could say the same thing of the opposition in Botswana.

The leadership in a country is responsible for educating the population. From day one, when *Domkrag* came into existence until the day I left office, we carried out extensive education with the people. We believed from the beginning that the essence of a democracy is an informed public. When people choose, they must know the basis of their choice: Why choose A and not B? Otherwise, you might expect them to vote blindfolded.

Over the years, *Domkrag* consistently stayed strong in most rural areas, while the opposition parties increased their strength in the urban areas. I think this is in part, at least, because the people in the rural area are down-to-earth people. They know they cannot expect ten hectares yield from one hectare. They know if they are hired to help scare the birds from eating the corn and to help reap the corn, and the result is a yield of two bags, then if the owner gives them one, they know they could not have done better. The opposition grossly underestimated the intelligence and the common sense of the people in the rural areas. They often thought they could just tell the people anything, and they would accept it.

In the urban areas, we have been less successful in educating people about the realities and the real choices. When people come to town, they start to deal in the abstract. They may say they are not paid well without asking: What have I done, and what is it worth? If one is working for a business that is making a loss, one can't expect the owner to increase the pay just because one feels ill paid. One may not even know that someone could run a business at a loss for periods of time and not make money. Those in the rural areas are confronted with the stark realities of life, while in town the electric lights have given the people the impression that they see when they don't. But, if the urban areas have not been as misled as the opposition would like them to be, it was because we in *Domkrag* were able to counter the venom they spewed and to explain some of the realities we faced as a country.

The issue of the opposition ultimately taking over the country is a worrying thought, not because *Domkrag* is always correct, but because so far the opposition parties have not demonstrated coherent programmes, nor have they shown a capacity to govern. However, people like change, even if it is just for the sake of change. Therefore, they might say: "Let us see what these fumbling fellows can do," and they might give them a chance. This is why we in *Domkrag* have tried not only to educate the electorate but to educate the opposition as well.

During my time as president, I had periodic meetings with the opposition on all matters, including security. As far back as Dr Verwoerd's or Mr Ian Smith's time, the late president or I would say there were questions we could answer in the House, and some we could answer when we were sitting privately with both government and opposition members. But there were a limited number of things affecting national security that we could talk about only on the basis of "the need to know".

Mr Mpho was one who accepted that position, since he had an understanding of the importance and sensitivity of national security. Whenever we had a problem with the Rhodesians or South Africans, or if something was highly sensitive to be shared only on a need to know basis, we would say so, and Mr Mpho would say: "Yes, precisely, that is what I would do, if I were in government, since I would not risk the country's security." He was very respectful of those distinctions. On the other hand, someone like Mr Matante could not be trusted. He would blast us and say: "Nothing doing, you should be telling us all these things. These are not your private affairs, so the general public should know," and so forth. It was one of the many things about Mr Matante that would have made him completely unfit to govern.

We had meetings between the leader of the opposition and the president. We had others among all members of Parliament where we thrashed out issues among people of all parties, as when we were trying to deal with cattle lung disease in the north in the 1990s. We would call in all MPs to tell them what was going on and explain the rationale for the course of action government was pursuing. We would give them the opportunity to ask questions and make comments. We wanted to make sure that if they went to the people and said things that were untrue, we would know it was a deliberate act, and not because they did not know the facts. In fact, on several occasions people from the opposition did just that: They did not refrain from telling people untruths.

We had extensive all-party caucus meetings on matters of economic policy, too. In these cases the opposition, as well as our back-benchers, really did seem to learn. When we faced the first real crisis in the diamond market in 1981-82, our economic problems were substantial. We took an entire afternoon after the 1982 Budget Speech had been delivered, and we brought officials from several ministries to an all-party caucus to explain in detail what was going on. We told them what we thought our options were and why we were choosing the particular ways of dealing with the problems.

We did the same thing in the mid-1980s when we were experiencing what appeared to be a "surplus" of foreign exchange reserves. There were political pressures from all sides, both within *Domkrag* and in the opposition, to increase spending at a faster rate. At that time the political situation in southern Africa was deteriorating. Our contingency planning showed we had very clear challenges, and we needed to protect the country in case of severe disruption by South Africa or because of sanctions. We knew having extra foreign exchange reserves was critical to our contingency plans. It was important that all politicians understand the basic facts.

The weakness and self-destruction of the opposition is worrying because it in turn weakens the performance of *Domkrag*. If one does not sharpen one's arguments against an intelligent foe, one can get lazy or sloppy. Both Botswana and *Domkrag* would be stronger and better off if we had a coherent opposition that had good leadership and substantive policies that were actual alternatives to those of the Democratic Party. It is much healthier to campaign on the basis of policies than on the basis of slogans or personalities or empty sweet-sounding promises.

Opposition Leaders

The qualities and motivation of the leadership of opposition parties have been very mixed in Botswana right from the beginning. There of course have been many admirable people, but there were some who were not, as can be true of any group. My comments are not meant to be comprehensive, but they may give a sense of how I and my colleagues in the BDP leadership regarded some of the opposition leaders during my years in politics.

Mr Motsamai Mpho always struck me as a very honest man, of very good character, and he had picked up a few ideas about policy from South Africa. Bias Mookodi and I had met him at Tiger Kloof in Form III, and from school he went to Johannesburg, where he imbibed the philosophy of the ANC. He appeared to accept everything the ANC said as gospel truth and of universal application. He was a treason trialist with Nelson Mandela and others, and after he was deported to Botswana, he preached the gospel of the ANC. It was difficult to dissuade him from his views, though we tried to tell him that what he thought was true for South Africa was not necessarily true for Botswana.

Mr Philip Matante was an actor who had adopted the PAC philosophy in South Africa. He could invent stories, and he could captivate people, but he did so as an entertainer. Rather than talk about the problems facing the country, he would try to find things that would interest his audience. Shortly after independence when the Okoh Commission was reviewing civil service salaries, he was addressing a meeting, and he shouted: "*Le fatshe, le faaatshe!*" (The land!) and then he shouted "*la rooona!*" (Ours!), drawing out each word; and then he waited for a response. There was none, and so he asked: "Don't you want to know about Okoh?" Finally, the civil servants at the meeting showed polite interest, even though Mr Matante knew far less about the subject than they did. The *Hansard* shows that his remarks in Parliament seldom contained anything of substance. Any disgruntled person could take his case to Matante, and without examining the merits, he would take it as truth and shout it from the rooftops.

One time in Parliament when Mr Matante made one of his abusive and irrelevant speeches, I said he reminded me of a story of two men. They were walking along, and one said: "You know, buddy, last night I dreamt I was going through a valley that was full of melons." The other asked: "Did you think of sharing them with me?" And he said "No, buddy." The second asked: "Did you think of giving some to me?" And the first again said: "No." So the second asked "Why not?" to which the first responded: "Why don't you dream your own dreams?" The moral of the story is that while Mr Mpho could dream of what responsibilities he would have if he were the president of Botswana, Mr Matante did not even allow his dreams to go that far.

Dr Kenneth Koma is an inscrutable fellow. He came back from his training in Russia full of Marxist ideology and became the leader of the Botswana National Front (BNF) to bring together splinter groups of the BPP. He allied himself with Chief Bathoen, of all people—the Marxist and the chief in the same party! The two made "strange bedfellows", as Joe Podbrey of the *Mafeking Mail* once said in an editorial column. Actually, Koma's first political pamphlet proposed that we should have a federal constitution with a tribally based "House of Nationalities". This appealed to Chief Bathoen and also to Chief Linchwe, who had initially aligned himself with the BNF. However, Koma also argued in his pamphlet that the chiefs would have to be dealt with.

Kenneth Koma can be as dishonest as he can be honest, and you never know which he is being. The opposition came up with 13 seats out of 44 in 1994, but lost the elections. At the first BNF conference in Palapye after the elections, there were great disagreements, and they ended up throwing chairs and bottles. Mr Koma reportedly said: "*Thaka*! (Good gracious!) Isn't it fortunate that we didn't win the elections? Since instead of throwing bottles, we would have been shooting each other with real bullets." Then he was being honest!

Mr Koma would say publicly he did not know things, when, in fact, they were issues on which he had been thoroughly briefed and actually knew very well. When he was leader, I told him I would keep the opposition informed of all important matters, which I did. When we had to decimate 320,000 head of cattle in Ngamiland because of cattle-lung disease, I briefed the whole opposition in detail as part of an all-party caucus. I gave the reasons for our actions and what we were going to do. We felt this was a national crisis, and we needed to have all political leaders understand the situation so they could help the public understand. But, the opposition decided to go to the affected areas in Ngamiland to stir up trouble. They told people that government had been advised by the tourist industry that these areas were better for wildlife, and therefore government had infected the cattle with this disease in order to kill them. Their behaviour made it much more difficult to deal with an already complex problem.

So, in that case Mr Koma was very dishonest, as he told a complete fabrication despite his opportunity to question all aspects of our policy. During those difficult times, I would call Mr Koma in to tell him we had learned what the opposition was doing. Sometimes he would say: "It must be one of our people who sometimes speaks like a chicken whose head has been chopped off." At other times he would say "Is that true? Some of our people must have said these things because they didn't know." This was completely untrue, which he knew very well.

A number of politicians have switched parties over the years, and one of the most travelled was Daniel Kwele. Mr Kwele was able, but he seemed to be one of those who was only interested in what politics would bring him personally. Mr Kwele had been in all versions of the opposition at one time or another, and at one point the late president had attracted him to our party. I was not particularly interested in having him join us, because our attitudes toward life were diametrically opposed. After Mr Kwele had come into the party, and we had worked together, I thought perhaps I had been wrong. But, as I learned more about him and found him to be simply manipulative, I concluded I had been right in the first place.

When Mr Kwele joined the BDP, we brought him into government and appointed him as an assistant minister. However, he treated people as if they were his own menial servants. And, he would fish in troubled waters, including our most divisive issue, that of tribalism. The end came when he went on a tour from Gaborone to Ghanzi, Maun and Francistown, and it was as if he was engaged in a scorched earth policy. He spent the trip maligning both the government and government officials; so when he came back, I dismissed him. I announced to my parliamentary colleagues: "Gentlemen, I have released Mr Kwele from his duties, and he has resigned from the party." Many of them asked: "Was he ever in the party?"

Others in the opposition, including Mr Mpho, had their own views of Mr Kwele. Before the 1994 elections, we held a last party conference in Zwenshambe in the north-east. I invited the opposition leaders to meet me in Francistown. I owed it to them to explain to them why we had originally said that *Omang*, the new national identity card, would be used in elections, but we were going to be unable to use it that year for identification. The implementation had taken much longer than it should have. If we were to wait for *Omang* registration to be completed, it would delay the elections for a year, and according to our constitution we could not do that. Mr Kwele responded to my explanation by saying: "We knew you people would cheat, and you found that the *Omang* would keep you from cheating, so you are dropping it." And he went on and on.

By this time, Mr Kwele had formed a new party, the Botswana Progressive Union (BPU), the last party he was in. After the meeting while we waited for lunch, Mr Mpho said to Mr Kwele: "By the way, Mr Kwele, in which party were you before you formed the BPU?" Mr Kwele responded: "I was in the BDP." "And before then?" asked Mr Mpho. Mr Kwele said: "I was a member of Botswsana National Front." Mr Mpho asked: "And before then?" and Mr Kwele replied: "I became a member of the Botswana People's Party." Mr Mpho again asked: "And then?" At that point Mr Kwele became very excited and said: "Why are you asking me all these questions?" And Mr Mpho said: "I just wanted to see the long journey you have taken," and he drew out the word "joouurney" as he spoke. And this appealed to Kenneth Koma, who repeated Mr Mpho's response, drawing out at even greater length *mosepele*, the Setswana word for journey: "*mooseepeeele!*" This so annoyed Mr Kwele that he felt too worked up to have lunch with us, so he left.

Dealing with the Country's Security
The late president and I as leaders of *Domkrag* always faced the opposition as competitors for votes. But as the leaders of government, we also had to deal with activities of some opposition politicians that on occasion presented threats to our national security or to law and order.

The issue of external threats was always with us, and it was perhaps most serious during the apartheid era in South Africa and the Smith regime in Rhodesia. During those years, the communist and Western countries were stirring things up in southern Africa, which was one of the battlegrounds of the Cold War. We certainly did not trust the Soviets' motives to be consistent with democratic principles, and we did not think their objectives in the region were necessarily consistent with ours.

The Special Branch of the Police collected information related to possible threats to the security of the country. From time to time the Special Branch came up with reports about politicians, both in *Domkrag* and in opposition parties, as well as civil servants, private citizens, and non-citizens. Their reports were based on observations that sometimes could be confirmed and sometimes not. It would have been a mistake to take reports in their files as established fact. We had regular meetings with all the security forces, and if we had our own concerns, we would put questions to the police about individuals where we had suspicions. We heard on occasion that someone in Botswana was working with people outside the country whom we thought questionable. It was important that we knew whether the person was asking for help in his own political aims, or whether our enemies were trying to get the person to assist them. We had plenty of evidence of both South African and Rhodesian efforts to undermine our stability, as well as our economy, and it was important that we protect the nation as a whole.

The great powers were very active in southern Africa in the 1970s. China, the Soviet Union and the United States were intervening with arms and supplies. The Cubans sent troops to Angola, as did the South Africans on their own behalf and on behalf of the Americans, both of whom were supporting UNITA against the Angolan government. We knew we could be at grave risk if we were not careful.

In 1977, the Soviets invited representatives from all our political parties to a meeting in Cuba. They provided air tickets, but those issued to the BDP were routed first to Odessa on the Black Sea, and then to Cuba, while the BNF received tickets that would take them directly to Cuba. It was clear that by the time the BDP delegates would arrive in Cuba, the BNF would be back in Gaborone. We also received reports that the meeting was not to be just an innocent conference, but it also would include training for potential insurgents. And at that time, the BNF was talking about "going to the bush" to seek power by force, since they continued to lose elections.

In response to the situation, we suspended the passports of some opposition members so they could not make the trip to Cuba. There was an outcry, of course, about how we were interfering with the opposition's rights. However, it seemed clear to us that there was a threat, not to the Democratic Party government, but to the security of the nation as a whole, were the opposition to become allied with external enemies in an effort to destabilise or overthrow the government by force. Bathoen was the leader of the BNF at the time, and he was an interesting contradiction. He had been very strong as a chief, but he was very weak as a political leader. He was so anxious to get to the top that he was willing to do anything to get there. Knowing of Bathoen's motivation and of the connections to extreme leftists on the part of some others in the opposition, we were suspicious of their motives and had to keep an eye on them.

The opposition stirred up troubles within Botswana in a number of different ways over the years. There was an incident in the Tuli Block in 1978, when a BDF soldier named Tswaipe was accused of murdering a British tourist. We in government felt it was obvious that we should leave the matter to the courts and let justice take its course one way or the other. But the BNF raised a fund to defend the soldier on the basis that even if a tourist was killed, the soldier was acting in the line of duty, and there should be no prosecution. We thought this was clearly a case of the opposition trying to make political capital out of an issue that should have been a matter of administering justice under the law.

Tswaipe was tried and convicted and sentenced to two years in prison. As president, I then pardoned him. I think both actions were appropriate. On the one hand, he was found to have violated the law. On the other hand, at that time, and in the area where he was operating, it was not unreasonable to assume that any whites were Rhodesians making trouble. People were so on edge because of Smith's forces that even on my farm in Ghanzi, more than 600 kilometres from the border with Rhodesia, people were frightened. I once hired a helicopter to assist in a survey at the farm, and one of my men ran in fright when he saw it, since he thought it must be one of Ian Smith's.

There have been several instances where the opposition was involved in inciting serious civil disruptions that literally threatened the whole society. In 1986, a child in Gaborone who had gone to visit her aunt was later reported missing by her mother. The mother panicked when she could not locate her child, and a rumour began that a woman had taken the child for use in witchcraft. Mr Dabutha, the BNF MP from Gaborone North, connived with a man named Sam Mbaiwa in the Information Department. Mr Mbaiwa went all over town in a speaker truck in the morning to say there would be a very important announcement made in the afternoon at Bontleng. In the afternoon, Mr Dabutha took the floor at a Bontleng Freedom Square and said *Domkrag* was allowing children to be taken away to be used for witchcraft. He said: "The lady who did this is in a certain house in Bontleng and her name is Mmadirelang." The opposition claimed a witch doctor named Segobaetsho from Mochudi had pointed out the house where the child was hidden.

A mob formed and went riotous. They stoned the house and almost lynched Mmadirelang; they stoned passing cars and created general disruption. It was a huge commotion, and Gaborone nearly became ungovernable. It was clearly a political ploy by the BNF to create chaos on which they could feed. But even reasonable people seemed to believe the rumours and wondered why government would allow someone to do such hideous things. Mmadirelang was exonerated of the allegations.

Then in 1994, a schoolgirl in Mochudi named Segametse Mogomotsi was victim of what appeared to be a ritual murder. The police were called to investigate, but they were unable to determine who might have killed the girl. However, some of the villagers had suspicions about who might have done it, and they burned down the houses of the people they suspected. The police came in to stop the violence, but the villagers, instigated by the BNF, insisted that the government was protecting evildoers. The BNF then stirred up University of Botswana students to take part in the disturbances on the basis that innocent children were being murdered, and sorcery was being used, to make certain people rich and powerful. This set off a whole string of riots that once again nearly caused the whole country to become ungovernable.

After the riots were quelled, it was alleged that government could not properly investigate, so we asked Scotland Yard to come from Britain. They investigated and made their report, which failed to discover who had committed the heinous act. The opposition demanded that the report be made public. The police rightly said that since they had not closed the case, the investigation was continuing. It would be totally against proper police procedure to release such a report. The case was never solved; so, a report has never been issued. Even today, more than ten years later, whenever the opposition has nothing else to say, they will ask about Segametse, the Scotland Yard report, and the like.

We had clear documentation of the role of the BNF as instigators in the violence, including names of BNF members of Parliament who were at various meetings in Mochudi and at the university. But, it was difficult to preempt their actions. If we had gone after them, which we quite legitimately could have done, we would have been accused of political persecution. I knew the opposition would charge me with acting like the typical African despot that the media like to portray, though such measures would have stopped the troublemakers. But if government had prevented the riots, then people would never have known what those who promoted the disturbances were capable of achieving in destabilising the country. The opposition really got away with its misbehaviour. Yet, I am quite sure that the opposition is known by the public to play by these tactics. It is perhaps just as well that I didn't take steps; time does tell.

The Mochudi and Bontleng incidents were not the only times the opposition has stirred up trouble by taking advantage of a situation. There had been a murder of two children near the Notwane River in Gaborone, and a specific minister was accused. Upon investigation, the allegations against the minister were shown to have been made out of sheer malice. While these and other incidents are examples of some in the opposition parties in Botswana, they are not representative of all those in opposition. However, I think it is fair to say that the major opposition parties have been motivated more by a desire to defeat the BDP than to establish any coherent set of policies that would lead the country to greater prosperity, security, or unity.

Botswana as an Open Society

Our tradition in Botswana, based in the *kgotla*, has been one of open debate. Therefore, if somebody has argued against what you have said, you don't consider him an enemy; you just take it that you differed. It might be your cousin, or your brother or your brother-in-law; but just because you differed it doesn't mean the person hates you. The arrival of Western politics just provided different names or contexts to the way we had carried out our differences traditionally—*Mmualebe o bua la gagwe a re mana lentle a tle a letswe* (let him who knows not have his say, to give him who knows better the chance to correct him).

Nketsang Moditswane and Rapontsheng Kalabeng were great pals of mine in Kanye, and they almost always differed and argued with me. My uncle asked me: "Why do you like these people so much, since you differ with them about so many things?" I told my uncle I liked them because they spoke their minds, even if we disagreed. This is how it is with the opposition; where we think they sincerely hold a different point of view, we respect their right to differ with us.

Ntwakgolo ke ya molomo is a Setswana proverb that means "the big battle should be fought by words". If you really want to engage in a fight which will have a reward at the end, you had better engage in a verbal battle. It was not surprising to have gone to a Freedom Square and found Dr Kenneth Koma arguing vociferously with everything Quett Masire was doing, and in the evening found they were dining together. After all, my sister Gabalegwe married into the Koma family. Motsamai Mpho might have disagreed publicly with Tsheko Tsheko, but both recognised they were from the same place, and they could be friends. Even with the factions that developed within *Domkrag*, the issue is personalities. People from the two sides are often good friends and will go out and have a meal together. The issue between them is: How persuasively can each one argue in order to have his way?

Once when I was vice-president, a Zambian minister named Kalulu was in Gaborone for a meeting, and I invited him and some other people to my house for a drink in the evening. During our conversation I mentioned that Mr Matante had been at my house at the last drinks party. Mr Kalulu said: "If the vice-president in Zambia, Ruben Kamaga, had invited a member of the opposition for a drink at his house I would walk out." We in Botswana have somehow managed to keep even very strong political differences separate from our personal relationships, and this has contributed to the feeling of openness in political debate. Perhaps this accounts for some of the difference between our politics and those in some other African countries.

Chapter 11
Politics and Elections after 1965

Domkrag won overwhelmingly in the 1965 elections, and we continued to win a majority in Parliament, and therefore the presidency, up to and including the elections of 2004. Seretse Khama led us to victory in 1965, 1969, 1974 and 1979. While I was president we prevailed in the elections of 1984, 1989, and 1994. Festus Mogae continued to lead *Domkrag's* winning ways in 1999 and 2004. While this chapter is not meant to be a comprehensive history of our politics, I briefly review each election, discuss some other political personalities, and comment on a number of broader political issues that I believe have been important.

The Aftermath of the 1965 Elections
After we won the elections in 1965, Chief Bathoen was very upset. In fact, the shock wave came when he had seen the eagerness with which people turned up for elections. He clearly had miscalculated and failed to read the winds of change in the people's hearts. People who previously had known nothing about elections were overwhelmingly excited about voting. They came early in the morning in the dark to stand in line; women who were in confinement broke with tradition and left home to go and vote. The chief was so disappointed at the results that he asked to be allowed to preach in the Kanye LMS church the day following the elections. His text was from I Peter, Chapter 2, Verse 17: "Honour everyone. Love the family of believers. Fear God. Honour the Emperor." The Setswana translation of "Emperor" in the text was *"Kgosi"*, so it read *"Tlotlang Kgosi"* (honour the chief). He contrasted that message with how his own calls for people to do various things were being ignored. He didn't explicitly say so, but he implied: "Yet when these renegades call you to vote, you turn up in hordes."

At the end of the service, Rre Rapontsheng Kalabeng, a stalwart supporter of *Domkrag* was asked to pronounce the benediction. His benediction went like this: "Oh God the Almighty, who brought the children of Israel from Egypt to the land of Canaan, who arranged for Moses and Joshua to lead the people to freedom, we are thankful that you have raised from among us our own children who are going to lead us." He pulled the carpet from under the chief's feet, and his benediction became the talk of the town!

Chief Bathoen remained bitter, and his behaviour became very sulky, eccentric and negative. He tried hard to go back on some of the matters of constitutional and legislative change that we had already agreed upon. He also decided there was great merit in South Africa's Bantustans and that Botswana would be better as part of South Africa. He invited Kaiser Mantanzima, the leader of the Transkei Bantustan in South Africa, to visit Kanye. On his way home, Mantanzima travelled via Gaborone, where he wanted to pay a courtesy call on Seretse. Seretse refused to see him, since we did not want to be associated with the Bantustans. Reports from the Special Branch reached us that Chief Bathoen had been to see Dr Klopper, the South

African who was high commissioner for the Bophuthatswana Bantustan, to seek the incorporation of the Bangwaketse territory into South Africa. However, Dr Klopper had informed him that was not possible. Dr Klopper had told Chief Bathoen; the report went on, that if he would do as Seretse Khama had done and become the next president of Botswana then he could bring not only his own tribe, but the whole country, into South Africa.

After independence, *Domkrag* held a party conference in Kanye. We had established the practice that on arrival for a conference at any village we would send a few people to pay our respects to the chief so that we would be welcomed. My colleagues felt that this mark of respect should not be extended to Chief Bathoen in view of his attitude towards us, but I did not agree. I pointed out that neglecting to pay our respects would give the impression that we did so because the chief was opposed to *Domkrag*. Further, if we ignored him, it would compromise the position of those who did receive us in their villages. After a lengthy discussion, it was decided that we would follow tradition and pay our respects to the chief. We expected that he would reciprocate by coming to the opening of our conference to welcome us all to his village.

Instead of welcoming us, however, Chief Bathoen made a series of political remarks about our new government. He said we had wanted independence, but we had not achieved independence, since Gaborone was only for whites. He said Batswana were only allowed to stay at Naledi (the shanty town to the south), and that the constitutional talks had been a sham. I welled up with emotion and interrupted him in the middle of his speech to say that what he was saying was not true. He had never been challenged in that way in his 40 years as chief. To be interrupted and contradicted while he was speaking had never been done. As was to be expected, my intervention won me a yet another bad mark in Chief Bathoen's book. But it also made my own people in the party feel that I had not betrayed them into coming to the chief's place only to be slaughtered.

Over time, the late president quietly tried to persuade Chief Bathoen that he was pursuing the wrong course, but B2's hostility continued. Seretse finally decided it would be more effective if he told the chief in the Kanye *kgotla* that he was obstructing progress of our democracy. That way, if there was ultimately to be a break, the tribe would know and understand the cause. A meeting was planned, and Dr Kenneth Koma, who by that time had founded the BNF, saw it as an opportunity not to be lost. Koma had always thought *Domkrag* had won because it had been led by Chief Seretse Khama, and that it was time for another chief to come in to replace Seretse. Dr Koma came to Kanye and persuaded Chief Bathoen that since Seretse was going to depose him, which was not true, it would be better for Bathoen to take a pre-emptive action and resign before he was pushed out. He also proposed that B2 join the BNF as its leader.

When Seretse and I arrived at the house of Julian Tennant, the DC in Kanye, we found Tennant had received that morning a letter from Bathoen resigning as chief. We telephoned Alan Tilbury in Gaborone to ask him the legal position. He said Chief Bathoen's deputy, Mookami Gaseitsiwe, could act until a decision was taken as to who would be the new chief of the Bangwaketse. At the *kgotla*, Chief Bathoen announced his resignation. Seretse accepted it and immediately appointed Mookami Gaseitsiwe as the acting chief. The people were stunned! Bathoen had run the tribe since the 1920s and had even made speeches in which he said: "I have ruled for 40 years and no one can say I was ever at fault." People were just bamboozled by the fact that he had decided to quit.

1969
Bathoen became known as Bathoen Gaseitsiwe after he resigned the chieftainship and joined politics. Having teamed up with Dr Koma, he was ready to run for Parliament, and he chose to run against me in my constituency, Kanye South. During the campaign for the 1969 elections I, of course, talked about *Domkrag's* policies, explaining that the programmes we had started would continue to be pursued. As we had more funds available, there would be even more development programmes than in the past. I gave the basic Democratic Party message: We had told the country that we would do what we promised, and our record of action showed we had accomplished what we had promised. We had told people the country was going to become independent, and we needed to prepare for that. We had taken over from the British, and we had developed a track record. Bathoen's message to the people was simple. The very fact that he had resigned the chieftainship demonstrated he was in complete disagreement with what the BDP government had been doing.

I attacked Bathoen on his dealings with Dr Klopper and the Bophuthatswana Bantustan. The "Black Key", as the plan was known, was going to open South Africa to Botswana. I emphasised that we did not want to become a Bantustan, nor did we want to participate in the breaking up of South Africa. I talked openly about the issue and really went to town on Bathoen's role in it. His stance was that we should not go it alone; we were a natural part of South Africa, and we should go in their direction. He said that Seretse should not be critical of South Africa, since doing so was against Botswana's interest. I don't know if he really believed it, or whether his simplistic view of leadership obscured his vision.

There was serious apprehension among my colleagues about my standing against Bathoen. Doing so, they felt, was risking the political position of the country's vice-president. But I did not want to be seen to run away. I had to worry about the party nationally, since I was the secretary-general, and then, of course, about my own seat in Kanye. In the beginning, I had not thought that Bathoen would win, but over time I concluded that he would. Issues did not matter as much as tribal loyalty, this was now strictly tribal politics. I had won overwhelmingly in 1965, with my opponent Peter Maruping collecting only 57 votes. But in 1969, I lost dismally to the man who was still regarded by many as my chief. Bathoen Gaseitsiwe immediately became the leader of the BNF. He also campaigned successfully for two other BNF candidates in Ngwaketse, giving them three seats overall. The BPP also won three seats, so the size of the opposition doubled.

After the election, disappointed as I was, I simply had to resign myself to my loss and get on with helping to lead the party and the government. I was nominated to a specially elected seat in the House and came back as vice-president and minister of finance and development planning. I also continued as leader of the House.

1974

As the 1974 elections approached, Seretse became restive because he did not want me to stand in Kanye again. It was one thing to be specially elected once and continue as vice-president, but twice would be difficult, so he wanted to give me a safe seat outside Ngwaketse. He worked on me, and when he failed to convince me he asked Archie Mogwe to plead with me. I was reluctant for two overriding reasons. First, if I left Ngwaketse, we would virtually be giving all four seats to the opposition. Second, if we did not run a strong campaign in Ngwaketse, we would not be in a position to contest successfully for district council seats. The councillors would be better placed if I were by their side. But instead of running directly against Bathoen in Ngwaketse South, I ran in Ngwaketse/Kgalagadi, a constituency we had lost in the 1969 elections, and I won it back. People in the party had originally thought I had taken the wrong decision to stand for a risky constituency where Bathoen's influence was still strong. After the fact, people felt I had taken the right decision.

I started working on my new constituency early, well before the election. I toured it, and I caused questions that had come up in the constituency meetings to be asked in Parliament by other members. It was a matter of great amusement that Mr Mosinyi, who represented Shoshong, would ask a question about some small villages in western Ngwaketse. Of course, the late president was keen that I should win so he campaigned on my behalf as well and was a great help.

Seretse's message in 1974 was very subtle. He said that in 1965 we had only been tribes, not a nation, and we knew chiefs but no other leaders. As we progressed and became one nation, we needed to start to look amongst ourselves to see who the best people to serve the country were. He even said that although in 1965 he himself was probably elected because he was a Khama, in 1974 people should look to see if he had done a good job as president before voting for him again.

In 1974, Mrs Kebatshabile Disele was standing for election against Bathoen in my old constituency of Ngwaketse South, and I pitched up to help her out. The Johannesburg *Rand Daily Mail* asked me why I was spending so much time in a constituency I was not contesting. It was part of our strategy that if our candidate failed, we would have worked hard so she did not fail badly, and her morale would remain high. My campaigning there would also help those who were running for council seats. Our strategy worked well. We had controlled the council in 1969 even though we had lost three of four parliamentary seats; Mrs Disele lost to Bathoen in 1974, but we split the Ngwaketse parliamentary seats two and two and we kept control of the council as well.

Motsamai Mpho won in Okavango for his BIP that year, defeating Tsheko Tsheko, but we balanced the loss since Greek Ruele won for *Domkrag* in Mochudi. The opposition fell from six seats to five—two each for BPP and BNF, and one for the BIP. We also increased our share of the total vote to 77%.

1979

At the time of the 1974 elections, we realised that while we had many good people, some did not have much formal education. We needed to recruit educated people into the party to provide leadership for the future. We also knew that some very good people, such as Gaositwe Chiepe and Archie Mogwe, were soon to retire from the civil service. We recruited those two, and they were specially elected after the 1974 elections. Mr Kgari died shortly thereafter, so Dr Chiepe stood for and won his former seat in a by-election.

We felt confident going into the 1979 election even though the late president was by then very, very ill. The economy was strong, and the party was very strong as well, and we won 75% of the popular vote. Mr Mpho was defeated in the Okavango, and since we beat Mr Matante in Francistown as well, we added a seat at the expense of BPP. We had 29 seats, and the opposition fell from five seats to three. Bathoen Gaseitsiwe became the leader of the opposition, replacing Mr Matante.

Mr Matante lost because we had a strong candidate in Patrick Balopi. While Mr Balopi was executive secretary of *Domkrag* we had sent him to Mr Matante's constituency on party missions. This was a good example of the selection process we sometimes used. The party executive would meet to consider people we thought should become better known in a constituency. Then we would promote the person with the constituency executive in a subtle way. If we succeeded, the local party executive and members would see merit in the person, and he or she would become the constituency's candidate. That was how Patrick Balopi came to face Mr Matante.

Sometimes our selection system failed as in the Barolong. B. C. Thema, who was very able as a minister, had gone to Nigeria for a conference at Abuja and had contracted malaria. The disease seriously weakened him, and he decided not to run for office. The Barolong constituency executive wanted their own man, though we tried to propose other candidates who were quite able. Their reasons were entirely local: The man was someone who was willing to do small favours for people. So, that was one of the cases where one just could not go against the tide, and we had to settle for a weak candidate.

July 1980

Seretse's health was very poor leading up to the October 1979 elections, and he declined further after our victory. As I related in Chapter 9, his condition became critical, and in June 1980 he was flown to England for medical care. It was not effective, and he was brought back to Gaborone. When I arrived at the airport in Gaborone, having been recalled from a visit to China, two officials told me it was evident that he was dying. They pleaded that if I was asked to succeed him, I shouldn't say no. Many people, including members of the opposition parties, began coming to me to urge me to accept the role if I were asked.

On Sunday, 13 July, it was my sad responsibility to inform the nation on the radio that Sir Seretse Khama had passed away that morning. We declared a full month of national mourning; there were public prayer services throughout the country, and Radio Botswana played sacred music all day. There was a large memorial service at the national stadium attended by heads of state from many African countries and high level delegations from around the world. A funeral was held in Serowe where he was buried with his ancestors. I addressed both gatherings.

The transition after Seretse's death was very difficult for me for many reasons. First, I had lost a very close friend and a colleague whom I greatly admired. Second, there was the grief we all felt on losing the man who was the father of the nation. Then there was a feeling among the public that government was in too great a hurry to select a new president. Further, both the natural grief that everyone felt, and the public's concern that we were acting too hastily in choosing a successor, were focussed on government; and it was especially directed to me as the interim leader of the government. It was a very trying time.

People wondered: "Why not have the funeral first, and allow the nation time to grieve?" Cabinet and Parliament decided Attorney General Moleleki Mokama needed to go on the radio to read sections of the constitution to the people and explain that we had laws to follow in filling the presidency. He pointed out that the constitution specified a period of seven days within which we had to elect a new president. He also said that if we left the country without a head, there would be people who did not wish us well who might take advantage of the situation. His interview was carried in both English and Setswana and was printed in the *Daily News* as well.

I was a reluctant politician. If I had had my way, I would not have become a politician in the 1960s, but I felt I had to do it because there was a need. In 1980, if people had felt someone else should be president, I would have given him, or her, my full support. When some people in the party were inclined to be critical of Mout Nwako and David Magang for seeking the presidency and campaigning for it in July 1980, I saw no harm in their doing so; I felt we shouldn't be in a situation in which no one wanted to be president.

Many different people came to see me: representatives of the churches and groups of farmers, and people like Mr Mutsumi and Mr Mpho from the opposition. My uncle Kgopo Kgopo came from Kanye to urge me to accept. Six of the senior members of the party were officially detailed to come and see me: Ben Thema, Gaefalale Sebeso, Dikgothi Monwela, Mudongo Maswikiti, Boy Moapare and Goareng Mosinyi. I told them that if they really wanted me, I would be willing to stand. On Thursday 17 July, the BDP caucus met in Tsholetsa House and voted to nominate me to the National Assembly.

I think it was a great relief to people when I accepted, since many had thought I would refuse to serve. I was nominated and elected by the National Assembly on 18 July, and I believe people were pleased. When I was sworn in by the chief justice on that day, it was not a moment of celebration or joy for me. It was for me a time of reflection, quiet contemplation and silent prayer that God should be my guide in accomplishing the honourable tasks fate had entrusted to me. Despite the normal criticism I expected as a politician and a president, I felt the nation was behind me in overwhelming majority.

The Spoilers
I had taken office nine months after the 1979 elections, so there were four years before we needed to hold the next elections. Through those years there were, of course, some who were unhappy with my being the president; some were spoilers who exploited several incidents to call my presidency into question.

As president, Seretse Khama's picture had hung on the wall in every government office and most business establishments. Civil servants took it as given that after I became president, my picture should be on the wall. But, in the workings of government bureaucracy, it took many months before Seretse's picture was taken down and exchanged for mine. When the pictures were exchanged, some people, especially some Bangwato, were resentful. Similarly, although Botswana law prescribed that bank notes would carry the picture of the head of state, it took many months after Seretse's demise before my picture appeared on printed currency. When it did appear, at about the same time as the portraits in the offices were changed, the issue was raised in the Ngwato *kgotla*: "Masire is, after all, a commoner, and here his image is replacing Seretse who was a chief." Some objectors even inferred that the value on similar currency notes was not the same!

Such incidents harked back to the resistance against the constitution by the chiefs. On this occasion, however, tribal rivalry was at play; in the Bangwato mind, no one other than a member of the Ngwato royal family could be president. Some from other tribes thought: "We don't mind if Quett Masire is president, but Seretse's portrait should be on the walls and on the currency." I did not really place any importance on these matters, but they added to my troubles. Although it might have caused a debate, with hindsight it might have been better if we had done some explaining.

My role as a commoner who was president sometimes brought out interesting comments. There was a Mokgatla named Dihatlho Seame, who frequently spoke at *kgotla* meetings. At a meeting in Mochudi, after I had become president he said: "Masire, you are a commoner. You have to behave creditably, because if you don't these chiefs will think a commoner cannot do a good job as president, and they will want to have the monopoly of being president!" I had found the same fellow one night on the Lobatse road some years earlier. His vehicle had broken down and I stopped to help. When he realised it was the vice-president and that I was driving myself as I always did in those days, he scolded me: "Masire, you must not be doing that driving yourself. You are depriving someone else of a job!"

Another issue arose at the same time as the portrait and currency matters: the status of Seretse's son, Lt. General Ian Khama, who was at the time second in command of the Botswana Defence Force. In some people's minds

I was simply Seretse's lieutenant; and if I was president, it was as a kind of stopgap; perhaps I was even a regent between father and son.

The late president had installed his son as chief of the Bangwato in May 1979, and had established his full name as Seretse Khama Ian Khama. Apparently, Seretse's 1956 renunciation of the chieftainship himself had gone by the board. He was urged to make Ian a chief by people like Mr Nwako and Moleleki Mokama. Given Mr Nwako's opposition to chieftainship, I thought that was an interesting position for him to take.

I was very disturbed by Ian Khama's ambivalent role of being both a soldier and chief of the Bangwato. Chieftainship was divisive and obviously so, as we had long ago concluded. I went to the *kgotla* in Serowe to thank the Bangwato for allowing their chief to serve in the army, and to say that it now appeared there was a need for them to have him back. The Bangwato were surprised, and there were questions as to why he could not stay as a soldier for a while. I had discussions with elders from the tribe, and it was agreed that Ian would be chief-in-absentia, but he could not be chief and still remain in the army. Another person was appointed Tribal Authority to carry out the day-to-day duties of the chief. From then to the day I retired, I felt I enjoyed the support of General Khama and that of the Bangwato.

The real problem for the future was that it was incompatible to be a chief or a chief-in-absentia, or even to be a chief-designate, and to be a politician and a president. The late president had made that point clear both by his own example and by not allowing Bathoen to be both a chief and an elected politician.

The spoilers played on tribal feelings that were still strong despite our years of democracy. I can only hope that what some people have said is true: That they realised from the currency and portrait and Ian Khama incidents that tribalism was still an issue we had to face squarely.

1984

The 1984 elections were the first after I became president. Because we previously changed the constitution so the president would not run for a constituency, I vacated my parliamentary seat. Mr Tshipinare ran for my former seat, and he won. He was a good candidate: He had been active in the party and he had been deputy council secretary. He came from the area, so he was a son of the soil.

We worked very hard in the 1984 elections, since we were entering with a new team as compared with 1979. The other parties also worked hard, but they didn't have much of substance to sell. While *Domkrag* had a clear message that was consistent throughout the country, the opposition parties always told people what they would like to hear, so they ended up preaching different messages in different constituencies. The two BNF party leaders, Bathoen Gaseitsiwe and Kenneth Koma, were entirely different in their ideological orientation: Bathoen a traditionalist and an autocratic chief, Koma a rabid ideological socialist. The late president had wanted to woo Bathoen to *Domkrag* but I had argued against it. My former chief was a divisive factor within the opposition, and he helped to weaken them!

Peter Mmusi, who was by then vice-president, had won the election in Gaborone against Kenneth Koma, but someone had hidden a ballot box. The lost box meant there had to be a by-election, which Mmusi lost. It was a big personal blow to me as well as a setback to *Domkrag*. The BNF picked up three seats, including Peter Mmusi's. The size of the House had been increased to 34 following the 1981 Census and delimitation, so *Domkrag* dropped only one seat, from 29 to 28; the BNF won five and the BPP one. Our share of the popular vote declined from 75% to 68%.

Recruits to the Party
We continued to look for new people to bring into the party, particularly people who had done well in the civil service or the private sector. Recruitment into the party was sometimes complicated. Human nature being what it is, older members tended to think they had seen more than new ones and their judgment was based on a more realistic view of life. On the other hand, the younger ones often felt that simply because they had graduated from university, they could do better than others who had not. Sometimes we had gone all out to recruit young people who, unfortunately, thought we had ready-made positions for them and were disappointed when they didn't get to the Promised Land quickly enough. Some were realistic and stayed, but others became disappointed and left. One young man told me that when he first became a member of Parliament, he thought he would become a minister right away. He later realised how unrealistic that had been, though he did become a minister after some time.

Dan Kwelagobe was one of our early recruits after independence. I knew of him when he was still at school although I did not know him personally. Dan was a regular subscriber to *Therisanyo* even before we formed a youth wing of the party. When he came out of school, he joined the Information Department, and he was always keen to put government in the best light. When *Domkrag* came to involve youth in a formal way, Dan was an obvious choice since he was a streak ahead of all others politically. He stood for elections in Molepolole and won, and the late president made him an assistant minister right away.

Dan became a very hard-working member of the party, and his passion for the party was unsurpassed. He literally wept when a development inside or outside the party threatened the strength or stability of the party. He was a "man of the people", and it was not a surprise that he was elected secretary-general of the party in 1980 when I became president.

However, all people have their strengths and weaknesses—*motho mogakabe mo jewa ka ntlhangwe* (like a crow, one side is edible and the other side bitter). Dan was always a very difficult fellow in cabinet. He could virtually silence some of the senior ministers such as Messrs. Nwako, Haskins, Thema and Tsoebebe. If he knew anything embarrassing about a person, he would use it. If the person had coughed at a church service, Dan would work that into a remark such as: "It is not just that you coughed at the church service the other day..." And people would think there was more to the story than Dan was willing to tell. At one point I was so fed up with him that I was ready to throw him out of cabinet, since older ministers would rather keep quiet than argue with him. However, Mr Mogwe said: "This is just a youngster; you must expect him to misbehave sometimes." Dan did not know this, but Mr Mogwe saved him.

Dan Kwelagobe had great energy; he would go all out for anything he believed in, and he would be aggressive against anything that opposed him. Dan was also helpful to me in restraining ministers from raising our salaries, since he would put the argument on a personal basis, saying things like: "We should not be only interested in *go ja* (eating)."

Dr Chiepe and Messrs. Mogwe, Mmusi and Kedikilwe, all of whom were better educated than most other members of the party leadership, were made ministers immediately as each joined the party. Those who had come before, including founding members, accepted them happily, in part because they were respectful of others, adopted a low profile, and did not appear to take over the party. The established members also realised that these new recruits were being brought in as part of the effort to improve the party's ability to perform. But, if newcomers tried to come in both to hold high political office and to take control of the party, we would have risked losing the support of regular party workers and members, and that could have weakened the party.

One young lawyer who came into the party thought he could throw his weight around even at his first party congress in Serowe. He tried to interpret the party constitution to suit his purposes. He was playing the lawyer and telling us what the language meant in law. I remember saying to him: "We did not intend the party constitution to say that, and if you say that is what it means, then we must amend the constitution." Later when he and one or two other politicians became ministers, they felt that as ministers they should be given privileges that were not due them. They came with a sense of entitlement and tried to give personal directives to their ministries. A strong civil service has been important in keeping such people from overstepping their authority, even though civil servants themselves sometimes stepped over the line.

As a young man, Mr Kedikilwe stood a little on the side and seemed not to be too inclined to politics. As he became more senior in the civil service, his job became that of carrying out the government's policies, and when he retired he was director of public service management. He seemed very sympathetic to the objectives of *Domkrag*, so we approached him, and he agreed to join the party. He stood for elections in 1984 and won, and after elections I appointed him a minister.

Mompati Merafhe was another civil servant who I thought could bring talent to the cabinet if he joined the party after he retired from the army. He had been deputy commissioner of police, and in 1977 he was appointed as the first Commander of the Botswana Defence Force. He performed very well in his new responsibilities at a difficult time in our history. Under his leadership, the BDF became an effective and respected organisation. He also showed he was public spirited when he took a leading role in an NGO that built the National Stadium in Gaborone. He was a very effective minister, but over time his role in the party complicated things both for the party and for me, as I explain below.

Over the years, we in the BDP made it a point to ensure that all Batswana who are interested should be included in the political process, irrespective of colour or creed. It is interesting that despite the fact that the farms in Ghanzi, the Tuli Block, Tati Block and Molopo are still very largely owned by white citizens, there has been no discordant issue politically. The farmers in the largely white areas are virtually all members of *Domkrag*. Hendry Vickerman, in Ghanzi, is as good a politician as you could think of, though he has never run for Parliament. Dick Eaton, also from Ghanzi, has either been a councillor or a member of Parliament since we became independent. Jimmy Haskins, from Francistown, was a minister and later Mr Speaker. The Blackbeards, father Colin and son Roy, were both very active in the party and in local politics as councillors and chairmen of the Central District Council. Later each was elected to Parliament and each served as minister as well.

A number of Batswana of Asian origin have also been important to the party. Sham Khan was for long time a very active fundraiser. Satar Dada also has been active in *Domkrag*, and was a councillor in Nyorosi Ward in Kanye for many years. He attended many social activities such as weddings and funerals, courtesies that mean a lot to Batswana.

All these individuals recognised that as citizens of Asian or European origin they should not try to play a role that might be seen as inappropriate by many Batswana. They have been helpful to our efforts and have given meaning to our commitment to non-racialism.

1989 Elections and Development of Factions

In 1989, *Domkrag* dropped in its share of the overall vote, but we increased our majority in Parliament. The People's Party was eliminated, and the BNF dropped to only three seats. The economy was doing well; the party was well organised; and we had an experienced team in both government and the party. I went into the election expecting to retire during that term and hand over to a successor.

But after the 1989 election, we became weak as a party because of the development of two strong factions. My colleagues believed that I wanted to retire, and a jostle for the presidency started within the party. People seemed not to mind if I continued as president, but they started thinking keenly of their own positions, or at least those of the candidates they favoured, if I were not president.

Dan Kwelagobe and Mompati Merafhe were old friends. However, Dan was a great one for the status quo in the party, and I think he saw that Mompati's ambition was a challenge to Peter Mmusi, who was then vice-president. At that point the two factions formed, and Dan and Mompati Merafhe became permanently at loggerheads—*ya nna sa ntsa htsa le phiri* (they developed an intense disapproval of each other). After Peter Mmusi resigned as vice-president, both Kedikilwe and Merafhe appeared to be interested in the presidency, and Mr Kedikilwe was pushed by Dan as an alternative to Mompati. At the time I thought Mompati Merafhe was the best available, followed by Mr Kedikilwe. Dan seemed to like to be a kingmaker rather than the king. That was just as well, since the range of routine but very important things a president must do would have frustrated Dan.

Some people in the party, and some outside, saw Mompati Merafhe as being groomed to be a future president. In fact, four ministers in cabinet—Temane, Butale, Roy Blackbeard and Magang—joined with Merafhe in a group known as "The Big Five"—to promote his candidacy. I knew nothing about the group until I was asked about the "big five" at a *kgotla* meeting in Bobonong.

When there are factions within a party, reason abdicates and emotions take over, and this creates problems for a president. A president must, to the best of his or her ability, try to be seen not to favour any faction but should not be deluded: Each faction will accuse the president of belonging to the other camp. So long as they cannot prove it, one may be safe! And, that is the way I went about it.

As president and as leader of the party I had a difficult time dealing with Dan and Mompati Merafhe. I would talk with each of them individually, and then I would bring them together. I enlisted the party elders—people such as Dr Merriweather, Mrs Gagoumakwe Sechele, Greek Ruele, and David Maina—to talk with them. They, too, talked with them both separately and together, and they emphasised that personal rivalries would weaken the party. But it was to no avail. Dan and Mompati would swear by heaven and earth that they would mend their ways and work together. But later, not to make it obvious, they used surrogates to get at each other.

The problem was that the differences between the factions were not philosophical, they were personal. Each felt more *Domkrag* than the other, and this kept each from leaving the party. The differences had a spill-over effect to newcomers to the party. The new members might have been indifferent to begin with, but sympathy ultimately developed for one faction or the other. That, unfortunately, kept the process going. We took the matter to the party congress at Kanye, one that came to be known as *congress ya kgola disana* (the congress of removing stumps), but we failed to bring about a permanent peace.

There were several issues that we had to negotiate around the factions. One, perhaps the beginning of the factionalism, was where to locate the first diamond-cutting factory—Kwelagobe's home in Molepolole, or Serowe, which was Merafhe's home. Another crucial issue was the buying of shares in De Beers in exchange for Debswana's stockpile of diamonds in 1987. *Domkrag* had experienced an earlier difficult disagreement over TGLP, but in that case it was a difference of views on an issue, it did not involve permanent differences, nor were the differences personal ones. The factions are more personal or partisan—more like loyalty to a football club.

Both Dan Kwelagobe and Mompati Merafhe were very close to me. Dan had been responsible for the BDF as minister for presidential affairs when Mompati was the BDF Commander. In fact, they had been close friends of each other. They were among those one could count on to do things to strengthen the party. But, it did not take a prophet to tell us that these two party stalwarts could eventually bring down the party if their factions continued to fight.

If there had not been a bad split in the party, I would have been very pleased to retire as president and go back to farming in the early 1990s. But the divisions became so unbridgeable that I felt I had to stay until we could put together a transition to new leadership that would not divide *Domkrag* and give the elections to the opposition. I made Festus Mogae my vice-president in part because he was not associated with either faction. We subsequently amended the constitution to accomplish two objectives. One provided that the vice-president would automatically become president if the presidency became vacant, a provision we lacked in 1980. The second provided that Parliament would approve the selection of the vice-president. This ensured that the people's representatives chose the person who could succeed to the presidency.

1994

We went into the 1994 elections with factions in the party. The opposition, on the other hand, had done well in their recruiting and, if they kept it up, they thought they could win. Despite the hard feelings and even hatred between the factions, I did not think we would split, since both groups loved the party and hated the opposition. What kept the two factions in *Domkrag* was a feeling of what we had stood for since our inception. Each would rather have lost to the other within the party than risk a three-way vote that would result in the opposition taking over. We also used the troubles of the People's Party to illustrate to our own people the dangers of factionalism.

The party is almost like a religion; one does things because one is a believer. If the party is divided, one's enthusiasm is tampered with. In almost every constituency, *Domkrag's* candidate in the election was from the majority faction in that area. The divisions in the party lowered party morale and also resulted in voter apathy. If someone from one faction was running in a constituency, people from the other were less willing to work on his or her behalf. Those with no enthusiasm for *Domkrag's* candidate would refuse to vote for an opposition candidate, so they would not turn out.

As a result of our factionalism and despite hard campaigning, *Domkrag* was divided and weak in 1994, and our divisions enabled the opposition to increase their representation in Parliament. The size of Parliament had been increased to 44 seats following the 1991 Census and the Delimitation Commission Report. In a system of single-member constituencies, an increased number of constituencies will generally favour gains by the minority parties. The delimitation of Gaborone constituencies favoured the opposition, since a good deal of the BNF's strength lay in the urban areas. Gaborone was given two additional seats, and the BNF took both. BNF won three seats in Ngwaketse, and we maintained two. We took 55% of the popular vote, but in Parliament we held 31 seats and the BNF 13.

In the 1999 elections, 18 months after I had left office, the problem of factions that had affected *Domkrag* in 1994 affected the BNF and the rest of the opposition. The divisions in *Domkrag* had not been as well known in 1994, but in 1999 the opposition was very open about their internal disagreements, and they practically disintegrated. As a result, *Domkrag* picked up two percentage points in the popular vote and gained 6 seats in a Parliament of 44, bringing our majority to 37 against 7.

Personalities and Politics

Politics is about both policy and people. We were very fortunate in the quality of the people who took an interest in *Domkrag* from the beginning, and we worked hard to encourage good people to join the party over the years. Of course, the party benefited politically as people recognised that we were delivering the goods.

Seretse's team in cabinet and Parliament were high-minded people who bravely and honestly soldiered on. In my years as president, I tried to maintain the same standards. The vast majority of individuals who entered politics as members of *Domkrag* were unselfish and thought of the public good. However, even a few exceptions can make life difficult for the whole party, and even the whole country, and a few examples may make this clear.

One of the selfish people in the party was a fellow who influenced Dan Kwelagobe on a number of issues, including the exchange of Debswana's diamond stockpile for De Beers shares. I had appointed the man to a diplomatic post, but he then wanted to stand for elections in 1989. He made it his prerogative to decide where to stand, and even to decide when he would decide. He wanted to apply for the candidacy of both Gaborone North and Gaborone South. Because we thought he was interested in Gaborone South, we asked Peter Mmusi to go back to Thamaga instead of standing again in Gaborone South. The Thamaga people took us to task for thrusting a candidate on them, but the matter was settled amicably, since we were all Democrats.

The fellow won the nomination in both Gaborone constituencies, but even then he would not say in which one he would contest the general election. I was in Lobatse at my farm one Saturday when Dan Kwelagobe, as secretary-general of the party, came to see me. We referred to this fellow as *Mbisana* (the small boy), and Dan said to me: "You know, Comrade, *Mbisana* is being impossible. Now he wishes to stand in Thamaga. How about getting Mmusi back to Gaborone?" This time I hit the roof! I said "Do you think people are fools? Do you think people will accept us moving them like draught pieces on a board? Do you think we can push Peter Mmusi around for the benefit of this naughty fellow? And what of the constituency? We took Mmusi from Gaborone, where the people wanted him. We managed to talk the Thamaga people into accepting him. What do you think we could say to the people in Thamaga and Gaborone?"

Eventually, when the man stood for elections, he lost. He then expected me to nominate him to be specially elected, but I had had enough and I nominated Clara Olsen instead. She was intelligent, she had served the party as executive secretary, and she added another woman to Parliament as well.

Another fellow who put his selfish interests first had served as an assistant minister of finance in the 1970s. His portfolio included oversight of the

African Development Bank, and he and I had agreed that, even though it was Botswana's turn for one of our people to serve as an executive director, we should decline it. We had felt for many years that we should not encourage our people to take international appointments because we needed them in Botswana. While he was at a Bank meeting in Abidjan, however, he called to tell me he was under pressure to take the job. I said: "Well, you are on the ground, you are the best judge of what to do," and he decided to take the job. We then asked Peter Mmusi to resign from the Thamaga constituency and stand in the constituency that this man had vacated.

After his term in that high-paying international job had ended, the fellow returned and told me he wanted to stand in his old constituency. I said no, we already had Peter Mmusi as the MP for that constituency. While he appeared to accept my decision and said he would go into business, I later heard that people believed I had refused him something that was his due. The fellow decided to run against the BDP candidate in the next election, and he lost disastrously. When he had won previously as a member of *Domkrag*, he believed it was because of him and not the party. He thought he would show the party who he was, but instead the party showed him.

I have always worried that people with selfish interests, instead of national interests, would join politics. Perhaps we were simply lucky during my years in office that so many who were interested in the public good became politicians.

The Press and Politics

Having been a journalist and an editor before I entered politics, I have always had an appreciation of the role that the media can play in a democratic society. At *Naledi ya Botswana* in the 1950s, we tried to help educate people throughout the country about current issues and to provide information about public affairs. Of course, some of the articles were written to advocate particular points of view, and as editor I tried to be sure that news articles were separated from editorials or columnists' viewpoints.

An Information Department was started when government was still in Mafeking, and it published the *Daily News*, for many years the only newspaper in the country. It went well at first, since we began with people who had worked with private newspapers, and they knew what the work of a newshound was all about. As we started employing people who did not have previous experience, they thought they were like any other civil servant, and some would sit in their offices instead of going out to gather news. However, they also wanted to claim their independence as if they were journalists in the private sector, forgetting that private sector papers have their own editors, boards, and editorial policies to which reporters must adhere.

There is always an inherent problem in the government press between editors and reporters. When reporters go off at a tangent and the editor brings them back into line, the reporters might accuse the editor of interfering with the media. However, the main object of a government press is to provide information on what various ministries and departments are doing, not to give their journalists a field day. Ministers were often at loggerheads with Information Department journalists over their role. We tried to make it clear that their role was to inform the nation. Whether it was a minister or the opposition, they should report what was said, but they shouldn't editorialise about it.

The Information Department in Mafeking also started Radio Botswana from scratch. It was a small operation, and at the time we had no people with radio experience. The print and radio media had joint management, and what one provided as news, the other did as well. From the beginning, Radio Botswana also ran educational programmes, including programmes on farming and other practical issues.

The widespread availability of radios made this a good medium for us. While in some countries there was a tax on radios, we thought there should not be a tax, since radios helped us to reach people. As early as the 1960s, people were listening to the radio and getting news from it. We in *Domkrag* knew this because people would talk in our political meetings about news they could only have received from radio broadcasts. It became clear as we made our way around the country that radio was second only to our actual visits in informing people. The 1971 Census reported that there were over 14,000 households with radios, which meant one for about every 40 people in the country. The concentrations were greatest in the urban areas, but they were also spread throughout Botswana. In 1975 we undertook a major consultation on tribal land use through the radio, distributing several thousand to Radio Learning Groups that provided feedback to government on the proposed policy.

We did not add a government television station until after I left office, though the decision to introduce it was taken while I was still president. Some of us had opposed the idea of introducing a government television station. We believed that if resources were added for information, they should go to radio. It was clear we would reach a far larger number of people through radio. I still believe staying with radio would have been the right thing to do.

Botswana developed a private independent press in the 1980s, and its coverage was devoted heavily to politics. There is always benefit to genuine discussion of issues, and such discussion is central to the value of consultation, since it produces better ideas. So when the media come up with alternatives, they can make an important contribution in a democracy.

However, during my time in office, much of what the private press did was just mud slinging. By the time I retired from politics, we had five independent papers: *The Sun* and *The Guardian* under the same editorship, *Mmegi* and an offshoot, *Mmegi Monitor*, and *The Gazette*. *The Gazette* was started on the basis of good and accurate journalism, as a contrast to the earlier papers. But it quickly learned that rumour sold better than fact, and that was where it went. The papers were largely opposition newspapers under another name. Their editorial comment was in opposition to government most of the time, and that was how they reported what they said was news.

Our private newspapers did not have a proper sense of the roles of editors and of reporters, or the difference between editorial policy and coverage of news. I once asked a friend who was editing one of the papers why the paper didn't play a constructive role. Why did they publish stories that were not well investigated? The editor's defence was that it was the fault of the reporters! Well, I had been in the news business, so I knew a paper had to have a policy, and it also had to have an editorial board. Reporters needed to be accurate, since inaccuracies brought down the reputation of the paper and could even cost the paper monetary damages for libel. Reporters who would not abide by the policies of the paper should either be brought back to earth or be fired.

In public debates on issues, ministers or other politicians tried to provide factual material that would be helpful. However, they found that reporters often came with a story they had already written, and they would try to tell the story through quotes by the minister. If one gave answers that did not conform to the story they were trying to tell, they would report that the interviewee was not forthcoming!

The independent press has sometimes been sufficiently investigative to keep everyone—ministers, officials, the opposition and civil society generally—on their toes. At those times, as well as when the press is providing information or alternatives in a policy debate, the press can be a very positive force in a democracy. But, when the stories are misinformation or half-truths, this has to be a negative factor on the society and on the political process. The effect of the private press on the Botswana *Daily News* was to make the *Daily News* staff seek the same sensationalism, rather than trying to be factually correct.

The press often got away with murder in telling their falsehoods. One might ask whether we in government should have been more aggressive in going after the press for their misstatements and untruths. Morally, it might have been better to do so. In some countries, politicians have pursued and won major libel actions against the press. We chose not to bring such actions because we did not want to seem like some non-democratic regimes. Even if we rightly accused people, it would be said we were acting arbitrarily like oppressive regimes elsewhere that even arrested journalists. Unless there were big changes in the other circumstances, if I were to do it over, I think I would do the same thing and leave them alone.

Of course, it was not just in Botswana that the press published stories that were gossip or worse. One night I had worked late at the office, and on my way downstairs, I missed a step in the dark, fell, and tore the ligaments in my knee. It was a bad enough injury that I had to be taken to London to have it repaired, and I was sewn up like a sack of mealies. *Africa Confidential* reported that my injury had resulted when I tried to intervene between Kwelagobe and Kedikilwe who, the paper alleged, were physically fighting for the leadership of the party! That's when you begin to take everything in the press with a pinch of salt. If a story about things I knew was so distorted or so far from the truth, how could I believe stories about which I knew nothing?

Political Issues and the Opposition

We dealt with many important and controversial political issues during my presidency. Some, though not all, had a common element in that they either were stirred up or were seized by the opposition as places where they could make political hay at the expense of *Domkrag*. Here I review the creation of an Independent Electoral Commission, reduction of the voting age, the role of the president, increased gender equality, and our national identity card (*Omang*).

The constitution provided that the permanent secretary to the president would act as the electoral supervisor. He would do that work without any interference from the president or from the minister for presidential affairs. The opposition made unsavoury comments about it whenever they could. They suggested that the reason they kept losing was that we lacked an independent authority to supervise elections. Some people concluded that since the PSP was in the Office of the President, when he was acting as election supervisor, he must have been taking directions from the president. Since justice should not only be done but should be seen to be done, we ultimately felt that we should meet the concern and establish an independent body to conduct elections.

We waited for many years to address the matter because we saw nothing really wrong in the system that had been established in the constitution. We also felt it would be wrong to just click our heels in the face of baseless accusations. There had never been real trouble or difficulties other than some of the opposition making noises; they had never come up with any evidence of wrong-doing, and they knew it. We acted at a time when we were least expected to do so, in a sense as a pre-emptive strike. We established the Independent Electoral Commission to settle the matter and remove any doubt.

Because establishing an independent commission was a change in our procedures, we first took it to the party congress. We told them what we intended to do and why, and we received their blessing. We then made the change through the normal process for amendments to the constitution. Now that there is an Independent Electoral Commission, of course, the opposition picks away at the details of the arrangements because they continue to lose. But, that is what happens in politics.

Domkrag for many years resisted the reduction in the voting age from 21 to 18, primarily because at 18 most people were still at school. If they were able to vote, they needed to be accessible to the candidates for whom they would be voting. This would mean political parties would be invading the secondary schools and universities, a practice we did not consider appropriate. The opposition had been harping on the need to change, suggesting that *Domkrag* was unsympathetic to young people and their concerns.

We eventually did make the change in voting age, partly because we had investigated the voting age in Commonwealth and other countries. Louis Selepeng, who was then in my office, visited a number of countries, and his report showed that those that did not allow voting at the age of 18 were those with which we did not wish to associate. Those whose political ideals we shared provided for voting at the age of 18. So, we changed our minds. I argued the merits of the case at a party congress at Maun. I said we were not lowering the voting age just because some people were saying: "Let it be done." We were doing it because we had studied the matter, and we had considered how things had changed, particularly that people now left secondary school at a younger age. I presented what I thought was a reasoned case and asked for their agreement. We received approval of the party, and then we made the necessary changes in the constitution.

In our constitution, the president plays a dual role as head of state and head of government. As head of state the president is above politics and plays a ceremonial role. As head of government the role is the same as a Tony Blair or a Helmut Kohl or others who govern in parliamentary democracies. There have been some BNF proposals for a direct election of the president separate from the elections of members of Parliament. This has been a relatively recent development, and it has received support from some of the lecturers at the university who are associated with the BNF.

The degree of instability and potential paralysis of government that could come from having the president from a different party than the majority in Parliament would not be good for Botswana. We considered the idea carefully during the 1963 constitutional talks, and we looked at the experience of other countries before making the decision we did. I still believe it is important that the president should be the leader of the majority party in the National Assembly, and that the president should appoint ministers from among parliamentary colleagues. Both responsibility and authority are then clearly established in the leadership. There would be a great potential for conflict if the president and head of executive government was of one party and the majority in the legislature was of another.

The French and the Americans elect an executive president separate from the legislature, as do some other countries. However, we felt we should learn from the problems that sometimes occur. The French changed their basic form of government in the past 50 years, and the Americans have faced severe budget crises because the president and Congress could not agree. The prevalence of separately elected executive presidents in a number of African countries may reflect the history of so many one party states on the continent. A separately elected president in a one-party state would not have the effect of producing a stalemate in government.

Batswana are by tradition a patriarchal society, and we also had the heritage of Roman-Dutch common law, which did not treat women as fully equal with men. During my last years in office, we had the attorney general's Chambers comb through all our laws to find out where there were discriminatory provisions on the basis of gender that needed correction through legislation. We had done the same thing on issues of racial discrimination during Legco. The investigation was an important exercise because there were problems of discrimination in the acquisition of property, inheritance, and other laws. Since customary law must be compatible with the constitution and with statute law, amending the statutes had the effect of eliminating gender discrimination that existed in Tswana customary law as well. Of course, we had traditionalists in the Chambers who were not as keen on making changes as some of the rest of us. Their reluctance and inertia had to be overcome in order to find all the discriminatory language and get it changed.

The issue of gender had arisen in the 1980s when we amended the Citizenship Act. A number of emotional issues were involved in that piece of legislation. In the debate we had people who thought almost as if: Once a foreigner, always a foreigner. While many of us shared the view that a citizen should be loyal to his or her adopted country, we also felt we should not put up too many barriers. We had many examples of naturalised citizens who were making major contributions to the development of Botswana. In addition, many Batswana had married people from other countries particularly in southern Africa.

After we had passed the amendments to the Citizenship Act, a woman lawyer named Unity Dow brought a case challenging a provision of the Act. Under the amendments in the Act, her children were not recognised as citizens of Botswana since her husband was not a Motswana. However, if her husband had been a citizen and she had been the non-citizen, the children would be citizens. Why that provision was adopted should be seen in the context of the conditions when the Act was approved. At that time, many of our young women were being used in marriages of convenience. A man who married a Motswana could legally reside here, and it was an advantage for the man to be a Botswana resident. That was the motivation for some of the refugees, including agents of minority-ruled regimes in southern Africa, so this became an issue of the nation's security. Unity Dow argued that the law was unconstitutional because it discriminated on the basis of gender. She won her case on appeal; I later appointed her to the High Court as a judge, which clearly showed I held nothing against her for pressing her case.

We thought a national identity card would be a good idea, since we believed it was important to identify those who were actually citizens. The reason was that refugees were pouring in from all over the region, and we needed to know who was who. Further, we wanted no party to take advantage of refugees to boost its numbers when those people were not in fact citizens. All the parties agreed that we needed to find a way to determine who was a national for many purposes: voting, getting a piece of land, buying a rifle, or whatever. It was one of the many issues we discussed in all-party caucuses at the National Assembly.

Omang means: "Who are you?" It was the first question on the form every Motswana had to fill out in order to receive his or her national identity card. So, the cards themselves quickly became known as *Omang*. No one planned it; it was one of those ideas that in retrospect looked very clever!

When it came to implementation we gave the matter to Pelonomi Venson, a very dynamic woman in the civil service, but it turned out that the administration was not as easy as we had thought. In addition to requiring a well-run organisation, cultural taboos were involved. We hired young people to assist, and in our culture it was awkward for a man as old as I to tell a young girl when he was born and who his parents were, and similar personal questions.

Of course, as soon as there were difficulties and objections, the opposition incited the public against the idea. They asked why government was questioning people and why we insisted that someone older than that person must vouch that he was indeed born in a particular year or place. Why could we not just take Batswana at face value? Now, of course, *Omang* is taken as a matter of fact. Not even I can go into a bank and just say: "You know me, I have been president for so many years;" I have to produce my *Omang*.

The Chieftainship and Politics Again

When President Mogae chose his vice-president, I was in favour of his choice of Ian Khama, the eldest son of the late president, Sir Seretse Khama. However, I felt it should have been done differently in two respects. First, Ian Khama had just retired from the army. Like his predecessor Mompati Merafhe, he had led the BDF ably. He had not been elected to the House, and by law the vice-president must be a member of Parliament. There is a provision in the constitution that a minister can be appointed for a period of up to four months before he or she is elected, but this provision was put in for cases of dire need. President Mogae's own constituency had become vacant when he became president, so Ian Khama could have stood for election in that constituency, which he would have won easily. He then could have been appointed vice-president.

The second issue was Ian Khama's position as chief-in-absentia of Bangwato. In Botswana we had not allowed people to be both a chief and a politician; if Ian Khama remained a chief and entered politics, what would stop other chiefs from aspiring to be members of Parliament and ministers? There would be constant battles between a member of Parliament and the chief in that area. When elections came, what had happened between Chief Bathoen II and me could happen again, but without the person resigning the chieftainship. Seretse had told Bathoen in plain language, both in private and at the *kgotla* in Kanye, that he could not be both a politician and a chief. He had to make a choice, not for strictly legal reasons but for important political reasons.

As I explained earlier, the Bangwato had allowed Ian Khama as their chief-in-absentia to be in the army after that had been negotiated with them following my meeting at the Serowe *kgotla*. At the time of his appointment as vice-president, I thought he should have gone to the tribe to say he had now become a politician, and he would play a larger role to guide the interests of the tribe and that of the whole nation better than if he was their chief.

I could not see other chiefs holding back when they knew that Ian Khama was allowed to enjoy both roles. We know what happened in Ngwaketse when Chief Bathoen was elected—he just brought with him into Parliament his henchmen who were not able people. It would be a disaster for this country if that were to happen on a large scale. Kgosi Tawana of the Batawana proved my prediction before the 2004 elections when he tried to stand for Parliament. The proposed increase in the size of the House of Chiefs to accommodate the creation of new chiefs will make matters worse, since the potential conflicts will increase. Chieftainship and tribalism were potentially our most divisive issues as we sought to create a single nation in the 1960s. It would be a tragedy if they were allowed to emerge in that way again.

Vision 2016
As I was preparing for transition to the next president, I thought we should commit ourselves to something that showed we were thinking ahead. We had managed well for a long time on the Four Principles—Democracy, Development, Unity and Self-Reliance—and we had added a fifth, Social Justice. It was time to think about the future. Of course, it had become fashionable in other countries to create a "Vision 2020". In our case we chose 2016, since that will be the 50th anniversary of our independence.

I thought it would be a jolly good thing if this could be a national exercise rather than a party one. We went to all walks of life and involved school children, political parties, and civil society, or what the French call *forces vives*. It was very rewarding to see how people responded, including the members of the opposition. I thought; here is something that could unite us not as something that is partisan but as something that would strike a concordant note all the way through the country. Later, of course, the opposition reneged, but by then some of their people like Botshabelo Bagwasi had already served on the team that set out to compose the Vision.

To begin with, I appointed a nine-person task group in August 1996. After they had produced a booklet called "A Framework for a Long-Term Vision for Botswana", we expanded the group to 31 people in January 1997. The task group held more than 30 hearings and *kgotla* meetings throughout the country, arranged for consultations by a University of Botswana team in small villages and remote settlements, held an essay competition in the schools that resulted in over 700 entries, and received written submissions from Batswana, including those living outside the country. After careful deliberation, they produced a report, "A Long-Term Vision for Botswana: Towards Prosperity for All". The logo for the Vision was chosen during a public competition in which more than 400 people submitted ideas.

The Vision exercise worked from our Four National Principles—Democracy, Development, Unity and Self-Reliance. It examined how economic, political and social conditions had changed since independence. It concluded that we should expand from four to seven the number of broad goals, objectives or principles that should guide our national decision-making. The Vision is that by the year 2016, Botswana will be:

An Educated, Informed Nation
A Prosperous, Productive and Innovative Nation
A Compassionate, Just and Caring Nation
A Safe and Secure Nation
An Open, Democratic and Accountable Nation
A Moral and Tolerant Nation
A United and Proud Nation

The Four National Principles are embedded in the seven aspects of Vision 2016, but the Vision adds emphasis on such goals as tolerance, morality and justice, accountability, innovation and security.

I think the Vision has taken hold. It is frequently quoted, and the points are accepted as articles of faith. People do not challenge the idea of following the Vision 2016. Often the question has become: "Can we hope to achieve Vision 2016 if we do X, Y or Z?" It has become a kind of measuring rod, which is very satisfying. And as the saying goes: "Where there is no vision, the people perish."

When I made my farewell or good-bye tour in 1997 and early 1998, there were of course still some people saying uninformed things. But on the whole, people talked about the many things that we had accomplished. In many ways it was very flattering. By and large people were well aware of the many areas in which we made major progress.

Chapter 12
Managing Economic Development

In the next five chapters I try to explain how and why we made the choices we did to develop the economy and improve the lives of our people. From the beginning of Legco, those of us in the leadership of the BDP were concerned with the development of economic opportunities for all Batswana. We took it as given that economic development and meeting our political objectives were interrelated. Such things as improving opportunities in the livestock sector and securing greater financial resources to promote our development efforts were central to our political goals of creating a viable, unified and democratic nation. The Democratic Party's "Aims and Objectives" and our Four National Principles—Democracy, Development, Unity and Self-Reliance—laid strong emphasis on economic goals, not just political ones. The same was true of the principle of Social Justice that we later added.

World Bank statistics show that Botswana achieved the highest rate of growth of per capita income of any country in the world during the 35 years after we achieved self-rule. Of course, we had the good fortune to discover substantial deposits of diamonds. Over that same period, however, even the non-mining sectors of our economy grew at world-record rates. We had created our own procedures for planning, making choices among priorities, and implementing projects and policies, before diamonds became a significant factor. We learned from the experience of other countries that possessing minerals did not automatically lead to economic development. We needed to secure the benefits of our underground diamond wealth for our people.

We took it as given that we should try to provide opportunities for individual Batswana to better themselves economically. We did not subscribe to the view held in some countries, and by some in Botswana, that one person's success came at the expense of someone else. On the contrary, we in the BDP leadership believed that if a person was successful, the whole country would benefit from that success—for example; the person would pay taxes and would employ other people in his or her farm or business. However, we knew that some people would benefit disproportionately if we achieved success, and therefore we would need policies to mitigate inequalities.

People often ask me why Botswana behaved differently on matters of economic management from many other countries. I think some of it has to do with the nature of our people. We had always been subject to harsh conditions and uncertainties of drought, and "waste not, want not", had real meaning to us as a people. We also had examples such as that of our neighbour to the north, Zambia. Because of its wealth from copper, it had been moved to the status of a middle-income state by the World Bank in the 1960s. However, Zambia's many subsequent economic problems provided lessons on what we should avoid. As we met people from other countries, we discussed their problems. We could see which countries were getting into trouble, and we tried to look into why they were, and to find out what we could do to avoid such difficulties. We were pragmatic, not ideological, in our approach; we wanted to choose policies that would achieve our desired results regardless of whether they carried a particular label or "ism".

Before becoming president in 1980, I served for 14 years as minister of finance and development planning. When I'm asked about my credentials for those positions, I sometimes say I'm just a lay preacher. However, I had tried to make up for what I thought my schooling had missed, and, in the early 1950s I had taken a course by correspondence that covered commerce, bookkeeping, and general economics. Since I was mathematically inclined, and numbers were my main strength at school, I took to the study of economics as well. My facility with numbers and my economics background proved useful when we moved into negotiations on the Customs Union and with De Beers and other mining companies, and also when we developed our own currency and had to manage our exchange rate.

The close relationship I enjoyed with the late president while I was minister of finance and development planning (MFDP) was invaluable. Both politics and economics involve choices, and a president must understand the consequences of economic as well as political choices. While Seretse trusted me, I felt it was important that he be fully informed on why we in finance were recommending some alternatives and not others. After I became president, I maintained a close interest in our economic plans and policies and our budget choices.

Over time we were able to achieve a high degree of continuity of leadership in many important positions. We had concluded it was not necessary to change things for the sake of change. If someone was trained up in one area, and just as he or she learned the ropes was moved to a new ministry, then one had both wasted the training and deprived the country of the experience. Further, in dealing with outside parties—other governments, mining companies, or donor agencies—it was a great advantage for our people to know what had come before on a particular policy or programme or agreement. We were also aware of disasters in other countries. For example, when some presidents were in a bad mood, they would go to the rostrum and announce the names of new ministers at the drop of a hat. Such presidents ended up being the only ones who had knowledge of the various areas of responsibility, and in cabinet they would always claim to know more than the minister responsible for each portfolio area. Even though such a president might feel more secure, it was clearly not a good thing for the country. We consciously tried to avoid such a circumstance in Botswana.

We had many years of continuity of our personnel in finance and planning. Festus Mogae was director of economic affairs in the early 1970s, then permanent secretary in finance, governor of the Bank of Botswana, PSP, and later minister of finance and vice-president before becoming president in 1998. Baledzi Gaolathe has been involved in finance and minerals for more than 30 years, first as the PS responsible for minerals and then for finance; he next was managing director of Debswana, then governor of the Bank of

Botswana, and in 1998 he became minister of finance and development planning. Others had similar long periods of service, and we have benefited from having experienced people in charge.

Our Early Planning

The neglect of physical and social infrastructure by the Protectorate government is well known. Beginning in the mid-1950s, the pace of spending began to increase, but from a pitifully low level. Grants from the UK government grew from P252,000 in 1954-55 to P5.4 million in 1964-65, when they covered 55% of total expenditure. Peter Fawcus' lobbying on our behalf in London was a major reason for the increase.

As we came to understand the financial situation at Legco, we were shocked to discover how little money the British government voted for development in Bechuanaland each year. More shocking was how a large part was unspent by the end of that year and turned back to the UK Treasury. This return of funds happened because the government received the money first, and only then did they plan how to use it. As a result, plans were not ready by the time the annual authorisation for the money expired. What was lacking was the capacity to spend on a series of well thought out projects.

Our system of planning and budgeting has been modified over time, but the basis was laid during our first few years. In 1963, Peter Fawcus created an investment centre in finance, and we later moved it to development planning. Quill Hermans was the first executive officer, and Peter Landell-Mills was its first economist. They formed the core of the team that created a development plan for the territory. We were very lucky that the Peter Landell-Mills and Quill Hermans of this world joined us, and that the Alf Beebys of this world (who had managed finance in the colonial government) left us, because we were then able to anticipate resources.

We quickly realised we should have a document that related the projects and placed them in their order of priority. Our first plan was developed as part of a consultative process and was the basis for a £10 million expenditure programme over five years, twice the previous level. It was also the first attempt at a comprehensive plan for the country, rather than a list of a few possible projects. The plan was ambitious and contained a number of projects that were beyond the financing we knew about but could be undertaken if funding became available. Producing this plan made us confront choices among priorities, and it also led to understanding the importance of efficient implementation. This practice started during self-rule, and the exercise enabled us to carry with us our Transitional Plan for Social and Economic Development when seeking post-independence external assistance.

A great deal of debate went into setting the priorities for the transitional plan during self-rule in 1965-66; we also set the stage for future procedures. We linked the development plan to the annual budget through the Estimates Committee of Officials. The individual ministries, of course, were the ones who needed to propose the projects. I told ministers that if they wanted their projects to be included, they would have to come with a convincing case. It was not a question of allocating equal funds to ministries, but rather that we had to follow our established priorities. Since we had to balance the demands, we had to discuss them openly among people from finance as well as other ministries. It had to be teamwork all the way.

Planning and Priorities

We had a great deal to do on all fronts, and we tried to make sure no one thing ran too far ahead of the others. In planning and budgeting, while the ministries, and later the districts, needed to propose specific projects, we also had to take an overall look from MFDP at the levels of resources that might be available and the broader strategies we needed to follow. At the beginning, priority for spending on social and physical infrastructure was adopted for two reasons. First, there were very few employment opportunities in Botswana outside of agriculture. We knew that without water supplies, education, roads or communication, we could not establish enterprises that would employ people productively. Therefore, we concluded we needed to focus our resources in the beginning on building the basic social and physical infrastructure. Second, our people had told us directly that they wanted clean water, educational opportunities, and access to health care for themselves and their families. They also wanted the ways and means of transportation, communication and marketing for crops and cattle. Therefore, our focus on social and physical infrastructure responded directly to people's desires and also provided the basis for further investment and employment.

A prominent section in our early plans was entitled "The Need to Plan". This was an answer to the people who felt we should just decide things as they came up. We felt there was a clear need for a road map, so we would know where we were going, and for a carefully considered sharing of resources by the various sectors of the economy. If we didn't plan, then Ministry A might be very vocal and generate projects that required recurrent expenditures in future years for functions that were in fact less important than those of Ministry B. We also needed to be sure we were being internally consistent, so that, for example, the expansion of teachers matched that of school classrooms and of the planned intake of students. We wanted to be certain to spend our full allocation of British Grant-in-Aid each year; therefore, projects needed to be prepared and available. We also wanted good projects of high priority that we could propose to new donors. The British and other potential donors needed to see that we knew what we were doing and had thought through our priorities.

Of course, there were always those who were not happy with the budget allocations. Simon Hirschfeld, the commissioner of police, once came to see me to ask why we hated him and his police so much, since we had not given them a large enough allocation. I told him first that he had not yet spent the funds that had already been voted for police projects. I also explained that if we spent money too rapidly, given our limited capacity to implement projects, we would just drive up the cost of the projects and not really complete more of them. I reminded him of the Setswana saying: "*Mmu otleste boleke*" (you cannot put more soil in a container that is already full; if you try to add more, the extra will just fall out). The same was true of the capacity in our construction industry on a number of occasions, the first in the early 1970s. If we had pushed out more spending, we would have just caused more inflation without receiving value for money. There have been a few times in our history, as I relate below, when we did generate inflation by trying to spend too quickly.

We were clear that every project had an opportunity cost, and we faced some very difficult choices, such as the location of schools. For example, for the cost of building a school at a remote place like Kang, a village 350 kilometres west of the railhead at Lobatse over dirt roads; we could have built two or even three schools in towns along the line of rail. But one of our guiding principles, social justice, demanded that these remote places should have their share of development. In another case, we had some money to help us with refugees. Should we build schools and make them for refugees only? Or, should we build Botswana schools that would take some refugees? I felt very strongly that we should adopt the latter strategy, and I once travelled throughout the night from Ghanzi to Gaborone to take part in the discussions before a decision was made. While my view prevailed in that case, it was very difficult to deal with such choices.

To a large extent, the choices we made were dictated by the circumstances we faced. We had limited resources, and we had to undertake the practical things that would help develop the country. For the most part, these choices were also obvious to the donors. In the case of roads, for example, the main north-south road was obviously a necessity to improve transportation and communication for the economic development of the country. It also provided an alternative route of transport to the north, independent of South Africa. As we decided which roads to complete and tarmac, that route had to be our first priority. Once the north-south road was completed, then we had the luxury of thinking of roads that would serve places with smaller populations. But things had to be taken in a logical sequence.

From time to time we politicians would do something that might seem a bit perverse. Some of us felt that one should be able to travel from Orapa to both Francistown and Serowe by tarred road. The road to Francistown and its railway access was the most obvious, but we decided to build the road to Serowe first. Economic imperatives would eventually result in the construction of the Francistown-Orapa road. If we had built the latter road first, there would have been no subsequent compelling economic justification for a Serowe-Orapa road.

Development plans for each district started in more or less the same way as the national plan, but somewhat later. To begin with, we sent university students to *kgotlas* in all districts. We asked them to compose a shopping list of what, in the view of people there, were their needs. After that, we had them ask: If you could do only one project, what would it be? And then, if there could be a second, what would it be? In this way we got a sense of what the needs were, and how people would order their priorities. The process of public meetings and acclamation provided the materials that led to the first district plans. Later plans were done by the district councils themselves, and we seconded planning officers to assist them.

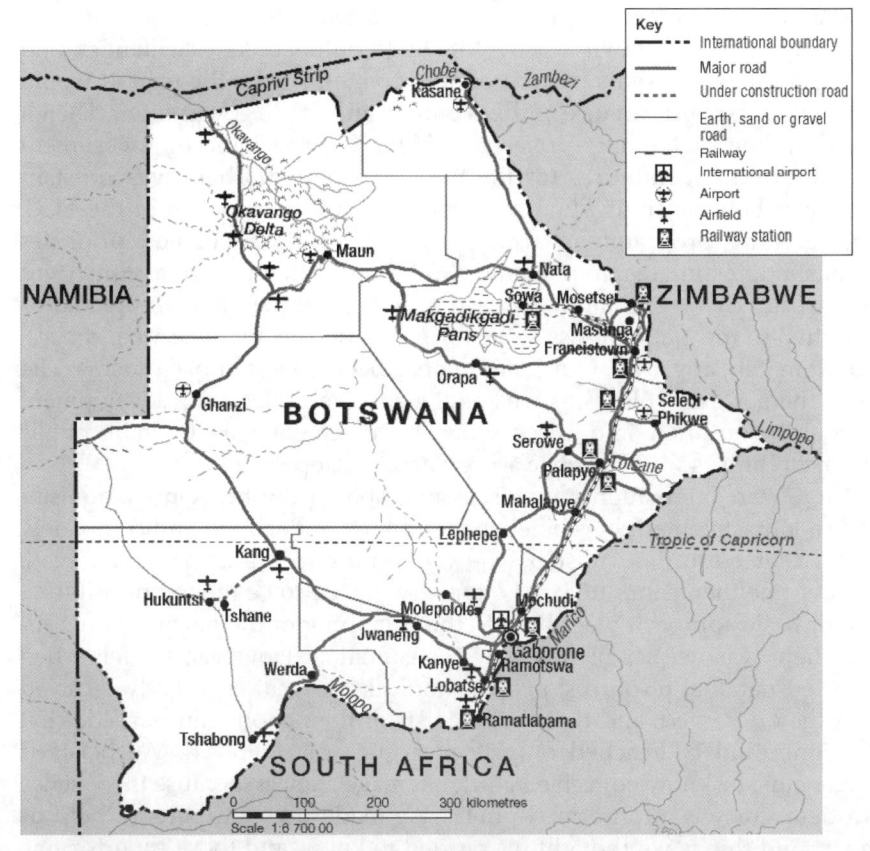

Map of Botswana transport network, virtually all built since 1966

The Planning Process

Our process of national planning evolved over time. When we started out we began with five-year plans, which were then very common in developing countries. However, our circumstances were changing so rapidly that we decided we would overlap these plans, and we began the next before the first plan period was over. Our first development plan was the Transitional Plan for Social and Economic Development. Shortly after independence, it was clear that our circumstances had changed substantially, and we produced a 1968-73 plan, and then the 1970-75 plan. This pattern of overlapping five-year periods, which we called a "rolling plan" was continued until the late 1970s.

The formulation of a National Development Plan involved a complex process of consultation with each ministry and within the Economic Committee of Cabinet (ECC). The annual recurrent budgets were linked to the long-term planning process through the annual development budget that allocated finance for projects in the plan. We saw planning as an ongoing process. Each year ministries would bring proposals for new development projects to be considered by Parliament. If approved, the projects would become part of the National Development Plan.

The process of preparing a plan usually started with the ECC considering an "issues paper" drawn up by MFDP. It outlined key challenges and strategies and proposed a macroeconomic framework for the plan. It would review the past performance of the economy and of the government. Then it would outline preliminary projections of the economy and of government revenues and expenditures for the next plan period. There was constant discussion between individual ministries and MFDP, and within the ECC. Projects and programmes were proposed and discussed, priorities established, estimates made, and MFDP put them into a consistent framework. There was ultimately a decision in cabinet, and the plan was submitted to the National Assembly for public debate, possible amendment, and ultimately approval. Our planning has been a very public process. The major themes and policies as well as the specific projects for development were fully outlined and discussed. The objective was to gain public understanding as well as public acceptance and approval.

There were often interesting discussions about priorities. Once a minister made a long statement in cabinet about how he understood and completely agreed that education must be the top priority for that particular plan. However, he then continued: "My ministry must also be the top priority!"

Our basic approach went back to the beginning of the party. Before self-rule, there was neither planning nor consultation. However, we felt when one used national resources, people should know that everybody received what they deserved, and that the interests of the nation were served. That situation could be reached only if everyone was involved. We believed people must be knowledgeable in order to make choices, because the essence of a democracy is an informed public. We made use of experts to help us understand things we thought we needed to know, and those experts came from wherever we could find the best people and best ideas, whether within Botswana or outside the country. It simply seemed to us to be the logical way to proceed if we were to be both democratic and effective.

In the early 1970s, as our capacity for planning and execution within government was growing, we developed a process of sharing the planning officer cadre from the MFDP with the various operating ministries—agriculture, health, education and so forth. We thought the planning office of MFDP should be running a coordinated development effort, but in order to do this it had to be aware of what was happening in all ministries. The ministries were ambivalent about having planning officers. They appreciated that they could be advised in certain things by their own planning officers, since without that advice they might have gone off at a tangent. On the other hand, they hated the fact that their planning officers also reported back to the Ministry of Finance and Development Planning. And, being human, they were vocal about the things they disapproved of but did not give credit for the parts they liked.

The extent of consultation made planning a very time consuming process, and in 1979 we changed to a six-year plan, with a mid-term review conducted during the third year. Since the economy usually developed in a different manner from the way the plan had projected, we had an opportunity to make changes where needed without going through the entire elaborate process, including producing a new plan document. After the third year, a draft mid-term review document was produced and debated, and a final one was adopted and published with new economic, financial and government budget projections.

We had three categories of projects in our plans—the first for which we had money, the second for which we did not have the money but where there were reasonable prospects, and the third for which we did not have money and saw no likely prospects but nonetheless were things we felt should be done. By having this third category, we were able to take advantage of the fact that many other countries were not spending all their development assistance. Because we had projects prepared and waiting, we were frequently able to obtain more assistance from a donor agency than it was initially willing to commit. We learned that donors have budgets, and sometimes they could not disburse their funds because other recipient countries were not implementing their projects. We would approach donor agencies toward the end of their fiscal year and suggest that a worthy project in Botswana could use further funding! That was how we financed the purchase of some of the Tati Company land in Francistown.

We also tried to execute and implement our projects so that donors would be well satisfied. Obviously, they had to be good projects, both in the sense that the money could be spent and that the projects would be seen to be worthwhile. However, had not the donors been convinced that we were implementing good projects, we would not have been able to continue. Even 35 years after self-rule, we were still able to benefit when donor agencies were not able to use all their funds in other countries. Partly as a result of our approach, Botswana often received more aid per capita than any other country in Sub-Saharan Africa.

Donors and their Importance
Botswana has been the recipient of very generous support from the international community. We received assistance from individual countries, from multilateral institutions such as the World Bank, and from private foundations and organisations. We would never have been able to achieve our successes without provision of finance and personnel from other countries. Before 1972, every thebe of development expenditure was funded by donors. In the late 1970s, over half was donor-funded, and in the late 1980s, one-third of our development expenditures were funded by donors. Even during my last few years in office, donors contributed 10% of our development budget, and donor aid was substantial in absolute amounts.

All Batswana must understand how grateful we as a people should be for the generous support we have received. We Batswana must also remember this support was given, or was loaned on very reasonable terms, by people and governments who believed in what we were trying to accomplish: to build a viable, non-racial, democratic country.

Britain was our only major donor and financial supporter at independence. We could never have succeeded without that aid which initially provided over half of our total expenditures of P12 million. However, we felt we would get more assistance if we were able to diversify our donors, and also we would not be too much of a burden on any one donor country. Our first attempt was a good one. We wanted to look at the uses of the waters of the Okavango, and we had no money to pay for the counterpart contribution—that is, the funds normally provided by the recipient country for part of a project. The money that was given multilaterally came from the Scandinavians, and then the same countries came in bilaterally to give us the counterpart funds.

Around independence, we had a number of sources of support for drought relief, and our experience with drought relief taught us how best to utilise our donors. We established the principle that government would set the priorities, and we would coordinate the efforts. Then the individual organisations, such as Oxfam, Catholic Relief, and the World Food Programme, would execute their particular projects or programmes. We made sure from then on that we did the coordinating and set the priorities; donor-financed projects had to be part of our development plans.

Over time, we added to the list of both bilateral and multilateral donors: the United States, Canada, all the Scandinavian countries, the Germans, and eventually French and Japanese agencies became involved. The European Community (now the European Union) was very helpful. The United Nations Development Programme was an early donor, and we became members of the World Bank, the IMF and the African Development Bank. Following the oil price increases in the early 1970s, the Arab countries began major programmes, and we received support from Saudi Arabia, Kuwait, and multilateral Arab donors as well.

Our lack of trained and experienced personnel at independence could not be overcome quickly, especially after our economy began to expand so rapidly, so we also benefited from technical assistance personnel provided by our donors. Expatriates have been vital to our ability to train our own citizens, and our need for expertise in some areas continues even today. Agencies such as the Ford Foundation and the Commonwealth Fund for Technical Cooperation were important sources of short-term and long-term technical assistance personnel, and the British Overseas Aid Scheme and other individual country programmes furnished us with thousands of people over the years. We often used technical assistance personnel to provide expertise in dealing with other external parties and in negotiations: with donors, with the South Africans during apartheid, and with international companies and commercial banks. There have always been political pressures to fill positions with citizens instead of expatriates, and, of course, we as a BDP government wanted to localise as well. However, we wanted the country to develop rapidly, so we needed to be sure we maintained the capacity to execute policies and projects well, even if the staffing was not entirely by citizens.

Dealing separately with each donor became our mode of doing things, and we did not go in for big donor conferences. We brought groups of donors together only when we needed a consortium for financing a particular project, such as a large dam or the Francistown-Maun road. We had seen other countries lose control of their planning process and the setting of their priorities by depending too much on donor conferences. We wanted to be sure that any assistance we received was directed to Botswana's priorities. We also tried to match our priorities with what we saw as the donor's particular interests. This approach led to a long collaboration with the Swedes on water projects, in which they had a major interest and talent and Botswana had a continuing need. Of course, the fact that so much of the work was done with Swedish companies helped, since the companies lobbied their government to keep the expansion of programmes going.

The Europeans, through what became the European Union, have been well disposed to Botswana, as well as to the Southern African Development Community (SADC), but their rules are almost impossible. The problem is that they are an amalgam of nations who have had various experiences with aid. It almost seems as if they decided to give aid and then developed a set of rules that made it impossible to dispense that aid. We even had to decide on occasion that it was better to raise a commercial loan than to depend on a concessionary European loan that carried too many conditions.

However, the Europeans' willingness to give our beef preferential access to their market was very helpful. We worked out with them a way to be sure that higher prices would come directly back to our cattle producers. There were difficult battles in ensuring access to European markets, and for many years access was available only on a six-monthly basis. We also had competition from countries like Ireland who for years earned most of their exports from agriculture, including beef. The European veterinary requirements are such that our director of veterinary services became the only dictator in the country, with powers that even the president does not have! He also needed disciplined people who would adhere strictly to the requirements. The veterinary restrictions also led to the need for the cordon fences that have been the subject of much controversy because they inhibit game migrations.

As donors, the Germans were particularly difficult, and I remember making jokes with them that they sometimes did not appreciate. On one occasion an official from their ministry came to visit. I told him one of Germany's assistant ministers had given me a pair of binoculars, and I had concluded that the purpose of the gift was to tell me that German aid was coming, but it was still very far away! Later, the Serule-Francistown road was under discussion when Ian Smith's government was at its worst in Rhodesia. The Germans were willing to finance part of the project, but they did not want to finance a bridge, since they said there was already was one on the road from Francistown to Nata. We felt two bridges were necessary, since Smith would have had a real temptation to destroy a single bridge into Francistown. I said: "Okay, we are grateful, and we will build the road up to where the other bridge ought to be, and we will put up a sign that says: 'Here is the road that the Germans would not complete'." That did not amuse the Germans.

The Americans were helpful in providing technical assistance personnel, the Peace Corps, and a number of important infrastructure projects. The Peace Corps volunteers were very useful to us, and we welcomed them. They met a sore need by teaching at secondary school level, since in the early years we had to import over 80% of our secondary school teachers. We needed manpower, but we were training our own people, so it was helpful to have people come to us only temporarily. People who came from abroad were sometimes viewed as a threat to Batswana who were in training, since there was a suspicion that a foreigner would want to stay forever. Some of the volunteers did very well indeed, and overall they were very good, though a very few had to be sent back for misbehaviour.

The road from Nata to Kazangula provided us with an alternative transport route independent of South Africa and Rhodesia. It was officially opened by the American ambassador, Donald Norland. His presence at such an occasion was a most helpful public symbol during the difficult years of the late 1970s. Around the same time, we were receiving many offers of assistance for specific projects, but we faced a shortage of funding for general development purposes. Ambassador Norland argued successfully with his colleagues at USAID that our annual assistance from the American government should be a grant for general purposes, rather than funding for specific projects. As often happened, some of our foreign friends were helpful in dealing with others—in this case within the same government.

We always urged donors to design their aid to Botswana to meet our priorities. Therefore, we took the initiative in approaching donor agencies to participate in financing appropriate projects in our development plans. We coordinated our approach to donors in order to make the best use of each one, since each agency had particular strengths or weaknesses. We also found it was important to decline an offer of assistance if it did not meet our needs, or if it imposed conditions that did not match our priorities. Our decision not to pursue IMF assistance during our first balance of payments crisis in 1982, as I explain below, was one example of when we said "no" in a polite way.

Becoming Financially Independent

While we had achieved political independence in 1966, we needed to become financially independent as well so we could manage our own affairs. It is easy to look back and say that in 1969 we negotiated the new revenue sharing formula under the Customs Union in anticipation of the large imports that would be coming from investments in the mining industry. But that would be wrong; we negotiated the new formula on the basis of what we felt was just and fair. And, we were very fortunate; no sooner had the Customs Union deal been clinched than the imports for the mining developments at Selebi-Phikwe and Orapa started to come in. Our revenue position improved because of the customs revenues generated by those imports under the new revenue sharing formula; major diamond revenues came later.

We achieved budgetary independence in 1972, well before anyone had thought possible. We also focused on attracting new bilateral and multilateral donors and on managing relationships with those donors carefully. Finally, our financial negotiations on mining projects emphasised getting the best possible terms for Botswana in exchange for granting mining leases. Together, these things brought us financial resources in the early 1970s that we could not have even imagined in 1966.

Budgetary independence meant we no longer relied on British Grant-in-Aid to support our recurrent budget. While this had been an important objective, as minister of finance I became very worried that the demands would be so great that we would pour money into projects where we had no capacity to implement. Instead of worrying only about the search for donor funds, my new concern was how to optimally use the funds we had. So, we in the ministry came up with the idea for a Revenue Stabilisation Fund (RSF) and a Public Debt Service Fund (PDSF).

The idea behind RSF was that we could put aside some money in years when revenues were plentiful so that we could maintain spending in years when there were revenue shortfalls, a situation we were sure would occur. The concept for PDSF was that we were borrowing money from the World Bank and others to finance development projects, and those monies would have to be repaid in the future. If we could save some surplus revenues and put them aside, we could build up a fund that could be used to repay the foreign loans when they became due. In the meantime, the monies appropriated to PDSF could be lent to domestic projects as and when good ones came along. Since such projects would pay interest and repay principal, those monies would cover our public debt service.

I had the task of selling the idea to the late president, and then to cabinet and to Parliament. We made the argument that Botswana's economic and financial base was very narrow and we needed a kitty that would take care of us if things went badly. The arguments carried the day and, somewhat to my surprise, the idea was accepted. RSF was lent short term, and PDSF funds were lent on a long-term basis. They eventually financed a large part of our investment in power, water and housing by parastatal organisations.

The establishment of these two reserve funds provided a good precedent when we established our own independent currency, the pula, in 1976. Since we had been using the South African rand, handling foreign exchange was a new concept for us. We had only been thinking of conserving government resources for future needs. Once we had our own currency, we needed to develop policies on foreign exchange reserves for the whole nation. So, our educational efforts on reserve funds in 1972 paid further dividends.

The Pula and Its Implications

We had been thinking of going it alone with our own currency for some time, though we had been in discussions with South Africa, Lesotho and Swaziland about creating a formal monetary agreement for the rand area. We had argued strongly for favourable terms for the BLS countries, right up to the last meeting, even though by then we had taken a decision that we would establish our own currency. We had stayed in the discussions in part because we thought it would help Lesotho and Swaziland in their own negotiation. The pula, as we named our currency, was formally launched on Pula Day, 23 August 1976. We chose Quill Hermans to be the first governor of our new central bank, the Bank of Botswana.

We decided to have our own currency for two reasons. First, South African foreign exchange reserves depended to a large extent on exports by

Botswana and Namibia from the Rand Monetary Area. However, the South Africans treated us shabbily. We contributed to the South African foreign reserves but received no income from our share of them. Second, we were unable to control our own economy, since we could not adopt our own monetary policies while we used the rand. The South Africans already controlled customs revenue rates, and to control the currency as well was too much for us. We were fairly confident about the level of reserves we would have after the pula was introduced, but our initial reserves after Pula Day were far greater than we had anticipated, which was a pleasant surprise.

Once we had formally decided to adopt our own currency, we faced new policy choices. We had not dealt previously with foreign exchange reserves, balance of payments, the exchange rate for the pula, monetary, credit and interest rate policies, and so forth. So, for nearly two years before Pula Day we brought in experts, and we held a series of educational seminars for ministers, permanent secretaries, and members of Parliament from all political parties. We wanted to be sure people were exposed to these new issues, and that they understood the choices and the new constraints we faced. We involved civil servants, including permanent secretaries and heads of departments in MFDP and the Bank of Botswana, as well as economists and other technicians, in these sessions. Some of these seminars seemed quite tedious as officials talked on and on about reserves and balance of payments. At the end of one long session during all-party caucus in 1976, a member of Parliament addressed the officials with a serious look on his face. "I've tried to follow and understand all this as best I can," he said, "but I have one question about these reserves and other matters: Do we have any money, really?" People tried hard to deal with the concepts, and the effort to educate them paid off handsomely in the future.

When I was dealing with the Congo in 2002, I had a revealing conversation with Jean-Pierre Bemba, the leader of Movement for the Liberation of the Congo. He was criticising the Congolese government for holding foreign exchange reserves; he assumed if there were foreign reserves it must mean government was not using the country's resources for development. I explained to him the functions that foreign exchange reserves perform. Bemba was quite dumbfounded and seemed impressed by my knowledge of these things. Then one of the other Africans in the group said: "Well, you have to understand that he comes from Botswana—where things work!"

Managing the exchange rate of the pula was part of our overall management of the economy, and we pursued an active policy of analyzing our exchange rate on a regular basis. The exchange rate was important to our development efforts as well as to controlling inflation. We made the first change in the par value of the pula in April 1978, when we revalued the pula upward by 5%. The revaluation was done in part to mitigate the effect of the growing inflation in South Africa, since revaluation decreased the pula price paid for imported goods. In 1982, after diamond sales had collapsed, we devalued the pula for the first time as part of the package of policies to deal with our first balance of payments crisis.

We had originally pegged the pula to the United States dollar; that is, we established a fixed rate of exchange between the pula and the dollar. This had the effect of pegging the pula to the rand, since the rand also was pegged to the dollar. But later, when the South Africans floated the rand, we had to make a new decision. Almost all our exports were sold for US dollars or sterling, but our imports were mainly from South Africa. If we stayed pegged to the US dollar, we would be pulled up in value relative to the rand. While this might have reduced inflation, it would also have put our newest local enterprises—manufacturing and service activities that competed with South Africa—at a competitive disadvantage. A rising value for the pula would have worked against our objectives of economic diversification and employment creation.

We ultimately decided to peg the pula to a "basket" of currencies, comprised of the SDR (the Special Drawing Rights of the IMF, itself a mixture of currencies) and the rand. As the rand sank in value during the 1980s, we were faced with regular decisions about what to do with the value of the pula. Some of our officials seemed to think that if we could only find the correct mixture of currencies to put in the basket, then we could avoid having to make so many decisions. I had to point out to them that changes of the relative values of currencies within the basket could also affect our economy, even if we remained pegged to a particular basket.

The extensive seminars we carried out at the time the pula was introduced were very important in helping the public to understand what we were doing. There were good discussions in Parliament and in all-party caucuses, with members entering the debates on such issues as the prudent level of foreign exchange reserves, or whether the value of the pula was too high or too low.

Macroeconomic Management
In 1975, when we decided to adopt our own currency, we created a new macroeconomic planning unit within MFDP. This unit would look at the full range of issues: how the budget related to the whole economy, the effect of our policies on our external balance of payments, how the exchange rate should be modified, and so forth. (Some of us joked about the name "macro" unit, since two of its first officials, Jan Isaksen from Norway and Geoff West from the UK, were each nearly two meters tall!) We knew that we needed to tie the whole planning process together and to keep a careful eye on macroeconomic balance; and those tasks fell to the macro unit.

As our economy developed and became more complex, and as diamond revenues became more important and plentiful, we made further changes in our planning and budgeting. In the 1976-81 National Development Plan, we introduced the concept of alternative forecasts of development. The plan showed a basic projection of growth of GDP, exports, and so forth, and then three possible disruptions, such as a delay in the expansion of diamond production. In the next plan, we had expanded the concept to include the impact of different developments on government revenue and, therefore, on expenditures. These alternative forecasts were discussed in ECC and in

Parliament, and they helped people understand the uncertainties we faced and why we needed to proceed prudently.

During preparation of the 1976-81 plan, we developed another new concept to deal with the shortage of trained staff. As our revenues increased, our financing capacity exceeded our administrative capacity to implement projects and manage programmes. Therefore, we introduced a "manpower budget". This gave us another method of allocating resources, in this case skilled people, on a priority basis: It helped control the growth of expenditures and kept us from spending money wastefully. The manpower allocation also was a part of sharing trained people with the private and parastatal sectors.

In the late 1970s and early 1980s, we were being criticised by some members of *Domkrag*, the opposition, and some academicians for being too conservative in our attitude to government spending. MFDP, in particular, was seen to be holding things back. In fact, however, the growth of government expenditure from self-rule through 1985 was the fastest of any country in the world, after adjustment for inflation, and it was twice as rapid as in the average developing country. We did not have the capacity to increase spending any faster without a substantial waste of funds. Experience with the Accelerated Rural Development Programme in 1973-74 had taught us that we had limited capacity, especially in the construction industry; more money spent did not necessarily mean more projects completed. The manpower budget helped us keep a degree of control, and it saved resources.

A third idea was introduced in the mid-1980s because of a very unusual development. As the South African economy deteriorated, the rand declined rapidly against other currencies. As a result, we received a very large windfall: Every dollar of diamond exports bought more of the rand that we used to purchase most of our imports. As a result, both foreign exchange reserves and government cash balances rose. We knew this was a one-time change, and that it could be reversed (as happened after I left office). Therefore, we knew we could not increase our spending on projects or programmes that would need continued operating support, such as new schools or hospitals. We introduced the concept of the "self-liquidating project". Ministries and parastatals could propose new projects for funding, provided such projects either would require no operating costs from government or, preferably, would be income generating. Developing serviced land (providing power, water, roads and telecommunications) that could be sold to private owners was one example of such projects.

Another innovation in our economic management was the introduction of the idea of a "sustainable budget". Mineral revenue by that time exceeded half of our total revenue, and it came from selling a national asset. As long as we spent mineral revenue to create new capital assets above the ground— educated people, productive enterprises, roads, schools—we would be exchanging one asset for another. If minerals were to run out, or to decline in value, we would have accumulated new national assets that replaced the diamonds in the ground. While this was a rough-and-ready idea, it proved to be a useful discipline on our overall spending. It also helped us emphasise the need to develop government revenue from sources other than minerals.

Such non-mining revenue was useful right away; it would become essential when mineral revenues declined.

We had many discussions over the years about the appropriate level of foreign reserves and the extent that revenues could be put into long-term investments abroad. In the mid-1980s, we had a number of debates in Parliament and in all-party caucus about the appropriate level of reserves. Botswana faced special factors—a narrow base to our economy, vulnerability as a land-locked country, apartheid South Africa as our neighbour, likelihood of drought, and so forth. Therefore, we needed a level of foreign exchange reserves higher than would be appropriate for a country in more normal circumstances. We also felt we needed to be prudent in the spending of our resources, since so much came from donor agencies.

By the mid-1980s, we had built up reserves we thought would be sufficient to meet the shocks that might come from political or economic disruptions in the region. After the Jwaneng mine had been fully developed and we experienced the windfall from the depreciation of the rand, Festus Mogae, Ponatshego Kedikilwe, Peter Mmusi, and I looked around to see what we could do with the diamond revenues besides investing them in Botswana. We sent officials to find out what other countries with similar circumstances had done. As a result of these investigations, we developed the concept of the Pula Fund. It was managed by the Bank of Botswana and invested in long-term financial assets in other currencies. The earnings on the Pula Fund flowed back to support the government budget. So, some of our mineral revenues were invested in a new type of asset that produced income for our future.

A counterpart of the increasing balances in various development funds (e.g. PDSF and RSF) and in the foreign exchange reserves was the growth of liquid assets in the banking system. This led to what became to be known as "surplus liquidity". Its presence created political and public relations problems for us, as it was difficult to explain to people that these funds in the banks could not be spent without other consequences. In our planning and budgeting, we did not just concentrate on the amount of money available. We looked at our needs and then focused on how we could, as frugally as possible, finance them. We did a lot of explaining, especially among our own party members, about the difficulties other countries had experienced in managing economies that depended on mining revenues. Some of these economies were even on the verge of collapse. With the decline in gold prices and the closure of mines, South Africa was an obvious example during the 1980s. While we did not want to go around publicly mentioning other countries by name, it was often very obvious about whom we were talking. "Surplus liquidity" was a public relations problem, but for the most part we were able to deal with the consequences of our prudent management and to avoid foolish mistakes in spending. However, we did fail to control spending in the late 1980s, as I discuss below.

Contingency Planning

Our geopolitical position meant we were always very vulnerable. We were entirely surrounded at independence by well-armed apartheid regimes; our transportation routes, food supplies, communications, marketing for our beef and other exports, and supplies of fuel all were dependent on travel through a hostile country. We knew that if we were too vulnerable, we could not be truly independent, and the fruits of our development efforts would be at risk. Therefore, we engaged in a substantial effort to plan for contingencies we hoped never would arise, and we undertook a number of projects primarily to increase our economic security.

When the first oil crisis arose in 1974, African, Arab and some Western governments increased their efforts to isolate South Africa, and they embargoed oil sales. We were afraid we could be directly affected, since all of our petroleum products came from or through South Africa, and we were part of the South African petroleum distribution system. We held a series of meetings at which we worked out arrangements for ensuring oil supplies. Most were at official level, but on one occasion Mr Mogwe and I met the South Africans at ministerial level at a secret location near Pretoria.

As soon as the oil embargo began, I took Mike Stevens, director of economic affairs, and Charles Tibone, secretary of external affairs, to some of the Arab countries—Algeria, Tunisia, Libya, Egypt, Kuwait—looking for assurances about supplies of oil and for development assistance—but we came back with nothing. In Kuwait, we found people somewhat willing to help, but they seemed to think we wanted reparations for slavery, and they argued that they had had no hand in slavery. Of course, we could have followed that route, since they had played a role in the slave trade, but we chose not to do so. We thought it over and ultimately abandoned the mission; we concluded that we needed to see our traditional supporters and donors and tell them the contingencies we faced.

So we went to Britain, the Scandinavian countries, Canada, and the US. Norway coordinated a consortium of countries to finance and build the Francistown-Nata road, and the US helped with the Nata-Kazangula road. These were known as the "lifeline" projects to provide an alternative transport route to our neighbours to the north. The British took some interest in a new airport that could take large commercial aircraft in case we needed an airlift for imports or exports. We engaged Sir Alexander Gibb and Partners to do the feasibility study. We asked the Tanzanians for the use of their harbour facilities for import and export, and we made tentative plans to engage meat trucks to export our beef through the north. We quietly made inquiries regarding fuel supplies from other countries such as Angola. We talked with the South African government not only about sharing whatever fuel they received but also whether, if we had access to crude oil, they would refine it for us. We expanded our oil storage capacity and arranged for the oil companies to manage a strategic reserve for us. While we never had to use any of the more complex contingency plans, the roads and the airport project have served us well.

We also established an inter-ministerial contingency planning committee. It analysed various scenarios, and examined issues such as strategic oil storage, food storage requirements, transportation plans for road, rail and air for both imports and exports, inventories of other goods that we would need, and so forth. One reason why we decided to have a relatively high target for foreign exchange reserves in the early years of the pula was to deal with the many contingencies we faced. We thought we could depend on friendly donor countries for some assistance in a crisis. However, if there were really an emergency, we would require funds immediately to pay the higher costs of imports, or to absorb higher costs of exports, if they had to be sent via alternative routes. Adequate foreign reserves became an important part of our overall contingency plans.

At independence, the railway that served us internally and connected us with both South Africa and Africa to our north was owned and operated by Rhodesia Railways. The railway played a critical role in large parts of our economy. It transported cattle to the abattoir, beef and copper-nickel matte to export markets, and before our roads were developed, it carried virtually all of our imports. There was racial segregation in the trains on both sides of the border, but we insisted there not be discrimination while the trains were within Botswana.

There had been discussions for many years about whether we should take over the railway and run it ourselves. In September 1974, without any discussion or decision in cabinet, the late president made a statement during a speech in Selebi-Phikwe: We were going to take over the railway line. One might say in this instance we behaved like other African countries! However, while there had not been a specific cabinet decision on the takeover, his statement reflected a basic position we all espoused. Once the president had announced it, the only issue became the timing. We just had to see how best we could carry it out.

The takeover of the rail line and the creation of Botswana Railways was a long and deliberate process. It was essential that we know how to run and maintain it properly before we insisted on any transfer of the authority and ownership. We had to purchase rolling stock, bring in technical assistance personnel both to hold senior positions and to train Batswana, and make all the necessary arrangements with the neighbouring systems so the trains would run smoothly. In fact, we did not complete the takeover until 1987.

In taking over the railway, we spent a great deal of capital and allocated a large number of skilled people to replace a system that was already in existence. The strategic oil storage depot and other projects added capacity we would not need if there were no emergency. The extra foreign exchange reserves we carried might have been invested either longer term in a larger Pula Fund or in other productive ways. However, given the uncertainties in southern Africa from the 1960s to the 1990s, we felt these expenditures on our contingency plans were necessary, both to ensure our independence and to protect the rest of the economy. In fact, apart from the 1981-82 diamond crisis, we were never forced to cut back on recurrent or development expenditures due to external disturbances to our economy.

Macroeconomic Strategies

The risks to our economy have always been large. As farmers, we have always known the importance of saving for a rainy day, or in our case for a dry day. So it was easy for us to adopt the idea of a budget policy that would build up reserves of foreign exchange or government cash deposits in relatively good years, knowing we would have to use them in years of difficulty. The development of the PDSF and RSF after budgetary independence was our first effort at budgetary stability. With the introduction of the pula in 1976, we added the notion of building up and running down foreign exchange reserves in good and bad periods. My budget speeches as minister of finance, as well as those of my successors, always played that tune, so that the public as well as the Parliament would understand what we were doing. We wanted to adopt levels of spending we could sustain over the long term. We did not want start-and-stop spending that could lead to political frustration as well as economic inefficiencies

In addition to maintaining macroeconomic balance that would avoid inflation or recession, we used macroeconomic management as part of our development strategy. From the very beginning of Legco, we knew we needed to develop other kinds of economic activity if we were to raise the standard of living of our citizens. Peter Fawcus' first address to Legco in 1961 had emphasised that we had to develop our agriculture, mining and other diversification activities if we were to succeed as a country.

By the mid-1970s, we were becoming a major mineral producer, and we realised we faced a new set of issues. Other mineral producers in Africa had encountered serious problems in diversifying their economies and in sustaining development. As I explain in the next chapter, we introduced a number of programmes that would use our mining revenues to provide direct assistance to Batswana who were trying to increase their incomes from productive activities. We knew we would have to provide a competitive environment for those activities. Imports could not be so cheap that our people could not sell their goods or services; and exporters needed adequate prices as well. We also learned that many mineral-exporting countries had experienced very high wages that discouraged local production (other than minerals) for both local markets and exports.

Because of the above factors, the macroeconomic part of our development strategy included two other ideas. First, we would keep a watch on the value of the pula to prevent it from becoming too high. Second, we could not allow wages and salaries of the minority who had good jobs to increase so rapidly that our products and services became too expensive to compete. The Incomes Policy we developed in 1972 was an important part of our strategy to diversify the economy and to increase jobs. We managed to achieve a growth rate of jobs in the modern sectors of the economy that was two to three times the growth rate of our labour force, and our macroeconomic strategies were critical to that success.

Economic Crisis, 1981-82

The investments we made in educating Parliament, cabinet, civil servants, and the general public about macroeconomic management paid off in 1982. During the late 1970s, there had been worldwide speculation in all commodities. Gold, oil, diamonds and virtually every other commodity had reached historic high prices by 1980. The readjustment started in 1981, and the diamond market was particularly hard hit. De Beers imposed a quota on its purchases from regular suppliers, including Debswana. Diamond exports in 1981 were P100 million lower than they had been in 1980; for several months we did not sell a single diamond. As a result our foreign exchange reserves fell rapidly.

We knew by mid-1981 that the international economy was headed for trouble and we would face declines in diamond and copper-nickel exports as well as in government revenue. However, rapid inflation over several years had increased pressure for a major increase of wages and salaries in the public sector. Civil servants were expecting that a salaries commission would be appointed in early 1982, and that it would recommend a large adjustment. So, we took some pre-emptive actions to avoid political pressure in a year of a very poor economy. We announced in August 1981 an immediate 7.5% increase in public sector pay. Over the next few months, the wages councils for various sectors of the economy met and made comparable adjustments in minimum wages in each sector. We also announced that we would no longer appoint a salary commission for the public sector every other year, as had become expected.

We undertook a number of other steps to stabilise the economy. The National Employment, Manpower and Incomes Council (NEMIC), composed of employers, labour unions and government, met several times to discuss the macroeconomic and budget situation. In light of the circumstances, NEMIC decided to recommend there be no wage or salary increases in the public sector in 1982. At that time, the private and parastatal sectors tended to follow government in salaries, so this was in effect an economy-wide wage freeze. The Bank of Botswana increased interest rates, which tightened domestic credit.

In his February 1982 Budget Speech, Peter Mmusi gave the bad news about the economy and the budget. He indicated we would be using the Revenue Stabilisation Fund (RSF) to help meet some of the revenue short-fall from diamonds, but we would also have to restrain both recurrent and development spending, as well as lending to parastatals. He sounded a warning about the copper-nickel mine at Selebi-Phikwe known as BCL; it was our largest private sector employer and was in danger of liquidation. He indicated that further fiscal and monetary measures would be needed to bring the economy into balance. While the purpose of building up reserves in good years was to cushion the bad years, this crisis was so serious we had to adjust our plans further. At the end of his speech he said: "None of the options open to us is a pleasant one, and it is clear that we must take concrete measures to live within our means."

Members of Parliament were shocked. While there had been talk around Gaborone of problems in the economy, in 15 years of independence we had never been faced with this sort of financial crisis. Instead of beginning the debate on the budget speech as planned, members demanded an all-party caucus to discuss matters privately. So, officials and ministers from the various economic ministries and the Bank of Botswana spent an afternoon giving explanations and answering questions. Discussion in the caucus built on the earlier seminars on the pula, foreign exchange reserves, and macroeconomics.

In addition to the austere budget in February 1982, we continued to examine options and to take action. The IMF sent a team to visit, but it was not very helpful. For one thing, the level of funds to which we would have access was very small. In addition, the IMF was very rigid about the size of the budget deficit they would permit. We pointed out that the purpose of our macroeconomic strategy was to build up reserves in domestic currency and foreign exchange when times were good so they would be available in the lean years. However, the IMF made it clear we would receive no recognition for our past prudence.

In the end, we developed our own strategy for dealing with the crisis, and we implemented it without assistance from the IMF. Interest rates were increased again, and we devalued the pula by 10% in May 1982. We drew down a commercial loan of $45 million that had been arranged in 1978 to help pay for our share of the equity investment in the Jwaneng mine. In a supplementary budget in August 1982, Peter Mmusi introduced a new sales tax to increase domestic revenues.

In designing our response to the crisis, we had several objectives. First, we sought policies that would spread the burden of adjustment fairly. Second, we involved politicians, civil servants, employers, unions and the general public in the discussions of macroeconomic policy, and we shared the facts, good and bad, so people would know what we were doing and why. Third, we were determined that our development efforts should proceed and not be seriously interrupted. We had intentionally restrained the growth of expenditure in the late 1970s when our financial capacity exceeded our ability to execute projects. This prudence gave us the financial cushion in 1982 to adjust to a difficult time without reducing the momentum of our development programme. Finally, we wanted to make the adjustments as quickly as we could, so we could get back to the business of development. We had seen other countries hope their problems would go away, when delay in taking action actually created more problems and ultimately the need for more severe measures. We did not want that to happen to us. I think we learned that, while prudent macroeconomic policies were not enough to ensure success, the failure to adopt prudent policies would make success unattainable.

Overheating the Economy
During the late 1980s, we seemed to forget the earlier lessons about the limits on our capacity to spend. Jwaneng had been completed in 1982, and it proved to be more profitable than expected. Our exports grew rapidly, as did government revenue (over 30% per year) and the liquid assets in the banking system. The South African rand depreciated against the US dollar, adding further to our financial resources. There was great political pressure to spend government revenues, despite the fact that skilled personnel were still very scarce.

Between 1985 and 1991, commercial bank lending expanded by over 30% per year, lending from PDSF and RSF to parastatals grew almost as rapidly, and government development expenditures increased by over 35% annually. The increased spending led to increased inflation in consumer prices—inflation was less than 7% in 1984, but it increased to 12% in 1990, and 16% in 1992.

We tried to overcome the shortage of serviced land in Gaborone and other major centres, which accounted for some of the increased expenditures. However, credit was available at interest rates that were lower than inflation rates, so people borrowed heavily to make investments in property and to purchase cars and household furnishings. Employment in the construction industry tripled in six years, and the industry started to experience serious shortages of both skilled workers and materials of all kinds. Prices for construction increased more rapidly than general inflation, and property in urban areas, particularly Gaborone, became overpriced in terms of people's capacity to pay.

The expansion came to an end in 1991. Property values declined, and employment in the construction industry fell by 50% over the next five years. This was the time when I had disagreements with my cabinet colleagues over providing assistance to small citizen contractors, who were not as strong financially as their larger counterparts owned by expatriates. It was a difficult time in the society. Many families and small businesses had become overly indebted to the banks and the hire-purchase companies. For many months the legal notices in the papers announced "sale in execution" of debts, or legal proceedings "in the matter between" creditors and debtors, who, of course, were named publicly. It was not a mere coincidence that the first serious cases of financial corruption in government and the parastatals, especially the Botswana Housing Corporation, emerged during this time of excessive spending.

Overall, the late 1980s represented one of our failures in macroeconomic management. Perhaps we had become too lax in our disciplines. Perhaps the systems of restraints we could rely on in our earlier and poorer days were not sufficient to overcome the political and social pressures to spend and to lend when money was seen to be available. We had established the Pula Fund, and in 1987 we exchanged Debswana's stockpile of diamonds for shares in De Beers. However, it would have been better if we had been willing to increase our financial saving even more during those years. We could have made a better match between our physical capacity to implement projects and our financial resources, and we would not have wasted resources by pushing up the real costs of implementing projects.

Over my years in politics, I gave many speeches, first as minister of finance and then as president, in which I talked of the importance of maintaining macroeconomic balance. Of course, I believed what I was saying about macroeconomic management was intellectually correct. But by the late 1980s, I had observed how some of our sister countries had made a mess of their economies, and we had experienced some close calls in our own economy. I was able to appreciate even more vividly how important sound macroeconomic policies are for a country's development.

Chapter 13
Economic Strategies and Programmes

Our strategies of development evolved as we achieved some of our objectives and our level of financial and human resources improved. To begin with, we had so much to do that we knew we must set our priorities clearly, prepare good projects, and implement them well. In the Introduction to our 1970-75 National Development Plan, I summarised our economic goals and strategies:

(i) to secure the fastest possible rate of economic growth in a manner designed to raise the living standards of the great mass of the inhabitants of Botswana;
(ii) to achieve budgetary self-sufficiency in the shortest possible time consistent with rapid economic growth;
(iii) to maximise the number of new job opportunities;
(iv) to promote an equitable distribution of income, in particular, by reducing income differentials between the urban and rural sectors through rural development.

It was clear from the very beginning that if we were to succeed in raising the living standard of our people, we would have to find the greatest amount of financial resources possible, invest them to achieve a high rate of economic growth, and create productive employment opportunities.

Our selection of government projects in the early years was in large part a response to the priorities expressed by our people: physical infrastructure such as roads, schools, and clinics, and services such as good water supplies, education, and health care. We also felt new institutions were needed to promote productive developments by Batswana and in Botswana. So, we created a number of parastatal organisations—bodies that were chartered by government with public funding, and an ability to act like commercial organisations, but under the direction of boards appointed by government. The Botswana Meat Commission (BMC) provided better prices for cattle farmers. The National Development Bank (NDB) was established in 1965 to provide needed capital, especially for agricultural development. The Botswana Development Corporation (BDC) was formed in 1970 to provide a catalyst for other development projects and as a partner for foreign investors.

Once we had made progress in developing physical infrastructure, establishing development institutions, and providing basic education, we could then turn our attention to promotion of productive activities, as I explain below. At the same time, we were investing in health care, water and other services to ensure all Batswana were participating in our progress.

Developing Physical Infrastructure
A large share of our public sector resources was devoted to providing physical infrastructure: roads, water and power supply systems, telephone and telecommunication services, serviced land, and housing. Not only did we lack all these things, but we were one of the most sparsely populated

countries in Africa. The rest of Sub-Saharan Africa was ten times more densely populated; even large arid countries in the Sahel had three or four times Botswana's population density. As a result, the relative cost of providing services to all our people was very high. We knew that private investors would be unwilling and unable to undertake productive development opportunities unless infrastructure facilities and services were available. We provided some things directly through government departments, some through new parastatal organisations, and some through lending to private individuals and companies.

Roads were in many ways the simplest problem to solve; the choices were obvious, even though the costs were high. At independence, we had only eight kilometres of paved roads, and by the time I left office the network of paved roads totalled more than 4,000 km. Most of the early road projects were financed by international donor agencies, so their economic and technical criteria as well as ours had to be met. (Their evaluation forms asked about numbers of vehicles per hour—while in the beginning we were still counting vehicles per day, or even per week!) By the end of the 1980s, we had completed most of the projects involving the heaviest traffic, and we then had the luxury of adding smaller and more remote settlements. With the independence of Namibia in 1990, we undertook the Trans-Kgalakgadi highway through Ghanzi and on to Gobabis.

I disagreed with my colleagues on one important issue in our road development. I thought we should charge a toll on the Ghanzi road across the Kgalakgadi to Namibia. First, some (like me) who used it would have been willing to pay tolls to fund its maintenance. Second, the people who would really break down the road would be the Namibians and the South Africans with their transit traffic; they should pay something to use it. But, people like Dan Kwelagobe and David Magang opposed a toll: Mr Kwelagobe because he always wanted government to provide everything free of charge, and Mr Magang because he was the minister responsible for roads at the time and did not want to be seen to be charging people. So, we did not use tolls.

Urban Housing
In the early days, government provided rental housing in Gaborone and many other areas. We did not see ourselves as permanent urban residents. People who worked for government expected to return home to their village after retiring. In the villages, all Batswana had access to tribal land on which to build a home—land on which they would not have to pay any rent or service levy. Urban areas were different. We had to provide services and land was not tribal. As these urban areas grew, we saw the need for more housing for both public and private employees. We created the Botswana Housing Corporation (BHC) to provide rental housing, and we handed over the stock of government housing to BHC as its initial capital. There was a shortage of rentable properties in Gaborone, and for a period of time the BHC served a major purpose.

I have always thought of housing as a kind of public utility. We needed to strike a golden mean, whereby people were not asked to pay punitive rental charges, but at the same time we didn't want people to be over-housed compared to their incomes. BHC rents had been intended to be at full economic rates, covering both capital charges and operating costs. We were at times able to achieve that objective, but housing costs are a political issue as well as an economic one. Our Incomes Policy created a necessary restraint on wages and salaries. A part of the quid pro quo in getting acceptance of the incomes policy was an exercise of restraint on BHC rentals. We no doubt created some problems, as one could see from the long lists of applicants for BHC housing. People knew they could have a larger house at a lower cost if they could rent a BHC house or flat than if they purchased or rented on the open market. Overall, however, we were able to provide reasonable accommodation for the vast majority of people in urban areas, despite the very rapid increase in demand for housing. We did so without having to give in to larger demands for wage and salary increases.

One of the housing developments that worked very well for us was the Self-Help Housing Agency, known by its initials: SHHA. Quill Hermans picked up the basic idea from Zambia, and we refined and then adopted it. It helped us avoid the worst aspects of urban slums that plagued so many countries, even though our urban population grew faster than that of any other country in Africa.

The concept was simple. First, as with tribal land, one did not have to purchase SHHA land. Second, the title (called a Certificate of Rights) was similar in concept to tribal land: One could bequeath the title to a person but not sell it. Third, we provided a modest interest free loan for building materials. This enabled a person to put up a very small house and a pit latrine using his or her own labour. Fourth, we laid out plots and streets and provided standpipes at frequent intervals to deliver potable water. Since we did not provide a water-borne sewerage system, electricity, or water directly to each plot, SHHA housing had very low capital costs. As a result, we could afford to provide plots and loans roughly in line with the growing demand for housing. At the time I left office, over 60% of urban households lived in SHHA developments.

Visitors familiar with urban areas in other developing countries sometimes came to Gaborone and asked a taxi driver to take them to the poorest part of town. They were invariably taken to Old Naledi, an area of Gaborone that initially had been a squatter area. The visitor always told the driver he must have misunderstood, that Old Naledi could not be the poorest area—but it was. Even our poorest area did not have the characteristics one found in the urban slums of most other developing countries in Asia and Africa. After the SHHA concept had been developed, we went into Old Naledi and provided people there with SHHA facilities, including roads, proper plots, water, latrines, and title documents similar to SHHA.

Many homes in SHHA areas now are large, multi-bedroom houses. Some who took SHHA plots arranged for others in their family to acquire adjacent plots. The plots were then joined and the families built larger houses. We made arrangements in the initial design for wide rights-of-way so we could later provide upgrades in water, sewerage, and power supplies. As we found access to capital, and as people became able and willing to pay for services, we began to provide electricity, water and sewerage connections to individual houses.

The SHHA programme made it possible for us to provide decent shelter for tens of thousands of Batswana who migrated to our urban areas over the past 40 years. Naturally, it was of a lower standard than even the least expensive BHC house, so there were many criticisms, especially from the opposition. But it would have been impossible for us to provide the capital to house everyone in BHC type of housing. In addition, if we had tried, we also would have been faced with large and growing operating subsidies—for water, sewerage, power and the housing itself.

In dealing with urban housing, I think it helped that we Batswana have a tradition of living in large villages. Shortly after independence, when the populations of urban Gaborone and Francistown were in the range of 10,000 people when major villages Serowe, Kanye and Molepolole were each around 30,000 in population, and Mochudi and Mahalapye held 12,000 to 15,000 people. Coming to a crowded place was not a big change for many of us.

In addition to housing, we had the challenge of providing land that was serviced with power, water, roads, sewerage and telecommunications for commercial and industrial uses and for private individuals or firms wishing to develop housing. In Gaborone, we almost always had a shortage of serviced land—none of us could have imagined at independence that the city would grow to where it is now. In 1971, Gaborone and three main suburbs (Gabane, Mogoditshane and Tlokweng) had a total population of 25,000. By the 2001 Census, their combined population had reached almost 260,000. Each time we added to the area of serviced land, we found the demand exceeded the supply.

Starting in 1979, we tried to encourage private home ownership by citizens outside the SHHA areas by providing guarantees for mortgages. We also lent PDSF funds to the Botswana Building Society to finance mortgage lending. The BHC sold houses on a tenant purchase scheme, and it then rebuilt its stock of rental units through further development projects. The NDB and the BDC were both involved in financing commercial developments in urban areas. In the late 1970s, the BDC developed the first flats in Gaborone for the open rental market. Many of the original houses in Gaborone, built when we were very poor, have now been either substantially expanded or torn down and replaced by much larger homes. In recent years private investors, including many foreigners, have developed large commercial areas, especially in and near Gaborone, but also in other urban areas and in large villages. So, over time we have had a broad mixture of public funding and public management, use of parastatal bodies, and private sector initiatives in developing our urban areas.

Development Institutions

At independence, we lacked not only financial resources and trained people, but we also lacked institutions, public or private, to manage and promote development projects. We established parastatal organisations in which the minister responsible for the functions to be performed (e.g. for agriculture in the case of the Agricultural Marketing Board) appointed the directors after approval by cabinet. We needed such institutions to serve public aims without the restrictions of civil service rules. And, we wanted organisations that would be catalysts for economic development.

The National Development Bank (NDB) was started because of the wish and the hope that it would make resources available for farmers. During the colonial government years, arrangements for revolving finance were available only to white farmers. Some of us had raised a hue and cry that this was discriminatory, and the creation of NDB was an answer. It might have played a more catalytic role in Botswana if our agriculture were not so risky. (One time I was in Lesotho with Quill Hermans and Peter Landell-Mills, and I told them they shouldn't gamble at the casino. They said to me in a teasing way: "You are one of the biggest grain farmers in Botswana, so you yourself are one of the country's biggest gamblers!") For many years, NDB was quite conservative in its lending policy. But, in the 1980s, the more liberal it became, the more we farmers became indebted to it. When it got into trouble in the late 1980s, it swung to the other extreme and became very demanding on repayments. There was not an adequate matching of the payment schedule and the flow of cash both during the season and in terms of when projects pay off. At times farmers were at fault for not keeping bankers informed of the realities. But I think bank management was sometimes overly aggressive, both in making some of the loans without thorough investigation and in trying to collect on a schedule that was unrealistic in our climate.

The Botswana Development Corporation (BDC) was also established to be a development catalyst with several roles to play. First, it would provide information to prospective investors. Second, it could go into business where investors needed a local partner. Third, it could step in when something needed to be done but the private sector was not forthcoming. Fourth, it could do business as if it were another private company. It did well on many projects, for the most part combining with foreign companies but also with local investors. However, the BDC had a number of years when its management was quite moribund. We sometimes settled for second-best in leadership when we should have been more demanding. It was another area where we could have done better.

The Shashe project, which began construction in 1969, included the BCL copper-nickel mine at Selebi-Phikwe and all necessary infrastructure. The Botswana Power Corporation (BPC) began with the development of Gaborone and got a full boost from the Shashe project, and the Water Utilities Corporation (WUC) was also a child of the Shashe project. We had no choice but to use our own water supplies for the Shashe project, but the question of how best to obtain our power was both economic and political. We were being pressed by the World Bank and the project's investors to purchase power from the South African government's utility, Eskom. They would have been quite happy to sell us the power for both the Shashe project and for Gaborone. We would only have paid to extend the grid, and the price would have been lower than if we had generated electricity in small plants in Botswana.

However, we saw the Shashe project as an opportunity both to mine our own coal resources at Morupule and to develop the BPC. What was more important, we did not want to put ourselves further at risk with the apartheid government in South Africa. They withheld rail cars for our beef when we did something that displeased them, such as receiving high-profile political refugees. What would happen if they decided to shut off the electricity to the mine and smelter at Selebi-Phikwe, or to the capital in Gaborone? So, we made the case to donor agencies and to private investors in BCL that because of our vulnerability we should adopt the higher cost power, and they accepted the argument. In the 1980s, we developed a central power station near the coal mine at Morupule, and we also joined the South African electricity grid. We developed enough capacity to be able to withstand a South African disruption, and we were able to enjoy the benefits of cheaper power as well as back-up capacity for our own systems. As with most tasks, we did things in stages, and we tried to learn from our mistakes.

All of the capital funding for the Shashe project came from abroad. In addition, payment of the operating costs of the water and power supplies to the Selebi-Phikwe Township and to BCL were guaranteed in one way or another by the project's private sponsors. As a condition of the loans, both BPC and WUC undertook financial covenants that ensured both water and electricity would be supplied at full economic costs. This eliminated the temptation to subsidise such infrastructure services in order to keep rates down as costs rose, a practice we knew had led a number of other countries into serious financial difficulties. However, as the pula fell in value with the South African rand in the 1980s, we needed to raise water and power rates because BPC and WUC debts were in hard currencies. Doing so was very painful, both economically and politically.

Water was one of the areas where it was important for experts—hydrologists, engineers, economists—and us as politicians to understand one another as we reviewed our options and made decisions on major projects. Our only perennial rivers were in the sparsely populated far north in the Okavango and along the Chobe. Any other dam site depended on seasonal flow from rainfall; and in our climate evaporation losses from surface water were high. Ground water, which in the early years provided virtually all of our rural and urban water supplies, depended on aquifers, and we knew little of the hydrology of the country at independence. Therefore, we did not know whether increased water use would deplete the aquifers in different areas and whether, or how fast, they would recharge.

We faced some major choices in developing our water resources. When Bob Edwards worked in Bechuanaland before independence, he urged us to undertake a comprehensive study of the resources of the whole country. The one resource we knew we had was the water of the Okavango, and, as we are a dry country, we needed to investigate it very seriously. We established measuring stations to determine the rates of flow of the river, and we undertook ecological studies. We looked at the potential engineering issues that would be involved if we were to undertake any substantial use. In fact, these studies disillusioned us. The economic realities, the ecological effects, and the political impact, all argued against doing anything. Transporting the water for use only within Botswana would result in a cost that was equal to the heavens above. Exploiting the Okavango water would make sense only if we shared it with South Africa. But, during the apartheid era, we knew that if we were to be the source of a critical raw material such as water to the Northern Transvaal, it would provide a further excuse for South Africa to walk in to take us over under the pretext of protecting their vital interests.

Later, we did a study of the possibility of damming the Boro River at the southern edge of the Okavango Delta. It could have provided a supply of water that could be released along the Boteti River—at Makalamabedi, Moreomaoto, Xhumaga, Sukwane, Rakops, Xhumo—all the way to the mine and township at Orapa, which depended on groundwater. Water that was already flowing out of the delta toward Orapa would be put to good use, instead of evaporating and providing no economic benefit. We had consulted the local people in Maun, who had agreed. Cabinet unanimously agreed that we should proceed. We had actually assembled the teams in Maun to start the project.

At the last minute, however, the opposition, which always fished in troubled waters, learned of objections by some foreign ecologists. These ecologists were opposed to the idea and said the scheme was only for the benefit of the diamond mine at Orapa. That was not the case—though it would have been a legitimate reason even if it had been exclusively for the mine's use. The opposition stirred up the local people and even made spurious arguments related to tribal politics. The opposition got the safari companies involved, and they in turn used the Batawana people to say this project would take away their jobs in tourism. The safari companies thought we were going to take water out of the delta; but in fact we were going to distribute in a different fashion the discharge that was already leaving the delta. The water would be used economically, rather than simply going to waste in evaporation. We eventually gave in to political pressures stirred up by outside people, and we cancelled the project. Since we had already mobilised the contractors, we had to pay about P8 million in damages. This is one of those cases where I wish I had just put my foot down. I am sorry I became weak-kneed; I should have just gone ahead.

We were always under pressure to provide water, power and housing at prices below economic costs. In the urban areas, WUC and BPC maintained tariffs that covered full economic costs, in part because of the covenants in loan agreements. But, there have always been demands to provide power and water at subsidised prices in the major villages and in other rural areas. At independence, the demand for potable water was near the top of the list of priorities in almost every part of the country, so we moved rapidly to provide water supplies in the major villages and then in all other villages. For many years we provided village water supplies on the same basis as we did in SHHA areas in urban centres: We reticulated water to standpipes located at regular intervals throughout the village. Water was free, but one had to fetch it. We subsidised power in the rural areas, but we resisted the pressure to provide large subsidies.

Our basic policy was that in urban areas, where incomes were well above the rural areas, consumers would pay at least full economic prices. As our financial situation improved, we were able to respond more readily to demands to extend electricity and private water connections to the major, and then the smaller, villages. I believe we were right in the early years to resist the demand for more subsidies. Our funds financed investments, not consumption; those investments were the reason we were able to achieve our overall economic success and to spread the benefits of services widely.

At independence, we knew we needed some kind of airline. We were very isolated, we did not have a good road system, and internal distances were very long. Botswana National Airways, Botswana Airways, and Air Botswana, one after the other, were our national carriers. Many countries had internal political demands to establish an international airline, but we never experienced such pressures. We tried to make do with the minimum by way of air transportation within Botswana and to neighbouring countries. We also did things like leasing planes instead of buying them to keep our costs as low as possible. We wanted to avoid subsidising an airline, but for years the airline just didn't pay, and we had to bail it out several times. Members of Parliament used to ask me when I was going to stop asking them to salvage the airline again!

We have boasted, and rightly so, about our parastatals. This included the basic utilities but especially those that are agents of change, like BDC and NDB, and even WUC. They have provided reliable service and often have made good profits. However, I think they missed the purpose for which they were established. They didn't seem to take pride in their effectiveness as development agents. They wanted, instead, to boast about how profitable they had become. In that respect, they were just like any other private company or bank; but that was not why we established them.

As we made progress on physical and social infrastructure, we knew we had to do something to directly increase productive employment opportunities. We looked first to agriculture, and then to manufacturing and other sectors.

Arable Agriculture
Most Batswana were farmers, and, therefore, we felt we would have to raise agricultural incomes if we were to succeed in raising the living standards for the majority of our people. Cattle were the backbone of the economy before independence, and I discuss our programmes for cattle in the next chapter. However, almost all farmers grew crops. During the colonial era, we had agricultural officers and demonstrators to assist farmers. In the years after independence, we devised a number of new programmes aimed at arable agriculture in the hope of assisting the majority of Batswana.

The Arable Lands Development Programme (ALDEP) was developed in the 1970s to focus on the smaller farmers—those with fewer than five hectares of land under cultivation. ALDEP initially involved loans to finance purchases of improved inputs and draft power for ploughing and cultivation, as well as advice on techniques. It quickly became clear that providing financing via credit to the smallest farmers was very inefficient. So, in 1983 ALDEP was converted to a grant programme. If the farmer provided 15% of the cost of the improvement package, then government would provide the remaining 85% as a grant. Unfortunately, ALDEP was implemented at the time of the major droughts from 1982 to 1987, so its impact was limited. In response to these severe droughts, we introduced the Accelerated Rainfed Arable Programme

(ARAP) to assist farmers with ploughing, fertiliser, seed and the like. In 1986-87 over 16,000 farmers participated in ARAP.

Droughts have been constant features of our lives, and we decided in the early 1970s that it was time to investigate how we might mitigate their effects. Through the Overseas Development Institute we recruited Stephen Sandford, who was knowledgeable about livestock and drought from his work in other countries. He visited Botswana, studied our situation and produced a report called "Dealing with Drought". After we had received and discussed his report, we began to implement his recommendations. We established an inter-ministerial drought committee, which monitored the condition of grazing, water, grain supplies, and so forth throughout each year. With that information, we knew the extent to which each area had a problem, and we then developed recommendations as to what should be done in each locality.

Our drought relief programmes benefited from our earlier emphasis on the development of transportation and communication infrastructure. Many people criticised our expenditures on infrastructure, among them Mr Matante of the BPP, who used to complain in Parliament: "People can't eat roads." However, the road system made it possible for us to deliver either complete or supplementary food supplies to more than 60% of our people during several years of drought in the 1980s. Our experience during those severe droughts showed that, indeed, one can eat roads!

We established the Botswana Agricultural Marketing Board (BAMB) in 1974. BAMB had several objectives: to help stabilise grain markets throughout the country, to provide better prices than farmers had received from local grain traders, to hold grain reserves to deal with our fluctuations in weather and crops from year to year, and to provide stores of grain throughout the country so we would not have high transport costs during drought. Unfortunately, BAMB was a disaster. It bought grain from farmers at very low prices, and then due to large overheads charged such high prices that people would not buy grain from them. As a consequence, grain rotted in the silos, and the management was embarrassed. Part of our problem was that we had politicians who defended the mismanagement, including one assistant minister of agriculture who argued that large losses were an acceptable way of doing business. The failures of BAMB represent another area where our policies and projects simply were not implemented well.

Having had disappointing results in projects aimed at helping farmers improve their yields in traditional lands areas, we tried another approach in the north. The Pandamatenga farms project, located 100 kilometres south of Kasane on state land, was one project almost all of us thought would be successful. This area had good soils, was in a relatively good rainfall belt, had never been settled, and was raw bush. We saw it as a potentially important project, especially for food production.

The first results at Pandamatenga were very encouraging. The costs were relatively high, and as long as there was a grace period on repayment of loans, all went well. However, we soon encountered major problems. Wild game destroyed crops, rains were more irregular than had been predicted, and banks started calling in loans. Some of my ministers and officials felt that since the terms of the loans were clear, the farmers should just pay or lose their security, but I differed. I felt that the new factors should be taken into account in the loan repayment schedule—not that they should be forgiven, but the terms should be more flexible, with a period of grace. In South Africa, the Land Bank provided very long-term loans, and this was one of the factors in the strength of South African agriculture. In any case, the project did not produce the expected results.

We have spent millions of pula every year on agricultural development programmes, but the results have been very disappointing. In the years following independence, government spending on agriculture amounted to the equivalent of 12% of total income in agriculture. We had increased government spending to over 25% of agricultural income by 1980; it was over 40% by 1990; and public expenditures to assist agriculture exceeded 50% of total incomes in agriculture in the year I retired. Some countries in Africa failed to develop their agriculture because they did not invest in it. We failed despite very substantial investments that started as early as self-rule.

Many factors have worked against our development efforts in agriculture: our unfavourable climate, severe periods of drought, and growing employment opportunities in the cities and larger villages at much higher incomes than are possible in arable farming. As a farmer myself, it has been particularly disappointing to me to see how people have turned away from agriculture.

Manufacturing and Other Economic Opportunities

We had greater success in promoting activities such as manufacturing, transportation, and financial and other services. Value added in manufacturing grew at over 7.5% per year in the 35 years after self-rule, one of the fastest rates in the world. Further, even though agriculture grew very slowly, overall incomes in the non-mining sectors of Botswana's economy grew more rapidly than in any other developing country.

During the early 1970s, we had established the Botswana Enterprise Development Unit (BEDU) to provide technical assistance, facilities and financing to new citizen entrepreneurs. In 1977-78, the European Community helped us engage Professor Michael Lipton from Sussex University to do a detailed study of employment creation opportunities and policies, and we benefited from his analysis. We created an Employment Policy Unit in government; we developed new programmes for agriculture; and we established a Financial Assistance Policy (FAP) to provide cash grants for new projects that created productive employment. FAP became another use for mineral revenues, and, despite some abuses of the programmes, we had very rapid growth of both employment and production in manufacturing in the 1980s and 1990s. Employment also grew rapidly in financial and other services.

I believe our efforts in these areas succeeded in part because we did not encourage projects that were uneconomic or that would require a permanent subsidy from government. On a number of occasions, businesses facing competition from imports, or running losses in their export markets, came to us with a kind of blackmail: Either government should assist them directly or they would close their doors. We had watched other countries get into trouble by trying to subsidise losing businesses, and we did not want to go the same way. So, despite the unfortunate result of putting some people out of work, we decided government could not provide permanent financial support to failed businesses.

Our free trade agreement with Zimbabwe dating from the Protectorate era, and our membership in the Southern African Customs Union, created constraints on our ability to provide incentives to industries in Botswana. South Africa set the tariffs and excise rates for the entire Common Customs Area, but it did so to serve the interests of South African producers. The South Africans also had elaborate controls within their economy, most obviously in the motor vehicle industry, which effectively divided the South African market among a number of producers. We could not impose tariffs on imports from South Africa or Zimbabwe, nor could we impose restrictions on such imports to protect Botswana manufacturers.

In renegotiating the Customs Union in 1969, our arguments about the polarisation effects of a customs union with one large industrialised partner resulted in a special concession to the smaller member countries. We gained the right to impose a special import duty for up to eight years on goods coming from other partners in the Customs Union, if we could show that a new infant industry could supply the lion's share of our domestic market. We used this provision of the Customs Union sparingly, and, in the case of the Prinz Brau brewery, at serious cost.

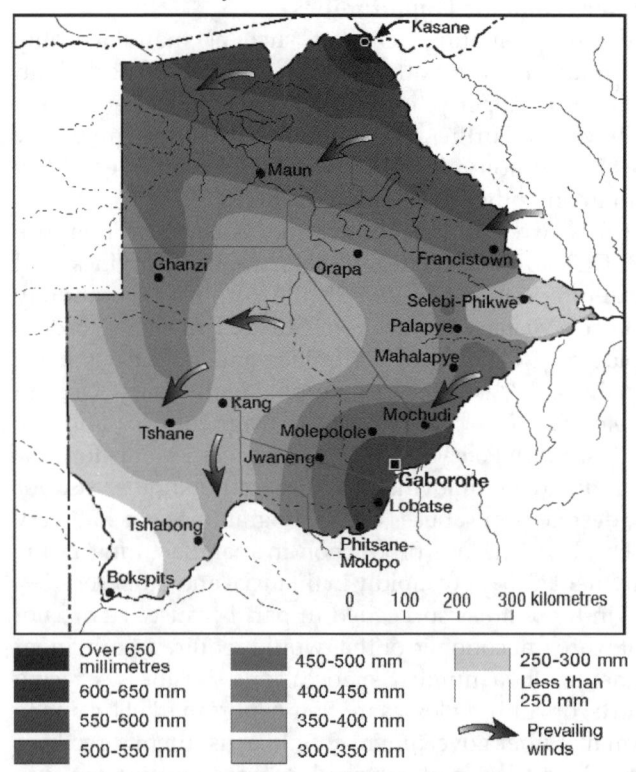

Map of Botswana showing rainfall pattern

In the 1970s, we thought it would be a good thing to establish a brewery in Botswana. It appeared we could do so economically with our size market, so we made our first use of the provision for temporary infant industry protection. BDC was our agent to find a joint venture partner, and we took a decision to diversify the sources of our foreign investments. Instead of approaching South African Breweries, which might have been the most logical thing since they were our largest supplier, we searched for a partner from outside the region. The Urtger group from Germany had a good reputation and had been successfully brewing beer for a very long time. They agreed to invest, and using the infant industry clause, we applied a 100% duty to all beer imported from outside Botswana. The new Prinz Brau brewery began production in Gaborone in March 1976.

This was a project that could have succeeded, but we were sabotaged by the South Africans. In much the same way, a brewery in Swaziland that had tried to compete with South African Breweries had been driven out of business a number of years earlier. In that case, shipments destined for northern Transvaal were somehow consigned to Cape Town, leading to losses and closure of the brewery. In our case, all sorts of foreign objects, including insects, somehow found their way into beer cans and bottles during production. This tampering took place in the hottest season of the year, during the Christmas and New Years holidays, when sales were traditionally the largest. Sales never recovered, the brewery made large losses, and we had to restructure the project. Not surprisingly, as soon as we brought in South African Breweries as the partner, everything was fine.

In the 1990s, we established a Hyundai motor vehicle assembly plant to take advantage of Customs Union provisions, but it was also sabotaged by South Africa. The South African motor industry was heavily protected by the external tariff, and we in Botswana paid very high prices when we purchased vehicles assembled in South Africa. Producers in South Africa were strongly opposed to having us do any assembly in Botswana. However, we established a partnership with Hyundai, which wanted to get into the market in southern Africa. This seemed to be a project where we could take advantage of the tariffs that South Africa had imposed. We could sell vehicles to South Africa and the other partners as well as meet some of the market demand in Botswana.

Once the Hyundai plant was established, the South Africans alleged that we were not assembling the vehicles, just uncrating them. Therefore, they said, we should pay the full tariff on assembled vehicles, not the lower tariff that was levied on components. So, we brought the South African officials to Botswana to show them assembly was indeed taking place. Then they said we were not collecting the appropriate customs and excise duties. Again, we brought them here so our customs people could show that all the relevant duties had been charged. Finally, I was awakened one night and told that our cars were piling up at the Tlokweng border gate—they were not being allowed to enter South Africa. I picked up the phone and called Chief Buthelezi, who was acting president. (Nelson Mandela was trying to make peace between President Mabuto and Laurent Kabila in Zaire, and Thabo

Mbeki, his deputy, was in East Africa trying to make peace in Burundi.) Chief Buthelezi was a good actor. He said, with great surprise: "Really! They are stopping cars from your place, when you have done so much for us!" Later I spoke with President Mandela, and exports began again.

South African authorities then accused the Hyundai dealers in South Africa of some illegality. We helped them fight that charge, and again we won. Finally, Hyundai's South African partner apparently siphoned off money, so eventually Hyundai gave up, and our plant was closed. This should have been a good project, in part because it was resulting in a good deal of training for our people. But it is a sad story: We now have a large empty building and we lost the jobs that had been created.

Both the brewery and Hyundai projects were among the largest in the manufacturing sector at the time they were undertaken, and both failed. Our good overall record in manufacturing growth seems to have come from doing a large number of small things successfully, rather than depending on one or two major projects.

Several initiatives on diversification were started around the time I became president in 1980. By then we had made a great deal of progress in developing our physical infrastructure, our financial position had become much stronger, and we were making good progress in all aspects of education. Our parastatal organisations were well established, and the Jwaneng diamond mine, then under construction, was projected to substantially increase government's financial resources. As Professor Lipton's 1978 report had made clear, however, we faced many challenges in creating employment opportunities for our citizens (e.g. expensive utilities, low skill levels, high transport costs). We were also aware that many Batswana felt there were insufficient programmes to enable them to improve economically. There were increasing calls for subsidies of all kinds, including water and power for both industrial and residential users. We needed to address these concerns and develop some positive programmes. Unless we did so, I felt we would be pushed to adopt policies that might be politically popular in the short term but that would be wasteful of resources, would not solve the problems, and would soon lead us into financial difficulties. By 1980, we also had the lesson of the brewery; once bitten, twice shy.

We established two groups in 1980 and 1981 to focus on strategies for increasing employment and income opportunities for Batswana: a working group on subsidy policies, and the Presidential Commission on Economic Opportunities. The commission was chaired by Peter Mmusi who was then minister of finance and development planning. It produced a comprehensive review of all our policies that were meant to provide citizens with the chance to improve their economic situation. Much of the emphasis in the commission's report was on the need to effectively implement the many policies we had adopted over the years. This was a continuing theme right up to the time I left office: We have had good policies on paper, but we sometimes failed to implement them effectively. The commission paid particular attention to the ways our licensing systems were restricting local entrepreneurs from doing business.

ECONOMIC STRATEGIES AND PROGRAMMES

The Economic Opportunities Commission emphasised that we were trying to equalise the opportunities for each person, not to ensure that each was equally successful. It was important for people to take initiative themselves. The willingness to take calculated risks was an important part of Botswana's success. If one wants political certainty, one has a dictatorship. If one wants economic certainty, one uses controls and not the market. When individuals in Botswana were successful, other people have often forgotten that those individuals took a risk at the beginning.

For example, we needed to make Gaborone a successful town, so I went to the UK just after independence to raise thousands of pounds to use as seed money for developments in our new capital. Then I hawked this money around to any enterprising person who was prepared to listen. I told them: "Here are these opportunities of land and of capital that are available." Only two people took up the opportunity; both were of Asian ethnicity. No one else was willing to take the risk, and in the 1960s, investment in Gaborone was definitely a risk. However, after we had become a successful economy, and Gaborone had become a highly developed city, others were resentful of the prosperity of these two individuals. They forgot that the two who invested might have lost everything.

The working group on subsidy policy examined how we could best use government financial resources to encourage viable economic activities. It consulted widely and brought interim reports and draft recommendations to the Economic Committee of Cabinet. Its main recommendations were incorporated into a White Paper on the Financial Assistance Policy (FAP) that was approved by Parliament in April 1982.

The FAP, as it was known, provided for direct grants to enterprises, primarily in manufacturing, that created productive employment. The enterprises could receive assistance regardless of whether their markets were for import substitutes in Botswana or for exports. Grants for small scale projects to meet start up costs were open only to Botswana citizens. Separate programmes for medium and large scale projects, open to citizens and non-citizens, provided various levels of scrutiny before projects were approved for funding. The basic idea was to use direct government grants instead of the indirect subsidies, such as protection by tariffs, which were used in other countries. We felt it was better to know exactly what the programmes cost so their effectiveness could be evaluated.

FAP was evaluated and modified several times, each time with an effort to provide better administration, more oversight, and more appropriate incentives. During its lifetime, FAP supported over 5,000 separate projects, 95% of which were small scale projects where the immediate beneficiary was a Motswana entrepreneur.

Almost all of these projects were in the manufacturing sectors. During the 19 years of FAP, employment in manufacturing rose from around 7,000 to over 30,000, an annual growth rate of 8%. Value added in manufacturing increased at an annual rate of 6.5% after inflation. Both were high growth rates by international standards. The Productive Employment Development Fund, which financed the FAP, provided another place to invest some of our diamond revenues. It helped diversify the economy and expand employment opportunities. In 2001, after I had retired, FAP was replaced by the Citizen Entrepreneurship Development Agency (CEDA). CEDA is designed to focus more directly on the entrepreneurs rather than create productive opportunities per se.

An Assessment of Our Record

In light of the four economic goals and strategies outlined at the beginning of this chapter, how might I assess our performance?

(i) We achieved the fastest growth rate of any country in the world during the years from self-rule in 1965 to my retirement in 1998. In addition, the overwhelming majority of Batswana participated in our economic development in one or more ways, through employment in newly created jobs, access to clean water and health care, receipt of an old age pension, education, and assistance during severe droughts.

(ii) We achieved budgetary independence in 1972, several years earlier than we had hoped. We did not have to sacrifice economic growth in order to achieve financial independence, as we at first feared might be necessary.

(iii) We created new jobs in the modern sectors of the economy at a rate that was two or three times faster than the growth of the labour force. While I would have wished for more new jobs, it was far higher than what we had thought possible at independence.

(iv) I address the extent to which we achieved equitable distribution of income, growing opportunities, and increased disparities in Chapter 16.

Chapter 14
Land and Cattle

Land and cattle were virtually the only assets we had before independence, and both continue to be of major significance socially, and politically, and economically. The two were interrelated, of course, since one needed land to graze cattle, and one needed oxen to plough the land.

The Land (*Le fatshe*)
The subject of land is one of the most sensitive issues in Botswana, as it is in much of the developing world. Traditionally our land was owned in common by the entire tribe, and such communal ownership of land has always been very important to us. When Peter Mmusi chaired the 1981-82 Presidential Commission on Economic Opportunities, he would frequently say at *kgotla* meetings: "Every Motswana is rich, because every Motswana has the right to land on which to build a home, to raise crops, and to graze livestock." Despite the shortage of land in certain parts of the country, that is still true. Our situation is very different from places such as South Asia, where a system of freehold land has resulted in millions of landless rural people.

Land for crops was given by the chief to each ward, and the people in the ward would determine how the land would be divided. Sometimes it would be allocated first at the chief's *kgotla*. Sometimes it would evolve that the people from a certain *kgotla* would settle in an area that had been unoccupied, and over time, by usage, the rights to plough the land would be established. Or, a person from one *kgotla* would come and ask to be allocated land in another. The people would decide whether he seemed to be a good person, and if so, then he would be allocated land.

Until the mid-1950s, there were no boreholes, so the only water available was either from wells dug by hand that could go to a maximum of 30 to 35 meters, or from seasonal surface water. The only land under use for cattle posts and ploughed lands would be where the water table was high. One could establish a cattle post virtually anywhere within those areas, since any tribesman could graze cattle on common land. Around 1956, the colonial authorities made the first development expenditures in Bechuanaland on boreholes, using the Colonial Development Welfare Funds. As boreholes of greater depth became possible, we could expand the areas of cattle grazing. But, that gets ahead of the story.

Land for homes was allocated to the wards by the chief. The land within the ward would be allocated by the headman of the ward. Sometimes the chief might say: "Your village is becoming too crowded. I want you all to move to a new place," and he would choose one within the tribe's area. A growing population could be accommodated on the tribe's common land. Allocations for commercial purposes were relatively few and were made by the chief himself or by his representative in the region.

Arrival of the Whites

There had only been tribal land held in common in the distant past. Because of the arrival of the whites and the subsequent colonial experience, by independence we had three types of land tenure: tribal or customary land with communal tenure, state (formerly Crown) lands, and freehold land. Today, about 70% of our land is held in customary title, 25% is state land, and 5% is freehold land.

Freehold land developed as a result of contact with whites in the 19th century. The Tati Company secured the rights to land in north-eastern Botswana in and around Francistown in a treaty with Chief Lobengula of the Ndebele, and the Tati Concession later became part of the Bechuanaland Protectorate. Some Boers had settled in Ghanzi in the 1870s, but the formal grant of land came from Chief Sekgoma of the Batawana in the 1890s. In 1898, 200 Boer farmers moved to Ghanzi, though most sold their farms to other whites in a relatively short time. The Tuli Block, along our border with South Africa, was granted by Chief Khama III to the British in 1895, and the British then made a grant to Rhodes' British South Africa Company (BSAC). The Gaborone and Lobatse Blocks were part of the same transaction to compensate the BSAC for building the railway through Botswana from South Africa to Rhodesia. These grants of land resulted in white settlement in Bechuanaland, and this land was used almost exclusively for farming. Strategically, the Ghanzi farms were an obstacle to German expansion from South West Africa, and the Tuli Block blocked Boer expansion from the Transvaal.

In all areas, Africans were displaced from their lands by the new freehold land, but the impact was uneven. Because of the low density of population in the west, the consequences were least for the Batawana, who had given up the Ghanzi farms. The effect of the Tati Concession on the Bakalanga in the densely settled Francistown area may have been the most serious in reducing land for tribesmen. The Babirwa were pushed out of the Tuli Block, and the Balete and Batlokwa also were crowded by the creation of the Gaborone Block. While the overall size of the freehold areas was relatively small, some Batswana felt the loss of tribal land more acutely than others.

The large areas of state land were the result of the Protectorate. The Protectorate government demarcated tribal "Reserves" for the eight tribes living under paramount chiefs, as I explained in Chapter 7. All land not allocated to the Reserves or in the freehold areas became Crown land, even though many tribesmen lived there. After independence, we converted most of the former Crown land into tribal land so that Batswana in the Kgalakgadi, Ghanzi and the Chobe had tribal territories with the same land rights as those in the former Reserves. The balance remaining in state land is now in National Parks, Wildlife Management Areas, Forest Reserves, or the main urban areas. We purchased land in the north-east from the Tati Company in order to provide Bakalanga with tribal lands.

Land Boards

As part of our effort to remove the arbitrary power of the chiefs, we needed to create a new system for allocation of land. Any new approach had to respect customary title, but decisions would have to be arrived at more democratically, not by the chief. The ideas were developed during our debates in the African Council, and they ultimately resulted in the Tribal Land Act of 1968. The Act provided for the establishment of Land Boards to allocate tribal land, and to start with, Land Boards were very close to the local councils. The secretary of the council was secretary of the Land Board, and there was an assistant secretary to whom the actual work of the Land Board was allocated. In addition, one or two councillors selected in the *kgotla* sat on the Land Board so the council would be represented. To begin with, there were no particular qualifications for election to the Land Board. Later we decided there should be an educational qualification at least to Standard 6, so that members should be able to read the minutes of meetings and other documents.

Land Boards initially did not have their own finances but received subventions from councils. We thought that any rent should go to each council's consolidated fund, and then it should be allocated from there. Our motivation was to develop the country and the land, not to make money from renting it. I regret that we later allowed the Land Boards to retain income from rents. When Land Boards were permitted to keep the rental income themselves, they became tempted when allocating land to go for high rents and not necessarily for developments by the people. One Land Board, for example, chose to lease land to the CDC instead of to TGLP farmers because the CDC rent would be higher; and then it used the higher rent to buy double-cab *bakkies* (pick-up trucks) for their own use!

We made a number of amendments to the land acts, and each time the change involved study and consultation by a presidential commission. One change involved the concept that any Motswana can go to any Land Board— he or she does not have to come from that tribe or area. Take the example of Tlokweng. Land there was very scarce, and because of its proximity to Gaborone, it was in high demand by people from all over. How would a Motlokwa feel about giving access to land in Tlokweng to a Motswana from elsewhere? But in fact, it was the land-scarce areas we were concerned about when we proposed the change. We felt it should be possible for any Motswana to have land, regardless of whether he or she was from a tribe with surplus land or very scarce land. If someone from Tlokweng wants to go to Ngwato territory where there is excess land, that person should not be denied land just because he or she comes from Tlokweng, outside the tribal area of Bangwato. Or suppose a man who has spent his life in Tshabong as a policeman decides he wants to retire there. Even though his home was originally in Bobonong, he should not be denied access to land in the place he served during his professional life.

Adoption of the idea that one could have land anywhere was not easy, because people thought of availability of land for their children, not just themselves. But, we pointed out that their children could find land elsewhere under the new policy; they would not be restricted to what was in their ward or village or tribal area as had been the case in the past. When one applied to any Land Board for an allocation, one had to declare where one already had land, and for what purpose it was being used. For example, if I had

Map of Botswana showing land use

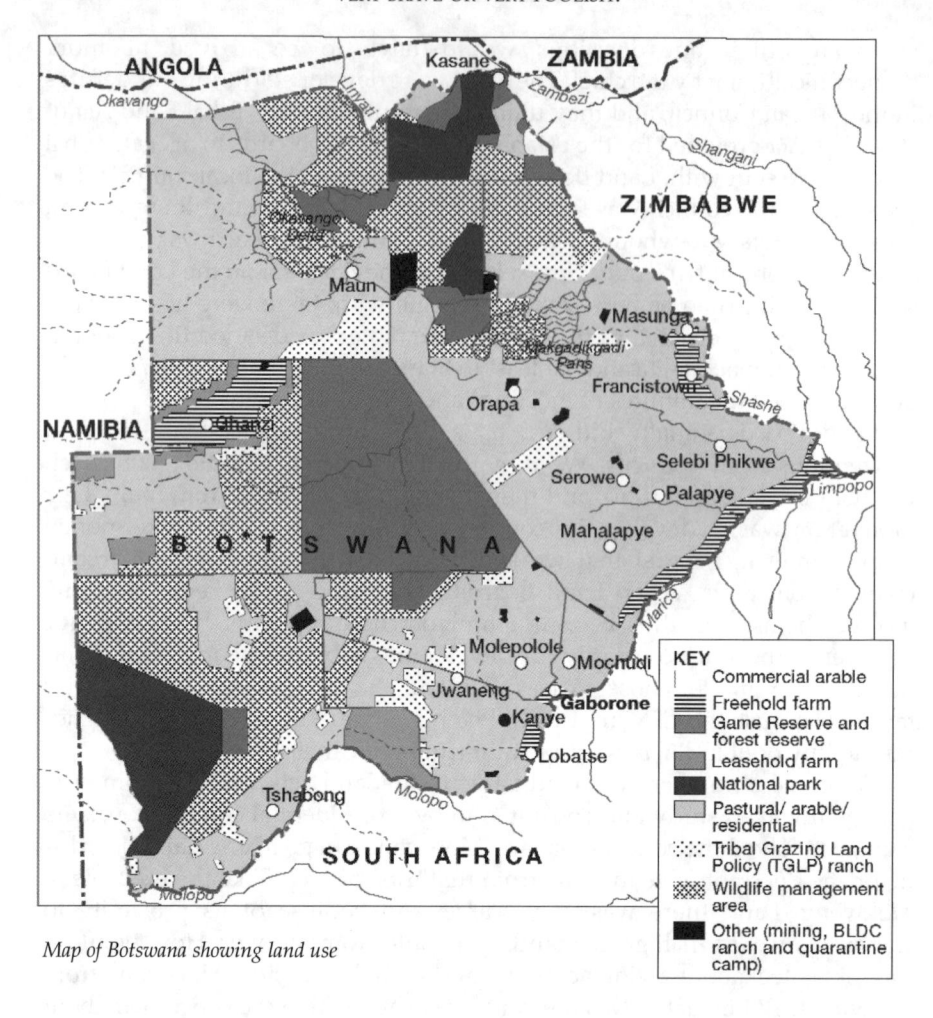

ploughing land in Ngwaketse but wanted to open a retail store in Mochudi or elsewhere in Kgatleng, then that might be acceptable, while I might be denied access to more ploughing land in Mochudi, since I had plenty of land for ploughing in Ngwaketse.

Our consultation on all land issues took place at *kgotla* meetings throughout the country. People from commissions went to Serowe, Kanye, Maun, Bobonong, and so forth, to say: "We have been detailed by government to find out your views as a tribe about whether the Land Board should allocate land to Batswana who do not necessarily come from your area." They also enquired about issues of land allocations of different sizes. They gathered opinions and eventually arrived at conclusions that enjoyed the consensus of people around the country. The report would be circulated by the Ministry of Local Government and Lands, and after further consultation resulted in a paper to cabinet. The specific legislation amending the Land Act was adopted by Parliament. Each decision regarding land use was taken in this way.

The Tribal Grazing Land Programme (TGLP)

The concept of finding better ways to manage communally held land started even before self-rule. Communal ownership gives a false sense of ownership since the land is yours to use, but in practice it could be taken from you by the tribe. The other problem of communal land is that what belongs to everybody belongs to nobody. Nobody can be held responsible for it, and no one has the responsibility for such things as preventing veld fires, soil erosion or overgrazing. On common land, if I reduce my stock to prevent overgrazing, others may use the grazing that my cattle might have used. If we say the land should not be overgrazed, to whom are we talking? And if it is overgrazed, no one would take responsibility, so whom are we to punish?

The problems in communal areas were obvious: veld fires would clean out the grazing from huge tracts of land; there was land degradation around existing boreholes; and people were ploughing in delicately balanced ecological areas. During a serious drought, cattle perished because communal areas had been overgrazed. The idea of stock limitation was floated, but Batswana had always had a right to own as many cattle as they could afford and a right to graze them on tribal land, so that was a non-starter. One could consider grazing control instead of controlling numbers of cattle, but such control could not be done without fences.

Some of us thought: We have plenty of land, and if we could provide exclusive access for those who could afford to drill boreholes and manage their farms, we might better preserve all of our land. Each farmer could make his own fire breaks, control his grazing, know when he should de-stock as grazing was diminished by drought, and so forth, since the land would be his alone to manage. Moving the large ranchers to new farms also would reduce pressure on communal areas.

All these concerns led to the examination of land utilisation, even during the Protectorate days. I was one of those who felt that a new system of managing the land would help us solve the problems. Alan Bent, an officer responsible for development before independence, was one of the first to look into it, followed by Bob Edwards, the future Kgosi Seepapitso, Rapontsheng Kalabeng, Luke Mosinyi, and some others. We talked about the subject with successive ministers of agriculture—Tsheko Tsheko, Amos Dambe and Setlhomo Edison Masisi—in the 1960s and 1970s. However, there were many difficulties and a big division of opinion. Any suggestion that involved exclusive, rather than communal, use made reform seem like a land grab by the rich. Some thought those who came first to establish boreholes would control the land, and those who came later would have nothing. Others argued that was not the case, since we were leasing the land for a fixed period, not giving freehold title. Also, just because one is a farmer, one's children may not wish to be farmers; if they live in a town they may want to sell their lease. The proponents of reform felt we should have three types of grazing land: common areas, leased TGLP areas, and areas that were not allocated but reserved for the future.

We envisaged that communal land would be undisturbed, but that unused land, where no boreholes existed and of which there was a good deal, would be cut into two parts. One part would be made available on leases to those who wanted to farm the land properly, and the other would be reserved for future generations. The tribe would receive rent from individuals or syndicates of farmers who were given exclusive use of land for TGLP ranches, provided they made the appropriate developments on it. An individual or group with exclusive rights would have the incentive to manage the land properly and to avoid overgrazing. Large owners were expected to move their cattle out of communal areas to TGLP ranches and leave the smaller owners—those who could not afford the fencing, boreholes and other management tools—on communal land. The decreased cattle population in the communal areas would reduce the overgrazing there.

We had to be very careful not only in what we proposed but also in how we went about proposing it, and we wanted to take the issue to the whole country. We undertook an exercise in 1975 that turned out to be our most comprehensive and expensive consultation: the radio learning campaign. We distributed thousands of small radios so people in every village could participate in the discussion and consultation. We trained more that 3,000 leaders for the radio learning groups, and each submitted forms collected after the meetings. More than 55,000 people participated in the learning groups. Over 25,000 written forms were analysed by the computer bureau, and we used the results as we discussed the ideas and their implementation.

After the radio learning campaign, tribes were again consulted, and ultimately TGLP was agreed in principle. The next step was to demarcate the areas in each tribal territory. In some areas, individuals had existing boreholes, and they were given TGLP leases if they applied for them, provided there were no other competing claims to that land. In other areas, there was to be immediate allocation. However, we encountered a number of serious implementation problems. In some areas that were thought to be unoccupied, we found people had been hunting or gathering or had settled there. Their claims had to be adjudicated before farms could be demarcated and leased. Then, for some reason, the survey instruments (spiro navigators) that the Ministry of Agriculture proposed for demarcation did not arrive in Botswana for many months.

Some people changed their minds during the delays in implementation. As in all democratic decisions, the minority have their say, but the majority have their way! Some who had thought they were in favour changed their minds when the concrete results of the decision started to become clear. People in the Kweneng saw that the initial allocations of land resulted in a very large percentage of the unused land in the Kweneng going to TGLP ranches. So, halfway through the process, the Kweneng *kgotla* just stopped further allocations. I sent Minister Kgabo to find out what was going on, and they told him: "Yes, we had initially agreed to this large allocation to TGLP, but we have changed our minds." That was, of course, their right: It was their land, held communally, until it was actually allocated and leased to an individual.

In the Central District, cattle barons who controlled many boreholes wanted to grab all the land, and there was naturally controversy about it. Mr Nwako was one who had not shared my view on the virtues of TGLP, but he had come around to support the general drift. In the discussions after TGLP was adopted, he and Mr Gaolese Koma brought us a new proposition. They argued that if X and Y wanted the right to drill boreholes in areas that were unoccupied, they should be given that right even without first receiving a TGLP lease. We didn't know who these hypothetical people X and Y might be, though we were sure they included Mr Nwako and Mr Koma! Of course, we refused.

I was a proponent of TGLP, since I felt the problem of degradation of the veld was very serious, and I still think it is. I thought once we had the allocation completed, we should have a land utilisation committee that would travel around to make sure the land was being used as it was intended. Obviously, one can't impose conditions on the use of tribal land, since it belongs to all; but one can do so if people have leased the exclusive right to use the land. The individual has been given the land to look after, and that implies obligations to look after it properly.

TGLP has had its critics, of course, both in Botswana and abroad. Some have said that the farms created too many fences, or the farms interfered with other traditional land uses, or TGLP was just a land grab by large cattle owners. Other criticisms were that fenced farms interfered with the movement of game, and, of course, there was the international lobby that wrote dramatic articles about the "fences of death" on which migrating animals became entangled and perished. As to the latter, I only look upon them with scorn. I have said, perhaps cynically, that those who harass us about game are those who have decimated their own wild animals and may just be jealous. Everyone is entitled to his or her own view, but to take a position that one's view is the only correct moral view, as our critics often have done, seems quite inappropriate. After all, we are a democratic country; we have adopted approaches we thought would solve a serious and difficult problem: that of managing land that is held in common. And, we have tried to adjust our policies as we learned during their implementation.

I remember driving through the night to meet one of the senior people from Sweden, Ernst Michanek of SIDA, who had been a major critic of our cattle policies. I wanted him to provide funds to fence the Western State Farms and the farm at Dong-Dong, and for the TGLP development projects in the Nojane area. Developing a paddock system, rotating cattle from paddock to paddock, and watering them at each place while the grass regenerated in the other paddocks, were crucial parts of the system. But one needed both the capital investment in fencing as well as improved management practices to ensure the maximum production from that area. I explained that we did not have adequate financing to support TGLP, and I asked for his assistance. He criticised me for coming to talk with him after people were already preparing to move into the area. He said I was just like all politicians: We promised people something when we didn't have the money. I then asked him which he would prefer: Should I propose a project when I did not know if people were ready to take it up, in which case he could complain that I did not yet have a viable project? Or did he want me to convince people to do it, and then tell him that our only constraint is the financing? He did not really have an answer, but he did become convinced that they should help us with the financing.

We had hoped and planned that the larger cattle owners would develop TGLP ranches and move their cattle from the overgrazed communal areas. That occurred in some areas, but in many others it didn't. The Western State Farms in the Nojane area were large enough to mop up all the cattle in the Ghanzi communal areas. But, those who developed the farms then restocked in their former areas. The same thing has happened in other places, and many of those with TGLP leases continue to graze cattle in the communal areas as well. We have never been able to adopt measures that would prevent TGLP lease holders from grazing their cattle on common land. I hope this change will come sooner rather than later.

Some of the TGLP farms have not yet been fully developed; critics have called them glorified cattle posts. We have not been as effective as we could have been in combining the leases with good extension services to promote better management and higher off-take of cattle for the market. But, a start has been made, and now those farms could be turned into what I would call real farms within a year. Some of those who took up TGLP farms had spent all their lives worrying about their cattle straying and becoming lost. So, their first emphasis was not on management but simply on containing their herds; the result was fenced farms that were not well managed. The price of fencing has doubled since allocations were made, so one wonders if the proper fencing and paddock systems will be completed.

My attitude to land and also to game is the same: We should semi-privatise both, with appropriate safeguards. People look after cattle because there is an economic reward to it. In the same way, if we allow people to look after the land, or to look after the game, and to keep the rewards from doing so, then they will manage and conserve the land and the game. Unfortunately, TGLP farms have not become the roaring success that some of us hoped they would be, but at least TGLP introduced and kept alive the idea of better husbandry; and I hope it will one day be highly sought after. In fact, the idea behind TGLP has been taking another form. In the early 1990s, farmers in the communal areas started to ask that they be divided into smaller farms so they could be better managed. Just before I left office, Land Boards started to make such allocations after consultation with the adjoining farmers. I think over time the TGLP concept will become the way we manage our land for grazing in Botswana.

Other Issues in Tribal Land Tenure

Banks would not make loans against the security of land held under tribal title, since they could not be sure the Land Boards would transfer title to them in the event of default. Therefore, to facilitate development, we developed a policy that tribal land could also be subject to common law leases. Title to the lease would be transferable, and the lease could be used as security for loans from the banks. In addition, Land Boards have allowed leased land to be transferred at a market price, but only to those who would be entitled to an allocation of tribal land. There was never a formal decision to do so; it just happened. So, in fact, we have evolved from the traditional tenure into a leasehold system, provided the land continues to be used for the purpose for which it was allocated: agricultural, residential, commercial, and so on. The only issue is whether the leases are registered under common law for a fixed period or whether the land is held indefinitely under tribal allocation. Common law leases have certain commercial advantages in being used as security for a loan. In fact, however, tribal title is more secure to the individual than leasehold title. Under tribal title, my great-grandfather's land is my land; nobody can challenge that. I can only lose it if I don't use it for some period of time. But in the case of a lease, I have it only for a period of years, and it could be terminated by the Land Board at the end of that time.

There are some special cases in tribal land, such as the leases of shorter duration in the Okavango and the Chobe for tourism. A number of years ago these leases were reallocated. Some people argued that we should not give a first right of refusal to those who had developed property under their previous lease. However, sanity prevailed, and those who were refused a renewal have tended to be those who had sat on the leased property without developing it. The new leases now have clear development obligations as a condition of the lease.

Since the Land Board system depends on human beings to make the decisions, there is, of course the prospect of wrong-doing, and our most famous case involved land in Mogoditshane. Rumours of questionable practices of land allocation in that area began to circulate, so in July 1991 I appointed a commission chaired by Mr Kgabo to look into the question of whether there had been inappropriate influence within government. The commission concluded that the allocation had happened inappropriately, as alleged. In addition, it found a number of other irregularities. I read the report and talked with the individuals involved. Two very senior ministers resigned from the cabinet, which was no small thing. But, for the good of both the country and the party it was the right thing to do. Both of them said publicly that they should be out of cabinet while further investigations were made and government took any action in the matter.

The Kgabo Commission made a number of other recommendations. It said all plots of land that had been allocated without appropriate authority should be repossessed by the Land Board, with reimbursement for any permanent improvements that had been made to the land. It also recommended that the Kweneng Land Board and the Thamaga Subordinate Land Board should be dissolved and be reconstituted with new members in order to restore confidence in the Land Board allocation process. Government accepted and implemented those recommendations.

Urban Land

At independence, the situation with urban land was very simple. There was adequate urban freehold land because there was so little urban development. However, our economic growth proceeded rapidly, and without agricultural development to hold people in the rural areas, almost every Motswana came to wish he or she could have a plot of land in the urban areas. Our success in overall economic development led to a shortage of urban land for virtually the whole time since independence.

The shortage of urban land was very severe by the 1980s. In Gaborone, the growth was beyond any expectation we could have had at independence. At the time of the 1984 General Elections, when Peter Mmusi was standing in one of the Gaborone constituencies, he talked of our plans to develop Gaborone West. At the time, the area west of the line of rail then held nothing but empty freehold farms. People accused him of just making election promises; but Gaborone West was quickly occupied, and we had to add more than twice the area soon after that. Later, when he was minister of local government and lands, he persuaded us that we should provide serviced urban land in all parts of the country, and we undertook a number of major projects. But even so, there has continued to be unmet demand.

I have explained our approach to low-income urban housing through site-and-service plots in Self Help Housing Areas (SHHAs). A key element of this approach was the adoption of a form of land tenure, a Certificate of Rights, very similar to the rights one would have to tribal land. One did not buy the land, nor could one sell it, but it could be inherited by one's family.

The shortage of urban land and the increase in its value have led to continued controversy about land policy. There have long been arguments that no one should be allowed to own more than one house, or one plot of land. There also have been strong feelings against allowing foreigners to own land anywhere in Botswana. It was natural that there should be such attitudes when by tradition land was seen as belonging to the people collectively, and every Motswana had a right to land for a home or for farming. Urban plots, however, were limited, and there has always been a political demand that newly available plots of serviced land be allocated and sold at only the cost of development. The price paid was less than if the land had been sold at auction to the highest bidder. At the same time, however, the market in existing plots of serviced land, houses and other buildings, operated freely. As prices increased rapidly over time, plots purchased through administrative allocation immediately commanded a higher price in the market. As a result, the excess demand for new plots continued.

I had personal experience with allocations of urban land. When Gaborone was new, everyone who lived there was assumed to be a temporary resident. We had a policy that as ministers we would live in institutional houses (i.e. those provided by government). We would not apply for plots of land in Gaborone. This policy continued until the late 1970s, by which time Gaborone had become a place where people were putting down roots; when one ceased to be a minister, one would be out of a house. So, the policy was changed to allow ministers to apply for plots like anyone else. I applied, and

I was allocated a plot opposite State House. The late president objected, since he did not want that plot privately owned. Mout Nwako kicked up a row on my behalf and asked: "Even by your vice-president?" But Seretse said I would not always be the vice-president, and another government might be elected in the future. Therefore, there should not be a private plot so close to State House. So, I applied again and another plot was allocated to me.

I had been developing and saving my resources for over 25 years, so I applied for a large plot, whereas most people had applied for small plots. A few years later, I was given permission to subdivide it into two plots, so I built two houses. I planned that I would rent them out in order to pay the mortgage bond, as many others were doing by that time, until I left politics and needed a home in Gaborone. A cousin of mine later told me he was travelling to Lobatse with another man, and as they passed a large house at Notwane, the fellow asked: "Is this one of the houses Quett is building with our money?" Many people just assumed that if I appeared to have material success, and I was in government, I must have used my position of influence to make it happen. While I often complain that our bureaucratic procedures have retarded our development, the point of such procedures is to be sure that politicians or civil servants do not take advantage of their positions, or do inappropriate things. I had to follow the rules just as any other Motswana would have to do.

While the growth of cities, especially Gaborone, put pressure on adjoining areas and led to problems such as the Mogoditshane land affair, it also resulted in private development on freehold farms adjacent to Gaborone. In one case, Ian Kirby, a lawyer who took citizenship after independence, bought freehold farms ten kilometres south of the city in the Gaborone block, and later turned them into smallholdings. But he also saw the potential for conservation, tourist development, environmental and wildlife education, employment, and protection of the areas adjacent to his personal land. The Kirbys gave a portion of their land to the Mokolodi Trust to be run on a non-profit basis. It was stocked with game, including elephants and rhinos, and the Trust runs a series of educational programmes along with game viewing, overnight accommodation and a restaurant. Since it is only a short distance from Gaborone, it has become an important attraction and destination for tourists and school groups, and Presidents Clinton and Bush each visited there when on state visits to Botswana. It developed a conference centre and created a good many jobs. The Kirbys provided a good example of what could be regarded as enlightened self-interest.

David Magang, another lawyer, proposed a major commercial and residential development at Phakalane, a freehold farm north of Gaborone. The late president refused to support the necessary changes in land use plans to make it possible for Mr Magang to develop his township. Seretse did so in part because he felt we could not approve Phakalane since we had refused a similar proposal at Notwane, and in part because he felt that others who owned farms around Gaborone would want to do the same thing. I felt the Notwane development had been properly denied for environmental reasons; the project was upstream of the Gaborone dam, and there was a serious risk of water pollution. The pollution problem did not seem to apply to Phakalane, since it was downstream of Gaborone, so I had sympathy for Mr Magang. After I became president, Mr Kgabo as the minister, and Peter Molosi, the PS in the Ministry of Local Government and Lands, and I pursued the changes in land use plans so Mr Magang could develop Phakalane. It has helped to ease the land pressure in Gaborone, and he deserves praise for what he has done with the development there.

In the course of the development, Mr Magang had to put up a water tower, provide sewerage treatment, and all the rest. When the project was underway, the city of Gaborone proposed to take over the infrastructure and manage it as part of the larger urban area. Mr Magang agreed, but the city refused to refund him payment for the cost of the water tower. He came to me to ask me to issue a presidential directive to require Gaborone to pay him for all the improvements. I told him that, if there was a dispute, it was not a policy matter but a legal matter; it should be up to the courts to decide. He has never forgiven me for that decision. At the opening of his new development, he even talked about how those in authority totally disregarded the efforts of those who want to make Botswana a better country. It was obvious about whom he was talking. It was not enough that I had made it possible for him to go ahead in the first place. But despite his criticism of me, if I had to do it again, I would make the same decisions.

Any system of land tenure has its drawbacks. The potential for abuse is always present when land is allocated administratively, whether by government officials or by a Land Board. However, since ownership of most of our land is vested in the community rather than the individual, inequities and misallocations can be corrected over time. In a country that was developing fast, especially where there were inequalities in the beginning, a purely free market system would have its problems as well. The continuing issues of land ownership in Zimbabwe, South Africa, Kenya, and other African countries with a colonial heritage illustrate the problems when a heavy reliance is placed on freehold land tenure, and where the only basis for land transfer is the market price. On balance, I think we developed a good system for a reasonably equitable allocation of land and land use that supports our development efforts.

Cattle (*Moraka*)

Cattle have played a major social and economic role in Botswana throughout our history. We have always been sentimental about our cattle; even though their relative importance in both social and economic terms has declined, the sentiment remains. Changes have taken place somewhat imperceptibly, and despite the fact that times have changed, there are still old folks like me who think in terms of *moraka*.

Cattle were the backbone of Botswana's economy in 1965, and cattle affected everybody's lives. Until the late 1960s, exports of cattle, beef and livestock products accounted for more than 75% of our total export earnings. Income from cattle, including milk consumed by households, amounted to more than half of rural people's incomes. More than 90% of our total population was rural and 70-80% of rural households had some cattle. Those who did not own cattle either worked for those who did, or they would use the *mafisa* system. Under *mafisa*, owners of cattle would arrange for others to look after their cattle. In exchange, those caring for the cattle could use them to plough their own lands, or as draft power for haulage, and could drink their milk. In some cases, those caring for cattle under *mafisa* could keep some of the calves and start their own herds. The disappearance of cattle in those days would be like the disappearance of diamonds from today's Botswana. Whether one did or did not own them, one knew that life depended on cattle.

If one reads through the debates in Legco, one will see how all of us—white and black, colonial officials and locals—talked about the need to develop and improve cattle husbandry and increase income from cattle. It was the basis of the economy; cattle were valuable in themselves as well as essential for cultivating the lands and for transporting goods. Those who argued for the welfare of their cattle were also talking of the welfare of the whole country. At the time, cattle were all we had and all we could look forward to.

Cattle also were the place where we would save our assets; they were like our bank accounts. If one had extra money, one bought cattle; if one needed money for school fees, or a wedding, or a funeral, one sold cattle. If someone raised a loan to start a business, he was likely to use part of the loan to buy a few cattle. We are social beings; the way of measuring one's wealth was seen to be how many cattle one owned. So, one wanted to be seen to be owning cattle, even if one may not have believed in them as the best investment.

As we thought about development projects related to cattle, we felt that the public good should be served. If people could help themselves with the assistance of development projects, and they could make cattle more profitable, that would be a good thing. While more families raised crops than owned cattle, income from the lands was only 10-25% of rural household incomes, depending on whether the rains were bad or good. Cattle, being already a much more important source of incomes, seemed a promising area to help people become better off.

I had known well before independence that the 16 government ranches around the country had proved beyond doubt that one could double the calving rate achieved under traditional methods with very simple management measures. Under better management, farmers could afford to lease land and pay for improvements. That, of course, was the origin of TGLP. With the help of donor funds, we were able to provide assistance in the form of loans for improvements and advice in management for farmers who wanted to ranch in a modern fashion on TGLP ranches.

With economic development, we have moved into a period where small cattle holdings are increasingly unviable. Since almost all children are now in school, and some 70% of all able-bodied people are in wage employment, the only people who are available to look after cattle are those who are paid to do so. Therefore, they must be paid a wage that is commensurate with what those of comparable education are earning in town. Many large cattle owners still lack management skills, and their off-take rate is still low, so they do not earn the income they could. Ultimately, the economic realities will force farmers to manage well or to leave farming.

Controlling Animal Diseases
Combating communicable diseases such as Anthrax, Foot and Mouth Disease (FMD), contagious abortion, quarter evil (or blackleg) and so forth, has been crucial to the whole nation. If these diseases develop in a single herd, they spread rapidly, as has happened many times in our history. Everyone in the country has known the dangers of these diseases and the need to take measures to control them. We decided early on to make inoculations free of charge rather than take a risk that a farmer would try to save money by not vaccinating. Some of the young experts from other countries did not understand why we were doing this, and we were sometimes accused of subsidising large farmers. However, we wanted to make certain that every animal was properly vaccinated.

An outbreak of Foot and Mouth Disease has an immediate effect throughout the country, not only in the infected areas. Once there is an outbreak, we have to stop all movement of cattle in order to inhibit the transmission of the disease. The director of veterinary services will announce: "From tonight, all movement of cattle must cease." And, everyone must obey. The abattoirs close, there can be no slaughter and no sale of meat until things are cleared by the veterinary officers. When they determine that the disease is confined, the uninfected areas are free to transact business; but while it is not confined, the movement of cattle is forbidden throughout the country. This means movement for all purposes: cattle going to the lands to plough, cattle being used for transport, cattle moving to slaughter for local consumption, the whole lot. The system of cordon fences we developed throughout the country meant we could permit movement within disease-free areas while containing the disease.

Because our most valuable market has been the European Union (EU), we have had to do everything in accordance with the veterinary regulations of the EU. We have earned ourselves a good name for the way we treat animal diseases, so we have retained access to good markets for our best quality beef. The development of cordon fences to meet EU requirements was critical for the livestock industry as well as the entire rural economy. While other African countries were looked at askance for being unable to control disease and have been denied the European market, it was because of these stringent controls that we were given the green light.

FMD is highly contagious, but it is not fatal to cattle. Cattle lose condition for a period of time, but they recover. However, when there is an outbreak of FMD, farmers immediately lose cash income. They cannot sell cattle, but all their other operating costs, for diesel to operate boreholes, for wages, for supplementary feeding, and so forth, continue. In 1977, we had our first serious outbreak since the one at independence. Fortunately, we were in a better financial condition, so we established a programme to provide loans of P50 per beast to carry farmers over until cattle movement and cattle sales could start again. We chose P50 in part because even a beast of low grade would fetch at least that much when it was sold at the abattoir. Cattle were branded when they were used as security for the loans, and the loan was repaid as the first claim when the cattle were sold to the BMC. Of course, there were some financial risks to government. However, given the importance of cattle to the whole rural economy, we felt it was the right thing to do.

In the late 1990s, an outbreak of cattle lung disease in Ngamiland created a very serious economic, social and ultimately political issue. The disease gets into the lungs of bovines. They are permanently impaired, and they also become permanent carriers, though the disease is not infectious to humans. The initial infections came from neglect of the fences between us and Namibia. We had tried to create a buffer zone with fences to confine cattle until we had done the necessary veterinary diagnostics. But some people started moving their cattle beyond the buffer zones, so we had to establish another fence, and so forth. The whole of the Maun area was affected very quickly.

There were some interesting issues at the time between politicians and officials. Roy Blackbeard was the minister of agriculture, and he visited Ngamiland and found that the pumping system from the river to Kgomo-Kgwana was badly designed. There was no back up, and if the pump had failed, it could have caused the death of thousands of cattle before we could provide a replacement. The minister happened to have a spare pump at his farm, so he took it there as a backup. On another occasion, Ronald Sebego, the assistant minister of agriculture, supervised the loading of pipes to make sure they got to an area needing more water. In both cases, senior officials came to me to complain: "Ministers are taking over from officials." But I said: "Now look, we can't just let things stall when there are obvious solutions. If those responsible are not doing the job, anyone including ministers should be free to help."

We ultimately learned that nothing short of killing the cattle would solve the problem. Until we killed all the cattle in the area, the disease would continue to spread throughout the country. We knew that if government was to take people's cattle and kill them, we would need to have some system of compensation for the farmers. The first approach we developed was a plan that farmers would be paid P500 each for the first 25% of the beasts, irrespective of the condition or type—oxen, bull, heifer, or calf. The balance of the compensation would be provided by replacement stock. Then as the programme expanded to the hundreds of thousands of head of cattle, we became concerned about where we could find the replacement stock, so we reversed the proportions to 75% cash and 25% replacement.

Once we had decided what needed to be done, officials advised that I should delay making the announcement about killing the cattle until after the forthcoming Easter Holidays. However, I did not want any word to leak before I had the chance to talk to people directly, so I did not delay. I went to the Maun *kgotla* to announce what was to be done, and after I had told the people, I was a lucky fellow to have got out alive! The initial political reaction was very violent.

Mr Sebego went to talk at the Xamasere *kgotla*, and he was almost crucified by the crowd. However, we were helped there by a shopkeeper who said: "This is certainly something that has not happened by design but by accident. But, we might come out better off. First, we have never sold cattle for P500, and this time we get P500 whether it is a calf or a cow or an ox. Second, we have been promised that we shall have replacement cattle, and these will certainly be better than any we have had here." This was an example of the common sense of many of our people. While others may have thought it, he was the only one brave enough to say it. Many people now feel that our response to the outbreak was one of the best things that could have happened to that part of the country, as the new cattle there are of much higher quality. Politically, we figured we would lose the constituency in the 1999 elections, but we felt we had to adopt the right policy to benefit the whole country regardless of the political consequences.

Cattle and Politics
Today, despite the fact that our overall economy has developed and become more diversified, most Batswana still think in terms of owning cattle, and nearly half of all rural households still do so. Therefore, cattle continue to remain an important sector in the economy of Botswana. In economic terms, cattle may not be as large a proportionate contributor to national income, but in social terms they are very important and are still an index of wealth. Many more people consider their economic interests are directly related to cattle than to diamonds, even though diamonds are much larger in national income and affect everyone's welfare to a much greater extent.

Cattle have always been important in politics and one often hears cynical remarks about "the cattle lobby" in Botswana. But, it would be very strange if there were not a lobby for cattle in this country. It is a lobby as there is a lobby for other parts of the economy—transport providers, industrialists, employers, unions, and the like. This is a normal part of the democratic process. In the early years, many supporters of *Domkrag* were farmers, of course, since almost all Batswana farmed. The opposition parties may talk about the BDP being the party of cattle owners, most of their leaders are quite happy to own cattle. Kenneth Koma's father was said to have been a cattle baron, though Mr Koma claims to be a socialist. K. T. Motsete, a founder of the BPP, was reputed to be a major cattle owner, and Chief Bathoen, of course, had many, many cattle. *Domkrag* certainly has had no monopoly on the cattle owners of the country.

Late politics

With President Jomo Kenyatta and African Finance Ministers (I'm third from the left in the front row).

As OAU Vice-Chairman at a meeting in Addis.

With Quill Hermans (to my right) and Festus Mogae (taking notes behind us) at a World Bank-IMF meeting.

Speaking at Sir Seretse Khama's funeral in Serowe, 1980, during a difficult time for our young nation.

Being sworn in as President in 1980 by Chief Justice Hayfron-Benjamin.

An official presidential portrait.

With His Royal Highness the Duke of Kent.

MmaGaone and I greet Chief Justice Moleleki Mokama and Mr Speaker Moutlakgola Nwako after my swearing-in ceremony in 1994.

A meeting with Somora Machel in Gaborone. Some of Botswana's ministers in attendance included Archie Mogwe, Colin Blackbeard, and Ketshabile Disele.

Dancing with MmaGaone; as President I was always on hand to open the dance floor.

A Front Line Heads of State meeting (L-R): Vice President Dos Santos representing Mozambique, and Presidents Neto, Nyerere, Kaunda and Masire.

With President Chissano on his State Visit to Botswana.

Receiving flowers at the Indian High Commission.

With Ian Khama, MmaGaone and Mompati Merafhe in front of a new BDF helicopter.

With German President von Weizsäcker and the two first ladies in Bonn, Germany, 1985.

As Chancellor of the University of Botswana conferring an Honorary Degree on Isaac Schapera, as Lebang Mpotokwane, Chairman of the Council, and Professor Thomas Tlou, Vice Chancellor, look on.

With MmaGaone and Lady Ruth Khama at a State Banquet in Gaborone.

Receiving the Naledi ya Botswana award from Vice President Peter Mmusi in 1986.

With President von Weizsäcker and Botswana's Foreign Minister, Dr Gaositwe Chiepe, during our 1991 visit to Germany.

With Boutros Boutros-Ghali, UN Secretary General.

With long-time friend Quill Hermans, founding Governor of the Bank of Botswana.

Calling on the Japanese Emperor in Tokyo.

With HRH Princess Diana and MmaGaone in the UK.

With Margaret Thatcher at No. 10 Downing Street, London.

Chatting with Baroness Chalker.

An audience with Pope John Paul II at the Vatican, 1996.

President Diouf welcoming us on a State Visit to Senegal in 1996.

Receiving an Honorary Degree of Doctor of Laws at Carleton College, Minnesota, USA, in 1996.

With Professor Stephen R. Lewis, Jr., President of Carleton College, 1996.

Exchanging our nations' highest honours with Nelson Mandela in Cape Town, 1996, while MmaGaone looks on. I received the Order of Good Hope and President Mandela received the Naledi ya Botswana.

With President Jacques Chirac in Paris, 1997.

Introducing President Bill Clinton at the start of his State Visit to Botswana in 1998.

Family and friends with President and Mrs Clinton at State House, 1998.

Official portrait as Chancellor of the University of Botswana.

At a diplomatic reception hosted by President Mogae, with Foreign Minister Mompati Merafhe at right.

With President Mandela during a visit to Botswana.

Holding the Vision 2016 torch in Gaborone with members of the Vision Council (L-R): Professor Sheila Tlou, now Minister of Health, Dr Gloria Somolakae, then Vision Chairperson, and Dr Collie Bathusi Monkge, Vision CEO.

With UN Secretary General Kofi Annan.

An informal chat with President Mogae.

Addressing a BDP final farewell party in Gaborone, 1998.

After retirement, I had an opportunity to show President Mogae my new cabbage farm at Mamokhasi.

Family and friends during my 80th birthday party, 23 July 2005.

Our grandchildren at my 80th birthday.

Chapter 15
Diamonds and Other Minerals

One of the major issues we faced as an independent government was the ownership of mineral rights. We in the Democratic Party believed that minerals belonged to the whole nation, not just to one part, so mineral rights should be vested in the state. Before independence, mineral rights belonged to the owner of the land. Since most land in Botswana was under tribal ownership, the biggest challenge was to change the ownership from tribe to nation. Fortunately, because we did not have a large number of private concessions, unlike many other former colonies, we did not have a major problem in finding ways to vest private mineral rights in the state. Of course, rights on state land, formerly Crown land, were not a problem. After we had dealt with the ownership of mineral rights, we needed to establish a legal framework for exploration and mining and decide how we would manage the financial and other arrangements with companies that wished to explore for and mine our minerals.

Ownership of Mineral Rights
Since the real issue was mineral rights in tribal areas, we pursued the transfer of mineral rights in stages, and we did so with full consultation with our people. We began our national discussion of mineral rights in the African Council through the work of a committee on local government. The committee's report recommended that mineral rights should move from the tribes to the central government. It noted that only one tribe had agreed by June 1964, and that "the matter had not yet been fully discussed by all tribes."

In the 1950s, Tshekedi Khama had discussed the rights to mine copper and nickel in the Ngwato territory with the Roan Selection Trust (RST) of Rhodesia. He convinced the tribe to grant RST a mining concession, and in 1959, three days before he died, Tshekedi signed an agreement with RST creating Bamangwato Concessions Limited (BCL), which eventually led to our first large mining development. It was fortunate that the first mineral indications were in Central District, the former Bangwato Reserve, where the Bangwato tribe held the land. Seretse was able to go to his tribe in 1965 not just as prime minister, but also as the man most Bangwato still considered their chief. His view was: "Let us share any wealth we find underground with the whole nation, irrespective of where it is found." He proposed that the tribe cede the mineral rights to the government of the nation. They discussed the matter fully and agreed, and Seretse talked with the chiefs of the other tribes one by one. The others seemed to think: "Well, if he and his people have given their rights to the state, why should we not do so also?" We also were fortunate that at that time there was not even a rumour of any possible minerals other than in the Bangwato area. We took the issue to the BDP Congress, and they, too, accepted the idea of transfer of mineral rights from the tribes to the state.

However, after the tribes had made the preliminary decision to surrender their mineral rights to the state, Chief Bathoen changed his mind. He went to see the Queen's commissioner, by then Sir Hugh Norman-Walker. The commissioner asked what it was about, and when Chief Bathoen said he wished to discuss mineral rights, Sir Hugh said: "We are only in charge of foreign affairs and finance; the country is run by the Democratic Party. I can only see you if you are with the prime minister." When the matter came to Seretse, he said: "Quett, go and talk with your chief." Chief Bathoen was very disappointed that I was the one to meet with him and not Seretse. We discussed the matter, and he made his points. I was able to take apart each one of his points, and after that he dropped the matter. In fact, I never enjoyed a tussle with my chief as much as I did that day.

It took time to complete the process, of course, since full consultation with each tribe was needed. In fact, it was not until 30 March 1967, six months after independence, that I announced in the House that the president had attended Ngwato *kgotla* in Serowe the day before, where the tribe had agreed to the Central District Council's recommendation that their mineral rights should be ceded to government.

Between April and July 1967, the tribes signed vesting agreements with the late president on behalf of the government. Englishman Kgabo as minister of local government and lands brought the Mineral Rights in Tribal Territories Bill to the House later in 1967. The House of Chiefs unanimously agreed that the Bill be allowed to pass.

The law ceding mineral rights to the nation was terribly important; it ensured that an issue that could have been very divisive never was allowed to arise. One only had to look at the effects of regional and tribal conflicts over natural resources in other countries to know we had to deal with the issue and put it to rest if we were to unify the nation.

After we had dealt with tribal mineral rights, we turned to the freehold areas. Gold had been discovered in the Tati Concession near Francistown before the Bechuanaland Protectorate existed, but production at the Monarch mine had peaked and run out long before our independence. There were private mineral rights in some of the Tuli Block farms. In dealing with the latter, we sought the help of Roland Brown, a British lawyer who had been attorney general in Tanzania. He came up with an approach: Since minerals under the ground were national assets, they should be taxed as such, and the owner of the land could write off exploration costs against any tax owed. Since this was unlikely to be an economic proposition for the owners, they voluntarily surrendered their mineral rights to the state in the years after independence.

The rights of the Tati Company were more complicated. Unlike the Tuli Block farmers for whom mineral rights were an incidental part of the asset, the Tati owners were speculating in mineral rights and wanted to strike a hard bargain. They were very difficult, and we did not complete negotiations to acquire their rights until well into the 1980s.

Even before we understood our potential mineral wealth, we knew that vesting mineral rights in the state would be critical for both our overall economic development and our political unity and stability. It was well worth the years of discussion and negotiation to have achieved that goal without resort to nationalisation or forcing a decision of the majority on an unwilling minority.

Mining Legislation
Once we had vested mineral rights for most areas in the state, we needed to establish a legal basis for prospecting and mining companies. We knew we had to provide investors with a reasonable return if we were to expect them to come to Botswana to prospect and to develop any deposits they found. But we also needed to ensure that any mineral development benefited the nation as a whole. We solicited advice from international experts in drafting the legislation, and the resulting Mines and Minerals Act was passed in 1967. Adjustments were subsequently made in the legislation in 1976 and 1977, and we adopted legislation to govern exploration and development of petroleum in the early 1980s.

The 1967 Mines and Minerals Act provided for prospecting licenses of limited duration and required minimum prospecting programmes and expenditures. Investors could not keep a potential deposit off the market and fail to develop it. After a prospect had been found, application had to be made for a mining lease. An investor was required to propose detailed plans for mining, marketing, financing and infrastructure. We felt that each potential mineral project would be unique. Therefore, each project should have its own specific provisions on the scale of the operation, marketing, design of the infrastructure, royalties, and so forth. The wide scope of discretion in the Act was troubling to some investors who preferred to know the terms on which a lease would be issued before they invested in prospecting.

A mining lease was specified to have a 25-year maximum duration, and it could be renewed on terms agreed by the government. The minister responsible for minerals was listed as the authority in the Act, but in practice all major developments were submitted to cabinet for approval. Seretse made sure this practice was followed from the beginning, so that the full cabinet would know the terms of any lease and would agree to it, and it was a practice I followed while I was in office.

Negotiating Mining Agreements
Early on we developed an approach to mining agreements that served us well. We created a Mineral Policy Committee (MPC), composed of four officials: the permanent secretaries for minerals and for finance; a senior official of the Office of the President; and the attorney general. They made use of other technical experts on mining, water, geology, finance and law. The minister responsible for mineral resources, acting on advice of the MPC, would propose overall objectives and a negotiating strategy to cabinet, and cabinet would amend or approve that strategy. The dealings with the mining companies were carried out by the civil servants on the MPC. It was agreed that if we reached an impasse at the official level, the minister or someone

higher could come in to bail out the officials. When I was vice-president I was designated as the one to meet with Harry Oppenheimer from De Beers to break any deadlock at ministerial level, and it was understood that if I came to an impasse, Seretse would be called upon. De Beers and other mining companies followed a similar approach. Harry Oppenheimer or his equivalent would stand ready to come in to break a deadlock. In fact, our process worked so well we never needed these measures; the negotiating teams from government were always able to settle the terms.

As with other policy issues, politicians, civil servants and other technicians worked closely together, and this was the source of our strength. We tried to ensure that ministers fully understood the technical issues and the consequences of the choices, and that the officials who were in the actual negotiations understood the political dimensions of their negotiating brief. We wanted to avoid the prospect either of officials being undermined by ill-informed politicians, or of politicians thinking they had been sold a bill of goods by officials. This process also provided transparency within government: Since the whole cabinet was involved, and since each PS had to advise his or her minister, the possibilities for collusion or corruption were minimised.

The Shashe Project

Our first ray of hope for a major mining project was at Matsitama in the BCL concession that Tshekedi Khama had signed in 1959. When RST finally decided to go ahead, however, it was to mine the deposits at Selebi-Phikwe, not at Matsitama. The overall development—mine, township, dam on the Shashe River, and other infrastructure—became known as the Shashe project. In 1966, I said in the House: "The Shashe Complex, as we are calling it, is a major development scheme, capable in the next ten years of making a dramatic impact on the economy of Botswana."

The Shashe project gave us not only a mine with many jobs but also the opportunity to develop infrastructure, a new urban centre, modern parastatal organisations to produce and deliver electricity and water, and exploitation of coal deposits at Morupule for the power station.

The negotiations on the Shashe Project were long and complex. It was a very, very large project for our economy. The original investment was P160 million. Our *total* national income in 1968-69, the year before investment began, was P50 million! The financing package involved the World Bank, USAID, Kreditanstalt für Wiederafbau and a consortium of German banks (since the Germans were interested in securing the nickel from the project), an export credit from the IDC in South Africa, commercial bank credits, and loans and equity investments by the Anglo-American Corporation (De Beers' sister company) and American Metal Climax (AMAX), which had taken over the RST investment. AMAX planned to use its refinery in the USA to do the final processing of the copper-nickel-cobalt matte that was produced by the mine. A public company, Botswana RST, controlled by Anglo and AMAX, owned 85% of BCL, and Botswana RST shares traded on stock exchanges in London, Johannesburg and New York. Some of the loans were guaranteed by the German and South African governments. The agreements ran to thousands of pages.

There was obviously no possibility Botswana could guarantee the repayment of loans as large as those required by the project. Therefore, the agreements also involved guarantees of various kinds from Anglo and AMAX, the major investors. We ultimately achieved our objective of shifting all the commercial risk either to Anglo and AMAX or to the government guarantors of the German and South African loans. Botswana received 15% of the equity in BCL as part of the compensation for granting the mining lease. We were also entitled to royalties based on the value of the metals in the matte and to income tax on profits of the mining company. Our team of negotiators, led by Quill Hermans, succeeded very well in protecting Botswana's interests in the project, informing cabinet of the progress at every stage of the negotiations.

The German government was very difficult, and at one point Quill and I made an emergency trip to Germany. When we arrived at the airport in Germany, I found I had come with a temporary passport that did not have a German visa. The immigration officials were not very cooperative; one even said to me: "Do you think Germany is your farm and you can just come in and out as you please?" We were eventually admitted, and I later joked about our experience with Helmut Schmidt, who was then their minister of finance.

Hugh Murray-Hudson, who had previously done a good job managing the development of Gaborone, headed the Shashe Project Management Unit in government that oversaw our responsibilities for the infrastructure: the township at Selebi-Phikwe, the water, power, roads and the like. All parts of the project for which government was responsible were completed on time and within their budgets.

We were dealing with two of the largest mining companies in the world, but one risk we had not properly evaluated was that they would not be able to develop the mine and its smelter properly. In fact, the original smelter failed; the mining and smelting portion of the project cost more than twice the initial estimates; and production and sales were delayed. The target level of output was not reached until the eighth year of operation. Before the mine achieved full production, it was headed for bankruptcy. What had been our hope for a profitable mine that would add to government revenue as well as to productive employment turned into one of our greatest disappointments. We received little royalty, and we never received taxes from the mine or dividends on our equity. We learned some valuable if costly lessons, including the importance of ensuring that foreign investors could not abandon a bad project and leave the host country with the liabilities.

Nonetheless, despite the disappointing results for BCL, the Shashe project contributed substantially to achieving our financial independence. Because of the revised revenue arrangements in the 1969 Customs Union Agreement, our customs revenue depended on the value of our imports, regardless of the country of origin. The hundreds of millions of pula of imports for the development and operation of the mine and infrastructure generated tens of millions of pula in customs revenue for Botswana. In addition to the revenue, of course, we had developed another major urban area; we created over 4,000 new jobs in the mine and smelter; and we established the Botswana Power Corporation and the Water Utilities Corporation as major parastatals.

Diamonds

We had dealt with the Anglo-American/De Beers group of companies since the 1950s. While I was in politics, Anglo-American was one of the world's largest mining companies and the world's largest producer of gold, and it controlled many industrial companies in South Africa. It also operated mining and other ventures either directly or through sister companies in many parts of the world. De Beers was the world's largest producer of diamonds, and it controlled most of the world market through its Central Selling Organisation (CSO). Anglo and De Beers had large share holdings in one another, and both were controlled by the Oppenheimer family. While the companies were separate legal entities, we always knew that we were dealing with one organisation. The group's interests in Botswana eventually included BCL and the Shashe Project, our diamond mines, the soda ash project at Sowa Pan, and the coal mines at Morupule.

De Beers began to explore for diamonds in the Protectorate in 1955. Shortly before independence, Harry Oppenheimer, then chairman of both Anglo and De Beers, told Seretse and Peter Fawcus in confidence that De Beers believed it had found a viable deposit of diamond-bearing kimberlite at Orapa in the Central District. This discovery was publicly announced in 1967. We were pursuing the Shashe Project at the time, so De Beers undertook the financing and execution of the entire diamond project, including infrastructure, mine, and township. Orapa was developed as a closed town; for reasons of diamond security, permission was needed for anyone to visit the township. Only mine employees, township staff, and their families were permitted to live there. Production began in 1971, and full production of 2.5 million carats per year was reached by 1972. Orapa then provided over 10% of government revenues and one-third of our export earnings.

In reaching our agreement with De Beers, Quill Hermans again led our negotiating team, with legal and other experts as consultants. The pattern of fiscal arrangements at Orapa was similar to those at BCL. Government received 15% of the equity in the mining company in exchange for granting the mining lease, a 10% royalty on diamond sales, and income tax on the profits of the mine. It seemed at the time to be a very fair deal.

Diamond Strategy

We debated within government whether or not we should mine the diamonds from the ground as quickly as possible. We discussed the question first in the 1960s, and then again after diamonds were discovered at Jwaneng in 1976. To mine the diamonds quickly might give the appearance that we were wealthy, and we might later on find that the diamonds were exhausted and we had nothing to live on. Would it not be wise to mine them on a slower basis? We realised, however, that we were dealing with a commodity that had a fictitious or ephemeral value. Therefore, the sooner we could get the diamonds out of the ground, sell them, and conserve the value in another form, the better. The money that came from diamonds was our capital; it needed to be converted from a resource underground to a resource above the ground. If we used the revenue for consumption, then we were really consuming capital; it would be like eating a dairy cow that should have been saved for milking rather than eaten as beef.

However, we did not have the capacity to absorb the money immediately and convert all of it into productive assets in Botswana. Therefore, we did a number of things. First, we had the development budget, where funds could be appropriated immediately and then spent as projects were ready for implementation. We could also use part of the funds to increase our absorptive capacity, which would then generate alternative sources of wealth in the country. Naturally, we had to be careful, since we knew there would be political demands for projects that would not necessarily be economically viable. We also appropriated funds to the Revenue Stabilisation Fund (RSF), the Public Debt Service Fund (PDSF), and the Productive Employment Development Fund to support the Financial Assistance Policy, and we ultimately built a long-term reserve of financial assets outside the country in the form of the Pula Fund.

Relations with De Beers
Soon after Orapa opened, we realised that De Beers had not told us their true assessment of the potential of Botswana as a diamond producer. Kimberlite pipes, in which all diamonds had originally been formed, come in provinces, or clusters, that contain many pipes. The fact that there was an Orapa province suggested there might be others in Botswana, too. Another kimberlite province was discovered in Jwaneng in the south. I'm sure De Beers also knew long before we did the exceptional long-term potential of the Jwaneng deposit, which they announced to us in 1976.

Shortly after production at Orapa reached its capacity, De Beers decided world demand was such that we should increase production of diamonds in Botswana. De Beers asked for amendments to our agreement in order to develop new deposits at Letlhakane, just south of Orapa. Letlhakane was much smaller but contained a higher proportion of gemstones, which were De Beers' main interest. They also proposed to double the production at Orapa; the surface area of the pipe at Orapa is the second largest of any pipe in the world. Long before De Beers came with this new proposal, we had concluded that De Beers had not told us of Orapa's true potential in order to obtain a good deal from us. The original Orapa agreement provided for renegotiation of the terms if there were extraordinary circumstances. As soon as De Beers proposed amendments to the agreements, we took advantage of the opportunity to obtain our fair share.

The re-negotiation of the Orapa agreements was completed in 1975. It provided for new financial and governance arrangements for all of the mines operated by the mining company, which we called Debswana. The arrangements provided for the shareholding in the company to be exactly 50/50 between De Beers and government, with no casting vote for a chairman. It is a partnership; therefore both sides had to agree on anything important, and one side could neither act unilaterally nor wash its hands of the affair. We did not push for majority control. We were aware of what was happening in Zambia during the 1970s. When copper prices fell, difficult decisions on output and employment had to be made, and major financial resources had to be found to sustain the Zambian copper mines. The Zambian government had by then taken majority control of the copper mines, while Anglo retained a minority interest and a management agreement. As minority shareholders, Anglo and the other foreign investors had no responsibility for making the choices or finding resources. The Anglo people told us they were glad they no longer had such responsibility. In addition, we saw the problems we were having with the private investors in BCL, and we did not want to add to our difficulties.

We also had concluded that there need be no direct connection between the proportions of shareholdings, and the proportion of investment each party contributed, or the split of the profits from the mine. The 1975 agreements between government and De Beers provided for 50/50 shareholding, 100% of the investment to be provided by De Beers, and three-quarters of the profits to come back to government as the owner of the minerals (some as royalty, some as tax, and some as dividends). As a result of the 1975 agreements, production doubled to about five million carats by 1980, just in time to catch the boom in the diamond markets in 1978-80. Diamonds then provided half of our export earnings and one-third of government revenue.

The profitability and the size of our diamond deposits meant there was a great deal of money at stake in each of these negotiations. Baledzi Gaolathe, then PS responsible for minerals, led the negotiating team in 1975. The negotiations were very heated, difficult and protracted. In addition to the arguments with the De Beers side, we also had differences of opinion within the government side. We debated the overall approach, the strategy, the trade-offs among different objectives, how far we should go in concessions or in pushing the other side, and so forth. Our negotiating approach—the MPC as the negotiators working under a mandate from cabinet—served us well. De Beers tried to take advantage of us in various ways such as selectively giving information to politicians who were not part of the negotiating team. However, we retained a disciplined approach and were, I think, quite successful.

Shortly after the 1975 agreements were signed, an article that was clearly inspired by De Beers appeared in the *Financial Times* of London. Its headline read: "Botswana Joins the Rapacious League". The article made the allegation that Botswana was unreasonable in dealing with foreign mining companies, citing the deal with De Beers as an example. But, of course, De Beers made hundreds of millions of dollars of profits from Botswana's diamonds under the agreements they called rapacious.

Marketing Our Diamonds

Since the 19th century, producers of diamonds had tried to control the supply in order to maintain high and stable prices. The Central Selling Organisation (CSO), controlled by De Beers, was established in the 1930s to purchase diamonds from most major suppliers on long-term contracts. The CSO also bought diamonds on the open market in some producing areas in order to maintain its control. The CSO had long-term relationships with manufacturers who purchased rough diamonds to cut and polish them. For many years, over 80% of the world's rough diamond production went through the CSO. As part of the agreement with the CSO, most producers, including South Africa and Namibia, had provisions whereby the CSO could limit its purchases to a fixed quota, based on each mine's production capacity, when markets were weak. As a result, producers would have to either stockpile diamonds that had been mined, or reduce their production. We agreed to sell Botswana's diamonds through the CSO, subject to sales contracts that were periodically re-negotiated. We received a quota based on Debswana's production capacity.

Given the nature of the diamond trade, many people have said that if De Beers' CSO hadn't existed, we would have wanted to invent it so that prices would be stabilised in the marketplace. Each diamond mine produced a different assortment of diamonds in terms of size, colour, quality and value. Each manufacturer who cut and polished diamonds specialised in a particular size or quality or type of diamond. Demand fluctuated with the incomes of the countries that buy gem diamonds, and supplies of each type of diamond changed as new mines were discovered or old ones depleted. The CSO matched these differences and stabilised the market over time, largely by adding to or reducing its large stockpile of rough diamonds.

Diamonds are a highly specialised commodity. Two diamonds that look identical to a layman could have values in the market that differ by five or ten times. No one but an expert can say because diamond A was sold for so much, so, too, should diamond B. Sorting and valuing was complex; by the 1970s the price book at the CSO had thousands of categories of diamonds, with a different price per carat on each one, depending on size, type, colour, imperfections, and so forth. We needed a mechanism to ensure that Debswana was getting the right value for the diamonds when they were sold to the CSO, and that government would therefore receive the appropriate revenue. We decided to hire someone who was independent and knowledgeable, and we found a firm of specialists to do a "check valuation" of the diamonds after they had been sorted and valued. We did our best to ensure that we were being treated fairly by De Beers. However, in the diamond business, it seemed everyone knew everyone else. One could never be sure one was finding someone who was truly independent who would give us unbiased valuations.

As part of the 1975 agreements, we established a new company, the Botswana Diamond Valuing Company (BDVC), to sort and value all of Debswana's production. Previously the diamonds had been sorted and valued at Kimberley in South Africa. De Beers constructed a large, specially designed building named Orapa House in Gaborone, and we trained citizens to do the sorting and valuing. BDVC created jobs and income in Botswana and assured that the diamonds were valued before they left the country.

The question arose, of course, as to whether we should find an alternative buyer to the CSO for at least a part of the production of the Debswana mines. One argument was that we could then have an independent indication of what we might get for our diamonds. But, as we looked around, we found that almost everyone had some kind of relationship with De Beers, whether as an associate or a fierce competitor. The latter could not be trusted, either, since they would be determined to try to show that De Beers was being unfair, even if it cost them money in the short term. By the 1990s, when we accounted for perhaps a quarter of total world supply, a buyer could have purchased a portion of our production at better prices than that buyer would ever have paid for the total. There also were proposals that we should set up our own independent marketing operation to sell the entire production of our diamonds to the diamond cutting industry. Perhaps some day we will do so. But, up to the time I left office, we continued to sell our whole production through the CSO, while constantly monitoring the market to see that we were receiving the best prices.

Jwaneng

In 1976, only a year after we had finalised the new agreement for the 50/50 partnership, De Beers came to tell us that they had found another payable deposit. It was at Jwaneng, 80 kilometres west of Kanye in Ngwaketse. We again put our MPC to work. This time we developed a somewhat different strategy with a number of new objectives. In contrast to the closed township planned and developed by De Beers at Orapa, we wanted an open township, in the hope that other economic activity would be encouraged around the mine. We felt it should be designed by our own planners to be comparable in layout to other towns in Botswana. We also wanted to increase the technical and management capacity within Botswana, since the Debswana mine management was actually reporting to the engineers at Anglo-American in Johannesburg instead of to a chief executive in Botswana.

On the financial side, we knew De Beers wanted a high rate of return on all the equity it invested. We decided we might invest some of our own money in the equity of the mining project. If we did so, in addition to the large share of the profits that Botswana would receive in exchange for granting the mining lease, we would also receive a share of the profits as a "paying" shareholder; we would earn the same rate of return on our investment as De Beers. The Jwaneng agreement ultimately provided government with an option to invest up to 20% of the equity required for the project, and we exercised the option.

As we were negotiating the arrangements for Jwaneng, Mr Oppenheimer said they only wanted to mine 40% of the potential of the deposit. He argued that Botswana was a small country with few resources to protect the mine, and we would be an easy target for anyone who wanted to do us harm. He also said it would be no good for anyone if they exploited the whole deposit, since selling so much production would cause a glut and push prices down. I told him I understood his decision as a businessman, of course. However, if he didn't want to mine the other 60%, we would need to find someone else who would mine it for us, as we needed the revenue from that 60%. He looked up and raised his eyebrows as he asked me: "Who do you have in mind?" I responded that we didn't have anyone else in mind yet, since we had thought De Beers would do it. But in the light of the fact that he didn't want to do it, we would have to find someone. "Do you mean even our enemies?" he asked. I said, well, he would need to tell us who De Beers' enemies were. He leaned forward and replied dramatically: "The world is full of our enemies, Mr Vice-President!" De Beers ultimately decided that if we were going to look for others to do the mining, then they would do it all themselves.

In the negotiations over Jwaneng, we faced a problem we had not encountered at Orapa: availability of adequate water supplies. There was no surface water source near Jwaneng to serve the mine and township, and the project would have to depend on a well field based on underground water. A field was identified in the Kweneng, but we knew very little about its hydrology, including the extent of the water resource and the rate of recharge. It was possible that pumping the water needed for Jwaneng would lower the water table and adversely affect boreholes for both cattle and people in the region. Further, if the reservoir were depleted, how would we run the mine and township? It took the De Beers people many months to appreciate how serious a political and social problem we would face if we were to deprive farmers and villages of their water. They seemed to think we were simply trying to commit them to a large future investment, such as an expensive pipeline from Gaborone. We finally resolved the issue by acknowledging in the agreements that if there was not adequate water, then we would have to come together to solve the problem. In fact, the well field has recharged, and we have not had any problems with other boreholes in the region.

The negotiations lasted more than a year, and since Jwaneng was clearly going to be more profitable than Orapa, the stakes were very high. Julian Nganunu led the negotiating team as the PS responsible for minerals at that time. The negotiations with De Beers became so difficult that we sent a small exploratory mission to Canada and the United States to meet with other potential investors. We hinted to De Beers that we were making enquiries to make sure they knew we were not dependent on them alone. Our own valuers examined the prospecting samples, and our geologists and mining engineers reviewed all the data from the prospecting reports on the grades of ore in different parts of the deposit. Even so, De Beers knew more about the potential than we did, so we were at a disadvantage in discussing the terms of an agreement that would be fair to both sides.

The agreement on Jwaneng was finalised in April 1978, and the mine reached full commercial production by the middle of 1982. Jwaneng became the most profitable diamond mine in the world, and by the mid-1980s Debswana's annual production was 12-13 million carats annually. Diamonds then comprised over two-thirds of our export earnings and over half of government revenues.

The Market Crisis of 1981-82

At the time construction at Jwaneng began, the world diamond markets along with all the other international commodities were booming. De Beers had been selling from its stockpiles in the late 1970s to try to stabilise prices, but speculation had driven prices to very high levels. When the markets for commodities collapsed in 1981-82, so did the market for diamonds, and De Beers needed to stockpile diamonds in order to stabilise prices. They also enforced stockpiling on producers like Debswana. Early in 1981 we had been exporting over P20 million per month; exports had fallen to about P15 million by October. The CSO purchased none of our diamonds in November or December, and when exports resumed in February 1982, they amounted to only P10 million.

We had been the beneficiaries of the expanding market for diamonds in the 1970s; in 1981-82 we experienced how the marketing arrangement would work when times were difficult. Since the cost of producing Debswana's diamonds is quite low by international standards, all three mines—Orapa, Letlhakane, and Jwaneng—remained profitable even though we were not selling our entire production; we did not need to reduce production or lay off workers. We did, of course, have to deal with the macroeconomic problem of stabilising the economy in the face of a large loss of export earnings.

Debswana's Diamond Stockpile

Our overall financial position recovered quickly, in part because Jwaneng came into full production in 1982. Our sales quota at the CSO increased along with our productive capacity, so we became entitled to sell more diamonds. However, the markets remained depressed, and both the CSO and Debswana continued to stockpile diamonds. By the mid-1980s, we were concerned that a large portion of our output remained unsold. De Beers was also concerned, especially about stocks held outside the control of the CSO at Debswana and at other producers, particularly the Russians. They proposed that we exchange Debswana's stockpile of diamonds for shares in De Beers that would be owned by Debswana. De Beers and Anglo-American had a long history of maintaining or increasing their control of the market by exchanging diamond stocks for company shares, so we were cautious as we approached the discussions. In addition to our usual MPC negotiating team, we engaged Morgan Grenfell from London as independent investment bankers to advise us on the arrangements.

The proposal to exchange the stockpile for De Beers' shares bitterly divided cabinet. The main arguments against it were that De Beers was a South African company, and the country was a pariah state. What would happen to our investment when there was a new political dispensation in South Africa? But, there was no counter proposal from the opponents as to what to do with the stockpile. Those who were in favour of the exchange for shares pointed out that we could always sell the shares in the future, if we chose to do so. Since a substantial part of De Beers' assets were invested in shares of the Anglo-American Corporation, our shareholding in De Beers through Debswana would provide a further diversification of Botswana's foreign assets as well. In the end, arguments for the swap won the day. We were able to liquidate Debswana's stockpile for shares in De Beers. Government also received the right to appoint two directors of De Beers.

Our very large diamond reserves, our low production costs, and the partnership with De Beers have brought substantial financial benefits to Botswana. The arrangements at Orapa and Jwaneng have been extremely profitable to both parties. De Beers and government have continued to invest in expansion of operations and in new technologies at Debswana's mines. Orapa's production started at 2.5 million carats per year; the 1975 agreements increased our production to over five million carats. Jwaneng brought total Debswana production to around 13 million carats. Expansions of capacity at Orapa and Jwaneng, the development of a "recrush" plant at Jwaneng to re-process ore and extract smaller diamonds, and the movement to continuous operations added to our diamond production and to government mineral revenue. By the end of the 1980s, annual production ranged between 15 and 17 million carats, and by 1997 it had reached 20 million. Over three-quarters of exports and 60% of government revenues came from diamonds by the time I retired.

Diamond Cutting

The issues surrounding a diamond cutting industry were very difficult for us. The general argument on one side was simple: It should be the aim of a producer of raw materials to maximise their value. In Botswana, this would involve cutting and polishing the diamonds. While that would seem like an obvious way to add value to our own diamonds, the diamond cutting and polishing industry has many special characteristics. There are many possibilities for being cheated. Even if the weight of the diamonds before and after cutting is checked accurately, someone could substitute poor quality cut stones for high quality rough ones. Worldwide, the industry generally relies on very highly skilled people, very low wages, small family businesses, or some combination of these features. In South Africa, the industry is subsidised. When Charles Tibone was PS in Mineral Resources, he visited different countries to evaluate the industry. When he came back, he told me: "Only the Indians can do it." Their success was due to low wages, high skills, long hours, strict supervision, and intensive use of the same facilities for cutting, polishing, eating, and even sleeping!

We approached De Beers to assist us in starting a cutting and polishing operation, and they proved to be difficult. We surmised that De Beers did not want Botswana to become any more independent of them by knowing more about the diamond industry. Eventually, however, we prevailed, and De Beers agreed to participate in establishing a factory in Botswana.

Every part of the country wanted the cutting factory, and the Land Boards in Kanye, Ramotswa, Kweneng and Serowe acted more quickly than they had on any other issue. We had a major rift in the government as ministers argued over the location. We were as tribally divided as we ever had been in our history. To be objective, we sent a team with a scoring system to all the potential sites to determine which one would be most suitable. Serowe came out tops, so we gave the new company a license in Serowe. However, it has not really been a vital development: It produced up to its original design capacity but did not expand any further. I don't think De Beers was interested in making it a success. So, we gained a few jobs, but not a real stimulus to growth.

After the decision to establish the Serowe factory, Maurice Templesman, an American diamond man who was active in many parts of Africa, came to see us. He seemed to have a complex competitive relationship with De Beers in a number of countries. He proposed a package that would involve Botswana participation in a project through BDC. A cutting factory would be established at Molepolole, giving some geographic balance to the cutting industry. We agreed, and it was established. However, a few years into the project it began to lose money, and Mr Templesman wanted us to subsidise it. We refused to do so, as we had done in case of other demands for subsidies, and eventually it closed. We had identified the problems of why a cutting industry would have difficulties, and apparently these proved to be correct.

The Shashe Project Restructurings

The mining and smelting portion of the Shashe project turned out to be financially disastrous. Delays, cost overruns, increases in the project's debt and its interest rates, low prices of copper and nickel, even adverse changes in currency values, all worked against the viability of the mining project. The mine had barely opened before it was in need of refinancing. Even so, by 1975 BCL employed twice as many people as Orapa and more than the total employed in all of manufacturing. It supported the township of Selebi-Phikwe, and it provided a very large share of the total sales of both the Botswana Power Corporation and the Water Utilities Corporation. It purchased imported goods on which we received customs revenue. Its closure would have been terrible for the country, as well as leaving creditors and shareholders with nothing. In 1976, teams from the major investors, the lenders, and government (through our MPC) began a series of very difficult negotiations to keep the mine in business. We hoped to restructure or rearrange its debt so that the mine would remain viable.

BCL was a major challenge for us from the late 1960s until I retired. The company was financially restructured several times, but it continued to operate. The initial difficulties had been due in part to the technical and management problems of the project sponsors, Anglo and AMAX. These were finally overcome, and BCL became one of the world's lowest cost producers of nickel by the early 1980s. However, the financial structure of the original project, the cost overruns, and the fact that the mine and smelter reached their target output seven years behind schedule, made BCL extremely weak financially. As the finances of the project were restructured over time, government deferred or gave up its royalty payments. We also contributed to a liquidity reserve through which government, Anglo and AMAX provided cash on a short-term basis whenever the mine required it. The major lenders, including those in Germany and South Africa, eventually agreed to automatically defer payments that were due if there was insufficient cash. The project seemed constantly on the edge of bankruptcy and closure.

We believed it was in our interest more than any of the other parties to the agreements to be sure the mine did not close. Our officials regularly did analyses to show us how far we could go in making concessions. Because we received customs revenues due to imports for the mine and smelter, we knew we would be ahead if we could keep the mine and infrastructure running and our people employed without having to subsidise the operation from government revenue. Our studies of Anglo and AMAX also helped us understand how far they would go before they would walk away. We had continual difficulty with the German government regarding the loans they had guaranteed, and Dr Chiepe, who was minister of mineral resources and water affairs for many of the critical years, took her officials on emergency trips to Germany on several occasions. Interestingly, we never had a problem with the South African government, even though those were the apartheid years.

In 1978, when Dr Chiepe was presenting some of the legislation needed to complete the first restructuring of BCL, she paid tribute to the MPC, which had been led by her PS, Julian Nganunu, and to her cabinet colleagues. She also noted that: "Negotiations after all are a matter of give and take." It was clear that if any of the parties had tried to enforce its rights under the original agreements, the project would have closed.

Our diamonds played an important role in our negotiations over BCL and its financial problems. The principal interest of De Beers and its sister company, Anglo-American, was in Botswana's diamond production. This interest was important in bringing Anglo-American into the Shashe project in the first place; it became more important over time as production in Orapa and Jwaneng continued to expand. Mr Oppenheimer was very aware of the importance of Botswana's stability to De Beers' long-term interests. This helped us retain their interest when BCL was in continuous financial difficulties; chaos in Botswana from putting 4,000 people at BCL out of work would not have been good for the diamond industry. Anglo even joined with us in making it possible for AMAX to give up its interests and obligations to BCL. But, of course, De Beers always wanted to have such help recognised in the financial arrangements for diamonds.

Other Mineral Projects

While diamonds and copper-nickel have been our principal mineral projects, there have been others of lesser importance. We have very large deposits of brine in the pans of north-central Botswana, and from our earliest days we had hoped a project to produce soda ash (used in making glass) and salt would be possible. Such a development at the Sowa Pan had been discussed in our development plans since the late 1960s, but it was not until 1991 that we finally developed a project. Anglo-American was our partner once again. However, we encountered major difficulties in the marketing of the soda ash in South Africa, despite the access we should have had in terms of the Customs Union Agreement. The project provided modest development at Sowa, but it never developed into the scale we had hoped.

In the early 1980s, we came close to another major development. Energy prices—for oil, natural gas and coal—had reached new highs in 1980, and prices were projected to continue climbing for years to come. Shell Coal, a unit of the Royal Dutch Shell group of companies, discovered a major body of coal at Kgaswe in the Central District near the Morupule coal field. They approached government to discuss its development.

Charles Tibone was then PS in Mineral Resources, and he led the MPC negotiating team. He and other officials analysed the potential of the project, and Dr Chiepe as the responsible minister, brought the results to cabinet. We concluded that coal would not be a major source of government revenue, since its profitability was not high. We also realised a substantial portion of the export price of the coal would go for transportation to the coast. The most logical route traversed South Africa to Richards Bay on the Indian Ocean. After extensive discussions at official level and in cabinet, we agreed on our basic negotiating position with Shell: The project should bear the cost of a new Trans-Kgalakgadi Railway from eastern Botswana to Walvis Bay in Namibia on the Atlantic coast. In effect, we would use the value of our coal to provide us with an alternative route to the sea as well as a major addition to our infrastructure. We might have had, for the first time, an alternative to using South African ports and railways. The coal traffic could have paid both operating and debt service costs for the railway, so the railway could have been viable even without other traffic. Because of Shell's size, financial strength, and strategic commitment to coal, we thought they could provide a guarantee (in the form of assured traffic) that would enable us to finance the railway development.

In 1982, we reached an agreement with Shell that accomplished our objectives; Shell subsequently carried out its obligations to develop a full feasibility study. However, even before we had finalised the agreement, energy prices had started to decline. The feasibility of the Kgaswe project depended on a high and slightly rising price of coal, so Shell surrendered its rights to the deposit after completing their studies. Perhaps, when energy again becomes scarce and valuable internationally, our coal projects will again become viable. It is an ill wind that blows no good.

One exchange during the negotiations with Shell showed how we had learned to regard our natural resources. There was a contentious issue about what would happen to the proceeds from sales of coal when it was exported. We wanted Shell to sell the dollars they received from selling the coal to the Bank of Botswana for pula. We would add the dollars to our foreign exchange reserves, and Shell could then purchase dollars or other currencies as needed—for imported supplies or to pay dividends or debt service. Shell wanted to keep the dollars outside Botswana. At one point their chief negotiator asked: "What would you say about the fact that we think of the proceeds from the sales as our dollars?" Baledzi Gaolathe, then PS responsible for finance, replied: "We think of the coal as our coal."

The Shell man paused, and then said with a frown: "That's what I was afraid you would say." We knew that, if we had a resource others wanted to buy, we could take our seat at the negotiating table.

Chapter 16
Economic Opportunities and Disparities

From the earliest days of the party, one of our major objectives was to raise the living standards of all our people. We knew from observing the experiences of other countries that a fortunate few often benefited much more than did the great majority; we wanted to avoid such a situation in Botswana. In part because of our objectives, and in part because our government was so poor and understaffed, we also knew that our approach had to be based on the self-reliance of individuals.

Those of us who became politicians continued to live among the ordinary people, and we shared their difficulties. The first cabinets were composed entirely of people from the rural areas. My fellow politicians and I knew the problems of rural life; we were not theorising. For example, people in my village queued for water, and as a boy I stood in line so my mother would not have to do so. Seretse Khama and other royals who were among the leaders in *Domkrag* were by nature people's people. There is something to Kipling's line: "If you can walk with kings, nor lose the common touch." There can be a danger when the leaders start either from too low, or from too high, in society.

Because at independence more than 90% of our people lived in rural areas, it was clear that we had to make our major effort there. However, delivering services to the majority of people was difficult and expensive, since we are so sparsely settled. The 1971 Census showed that nearly 80% of our people lived in settlements of fewer than 5,000 people, and more than 60% lived in settlements of fewer than 1,000.

When asked how to promote equality, my stock answer is as follows: We must invest in education so that everybody will have the opportunity to acquire the tools to succeed. We concluded that if we could provide education, clean water, access to heath care, and a more democratic approach to land allocation, then we would have a basis for equal opportunity for most people to make a living and to succeed. After that, I believe, you leave it to individual initiative and to market forces, provided that you have two devices, a progressive income tax, and an incomes policy, to keep those with marketable skills from gaining too much advantage.

In our 1974 Election Manifesto we had said: "Every citizen must enjoy as far as possible the same access to education, health facilities, land, water and employment." I believe any objective look at the facts would show that we overcame the obstacles and accomplished a large share of those objectives.

Rural-Urban Drift and Rural Development

We knew from what we had read and from our travels that almost every developing country had experienced a drift of people from rural to urban areas. Such migration usually resulted in unemployment, slum housing and crime. During the March 1964 meeting of Legco, there was a motion by a white member, Mr Wharren: "That government takes steps to stop the flow of unemployed to towns." This reaction reflected the approach in South

Africa—the way to keep the towns orderly was to prevent people from moving there! In the debate on his motion, the speakers from *Domkrag* said that certainly there were difficulties created by the drift to the urban areas. However, we needed first to develop productive opportunities in rural areas so people would voluntarily stay, and next to develop productive economic activities in towns for those who did migrate. We said we did not want to depend on legislation to prevent people from coming to towns.

We in the BDP were also concerned about the drift to towns for social reasons. In the rural areas, people had a traditional way of making a living and carrying on with their lives. In the cities, they either got a job or they just become lost souls. The traditional safety nets—going to live at your uncle's place, or borrowing oxen from someone else to plough your lands if you had no oxen—had no parallel in the towns. Our focus on reducing the rural-urban drift was a very conscious decision. We talked about it in cabinet; we talked about it in party meetings; and we talked about it in parliamentary caucuses. It was very much a part of our thinking as we developed our economic policies.

Since the roots of *Domkrag's* leadership were in the rural areas, we understood the people and their way of life, and the consequences of the drift to the towns and the adverse effects on people's lives. And, of course, we also wanted something done in our constituencies. So, in the late 1960s and early 1970s, we developed long-term programmes for rural development. We subsequently spent large sums of money on rural services and on agricultural programmes. Our agricultural potential, though undeveloped, was the one thing that we thought might give everybody some productive employment in the country. Professor Robert Chambers of Sussex University, one of our consultants, once asked me if I really believed in the future of rural development, and I told him I did. He then asked me why, and I said: "It is the only thing that will keep us out of mischief while we are searching for something better." We had to find ways of helping people where they lived.

As soon as we achieved budgetary independence in 1972, we decided to use some of the resources to implement an Accelerated Rural Development Programme (ARDP). Most of the ARDP expenditures were for buildings, and most were executed either by the central government, or public works departments or private contractors, with only a small part executed directly by councils. After ARDP was completed, Professor Chambers undertook an evaluation of it for us. He said that one of the things ARDP accomplished was to show the government bureaucracy that if there was strong political will to get something accomplished, then, in fact, it could be accomplished. To take but one example, in my constituency a man named Japie built a school at Magoriapitse that still stands today. Before ARDP, no one knew Rre Japie had any capacity to do a thing such as that; but the availability of financial resources made it possible for him to demonstrate it. Many people's accomplishments really surprised us.

A cynical view was that we undertook ARDP just because we wanted to be sure we won the 1974 elections. But, it was the advent of budgetary independence that made it possible for us to do the things in the rural areas we had long wanted to do. Assistance in the elections would be a bonus. Previously under Grant-in-Aid, all our expenditures had to be approved by the British who were quite prejudiced against local government projects. If they did not like something we proposed to do with our own resources, they would reduce their Grant-in-Aid by the same amount. Their pretext was that, since we used it for something they did not think appropriate, we did not need the money! So, the opportunity to undertake a substantial programme that would bring major benefits to rural areas all over the country was one we wanted to seize. Of course, being politicians, we also hoped we would be rewarded at the next elections, and we were.

We first started rural development projects on a small scale in the 1960s, and we accelerated them in the 1970s and 1980s. TGLP, Communal Area Development Projects, ALDEP, ARAP and others were all part of our rural development commitment. They are still plodding their weary way, and while we still have agricultural demonstrators, extension officers, and so forth, they are unfortunately accomplishing next to nothing. We tried many different types of programmes to encourage farming of all kinds for which we provided financial and other forms of support. My colleagues in *Domkrag* and I were continuously frustrated by both the weather and, to some extent the bureaucracy, in our efforts to create productive activity in the rural areas.

I continue to plough and plant every year, and so far I have almost always succeeded in getting a crop. But very few other people I know are still involved to any large degree in arable agriculture. In the Kanye and Ngwaketse area, I knew of only a handful in the year 2002-03, although there may have been six or seven others. That year I journeyed the 38 kilometres from Kanye to my lands and did not see a single plot that had been ploughed. The droughts we have suffered have done incalculable harm. We have poured a great deal of money into drought relief to keep body and soul together for people, and that, of course, is of paramount importance. But perhaps the greatest damage from the droughts is that people have lost the will to continue farming.

On the other hand, the major villages—Kanye, Molepolole, Serowe and the others—that had been another focus of our early attention have been transformed into peri-urban areas. They have an impressive array of commercial activities. Before independence, men had worked in South Africa and brought back money to build houses and purchase cattle. In the past 30 years, financed almost entirely by their incomes from our own mines and urban areas, people have built larger houses in their home villages for their own retirement or for their mothers or grandmothers. As a result, there now are many small contractors, and a sprinkling of other kinds of productive activities. Most of the increased business has been in retail and wholesale trade, including construction materials. However, our early notion of the villages as places where we would do the processing of agricultural products from the nearby lands was simply unrealised. Since agricultural development has been so disappointing, it is hard to see how such an objective could be achieved.

Water and Health

If we were to equalise the opportunities for Batswana to better their circumstances, we had to do so by providing equal access to good health. We knew from our own personal experience, from our meetings with ordinary people throughout the country, and from district planning exercises begun in the late 1960s, that access to potable water was a primary concern. Through the Water Utilities Corporation (WUC) in the urban areas and the Department of Water Affairs in the rest of the country, we made good progress. By the time I retired, over 95% of our people had access to clean water, a percentage well above the rest of Africa and the developing world. Most rural water supplies in villages involve distribution to standpipes, though in major villages water reticulated directly to households has become increasingly common. Delivery of potable water has been a major factor in improving the general health of our people, measured by such statistics as infant and child mortality. It also has contributed to the rapid decline in communicable diseases, with the terrible exception of HIV/AIDS.

Health care involved difficult choices for us. On the one hand, there was a demand for specialised curative health care to deal with complex medical problems. On the other hand, there was need for preventive care and primary health care for everyone. We took the latter option of providing primary health care, and we created a network of health centres throughout the country. The needs were greatest in rural areas, and we tried to be sure these were served regardless of the comparative costs. We met a large part of the need for specialised care at two referral hospitals, Princess Marina in Gaborone and Nyangabwe in Francistown. However, many patients with specialised needs requiring expensive care continue to be treated outside the country.

At independence, we had only eight small hospitals and perhaps two-dozen clinics and dispensaries. By the late 1990s, we had 30 hospitals, more than 300 clinics or health posts with nursing staff, over 200 facilities with other trained health-care staff, and mobile health teams made stops at more than 650 other locations. Over 80% of our people in rural areas now live within 15 kilometres of a primary health care facility. The HIV/AIDS pandemic, our greatest national challenge today, has placed tremendous strain on the health care system. However, the extensive network of facilities has made it possible to offer services throughout the country and to add specialised HIV/AIDS services to existing facilities.

Education

Access to education had to be the primary way of providing our people with access to productive economic opportunities. During the Protectorate era, education was in the hands of tribes and missionaries; it was strictly a local matter. The colonial administration's role was to provide the curriculum and to appoint supervisors to see that things were done according to certain standards. A director of education supervised the inspectors of schools, who in turn travelled around the country ensuring that standards were met. There were a very few bursaries to send selected students outside Bechuanaland for secondary education, mainly to South Africa, and a much smaller number to university.

An overseas development mission from the UK assessed our economic future in 1965 and determined that of the 205 public service jobs requiring either a high school or university degree, only 34 were held by locals. If one included those requiring either a high school or a Junior Certificate, only 575 of 1,239 posts were held by citizens. Even by 1972, only 30% of the top administrative and professional grades of the service were held by citizens. Of our secondary school teachers, more than 80% were non-citizens, and large shares of both primary and secondary school teachers did not have training to be teachers.

In the last few years before self-rule, the colonial government had begun to improve things, but the long years of neglect had left their mark. While primary school enrolments had doubled between 1960 and 1965, fewer than half of the primary-aged children were at school in the latter year. Only one child in ten who finished primary school found a place at secondary school. The schools had a ratio of 45 pupils per teacher; 40% of the teachers were untrained; and many classes were held outdoors because of lack of facilities.

Secondary schools had increased from five to nine in the five years before independence, but there were only 1,500 students in secondary school in the whole country in 1966. They were taught by some 89 teachers, 45% of whom were untrained. In 1964, only 136 Batswana passed their Junior Certificate, and only 27 passed the Cambridge Overseas Exam at the end of secondary school. Of the latter, only 13 had high enough marks to qualify for the newly opened regional University of Basutoland, Bechuanaland and Swaziland at Roma.

In 1965, we recognised that primary education was in many ways of greatest importance, since basic education was the way to ensure opportunities for people. We also felt education must have the input of parents in education to the maximum extent possible. However, we did not have the money to do everything, and we had a dire need of qualified workers due to the past neglect of secondary and tertiary education. We decided to devote a great deal more resources to tertiary and secondary education. As a result, our expansion of opportunities in primary education had to be carried out very economically from the viewpoint of the central government budget.

Primary Education

In the days of Legco, Chief Bathoen was responsible for social services in the Executive Council, and at one point I was acting for him. The colonial government expressed a desire to take on the responsibility for primary education from the tribes, but I argued strongly against that idea. I did so because we were expecting to take over government for internal self-rule the following year, and we would face an enormous task. I thought we should be given the opportunity to see how we would go about governing before we added even more responsibilities.

As we looked to independence, a number of issues faced us in primary education: the low number of places, lack of facilities and of trained teachers for existing schools, and inequity in the allocation of trained teachers between poorer and richer areas. We had to provide more schools, more places, and more teachers; to ensure more equity in distribution of opportunities; and also to upgrade the existing facilities and teaching force. At independence, local authorities and church missions were providing facilities and hiring and paying teachers, and primary school children were paying school fees. Because local authorities were responsible, the richer councils had been getting good teachers and the rest had not, since there was nothing to induce teachers to go to the poorer areas. Therefore, we created a Unified Teaching Service, so that the Ministry of Education could both employ and deploy teachers. Every teacher would go where he or she was needed, and the whole system would be more equitable.

It was not until 1973 that we were financially able to reduce primary school fees, and we eliminated them in 1980. We then subsidised tribal administration or school committees or councils by the amount they would have received from school fees. The councils didn't like this approach; if there was to be more financing from the central government, they wanted us to provide buildings first, rather than ending school fees. They had a good argument, in a way, since they knew that without school fees more children would wish to come to school, and they would not have the facilities. But in light of our scarce resources, we thought it was the best way to serve more children and to do so equitably. I personally had been taught under a tree, not in a classroom, at the primary level, so I knew from my own experience it was better to be taught somewhere than not taught at all. As a consequence of reducing school fees, the numbers of children in school shot right up in 1974 and again in 1981, and correspondingly the numbers of entrants to secondary school also increased. But where there is a will there is a way; the private sector made a determined effort to put up new schools, even in very poor places.

Enrolments in primary schools grew very quickly. From 71,000 at independence, we exceeded 170,000 by 1980 (when over 85% of primary-school-age children attended). More than 300,000 children were enrolled by the time I retired in 1998. Over the same period, we reduced the pupil/teacher ratio from 44/1 to less than 30/1, and the percentage of untrained teachers from 40% to 7%. It was a massive effort, since we wanted to ensure that education was available to virtually every family in every part of the country.

We had a big debate early on about English as a medium of instruction in some primary schools. There was a clear view by some that such schools would be elitist and should not receive government support. Of course, many of the opponents later sent their own children to private English medium schools! The argument was that if the politicians and civil servants sent their children to English medium schools, they would not care about improving the standards in the Setswana medium schools. There was recognition, too, that we didn't have the resources to raise the level of education all over the country to the level of English medium schools. We in government said if families wanted to use their resources to send their children to such schools, then they should be able to do so. However, we provided no government support to English medium primary schools.

In the colonial period, primary schools had been established by and for whites in Serowe, Ghanzi and Francistown. Lobatse was so close to Mafeking and Zeerust that the white children from Lobatse went to those places for school. Not even the biggest of the chiefs, such as Tshekedi or Bathoen, sent their children to white schools, since those that did exist were even more racist in their practice than those in Rhodesia. There were also two schools for coloured children; one at Kganagasi, west of Ghanzi, and the other was Lobatse Crescent school, mainly for Indians and coloureds. Two of my children, Mpho and Mmetla, went to Lobatse Crescent in the 1960s.

Secondary Education
Secondary education was mostly in the hands of local communities at independence. In 1950, I had been the first headmaster of what became the Seepapitso Secondary School at Kanye, and there were secondary schools in three other tribal areas. There were two church schools run by the Catholics: St. Joseph's at Kgale near Gaborone and Mater Spei in the north. When Gaborone was established, we built Gaborone Secondary School as the first government school. The pressure for secondary schools was great, and there was a mushrooming of private secondary schools—some good, some not so good, and some just rubbish. Mr Kgabo, for one, started as many as four schools. During the 1970s, we decided local private schools should be helped so that government could approve the curriculum and provide inspectors, and we also built administrative facilities. We progressively gave as much help as we could, later providing funds to pay teachers, and still later to put up buildings, though the schools still had their own boards of governors, selected by the local communities.

Education was critical to our economic development and economic independence but it was a politically sensitive subject as well. We twice established presidential commissions to review our entire approach to education, and both commissions had a major impact on our policies.

The Thema Commission, which sat from 1975 to 1977, strongly concluded that secondary schools should be community schools, and they should be in local areas. That was the start of what we called *tse di nala* (brown-and-white) community schools, after the colours they were painted, and we covered the whole country with them. We helped finance community junior secondary schools. Some of these were very expensive, but politically it was very desirable both that they be sponsored by local communities and be established throughout the country. These were national schools, so students could come from anywhere, and we ensured that previously neglected areas would receive educational opportunity. We could have built schools with places for more students if we had concentrated schools with boarding facilities along the line of rail. But we felt it was also important that they should be dispersed, so children from all areas would have access and so the communities would feel responsibility. We also thought if we only brought people to Gaborone or Lobatse, no one would want to go to the rural areas later on.

Though I didn't realise it at the time, there was a very positive effect on the communities, what one might call a "civilising effect" on the people, from having community schools. First, people had to choose a board of governors; second, they interacted socially with the teachers; and third, the schools became reception centres for visitors from Botswana or abroad. There had to be cooperation with the Village Development Committees as well as with other local organisations. And, the children were still the community's children—they did not go to school and grow up in faraway places. These developments were part of what these days would be called the strengthening of civil society.

The Thema Commission recommended that we aim to provide universal access to junior secondary education through junior secondary schools sponsored by local communities. In the 1990s, the Kedikilwe Commission identified a number of shortages of facilities, and it also recommended (among other things) giving help to preschool efforts and day-care facilities.

Following the Thema Commission, one of our objectives became that, up to the ninth year, no child should be refused entry into school for lack of space. The commission found that as many as one-fifth of students in a grade might have been repeating it because they had failed examinations. Since spaces were limited, we decided not to allow repeating a grade unless there was a good reason, such as ill health. Parents were up in arms about the change, and they said we were just pushing the children through school like cattle through a crush. Our response was to point out that we had limited capacity; we could either clog the pipeline by making people repeat or move them through and give everyone a chance. Quality control would be assured by supervising the curriculum and the teachers, making sure they were doing their jobs, and by the school leaving examination. Each individual would get a certificate of completion, but the examinations, the most important of which was at the end of the nine years, would give an indication of what the child had achieved.

The language of instruction in public schools was always a political issue. The language of instruction initially was a matter of practicality—Setswana, English, whatever. Prior to the Thema Commission, Setswana was not a language of examination, out of concern for the Kalanga who spoke Sekalanga. But after the Thema Commission, teachers had to teach first in Setswana. Then in secondary school the language of instruction was English. We did this not because we loved the English more, but because English was going to be the working language both in government and internationally. The school leaving examination continued to be the Cambridge Overseas Exam. The Kedikilwe Commission recommended in 1994 that, where possible, students should be taught primary school in their mother tongue, but that has been a difficult recommendation to implement, since many families have a mother and father who were brought up with different languages at home. What, then, is the mother tongue? And in more cosmopolitan places such as Gaborone or Selebi-Phikwe, establishing schools catering to each mother tongue would be a difficult proposition.

At independence, the 1500 students enrolled in junior and senior secondary schools were three times the level of 1960. Within ten years, we increased enrolment to over 9,500, and by our twentieth anniversary of independence, it reached 36,000. By 1994, we had met the objective that every child would have access to both primary and junior secondary school. When I retired in 1998, over 140,000 students were in secondary school. Of these,

10,000 were in their final year studying for the school leaving examination, while in 1966 there had been only 80 such students in the whole country. We were able to provide nearly 40% of those finishing junior secondary school with access to senior schools, and we were continuing to add places in senior secondary schools. For decades more than 20% of our national budgets went to support education. I believe our efforts made it possible to achieve a good share of our goal of providing equal opportunities for all Batswana.

University Education

In the early days, everyone at the tertiary level had to go out of the country—to Lesotho, or to the UK. The three High Commission Territories joined together in 1964 to form the University of Basutoland, Bechuanaland and Swaziland, which after independence became the University of Botswana, Lesotho and Swaziland (UBLS). To begin with, all courses were given at Roma, in Basutoland, at a former Catholic mission university. We later adopted a policy of devolution of different courses to Botswana and Swaziland so each country would have a part of the university; but Lesotho wanted to keep everything that was worth keeping. In 1975, the three heads of government met in Swaziland to discuss the university, and I represented the late president. I argued that all parties would be better off cooperating within one university. However, Chief Leabua Jonathan made too many demands on devolution, and eventually he walked out, went back to Lesotho, and threw out the students from Botswana and Swaziland.

We welcomed back the students and any lecturers who wanted to come with them, and we put up tents at the old fairground in Gaborone. We started to raise funds, through the Botswana University Campus Appeal (BUCA), which had the slogan: "One Man One Beast". The idea was that everyone should contribute based on ability, whether it was a chicken or a dozen eggs or a goat or one beast or ten. It was a big success, and there was no looking back. Swaziland stayed with us for a few more years, but in 1982 went our separate ways, and we founded the University of Botswana.

One Man One Beast: The Botswana University Campus Appeal project was launched in 1976 to help build the University of Botswana

In the 1970s, we introduced a mature student entry programme to pick up some of those who had not had the opportunity of university study in earlier years. It was a good thing for those individuals, and it also put maturity into the student body of the university. We continued to expand the university and to add new faculties to teach more specialties such as Law in Botswana. In 1965, fewer than a dozen students were at university. By my retirement, more than 7,500 attended the University of Botswana, and when I last officiated over 1,000 were capped at the graduation ceremony.

Our local university, whether UBLS or later the University of Botswana, was unable to provide all the specialties we required, such as Engineering, Medicine or Veterinary Studies. We continued to send students abroad, and with the help of Norwegian financing, we developed a programme to send students to other countries (third-country training). Other donors, international agencies and private foundations also provided bursaries to meet our needs. The Canadians, for example, provided training for mining engineers over a period of many years. At the same time, they staffed our Department of Mines with Canadian mining engineers. Batswana first received formal training in Canada and then returned to Botswana to climb the ladder in the public service. As they gained experience, Batswana took over positions formerly held by the Canadians.

In the Protectorate days, government provided bursaries for a few students at university, so the cost to the student was nothing. When we started our own university, we considered whether we should provide the education free of charge. We thought about means testing, so students who were able would pay for part or all of their education, but we realised that means tests might discourage those who didn't know the value of education. Also, we didn't have enough raw material in the form of secondary school graduates with university qualifications. So, we decided we should make it possible for anyone who was academically able, to attend university free of charge. One consequence of this approach was that many students felt entitled to government support, even to meet the cost of their rooms, meals and books. They often complained that they didn't have enough money to spend, though they were more fortunate than the majority of Batswana. Of course, such students were also able to find jobs immediately when they graduated from university, and such jobs were very highly paid in comparison with what the ordinary Motswana could earn. High and unrealistic expectations have been a consequence of the successes we achieved.

Technical and Vocational Education
Given the thrust of our education system, which was based on a British academic model, we realised we might only be producing people who were interested in white-collar jobs. Because of inadequate training opportunities, we depended on skilled artisans from neighbouring countries in construction, auto repair, and the like. In the early 1960s, fewer than 50 people were engaged in either full time or part time training in technical and vocational fields. With the establishment of the Bechuanaland Training

Centre, the numbers increased to 250 or 300 by independence. These were still inadequate, so we travelled to countries that were known to be good at technical training, such as Germany, Japan and the United States, to see what we could learn about how to organise our vocational and technical education system. Over time, and with help from our donors, we established a number of different types of technical and vocational training schools, expanded the Botswana Training Centre, and established the Botswana Polytechnic. By the tenth anniversary of independence in 1976, enrolments had risen to 1,750. The numbers continued to grow, and by the time I retired over 10,000 students were enrolled in 46 different institutions studying auto repairs, electronics, and other skilled trades.

Brigades

Most countries have some formal system of qualifying artisans such as plumbers, electricians, or carpenters, and that was the focus of our effort in vocational and technical education. However, the British system we inherited, which was also in use in the rest of southern Africa, depended on a reasonably high academic qualification for entry into technical programmes. Given our deficit of both academically trained and technically trained people, there was a need for institutions that would accept those with lower academic preparation, give them skills the economy needed, and add to their own income earning potential. The brigades filled that need.

The brigade movement was a brainchild of Patrick van Rensburg, a South African who became disillusioned by the apartheid system and moved to Botswana before independence. He felt that if we could not take the children into secondary education because we lacked facilities and teachers, at least we should give them some skills. The first brigade was established at Serowe in 1965, and the idea caught on like wildfire. Almost every tribe and community had a brigade, but the most productive ones were the ones in which Van Rensburg himself was involved.

The idea behind the brigades was that education and production should go together. Therefore, a brigade would not only involve teaching students skills in carpentry, for example, but also would produce furniture for sale. Ideally, Van Rensburg thought each brigade would become financially self-supporting. The brigades were generally organised under development trusts with local people serving on the governing boards of the trusts. In this way, institutions of civil society were also developed and strengthened. Brigades developed in construction, carpentry, bricklaying, and even catering.

The brigades were a bit controversial for professional educators because of their reliance on lower academic qualifications and the lack of rigorous formal testing at the end of training. The Ministry of Education took over responsibility for looking after them, and we invested millions of pula in the brigades over the years. The costs of training people in the brigades was much lower than in other vocational and technical education and closer to the costs in academic secondary school. From small beginnings, enrolment in brigades grew to over 1000 by 1976. By my retirement, over 3,500 individuals were enrolled in 37 different brigades throughout the country.

Other Educational Institutions

The demand for education was much greater than we could meet from central government resources alone. Therefore, we encouraged private initiatives by individuals and groups, and we tried not to over-regulate schools. Our people seemed to like forming organisations in order to address problems or opportunities they saw. As a result, our education has had a variety of types of schools, of which the brigades are but one example.

In addition to the brigades, Patrick van Rensburg started the Swaneng Hill School, and it was the best of our secondary schools at one time. His original idea was that people who were fleeing from South Africa could go to his school. But, we were reticent about that, since those people didn't need education any more than our people—charity begins at home, so why not start here? The houses at Swaneng Hill were built to last ten years. We asked the CDC to have someone look at Swaneng Hill to see if the approach should be replicated elsewhere, but the man told us that the life of the buildings was five to ten years, and we shouldn't put money into such construction. However, we felt that if the school produced 40 students a year, at the end of ten years it would have produced 400 students. At the time, one could not dismiss such an effort, since it would have fulfilled an important function. Swaneng Hill School played a very important role in producing people who went on to achieve a great deal in Botswana. The Shashe River School was another Van Rensburg initiative. He was a great one for using local materials; one weekend I took Quill Hermans, Peter Landell-Mills and Hugh Murray-Hudson, and we made a convoy up north to help clear the land and to build a kiln for the new Shashe River School.

Patrick van Rensburg's contributions are an example of how we in *Domkrag* both welcomed good ideas and energetic people but were careful about which suggestions to accept. He was around near the beginning of things, and when we started the Democratic Party he made himself available to help, especially in education. He was also left wing in his politics, so because of his views on what would be appropriate for Botswana, there was always a kind of tension between him and those of us in government. He often seemed to bring us ideas that had never worked anywhere else and that we did not think would be applicable in our context. Although we sometimes differed on policy issues, I was very sympathetic to Patrick van Rensburg; he was committed to Botswana and to our democratic principles, and he personally worked very hard. He was always full of ideas, including the establishment of *Mmegi*, one of the first and now the largest of the private newspapers in the country.

Since I thought he ought to be encouraged, I visited Swaneng Hill on a number of occasions to talk with him and give him encouragement. I think he was somewhat discouraged because of the failures of the socialist-oriented governments in some neighbouring countries. He must have found the Botswana government much more tolerant of his ideas and activities and more prepared to listen to what he said, and he came back home to Botswana when others did not adopt his ideas. In some respects, this reflects one of the reasons we were successful: Botswana has been a good place to live and to work.

Another educational initiative was a private night school called Capital Continuation Classes. It was established after government moved to Gaborone to teach people who were working. It functioned using volunteer teachers who provided classes for Forms I, II and III. I taught Maths in the school for a number of years, but my teaching was increasingly interrupted by visits abroad, and so I felt I should give it up because it was too disruptive to the students. A number of civil servants were teachers in the school with me, including Serara Ketlokgetswe, one of our first trained economists, who later served as our ambassador to the United States.

Maru a Pula Secondary School was founded in 1970. It was the brainchild of a group including Archie Mogwe and Hugh Murray-Hudson, and the founding headmaster was a dynamic man named Deane Yates. It was meant to be a non-racial school to serve a diverse student body from both Botswana and southern Africa. It was hoped it would become an example for the region of what could be done in education when children of all races were brought together. Some of the rest of us were recruited to help raise money, and we brought in a fund-raiser from Johannesburg to give us advice as to how to go about doing it. Although there was criticism of the school as being elitist, we had the support of Seretse and virtually everyone else who mattered, including Motsamai Mpho and other prominent people in the opposition who sent their children there. Mr Thema, who was then minister of education, thought that a place like Maru a Pula could be a pace setter.

There was an issue of whether Maru a Pula should be allowed to offer an A-level course. The Cambridge Overseas O-level was the final secondary school-leaving examination in our publicly supported system, and A-levels were a two year specialised course that followed it in the British system. Most of us felt we could not afford to provide the A-level courses as part of public secondary education. But, if Maru a Pula could provide it for those who wanted and were willing to pay for it, so much the better.

I believe our willingness to encourage diverse efforts in education and other fields was a real benefit to our progress in economic development, as well as to promoting democracy at the local level.

Tirelo Setshaba

We in government thought long and hard about whether we should provide some form of national service for young people. We visited a number of countries to see what they had done and what their experience had been, and we found some programmes were militarily oriented and others emphasised social service. For *Tirelo Setshaba* (national service), we chose the social-service emphasis, in part because of our conviction that if most of our children grew up in Gaborone or Lobatse or Francistown, they would not know what was happening in the rest of the country. If we could disburse the young people around the country, we could give them a sense of what life was like in other places before they had to make choices about what they themselves would do.

Seretse was a strong proponent of national service, since he felt all Batswana who had received the benefits of an education at public expense should give something back to the country. We introduced *Tirelo Setshaba* in

1980 on a voluntary basis. By 1985, we had made participation in the programme a requirement for access to the University of Botswana, other government tertiary institutions, and government bursaries to programmes in overseas universities. By the late 1980s, over 1,000 young people were serving throughout the nation each year.

Parents in general, including many in the senior civil service, were opposed to *Tirelo Setshaba*, in part because it deferred their children's formal education, and in part because they did not want them to go to far off places alone at such a young age. But in the end, I believe, the children loved it and eventually so did most of the parents. When I travelled around the country, I often would invite the *Tirelo Setshaba* participants to talk with me after dinner. They were enthusiastic, and I even found they would return to the villages where they had done their service because of friendships they had made and things they had learned. One of them at Dutlwe, for example, told me sometimes he had acted as a court clerk, and sometimes he had acted as a chief. He truly looked back with nostalgia on his time in *Tirelo Setshaba*.

We did have a loss of some children whose parents did not want them to be in *Tirelo Setshaba* and could afford to send them abroad instead of having them attend University of Botswana or other tertiary institutions in Botswana. But *Tirelo Setshaba* was a plus from an employer's viewpoint. Despite the success, there remained resistance, especially among senior civil servants. After I left government, a presidential commission recommended stopping it. I think the commission was really biased against *Tirelo Setshaba* from the start, partly as a result of a carryover of the initial opposition. I believe it was a net loss to the country to have discontinued it; but by the time that decision was taken, I had retired.

Incomes Policy
From the start, we in *Domkrag* were concerned that economic development was likely to be uneven. There was an extreme shortage of skilled and educated citizens, and we wanted to be sure our policies would not result in those fortunate few deriving the lion's share of the benefits from new developments. We discussed this issue in our earliest campaigns and addressed it in our first development plans.

Many people thought that simply because we were going to be an independent country, Batswana with jobs would automatically be paid more money than people earned in the colonial days. As early as when I was deputy prime minister, when the UK was still providing more than half of our total budget through Grant-in-Aid, I had to handle the civil servants who wanted to be paid more generously. Rre Tumelo, who was the chairman of the Botswana Civil Service Association (BCSA), said to me: "We will go to the people and tell them what you are paying us." I told him: "The sooner you do, the better, because when they find out how much money you are getting they will be surprised. They will be very annoyed that you want more, considering what they themselves are earning!"

We wanted from the beginning to increase the number of jobs for our people. I remember addressing a political meeting in Naledi in the late 1960s with Tsheko Tsheko and Mout Nwako. We discussed the need for an affordable cost of labour in urban areas so we could attract industries to places like Gaborone. We said if we were successful in achieving this, then there would be competition for available labour, and wages would go up accordingly. People looked at us as if we were dreaming. But, this was what ultimately happened, and it brought benefits to a very large share of our people.

Our 1970-75 plan anticipated the mining developments at Selebi-Phikwe and Orapa, but it also expressed our concern that mining could result in a minority of workers who were fortunate to have jobs that enjoyed wages "substantially above that of the rural groups". We went on to point out the "gross inequalities" of wealth that had developed between urban and rural peoples in other African countries. We said that if we were to avoid such problems, we would have to restrain wage levels in the mines and in government, since those were the major employers. Then we would use the monies saved to promote rural development.

We engaged a number of consultants to study our situation, develop these ideas, and advise us on what had been done in other countries. Professor Dharam Ghai from Nairobi produced a major report in 1972, and Professor Chris Colclough of Sussex University assisted us in framing our policy. Our first White Paper on Incomes Policy, "National Policy on Incomes, Employment, Prices and Profits", was adopted in 1972. We established the National Employment, Manpower and Incomes Council (NEMIC), a tripartite body initially drawn from the Botswana Employers Federation, the trade unions and government, and it played a major role in implementing the Incomes Policy.

The basic ideas were simple enough. First, we knew we needed to keep unskilled wages in the towns from rising too fast relative to incomes in rural areas. Second, the severe shortage of skilled people meant that if the market were to set wages and salaries, there would be large differentials between the rewards to highly skilled and to unskilled labour. Third, we needed to address the allocation of skilled Batswana among the public, private and parastatal sectors. Skilled people should not just go to the highest bidder, but we should attend to national priorities. Finally, we had the history of the colonial service, where there were very large differentials between the salaries of the senior people, who were almost all white, and junior staff, who were all African.

As part of the Incomes Policy we established minimum wages in a number of industries. We also made it clear, as we stated in the 1973-78 Development Plan, that private and parastatal wages and salaries "should generally conform to and on no account significantly exceed those paid by the government to comparable grades of public employees". We established mechanisms for reviewing wages and salaries, as well as allocating new Batswana university graduates to the public, private and parastatal sectors. A salaries commission recommended that the spread between the top civil service salaries and those at the bottom be reduced, and we did so.

We had to pay attention to prices as well as to wages and salaries in the Incomes Policy. We realised we could do little about prices of most goods, since we were an open economy and imported so many basic goods from South Africa or Zimbabwe. However, we restrained the BHC rents, since BHC was the major supplier of rental housing in Gaborone. The SHHA programme provided people in urban areas with housing that was affordable even at low wage rates.

The Incomes Policy was difficult to sell at first, since people felt it would only work to keep wages down. There was a legitimate fear that employers, particularly non-citizens, would benefit and labour would lose, and any money saved in wages would not be invested to create more jobs. But we thoroughly discussed the policy before adopting it, and people began to understand. When we later had to keep wages down, people felt it was not being done irrationally, even if they did not fully understand it.

It was easy for some critics to paint the Incomes Policy as something to restrain wages and benefit profits. But in mining, our largest industry, wage restraint would not necessarily benefit the profits of a private owner. BCL never made profits; it struggled to be competitive in international markets, and it was constantly in danger of liquidation. Higher wage and salary costs at BCL could have resulted in the closure of the mine and the loss of thousands of jobs. In the case of Debswana, government received three-quarters of the profits, so higher wages and salaries would primarily have meant reduced government revenue. Since diamond revenues belonged to all Batswana, and were to be spent on education, health, water and other investments, we felt they should not only go to a few people who worked for Debswana. Finally, the largest single employer was government; higher salaries and wages in government would have meant fewer resources would be available for other public investments and services.

Parastatals and most private sector companies applied the principle of comparability with public sector wages only to employees who were citizens. Most of the non-citizens employed by government had their local salaries supplemented by donor agencies. Since expatriates were largely white or from South Asia, income differentials were visible not just by citizenship but also by race. In our early years, even BCSA accepted that there needed to be such differentials in order to attract skilled people for whom there were no Batswana substitutes. However, the obvious differences in the living standards of most expatriates and even of well-educated Batswana have been a source of discontent that the opposition has often sought to exploit.

By the mid-1970s, we started to gather better information about income distribution in rural and urban areas. These showed that our very rapid economic growth was, in fact, benefiting some people much more than others. We had achieved a narrowing of the differentials between the highest and lowest paid employees within the urban areas. But because agriculture had not achieved much and all other sectors had boomed, the gap between rural and urban incomes had widened.

We reviewed and modified the Incomes Policy over time as our circumstances changed. Reducing the large differentials of the colonial era in civil service salaries was the right thing to do in the early 1970s. Fifteen years later, however, the evidence showed that those with the greatest responsibilities in the country were not being adequately compensated. After Zimbabwe became independent, and the South African Bantustans started employing skilled Africans, some of our most highly trained and able people were choosing to emigrate to take higher paying jobs. We worried that if we restrained their incomes too much, we would lose our skilled and experienced people. Also, the 1982 Economic Opportunities Commission cited reports that Batswana in the private sectors were not accepting promotions because there was not enough reward for accepting supervisory responsibility.

Dr Chiepe, who was then minister of foreign affairs, chaired the 1990 Presidential Commission on Review of the Incomes Policy. The commission concluded there had been great wisdom in adopting the policy in 1972 and in implementing it over the years. By keeping wage rates competitive, it had contributed to the rapid growth of employment in many sectors. The commission reaffirmed some of the key elements of our approach since 1972: spending on health and education should not be "jeopardised by current expenditures on wages, housing subsidies" and the like; and "equality of opportunity to participate in a growing economy" continued to be an essential element in a socially just society. However, the commission concluded that substantial changes in the economy had rendered the details of our old Incomes Policy obsolete. It recommended and we implemented a "decompression" of pay scales, whereby those at the top received larger increases in salaries. We needed to recognise the value of their services. Expanding opportunities for all Batswana to participate in a growing economy through employment, entrepreneurship or investment would in the future be the best way of pursuing the original goals of the Incomes Policy.

Our eighth National Development Plan was approved in 1997, during my final year in office. By that time, we had experienced continued growth and complexity of the economy, as well as increases in skills and education for Batswana. The plan noted that market forces were increasingly effective in Botswana, and this reduced the need for more direct controls on wage differentials. As with other policies, we adapted the Incomes Policy to our changing circumstances.

Our explicit policy on how to set incomes, principally wages and salaries, proved to have been a useful device. We were committed to social justice, and the Incomes Policy provided a vehicle for discussing and resolving the conflicts that arise in any developing country, particularly one based so heavily on mining. We were always searching for a balance between rural and urban families, skilled and unskilled workers, and the interests of workers who are employed today compared with those who are now unemployed or who will come into the labour force in the future. The job prospects for these latter groups would depend on the money available to invest, particularly in their education. And, we needed to maintain competitive wage levels so our new industries could compete with goods from other countries, as I discussed in relation to our macroeconomic policies. The emphasis and the balance shifted as our economy developed and our educational system produced more trained people. It was never perfect, but it contributed to our overall success.

Unions and Labour

Political parties all wanted to be friendly with the trade unions. In the early days of *Domkrag*, Gabriel Mmusi, one of our key people in Francistown, was a trade union leader, and Lenyeletse Seretse also maintained good contacts with the unions. The difficulty was that when *Domkrag* became the government, we had to look at the economy as a whole, while the trade unions only looked at one aspect of it: How their members were remunerated and their interests protected.

We took trade unions into account for two reasons. First, we supported their general objectives; and second, if they were to decide to take the bit between their teeth, they had the potential to frustrate development of the whole economy. We didn't disregard their sentiments or rights, but we thought those rights should go with their obligations, too, and we told them so. The unions publicly acted as if they didn't believe what we said, but I think privately they understood.

Over the years, some opposition parties tried to hijack the unions. We tried to make it very clear that union members should be free to join any political party. However, we said it would be a pity if the union leaders started talking on behalf of a political party. That would destroy their relations with government, because government would not know whether the leaders were politicking and trying to win votes in elections, or simply fighting for the rights of their members.

One important issue in dealing with the unions was in the implementation of the Incomes Policy. The unions were represented in NEMIC, so they were always involved directly in discussions of implementation. In fact, we found the trade unions sometimes took a more responsible position than other members of society with whom we worked. This was especially so at the time of the 1981-82 diamond crisis, when they understood the problems we faced and supported the package of actions to stabilise the economy.

As part of our approach to labour relations, we adopted employment legislation and established an industrial court to adjudicate disputes between labour and management. Despite this, we had a number of industrial actions, or strikes, but none that came near to crippling the economy. When I was vice-president, I once went to Selebi-Phikwe when there was a threat of an industrial action by the workers at BCL's mine and smelter. I told the union: "Now look, you know better than I do that these boilers have to be tended carefully. If we sit here and don't take decisions, they may explode, and perhaps the last word any of us will say will just be a yell." And they said: "Of course we know that, and it is why we want a positive decision so you will not perish with us!"

The commissioner of labour can play a vital role in overall labour relations, including the relationships among government, labour and employers. Peter Mmusi was the most successful commissioner we had, though we lost him from that role when we brought him into politics. Klaas Motshidisi was very good; he had been an early member of opposition parties and had given evidence on behalf of BPP to the Legco Committee on Race Relations in the early 1960s. We knew of his politics when we recruited him to the civil service, and he worked hard to overcome some of the attitudes and prejudices he brought from his political background. Peter Mmusi used to tell Klaas: "As commissioner of labour you need to be either loved and trusted by both labour and management or distrusted by both, since only then can you play the role of conciliator."

Old Age Pensions

In traditional Tswana society, there were social networks that helped provide for people, particularly the elderly, who were unable to work for a living. However, as we began to modernise and become more urban, these systems started to decay. We had provisions in government programmes to assist destitutes, but the amounts of money were small, the system required a means test, and the instruments for measuring people's means were not very accurate and were costly to administer. Both our own observations as politicians travelling around the country and the statistics that were coming out showed us that many of the destitutes were old people, and we could see their conditions were really deplorable.

We discussed the idea of an old age pension scheme for many years. If one called it a pension, it suggested people would have either worked to earn it or saved something in a pension fund. But the real problem was the needs of people who had done neither. And, from where would we get the funding for something meaningful? However, by 1996, we felt we had enough revenue coming from diamonds, and those funds belonged to all Batswana. So we discussed it and decided to go ahead. The payment had to be enough to meet reasonable needs, but we did not want it to be so large that people would just stop doing useful things, such as looking after children of relations while parents were working. Age 65 had been agreed to be the age at which civil servants could retire from government, so we decided every citizen over the age of 65 would receive P100 monthly, and the amount has been increased to compensate for inflation. One must go to an office in person with one's *Omang* every three months to show that one was still alive and eligible. The old age pension was one of the things that made a real difference to thousands of the poorest Batswana.

Conditions of the Basarwa

The Basarwa in the past were known as Bushmen. They have also been known by other names, such as San. Basarwa are found primarily throughout the western parts of Botswana, and while many still pursue their traditional activities of hunting and gathering for subsistence living, most have varying levels of contact with the settled life of other Batswana. In terms of governance, Basarwa have always been under the chief, or paramount chief, where they lived. They have served as guides and trackers for hunters, and many worked for cattle farmers, especially in the Ghanzi area. Many white farmers in Ghanzi speak excellent Naro, a Sesarwa language. In some cases Basarwa have been treated with disrespect or discriminated against by other Batswana.

We in *Domkrag* recognised from the beginning that the Basarwa were the most economically disadvantaged people in the country. While Basarwa tended to keep themselves apart, we felt we couldn't just leave them alone, since it would be very unfair, especially to their children. As citizens, like all Batswana, they should participate in our improvements in health, medical care, and nutrition. We also wanted to ensure that their children had access to education so they could make informed decisions as adults as to what way of life they would pursue. We were serious about economic opportunities for all Batswana, and we knew from our own personal experiences with Basarwa that we would have to make special efforts. Among all groups in Botswana, the Basarwa have been most unwilling to avail themselves of the opportunities for education, health care, and participation in the modern economy. This has been a source of great frustration to me and to other leaders in the BDP.

I think part of the issue with the Basarwa is attitudinal; they sometimes think of themselves as unworthy. That, to me, was the attitude we needed to help them get away from. They are citizens, and they should take advantage of opportunities as other Batswana were doing.

Beginning in the 1960s, we established development programmes that were directed specifically at Basarwa, and they have continued to this day. Our National Development Plans, for example, have talked about government's "commitment to raise the standard of living of the poorest sections of population which have not benefited, due to cultural, social and geographic obstacles". In the case of the Basarwa, our plans noted that in many areas "their situation is one of impoverishment combined with dependence on other better off social groups". However, their sparse population, the lack of access, and the distances involved, made it impractical to provide such services to Basarwa scattered all over the country, especially in the western Kgalakgadi. We proposed re-settling Basarwa, since we wanted to be able to provide the same kinds of opportunities for education, health care, water and nutrition that we did for other Batswana. We long had a policy of providing services and facilities in an efficient manner, but we were also willing to pay higher costs in order to reach some outlying areas.

We thought about places to settle Basarwa so we could provide the modern services we were providing in other more settled and densely populated areas. We needed to find large areas located in ecological conditions that were familiar to them. Modern services then could be combined with assistance in such things as marketing of traditional products or handicrafts, as well as provision of livestock, technical assistance in farming, and the like. As time went on we added such things as hostels for schools, so parents did not need to live in one of the settled areas in order for their children to get an education. Projects to achieve these objectives were developed and executed by the Ministry of Local Government and Lands. Over the years I was in politics, we spent tens of millions of pula on both capital and recurrent costs of such projects.

We have invested in programmes and projects, and we have been frustrated by the failure of Basarwa to take advantage of opportunities. However, some people from other countries have loudly criticised how we have handled matters regarding the Basarwa. Yes, we have moved and resettled some Basarwa, but we did so to aid in their participation and that of their children in our economic progress. We have moved other Batswana as well, such as when we established mines at Selebi-Phikwe, Orapa and Jwaneng, or demarcated the TGLP ranches. In all cases, we provided adequate compensation to anyone who was moved.

Some of the complaints have been especially strange. We established a borehole for a diamond prospecting site in the Central Kgalakgadi Game Reserve. While the prospecting was under way, Basarwa in the region were attracted to the area by the availability of water. The site was later determined to be uneconomic for mining, so the camp was abandoned, as, of course, was the borehole. Everyone knows Basarwa had never relied on boreholes for water in their traditional life; but when the borehole was abandoned, the critics complained that we were discriminating against the Basarwa! For the romantics who talk of preserving the traditional Basarwa way of life to protest the removal of a modern convenience seemed hypocritical to me. In fact, virtually all Basarwa are in contact with modern society in various ways; many use cell phones and other conveniences and hunt from Land Rovers using high powered rifles. They have already entered the modern economy in some ways, so the question becomes: How can we best help them to avail opportunities for themselves and their children?

Our foreign critics may be well intentioned, but the extreme criticism is misplaced. Such people want the Basarwa to remain, or really return to, what they were; they see the Basarwa as a curiosity to be preserved. We have seen them as fellow citizens who deserve the benefits of economic development.

Of course, there have been Basarwa who have been glad to seek the support of our foreign critics. I had a white neighbour in Ghanzi, Thomas Hardbattle, who was at the time the second richest man in cattle in Ghanzi. He married a Mosarwa, and they had children together. He left a will that said when he died, the cattle should be sold, the farms should remain empty, and the children should be sent to England to be educated. When the children came back, they could decide what to do with the farms. His will stated that only the grandchildren, not the children, could sell the farms if they decided they were not worth keeping. One son, John, joined the British Army, and the other, Thomas, became a diesel mechanic. After the father died, John came back to Ghanzi to farm, but his farming was nothing to write home about.

John Hardbattle opposed the authorities and argued we should give the Basarwa better treatment, and in this he found supporters in Western countries. While he was alive he achieved a good deal of notoriety, but I think much of it came from people who enjoyed promoting those whom they really saw as curiosities. Once John Hardbattle heard I was travelling to the United States, and the people who were supporting him encouraged him to travel to the States to confront me. When we met there, I said to him: "John, why do you come to America to discuss and settle our differences? Have you ever tried to see me in Botswana and I refused to see you?" The answer of course was no. It was surprising to me how a man who had enjoyed so much education could be so misguided. After John Hardbattle died, others took up the cause. And, of course, the opposition and the opposition media provide them with publicity and half-truths, since it serves their interests to keep criticism of the government in the local and international press.

HIV/AIDS

During my time in office, our failure to deal with HIV/AIDS in an effective way in the early days of the disease arose from judgmental errors. It is one of those things I wish I had handled differently, and it is perhaps my greatest regret. The pandemic is now threatening to destroy so much of what we have accomplished, economically, socially and politically. We are creating orphans at an alarming rate. Since many of our nurses, teachers and police personnel are now HIV positive, the disease will substantially reduce our ability to deliver services in every area, from health and education to law enforcement. It is likely to increase the inequality of incomes within the country as well.

The first reported AIDS death in Botswana was in 1985. At the time, I think most of us in government took the view that AIDS was a Western disease, mainly having to do with homosexual men. However, there also was evidence that it was becoming prevalent in some other African countries. So, both government and private sector employers like Debswana started to provide publicity on HIV/AIDS, such as posters in work areas on how to stop sexual transmission of HIV/AIDS. Since we had generally anticipated problems and tried to deal with them, we also began to develop our first plan for addressing the threats of the disease.

We had a very good Ministry of Health to advise us, and we had put a great many resources into our health care system, so we thought we would be in a position to take further action if needed. When people from other ministries or from outside government tried to offer advice, the people in the Ministry of Health felt their professionalism was being called into question. Also, doctors tended to tell the uninitiated not to interfere with medical issues; they suggested that laymen would not understand these scientific and technical matters.

HIV/AIDS is an area where we failed to apply the model of policy-making that worked successfully in so many other fields, from mineral agreements to economic policy. Had we followed our usual procedure when we saw a major problem, we would have constituted a group from a number of ministries, involved experts from outside government, looked at what was being done in other countries, presented analyses and alternatives, held extensive discussions in informal cabinet and in parliamentary caucus, and then reached conclusions that had broad support. But for a long time we treated HIV/AIDS as a narrow issue of health, and the consequences have been tragic.

Of course, we were not inactive; since it was obvious we faced a problem. By 1987, we had adopted our first short-term plan for dealing with HIV/AIDS. It involved increased education and information efforts; and it emphasised the need to ensure a safe supply of blood for transfusions and supplies of disposable needles to all clinics to prevent accidental spread of the disease. Our first medium term plan to combat HIV/AIDS was adopted in 1989. It strengthened surveillance and reporting activities so we could better understand the scope of the problem, and it increased education on the sexual transmission of HIV. It also added an emphasis on preventing pre-natal transmission from mothers to children, and it established reporting and monitoring systems.

In retrospect, we failed at that stage because we did not fully involve other partners, including other ministries and politicians, and especially civil society—churches, schools, community based organisations and other NGOs. We did not see the problem broadly enough. For the first several years the unit that was set up to coordinate all our efforts was within the epidemiology department in the Ministry of Health. Partly as a result, the issue did not get the prominence it deserved in development plans, budget speeches, and other public statements and debates.

Even so, some of the signs had seemed promising. By the early 1990s, a very high percentage of the population, especially young people, reported that they understood the methods of transmission and were knowledgeable about the methods of prevention. However, it became clear that knowing how to prevent transmission and actually doing something about it were two different things. In our society, men by tradition had more influence in sexual matters than women. If both a man and a woman knew what should be done by way of condom use, there was no assurance it would be done if a man did not wish to.

The modesty of Batswana and the sense that one wants society's approval have also made it more difficult for us to deal with the epidemic. As a people, we have never talked openly about sexual matters, so we spent many years being euphemistic in talking about transmission of HIV/AIDS. It is only recently that we have stopped calling a spade an agricultural instrument and started calling it a spade. There is also a great deal of shame associated with being HIV positive, or having AIDS. Even at funerals, people are reluctant to say the deceased died of AIDS or complications from AIDS. Mothers who are HIV positive sometimes refuse to use infant formula and continue to breastfeed their babies, which will almost certainly result in an HIV-positive child. They do so because if they are seen feeding with infant formula, their neighbours and relatives will conclude they have the disease, and they do not want that fact known. As we knew from dealing with race and tribalism, matters of social attitude are the most difficult to change. For too long, we acted as if education and information would be enough to get people to do the sensible thing.

In 1994, we began preparations for a new medium term plan and a revised National Policy on AIDS. These took effect during the year I retired. These efforts emphasised the multi-sectoral approach, rather than treating HIV/AIDS as primarily a medical issue. We have been very fortunate to have many international partners in the effort, such as the Bill and Melinda Gates Foundation, major pharmaceutical companies, and such institutions as Harvard and Baylor Universities from the United States. We would not have attracted these partners had we not built a very effective health care system, with a high degree of professionalism, throughout the country. However, even if we were to achieve no new infections immediately, the legacy of so many infected people, particularly of prime working age, will remain a major burden for years to come.

I have a number of other specific regrets about how I approached AIDS. While it is important that those with the disease be respected and treated well, I think we did not take into account the dangers to those who were not yet infected. For example, I wish we had made it a requirement that people coming into the country would be tested for HIV/AIDS. The Ministry of Health and others in cabinet were opposed, saying it would be discriminatory. We already had a policy that if someone were suffering from TB they would not be allowed into the country. What is the difference, except that TB is less self-imposed than AIDS? But I lost the argument.

In addition, as the nature of the problem became more obvious, I emphasised the disease is indicative of a lack of morality in the nation. I was surprised that not even the church supported my view. I once had four reverend gentlemen come to see me, and they adopted the role of the protectors of those who were unfortunate enough to have the disease. They took the side of those already sick, rather than those still in danger. Perhaps if I had called together all the clergy for a broader discussion, we might have had more progress. When I raised the issue of HIV/AIDS and the reasons for its spread in *kgotla* meetings, the reactions were very hostile to the idea that I would talk about such personal and moral issues publicly. Only the Bakgatla, who are more candid about most things than other Batswana, seemed to be interested in hearing and talking about the matter.

I also said publicly that the use of condoms was not the be-all and end-all. A poor girl can be told there is a condom when there isn't one; I saw this as a way of cheating innocent girls into having sex with fellows who the girls believed had condoms. So, the health people criticised me for being against condom use, but that was not the case. I think we became so obsessed with condoms that we in effect said it is okay to have sexual intercourse with whomever and whenever, and I think it was most unfortunate that we gave that impression.

The way President Mogae has taken very active leadership is a great credit to him. He has correctly seen the issue as a very broad-based political and social one, not simply a medical or heath problem. He has spoken out regularly and forcefully about the realities, and he has also been very effective in bringing partners from other countries to assist in combating the disease. I just regret I did not do more when I was president.

Corruption
Corruption is a scourge in many countries, rich and poor. It has benefited some at the expense of the majority, and it has also wrecked whole economies. While we have been fortunate to have managed as little corruption as we have, we also worked to avoid it and then punish it if discovered. In the beginning, we were a poor country with a very simple administration and few resources, and it was very easy to operate in a transparent manner. We also had a legacy from the British of properly accounting for things, and the policies didn't give room for abuse. We Batswana had the long-standing practice of open discussion where anyone's views could be expressed, which, of course, encouraged transparency. If one had opinions about how policies or procedures might be abused, one was encouraged to point them out.

As we grew and became larger and more complex, we started to see such things as petty thefts from government departments. Also, as we saw what was happening in other countries, it became clear that corrupt administration would not be easy to identify or detect. We then experienced a few major instances of corruption, such as the BHC scandal in 1992. After holding meetings with people from other countries, we concluded that Hong Kong had a good model for anti-corruption measures. So, I sent Simon Hirschfeld, the commissioner of police, to take a look at the system there. We brought Mr Stockwell, an experienced man from Hong Kong, to develop the relevant legislation, which was adopted in 1994. We established an anti-corruption unit that is independent of the police. A number of experienced investigators from London's Metropolitan Police were recruited to set the unit up properly and to train our own people.

But more important than specific legislation and investigations was that we did not give too much power to any one person. No minister could make major decisions on his or her own but had to involve one or two or three other departments. In fact, we went through an elaborate process within government when a major decision, such as granting a mining lease, was to be reached. It involved consultation between ministries and ultimately discussion and a decision within cabinet.

In the early days, for example, Minister Segokgo, who was responsible for minerals at the time, felt that as minister he could issue a license on his own, as was provided for in the Mines and Minerals Act. But Seretse told him: "No, this is not something for one man on his own; it is too important. Even if you think it is right, if anything goes wrong, you must share the responsibility with your colleagues in cabinet. And, if the people later think it is wrong, then you will have others who participated with you in the decision to help you defend why it was thought to be the right thing to do." It became routine for those who had the portfolio responsibility for a matter to bring the issues to cabinet through this consultative mechanism. All the implications, whether administrative or financial, had to be mentioned and accounted for.

Our system also had checks and balances in the roles of ministers and officials. We opted for the British model for a professional civil service, rather than the American one with thousands of political appointees. Even after several expansions of cabinet, there were fewer than two dozen political appointments in an administration. Civil servants who provided specialist knowledge and advice were protected by the Public Service Commission. Ministers did not act on their own. Even materials for decisions by ministers that did not go to cabinet were prepared by officials. On many occasions that I know of, and I am sure there are many more that I don't, officials made sure their minister would not exceed his or her authority under the law. Interestingly, this often led to complaints from politicians of both the front and back benches of all parties that the civil service carried too much influence. But if we had not received such complaints, I think we would have been in trouble, since it would have indicated that politicians were exercising unreasonable discretion.

Over the years, we have had a number of instances where corrupt practices were discovered and penalties assessed. In one case, Dan Kwelagobe had become suspicious of what was happening in *Domkrag's* offices and proposed that the party's books be looked at carefully. The executive secretary of *Domkrag* was found to have been embezzling funds. He was prosecuted, and, in addition to his jail time, he lost his license to practice law. In another famous instance, a cousin of the late president, who was a senior civil servant, was found to be misappropriating funds. In his case, the normal administrative processes of following up claims for expense reimbursement turned up suspicious activity; ultimately he was prosecuted and convicted. We have had some good people in the administration who had a nose for such activity—people like Joe Shannon, who was in finance for many years. Having a few people who are suspicious by nature is a useful part of the machinery.

When serious allegations of potential misbehaviour were made, especially against people in official positions, the public would wonder whether such allegations were true or not. Sometimes we appointed a presidential commission to investigate and take an independent view of the matter. We sometimes decided that publishing a commission's report would serve no useful purpose. On the other hand, the report on TGLP lease allocations, for example, concerned an area where my younger brother Peter had a farm. Therefore, I felt it would be useful to provide a public report of the commission. The Kgabo Report on Mogoditshane land allocations was another example where we made the commission's report public. Of course, people who thought something was inappropriate were usually not convinced by the public report of the investigation, but at least those who were simply curious had facts they could digest.

The Christie Commission report on financial irregularities at the BHC resulted in a number of actions. I had to ask both the assistant minister and permanent secretary in the Ministry of Local Government and Lands to resign their positions. The PS was not criminally culpable in the BHC scandal, but "Nearest to the king, nearest to the gallows", as the saying goes. The assistant minister was criminally implicated in the matter and convicted, but his conviction was overturned on appeal.

There has often been a hue and cry in the press or from the opposition about abuses or corruption in government or parastatals. In all significant cases when I was in politics, we made investigations through the police or a special commission to find the truth and to take action against any who had done wrong. It is regrettable that we had instances of corruption and abuse of power. However, the fact that we pursued all serious allegations and did not try to hide the fact they occurred was important to our democratic system, and also to our economic development. The annual surveys by Transparency International have rated Botswana as having among the lowest corruption levels in the entire developing world, and this reflects the efforts we made to combat corrupt practices.

I knew about a few overt attempts at buying influence. I once was approached directly by an Afrikaner named Blacknote, who offered me shares in his company free of any payment. I declined, and I explained to him that while we wanted to have black citizens participate in businesses, we wanted it to be on a commercial basis, not as a favour. In another case, while Lemme Makgekgenene was a minister he was approached by an Asian trader with a similar proposition. He declined and then reported it to me. In addition, no end of letters came to me over the years offering to open secret bank accounts in Switzerland, which, of course, I ignored.

I never had any crude approaches, but I also tried to avoid situations that held dangers of conflict of interest. For example, Satar Dada wanted me to buy shares in a new Mercedes dealership. I was uneasy about this, so I discussed it with Festus Mogae, and he, too, was uneasy, so I declined. In retrospect, I am glad I did, since the dealership ended up selling equipment to the mines at Orapa and Jwaneng. While it was possible to have owned the shares without any element of conflict, the situation was exploitable; and that would have disturbed me, and it would have disturbed the mine—both very important things! Justice must not only be done but must be seen to be done.

Politics and Perceptions

In many countries, perhaps most, there is a perception that politicians are in the game to enrich themselves, and there have always been such accusations in Botswana. One of the reasons we developed open procedures with checks and balances was to try to minimise the opportunities for abuse of influence, especially by ministers and high-ranking officials.

We were both lucky and careful when we started the party. We were lucky that the first leaders of the party comprised a very honest group. They were hard working and dedicated to the service of the country. However, we also were careful as we selected people for major positions, and we took their character into account as well as other aspects of their ability. Seretse Khama set this standard by being very clear that politicians and civil servants should not see independence as a route to enrich themselves personally.

The problem in politics arises not because people are ambitious, since one should be ambitious. But when politicians selfishly want things, when there is disregard for the country and for other people, or for what is reasonable, and especially when they use their political position for personal gain, then it is not only unreasonable but dangerous for the country. These are the kinds of people who have wrecked other countries: They visit on all the sins of a few greedy people who get into a position of power and abuse it. We would have been in trouble as a country if we had had only a few more people who pursued politics in a selfish manner. I have wondered why it was that there were not more selfish politicians, and I think it may just be that we were fortunate during my years in office, or it was a reflection of the times we lived in.

I don't think our politicians were outrageously rewarded by salaries or perks while I was in government. For example, it was many years before we allowed any first class air travel, or official cars with drivers, for anyone except the late president, even though such perks were the rule in countries as poor as or poorer than Botswana. The traditional modesty of our people was helpful, of course. Minister Masisi once discovered that management of the BMC was staying in a first class hotel in Rome. He went to them and told them to move to a less expensive hotel, such as the one in which he was staying, since the money they were spending belonged to the farmers of Botswana.

When people are elected to office it is, of course, wrong for them to enrich themselves from their position. But, at the same time, they must not be paid as paupers; otherwise, we would not get people who can deliver the goods. I'm not in favour of lavish standards for ministers or councillors, but we must be careful that our political leaders and senior civil servants don't trail too far behind successful individuals in the rest of society. There is not an exact comparative standard; certainly we should not house our permanent secretaries in the kind of residence Debswana or Barclays would provide for its chief executive. At the same time, our top people need to have the kind of remuneration whereby they can be comfortable in inviting those executives to their homes.

Towards the end of my presidency, there was a controversy about building flats for members of Parliament. For many years MPs stayed in government flats built in 1964 when Parliament was meeting. Those flats were extremely uncomfortable, with no heating in winter or air conditioning in summer. They also were cramped and unsuited for meeting with constituents, or even for working on one's papers in evenings or mornings. For quite some time, we had looked for a space where MPs could be adequately housed. We decided on a plot of land that contained a number of badly built pre-fabricated asbestos houses that should have been taken down in any case, and we built comfortable flats for MPs on that plot. Of course, the opposition made a fuss about the flats as being too extravagant and even went so far as to say they would not occupy them. But, having made their fuss, they moved into them too. I thought the flats were reasonable under the circumstances; they were not particularly extravagant in the context of Botswana in the late 1990s, though they certainly would have been in the 1960s, or even the 1980s. In fact, beginning in the 1980s, people all over the country were tearing down older, smaller and less well-built homes and putting up private houses of a standard we couldn't even have considered in the 1960s.

If the good people in the public sector, the ones with get-up-and-go, were to go into the private sector, they could earn much more than in public life. Therefore, as private sector incomes rise, one must adjust those in the public sector as well. However, there are dangers of increasing salaries, allowances, and perks such as the provision of cars for politicians. There naturally is an adverse public reaction. But the real danger is that people will come into politics for the wrong reason. It is bad enough when those who are talented come in to make money. It is even worse when those who are useless come into politics to become wealthy, since they may operate by hook or by crook to get whatever they want.

Evaluating Our Overall Record

When we founded the party, we wanted to provide all Batswana with opportunities to improve their lives. However, we knew there were dangers that some could benefit more than others, and we did not want those in high office to take advantage of their positions. I'm often asked how I would evaluate our record.

We succeeded to a very large degree in our efforts to provide equal opportunities. Almost every Motswana now has access to education through junior secondary school, clean water, health care, and land. We localised virtually every middle and upper level position in the public sector, and we made substantial gains in the private sector. Even though non-citizens still were a major presence as employers in the main cities, Batswana owned businesses of all sizes. Our biggest economic failure, or disappointment, has been in agriculture, a sector we had thought would be an important source of growing incomes. The largest problem facing us as I left office was the HIV/AIDS pandemic, which threatened to destroy much of what we have built and also to widen the gap between haves and have-nots.

We were never satisfied with the progress we made in creating new jobs, but our efforts were not in vain. We have been more successful in adding to employment than most other developing countries, especially those that were blessed with rich deposits of diamonds or oil or other minerals. The restraint on wages and economic disparities through the Incomes Policy and sound macroeconomic management were two major reasons why we achieved the economic diversification that we did. In 1964, during self-rule, perhaps 14,000 people were employed in proper modern sector jobs—about 5% of the population age 15 or older. By 1998, over 240,000 people held such jobs—nearly 30% of those 15 or older. And, tens of thousands of young people over the age of 15 were in secondary or tertiary education by 1998, while there had been fewer than 1,000 in such schools at independence. Population grew by 2.5% annually over three decades, but modern sector jobs grew by more than 7.5% annually over the same time. In addition, the jobs in 1998 had considerably higher real wages or salaries than those in 1965. None of us in the leadership at independence imagined that we could possibly achieve such results for our people.

While our overall growth has been rapid, the inequality or disparity of incomes increased by most measures. There were three primary reasons. First, government policies, including our success in negotiating mining agreements, helped create well-paying jobs for tens of thousands of people, but still not yet the majority. Second, agriculture failed to improve, despite millions of pula spent on government programmes, so the incomes of the many people depending on agriculture did not increase. Third, while many individuals took advantage of the many new programmes of assistance or started successful businesses, many more failed to take up those opportunities. It also becomes harder to motivate people to improve themselves if they see people who appear to be enriched without great effort. I am very worried about the increasing disparities, but unfortunately I don't see how one can easily, or even not so easily, stop it.

The late president and I always believed we should provide people with the opportunity to better themselves, but we could not try to guarantee they would do so. Over time, we have developed into a society where most people expect to be given things by government. Students whose education was free expected larger allowances. Civil servants who were paid well expected a guaranteed loan to purchase a new car. Some who became quite wealthy thought it was because they were geniuses, like meteorites fallen from above. They did not recognise that they had done well because conditions had been created to enable them to succeed. Some even said they succeeded despite all the roadblocks government put in their way. They conveniently forgot that without all the things government had done over all these years, without assistance from donors, without the good fortune to have resources from our diamonds, and without our success at obtaining Botswana's fair share of the profits, it would have been impossible for them to be as financially successful as they had been.

The dramatic changes in our economy have led to changes in people's motivation, including the motivation for getting into politics. In the beginning, we knew we must fight the human weakness that desires more goods and possessions. We almost made it a punishment to be a minister, in terms of giving up one's livelihood as a teacher or farmer and taking a job that did not pay much or have many benefits. We felt people in politics needed to sacrifice, a fact that was not always acknowledged or appreciated. Now, however, presidents are under pressure to make everyone who is elected to Parliament a minister, and to increase ministerial pay and perks. If one would yield to these things, the country would get up in arms, and for good reason. When even the most frugal civil servants and ministers add on to the size of their offices and take advantage of the perks, it becomes impossible to impose greater discipline on others who are by nature less frugal. Farmers who have their property re-possessed, or even when called on to repay their loans, say: "So all of this is being done to make ministers and parliamentarians more comfortable?"

Those of us who began *Domkrag* and helped to found Botswana talked of how we needed to cling to a golden mean. That is still the case as we try to balance the need to attract the most able people into public service and politics and the dangers of extremes in salaries and perks.

In some countries, corruption has simply enriched some at the expense of the country; in others, corruption by politicians and civil servants has been so bad it has wrecked the whole economy. We most certainly avoided the latter problem, and I believe we did a good job of limiting the illegitimate enrichment of some at the expense of others. The growing incomes and perks at the top make it much more difficult to maintain the kind of discipline on corruption that we accomplished for so long. The increasing immodesty of life styles among private individuals who have become financially successful makes me worry. It may be an irony that our very successes will make it more difficult to sustain our record in the future.

Chapter 17
Relations with South Africa during Apartheid

Our relations with South Africa have been an important part of our history for many generations. As we moved toward constitutional development and independence, the realities we faced in the relationship were stark. South Africa was ruled by the white supremacist National Party. It was our biggest neighbour, shared our longest populated border, and was our largest trading partner. It controlled Namibia to our west and was influential with Ian Smith's illegal regime in Rhodesia to our north-east. We were in a Customs Union dominated by South Africa, and we used the South African rand as our currency. Our transportation to the sea was almost exclusively through South Africa's territory. Employment in South Africa was much more important to Batswana than was cash employment within Botswana. We knew we had to deal with South Africa, and we knew such dealings would be difficult and even dangerous.

Historical Perspective

Our ancestors sought the protection of the British largely because of the expansionism of the Boer republics from the east and the ambitions of Cecil John Rhodes' British South Africa Company. The white freehold settlements on our borders—the Ghanzi Farms in the west, the Tuli Block, Gaborone Block and Lobatse Block in the east and the Molopo Farms in the south—were granted by chiefs as part of the effort to create white buffers with our neighbours. They separated Batswana from the Germans to the west and the Boers to the south and east. The Tati Concession in the north-east formed a buffer with white-ruled Southern Rhodesia.

The agreements at the end of the Anglo-Boer War established the Union of South Africa. They also provided for the eventual incorporation of the High Commission Territories—Basutoland, Bechuanaland, and Swaziland—into the Union of South Africa, subject to consultation with the traditional leaders of the territories. The agreements also established the Southern African Customs Union that included the three High Commission Territories. South Africa was the principal partner, collecting duties, setting the level of tariffs for the Customs Union, and distributing a small share of revenue to the smaller partners.

A further link to South Africa was provided by the development in the 19th century of the system of migrant labour, first for its mines and later for its urban areas. Africans from throughout southern Africa, as far north as Malawi, were hired on long-term (usually nine to twelve month) contracts to work in South Africa. They sent wages back home and returned to their local areas between contracts. At independence, some 50,000 Batswana worked in South Africa, 25,000 on the mines alone. In the 1960s, over one-third of all men between the ages of 20 and 40 worked outside Botswana, virtually all in South Africa.

In addition, there were perhaps three times as many Setswana speakers in South Africa as in Botswana, and there were family ties on both sides of the border. Tens of thousands of border crossings took place each year as relatives visited one another. Due to the lack of decent roads within Botswana and the dispersion of our population, many parts of southern and eastern Botswana had much closer commercial relations with the border area in South Africa than with the rest of Botswana. Many seasonal rivers in Botswana and along our border with South Africa were part of a common watershed.

Our imports and exports (principally cattle and beef), our transportation links with the rest of the world, our newspapers, the destination for students seeking secondary and tertiary education, all were dominated by our relations with South Africa. Our capital was in the Imperial Reserve in Mafeking, in South Africa's Cape Province. The British official formally responsible for governing us was the British high commissioner to South Africa, and the resident commissioner for Bechuanaland in Mafeking reported to him, not directly to London.

After World War II, with Britain in economic distress, British investments in and trade with South Africa were of great financial importance to the UK. So, Britain's diplomatic relationships with South Africa heavily influenced the UK government's attitudes toward all three High Commission Territories. The British government treated Seretse and Ruth Khama shamefully in the 1940s, banning them from the territory and forbidding Seretse from claiming his hereditary chieftainship. British behaviour was determined by their desire not to damage relationships between the UK and the National Party government in South Africa.

From 1911 onwards, successive South African governments had tried to incorporate the High Commission Territories. Incorporation was opposed by African leaders in the territories, especially by Tshekedi Khama after he became regent of the Bangwato in 1925. He and other local leaders made use of allies in Britain, including the churches, missionaries and liberal politicians, to carry the message that incorporation into South Africa would be a disaster for Africans in the High Commission Territories.

The above factors alone would have meant our foreign policy as an independent Botswana would have to be very sensitive to South Africa. In addition, after the National Party won control of the South African government in 1948 and introduced apartheid, we were faced with a neighbour with whom we disagreed on all fundamental principles: the rights of individuals, racial equality, non-racialism, and political and economic freedoms. The policies of the Nationalists gave rise to opposition groups that were eventually declared illegal; they were driven underground and into exile, and they became armed liberation movements. As South Africa's neighbour, we became a destination for refugees leaving that country, and we later became a transit route for liberation fighters re-entering South Africa.

When the Cold War was at its peak, the United States, the Soviet Union and China each had its own objectives in the region because of South Africa's mineral wealth and its strategic location on shipping routes. Therefore, our relations with the major powers were influenced by what was happening in

South Africa. Well before independence we knew that managing relationships with South Africa would be one of our greatest challenges.

The Threat of Incorporation

The Nationalist government in South Africa was so extreme in its policy of apartheid that, by the 1950s, British politicians became increasingly opposed to sending us to the fate of absorption by South Africa, and the threat seemed to diminish. After the Sharpeville massacre in 1960, and South Africa's subsequent withdrawal from the Commonwealth, it became very unlikely that the UK would consent to the High Commission Territories going to South Africa. However, the South African government continued to press the issue directly with the three territories, right up to and even after our independence. They also promoted their own brand of economic and political domination until serious discussions on South Africa's own political future began in the early 1990s.

In 1963, South Africa's Prime Minister H. F. Verwoerd made a speech entitled: "The Road to Freedom for Basutoland, Bechuanaland and Swaziland". He reiterated the message two days later in a speech entitled, "That No Man May Doubt". On 22 November, Hendrik van Gass, a white member of Legco from the Tuli Block, moved that Legco "consider the advisability of approaching Dr The hon. H. F. Verwoerd, prime minister of the Republic of South Africa, to lay before council or the people of the Protectorate his views as to the future of Bechuanaland to enable them to be studied by us." Van Gass then read Verwoerd's speech into the record. The speech gives a sense of those fellows' thinking:

"I have most clearly stated on behalf of my government that South Africa has no territorial ambitions with regard to these areas. Indeed, were they under her guardianship, South Africa would free them stage by stage, just as she is doing in the Transkei. We could lead them far better and much more quickly to independence and economic prosperity than Great Britain can do. That would be our aim in accordance with our policy of separate development (apartheid).

What would the effect of our present policy be? Firstly, we would aim at making them democratic states in which the masses would not be dominated by small groups of authoritarians. Instead, natural native democracy and its leaders coupled with representative democracy—as in the Transkei—would lead the whole population to democratic rule over its own country. Secondly we would steer away from the principle of multi-racialism. Where Whites would be needed and must remain for some time in those areas and occupations, they would become voters in the Republic of South Africa."

Verwoerd went on to propose an exchange of land "to the advantage of the Bantu people of the High Commission Territories". He said South Africa would apply its border-industry policy, under which factories in white areas would hire blacks from adjacent homelands: "Employees would be able to spend their income within their own states so that these can be built up." He also suggested consolidation of land: "Were it possible for them to be joined to those High Commission Territories to which their people are ethnically linked, then the present difficulty of establishing one big Tswana area, or one large Sotho or Swazi area would fall away."

"For these reasons," he concluded, "I am now making an offer to Great Britain—I might also call it a challenge—to allow us to put the essentials of our policies before the inhabitants of these territories."

Verwoerd's speeches and the substance of his proposals were a surprise throughout the region. The debate on Van Gass' motion in Legco was lively, with passionate contributions from both white and black members. Bertie Adams, the white farmer from Lobatse from whom I had learned some farming methods, was especially eloquent: "I was born in South Africa ... but today my birthright is freedom of speech, freedom of thought, freedom from fear; not of a Gestapo Police who can come and knock on your door, take you away and lock you up for no rhyme or reason before you are brought to a magistrate or a judge and told what you have done wrong. I am ashamed of the way [South Africa] is going today. ...I will stand by Bechuanaland as long as it lasts, as long as it believes in justice, peace, equal rights and a multi-racial democratic government."

I entered the debate at what turned out to be its end: "I think we are engaged in the task of flogging a dead horse. Dr Verwoerd's so-called offer, I think is in fact Dr Verwoerd's threat, and I am jolly well pleased with the course of the debate this morning. ...Since the inception of the Legislative Council, politics in Bechuanaland have with increased momentum followed the course which is diametrically opposed to that followed by South African politics."

I went on to dissect the proposals in various ways from both white and African perspectives: "If we are going to feel that we should get into the fold of Dr Verwoerd's apartheid policy, these poor [white] people who may be here because they ran away from that very policy might be given back to that from which they have run away. Finally, Mr Speaker, my honest conviction is that South Africa has for obvious reasons decided to deal us a deadly blow by economic strangulation and she is merely seeking moral justification for doing so. She is probably not morally brave enough to endure the inflictions she has suffered about her apartheid policy. She is a little hesitant to deal that deadly blow in cold blood; she is therefore causing a little strife in the heat of which she will deliver."

> At this point in my speech the *Hansard* record continues:
> MR VAN GASS: Mr Speaker, I believe....
> MR SPEAKER: Does the hon. Member wish to reply to the debate?
> MR VAN GASS: No, I wish to withdraw.
> HON. MEMBERS: Hear! Hear!

My response to Van Gass was actually very much tempered; I had cleared it with Seretse, and he tore a lot of it away! Some time later, South Africa's president made a comment about not allowing "little Hong Kongs" to develop along the borders of South Africa. That also came up in the debate in the House, and I prepared a blistering speech and went to clear it with

Seretse. He was more temperate than I, and he said: "Please, please don't say things like that!" We were always treading a narrow path.

At about the same time as the Verwoerd speech, Dr Mayer from the Tuli Block claimed an island in the Limpopo for South Africa. Even after independence, Chief Bathoen held discussions with the South African authorities about bringing Ngwaketse into South Africa. The leadership in *Domkrag* reacted vigorously to oppose all suggestions that would either dismember our country or put us under the South Africans. I mention these events as a reminder of how vulnerable we were and how persistent the South African efforts were to pull us away from freedom and into their hands.

Guiding Principles

One country's relationships with another country are always intertwined. One cannot separate economics, finance, politics, diplomacy, movement of people, and security. However, I think I can best tell the story of our relationship with South Africa by discussing some of the issues separately.

As we thought about our situation, we started with a general proposition. When you are weak, you have to stick to principles, since they are the only refuge under which you can take cover. We certainly did not want to, nor could we, take on South Africa as a military power. But, rightly or wrongly, we thought that if we could prove in Botswana that a non-racial society could be established and could work to nobody's disadvantage, and that all the National Party said was impossible could actually be accomplished, our example would do one of two things: Either it would provide comfort to the South African government that, after all, they didn't need to fear South African blacks; or it would show that the South African government had all along known our approach of non-racialism would work but were afraid to admit it. So, whatever the thinking in the National Party government, we could prove them wrong. And, this would apply not only to South Africa but also to Mozambique, Angola, Zimbabwe and Namibia. We were very explicit about this from the beginning. All of us in *Domkrag's* leadership understood and believed in it. Further, we knew that though our approach was offensive to South Africa, it could not be challenged as a moral principle.

The facts of our situation meant we could not survive, literally, without engaging in trade with South Africa, using their roads and railroads, and accepting employment for our people. Although we did business with South Africa, we did not hide the fact that we hated the way they ran their country. Every year the president of Botswana, whether Seretse Khama or Quett Masire, wrote a letter to the president of South Africa to say that he should release Nelson Mandela and other political prisoners. When things like the Sharpeville massacre happened, we vigorously stated our disapproval of what happened. When they raided and killed our people, we said it didn't matter if it was South Africa who did these things, or if the Americans or England or Germany had done them; it was just wrong. We couldn't challenge them in any military way, but we stuck to our principles. To survive we managed to create a situation of "live and let live", since we had no other sensible choice.

Another principle we adopted was that we should not do anything obviously confrontational to South Africa. For instance, we did not want the liberation movements operating in Botswana, since it would give the South Africans the pretext for moving against us or attacking us under a "hot pursuit" rationale. In 1985, South Africa's patience finally ran out; the temptation to hit us with military force became too great, and they raided Gaborone. There were many other instances in which they exercised their economic and geographic stranglehold as well as their military muscle to demonstrate what they could do to us if they wished. The threats to withhold our petrol supplies in the 1970s, their willingness to let goods pile up in Mafeking instead of coming through to Botswana by rail, or to withhold refrigerated railway wagons to prevent us from exporting beef, all showed that they were fully capable of punishing us.

We asked ourselves: "Could our independence really be secure if apartheid exists in the surrounding countries, in particular South Africa?" The answer clearly was: "No." Therefore, we worked with others in the region and with friends from beyond to help bring an end to minority rule and to the threat that an apartheid South Africa posed to the whole of southern Africa. But, as we worked for change, we had to be careful not to rub those fellows the wrong way, since they could make life very difficult, even impossible, for us.

Diplomatic Relations

South Africa was after us right from the beginning to have normal diplomatic relations—exchange of ambassadors and the like. Seretse Khama made it clear at the start that we would never provide diplomats to a country where they would be second-class citizens. During the first debate in the National Assembly after independence, however, the opposition proposed sending diplomatic representatives to South Africa! It was clear they were out of step once again.

Our "live and let live" approach was followed consistently from independence in 1966 to the installation of the new government in South Africa in 1994. Because we often had more than 25,000 citizens working in the South African mines, and thousands more working in other sectors, we established a small Department of Labour office in South Africa to assist our citizens; but that was the extent of any regular government representation. We also developed a framework within the Customs Union for managing most of the day-to-day issues in our relationships on a businesslike basis. We were as correct as we could possibly be in formal relationships, and we avoided publicity even when we had meetings at the political level.

Of course, the South African government wanted to be present at our independence celebrations. We did not want them there, but we did not want to be openly offensive. The Afrikaner Farmer's Association in South Africa wanted to give us some bulls to celebrate our independence. We made arrangements to accept them and planned to give them to our Ministry of Agriculture for the bull pool. But then the minister of agriculture of South Africa came to make the presentation, which was of course a little embarrassing for us. As the ceremony concluded, I decided to be a bit naughty and use the Afrikaans I had learned at Tiger Kloof. I went up to the minster, Jim Fouche, who was later to become president of South Africa. I lowered my voice and said: "*Tot siens, my baas*" (Good-bye, my boss). And he responded in a low voice: "*Tot siens, my Kaffertjie*" ("Good-bye, my little *Kaffir*").

The experience taught us that South Africa's private organisations were under instructions to refer any contacts with the Botswana government to the South African authorities; they viewed any relationship with us as a political one. During the severe drought at independence, we were offered some maize from the United States, but there was a delay in its arrival. We were determined not to accept any gifts from the South African government, but we approached their private sector, the South African Maize Board. We proposed that we use South African maize and then replace it, ton for ton, with the American maize when it arrived. However, the Maize Board brought in the South African government, who said they would just give us the maize free of charge—provided we asked for it. We said: "No, we don't want a gift, we want to exchange." However, they wanted to be able to say they were giving, and we were accepting, their aid. Finally they came up with an excuse for why they couldn't make the exchange we proposed: They said American maize was inferior to theirs!

After independence, the South African government continued to behave as they had in the past. For instance, when they had trouble with an African working in the mines, they would ask: "Who's your chief?" If the person responded with the name of a chief in Botswana, they would send the person to Botswana, whether or not he was a citizen. Chief Linchwe in Mochudi, for example, was recognised as chief by Bakgatla living in the Northern Transvaal, so some of his subjects were not Botswana citizens. We simply sent non-citizens right back to South Africa, which took them a bit by surprise. It may have taken the South Africans a bit of time to realise what kind of a new neighbour they had; we were in fact an independent state, and we acted as such. More importantly, we defined citizenship in the nation, not in a tribe.

The South African government was always suspicious of us, in part because we did not behave the way they expected African governments to conduct themselves; we were strictly professional and businesslike. We would make our views about apartheid known, but we were neither noisy in our criticism nor did we come cap in hand. They would not really talk straight with us, but they tried to give the impression that "we are here if you want to do business with us".

Boundaries

For the most part, we had no boundary disputes with South Africa, but there were two issues in the Caprivi Strip to our north that created problems. Sedudu Island in the Chobe River caused a dispute first with South Africa and later with Namibia. There was a clear history that the island was a part of Botswana, but the South Africans wanted to patrol the border on the Botswana side of the river. They argued that the boundary was to the south of the island, which would have put the island in Namibia, rather than to the north, where the border had always been.

We consulted SWAPO, as the leading Namibian liberation movement, and they agreed that the Boers were just making trouble to get a strategic island. Fortunately, the survey of the island was well documented and carefully measured from border to border and bank to bank, as well as the depths of the channels in the river. In 1970, our attorney general and surveyor general went to the United Nations in New York to make a joint report for the UN that showed the boundary was where Botswana said it was, and it was accepted. In their usual way, the South African government did not challenge the outcome, but they did not write back to say they accepted it either.

Another issue arose over whether Botswana and Zambia had a common border. The South African government argued that the boundary of the Caprivi Strip of Namibia was directly with Zimbabwe, so there was no common border between Botswana and Zambia. The South Africans said if we had a road and a bridge to Zambia, it would create a "Ho Chi Minh Trail" for the ANC, and the Rhodesian government made a similar charge. We raised the boundary issue with the British authorities before independence, thinking they might be in a better position to settle it with the Rhodesians than we would be, since the boundary we recognised had been established at the 1885 Berlin Conference. By then the British were at loggerheads with Ian Smith's UDI regime in Rhodesia, so they said they would take on the issue only if we agreed to postpone our independence until it was settled! We had to live with the ambiguity for many years.

South African Intelligence Operations

We knew before independence that South African and Rhodesian intelligence services operated in Botswana. They recruited agents in Botswana, and they undertook operations, sometimes against refugees who were in the liberation movements. All of us had stories about tampering with telephone calls or mail; it was a very common thing.

The South Africans had informants throughout the government. In 1976, we undertook a detailed study in my ministry of the costs and benefits of being in the Customs Union. After I read it, I felt it was so sensitive that we should destroy all copies except one to be kept in the ministry's safe. Then in early 1977, a story about the vulnerability of Botswana to South Africa appeared in a South African weekly magazine. In addition to disparaging the idea of the independent pula, the magazine cited a "secret" report on the Customs Union done by the Ministry of Finance and Development Planning. The article said our government estimated we would suffer an annual loss of P37 million if we were to withdraw from the Customs Union. This was the main conclusion of the report that was in my ministry's safe! We thought the South African government had given the information to the magazine so we in Botswana would know that not even our secret reports could be kept from them.

The security of the state was and is a responsibility of the Special Branch of the Police. They kept an eye on not only the general public but also on members of the police. We would get reports that some of our government security people had been approached by either the Rhodesians or the South

African government to become their agents. Sometimes we just let these people go on with their business, knowing we could not trust them with information. And if someone in *Domkrag* was hobnobbing with the South Africans or the Rhodesians, then the Special Branch would bring it to our attention. Of course, humans being what they are, some were falsely accused, but we knew we had to be constantly on our guard.

By and large, our personnel, both politicians and senior civil servants, were well disciplined, though one could never rule out the possibility that someone could become a fifth columnist. Many times when our people were approached, they would tell us about it. Of course, once someone came to say they had been approached, we never knew if others had been tempted but had not come forward to tell about it.

The Rand and the Pula

One overture from South Africa as we became independent was that we join with them as members of a group within the IMF. As an independent state, we were entitled to IMF membership even though we used the rand as our currency, and we felt the African group within the IMF, which excluded South Africa, would better suit us, so we declined. They also wanted us to continue using the rand as currency. We had made up our minds that we were not going to be part of a formal Rand Monetary Area, and we knew we wanted to establish our own currency. Even so, we worked with Lesotho and Swaziland in the negotiations to revise the Rand Monetary Area, hoping to help them strike a better deal.

After we had established the pula in August 1976, there were a number of stories in the South African press about what a mistake we had made, and how the pula would soon go the way of other currencies in Africa and decline rapidly in value. How many of the stories were encouraged by the South African government or its Reserve Bank to try to pressure us, I don't know. In April 1977, following the announcement of a very inflationary budget in South Africa, officials from my ministry and the Bank of Botswana brought me a recommendation that we should increase the par value of the pula by 5%. I listened to their arguments for more than two hours and asked them questions. I thought it was risky to change the value of the currency only eight months after it had been established. Their arguments centred on the idea that we could mitigate the rate of inflation if we increased the value of the pula—South African goods would become cheaper in pula terms and this, in turn, would lower the rate of inflation we imported from South Africa.

After two hours of discussion, I said to them: "I will accept your recommendation, but not for the reasons you have given." I told them their logic might be correct, but we had so few traders that it was unlikely prices would be properly discounted from rand to pula. We also faced the problem that 25,000 mine workers would suddenly find they had 5% fewer pula in their remittances than they had the week before. However, I thought it was important to establish the principle that we would manage the exchange rate of the pula in the best interests of the country. It would also establish our greater independence from South Africa.

At the time the late president was in a clinic in Johannesburg. Even though I had full authority as acting president to change the par value of the pula, I felt he should be consulted and either be persuaded or overrule us, as this would be the first time we would be making such a change. So, Phil Steenkamp, the PSP, arranged for a small charter plane (the only aircraft available in Gaborone that day), and he and I flew off to Johannesburg with some officials from my ministry and the Bank of Botswana. We were all somewhat shaken by flying through a severe electrical storm on the way. I joked to my companions that it was disconcerting to be flying in such bad weather with a group of godless economists! After landing in Johannesburg, we made our way to the clinic where we briefed Seretse. He asked a series of questions and then said he thought we were doing the right thing for the right reasons.

On our return home, as we were starting out onto the taxiway, one of the plane's two engines failed! Fortunately it was a minor problem, and we returned to Gaborone at about 10pm. The ministers who were in Gaborone were all called to my house that evening, and we briefed them so they would know what we had done and why. The announcement was made the next morning, a Saturday, after foreign exchange trading had closed for the day. Quill Hermans was then the governor of the Bank of Botswana, and he phoned the governor of the South African Reserve Bank early Saturday morning to tell him what we were about to announce. The governor replied, in a condescending voice, that Quill must be mistaken—obviously, the pula was being de-valued, not re-valued. Quill explained that we were in fact increasing the value of the pula relative to the rand, and there was a long silence on the line. We had finally made the point that we were fully independent of the South African rand.

The Customs Union

The Southern African Customs Union is the oldest customs union agreement in the world still in operation. It was established in 1910; South Africa set the tariffs and rates of excise tax throughout the Common Customs Area (CCA), comprising Botswana, Lesotho, Swaziland and South Africa. Each of the High Commission Territories, later known as the BLS countries, received a fixed percentage of the pool of revenue collected in the CCA. Botswana's share was based on our proportion of imports into the CCA from 1907 to 1910, which was calculated to be 0.27622%. The colonial authorities negotiated our share up to 0.30971% in 1965. One piece of advice from the British authorities was that we should do nothing after independence to tamper with the Customs Union, since their renegotiation had provided us such a good deal. We did our own analysis and concluded their advice was incorrect, and we entered into negotiations to revise the agreement.

The agreement as revised in 1969 provided the framework for many of our relationships with South Africa. Consultations on animal and plant disease controls, guarantees of free movement of goods, regulations of transportation rates, location and operation of border posts that governed movement of people as well as goods, all were covered under the agreement, in addition to revenue sharing and tariff setting provisions. It provided for regular quarterly consultations among officials, and for an annual meeting at which the minister of finance of the host country would make an appearance. The South Africans, especially at official level but even at ministerial level, were often quite legalistic. Whenever we could demonstrate that South Africa had violated the agreement, or was proposing a policy that would do so, the agreement provided us with a vehicle for discussing the matter.

There was disagreement for many years over whether we should remain in the Customs Union. On the political side, membership in the Customs Union was regarded by many as bringing us too close to South Africa, and some opposed our being in it for that reason. However, the Customs Union provided a framework for substantive discussions with the South African government, and we were better able to resist having diplomatic relations with them. During the oil crises of the 1970s and 1980s, our access to petroleum products was threatened by the oil embargo on South Africa. We were part of the South African supply system for refined petroleum, and we paid excise taxes, so the Customs Union provided a mechanism under which we could discuss supply issues with their government; we did not have to pay a diplomatic or other price to have the conversations.

There were also economic arguments on both sides. Those favouring membership pointed to the benefits of the revenue-sharing formula. Under the revised formula, customs revenue rose ten-fold in real terms between 1969 and 1975. From 1970 to 1975, customs revenue provided 45-50% of total government recurrent revenue. It was not until 1984, after the opening the Jwaneng, that mineral revenues began to exceed revenue from the customs union. There was also the fact that we did not have to divert skilled manpower to develop our own customs, excise and sales tax staff. They also liked the fact that we denied ourselves temptations, since other countries had abused their use of protective tariffs. Those opposing the Customs Union pointed out that giving up our discretion in setting tariffs and excise taxes not only reduced our fiscal flexibility but also denied us a method of encouraging domestic manufacturing industry. Opponents of the Customs Union also argued that we could import goods more cheaply from other countries, and then impose our own tariffs or other taxes. Our rights under international law protected transit of our goods through South African territory. Proponents of membership argued that the Customs Union provided us with a legal agreement with South Africa guaranteeing transit rights, and this was better than relying on international law alone.

Beginning in the mid-1970s, we regularly reviewed the costs and benefits of being in the Customs Union, and I took a keen interest in those studies. The calculation of the costs and the benefits was not easy, but in fact the key issue was political: How would South Africa react if we were to leave the Customs Union? Those who argued we would be better off outside assumed we would be able to import and export through South Africa without any interference. I thought it was unrealistic to imagine South Africa would allow free movement of our goods if we were not in the Customs Union. While in theory international law assured our transit rights, the South Africans were unlikely to honour those rights without a *quid pro quo* unless we had a treaty with them. There were plenty of occasions when, after we had said or done something they did not like, they had made life difficult for us just to show us who was in charge. If we were to stop buying South African goods worth hundreds of millions of pula, the South African government would surely retaliate. Without the legal framework of the Customs Union Agreement, we would have been at their mercy.

Of course, we did not want to let the South Africans know of our conclusions, since it would undermine our bargaining position. Therefore, in our negotiations, we always insisted on talking about how the high protected prices of South African goods disadvantaged the other smaller countries, and how the lagged revenue from the Customs Union was not sufficient to compensate for the high-priced goods produced in South Africa—even though we knew that the comparison was with an unrealistic alternative.

We benefited from the fact that a degree of understanding and trust had developed among the officials at the quarterly meetings over the years. The annual meeting of the Customs Union Commission gave more senior officials opportunities to maintain contact and promoted respect for the quality and integrity of our people. We also followed developments and even learned of disagreements within different parts of the South African government, since most Customs Union meetings involved representatives of several ministries from each country—finance, commerce, industry, agriculture, and foreign affairs. Further, if circumstances made it necessary to involve ministers, the Customs Union provided the framework for those discussions as well. We did not advertise these benefits of being in the Customs Union, but they were very important factors.

In dealing with the South Africans, we also knew more or less who were the most inclined to apartheid and who would be to the right or to the left. Pik Botha, the foreign minister, for example, would be toward the left end, while those on the right included some like Andries Treurnicht (who was referred to in the South African liberal press as "Dr No"). We took account of the fact that one like Pik Botha might be a liberal, or a pseudo-liberal, but he also was working under instructions from cabinet. We knew there would be a mixture of what one did as an individual and what one had to do as part of a team. And, to the extent possible, we would try to use that knowledge.

Renegotiating the Customs Union Agreement in 1969

During the negotiations to revise the Customs Union Agreement in 1969, we learned some important lessons. They established the pattern for our approach to international negotiations, including those for mining agreements.

We conducted the negotiations as systematically as we could. We had the analyses and views of our officials, and we also invited professors of economics from outside to enlighten us on such things as the effects of a large economy on adjacent smaller economies. We learned about "polarisation effects" of such development. Since the agreement gave South Africa the right to decide the tariff levels, South Africa's interests, not ours, were considered when setting tariffs, and protected factories would be located there. We concluded that since BLS consumers would pay the protected tariff prices, we were paying to protect South African industries. These factors became part of our argument that the BLS countries needed some financial compensation if we were to be partners with a dominant South Africa. We developed the argument that, surely, we should get out of this what we put into it. Therefore, the revenue we received from the customs pool should bear a relationship to whatever we imported at protected prices, whether it was from South Africa or from abroad. So, those were the three main elements that we proposed be taken into account in a new agreement.

The practice we developed for negotiations was that officials, along with any outside experts, would develop analyses and make proposals to ministers, who would discuss the pros and cons. Cabinet and the president would then approve a negotiating strategy and set some boundaries. These established how far negotiators could go without returning to the relevant ministers or to cabinet. Officials were involved in the actual discussions, leaving ministers in reserve in case things did not go well. In the 1969 negotiations, our officials were rebuffed by the South African officials, despite the logic and persuasiveness of their arguments and evidence. Ultimately, the negotiations at official level ended in a stalemate. The ministers of finance from South Africa and BLS met in Cape Town, without any officials present. My officials were left outside the doors, wondering what we would come up with; and they were nervous about what I would agree to!

Dr Deitrichs, the South African minister of finance, was very condescending in the meeting. One really felt he was thinking: "Well, these beggars are here." I carried the message to the other finance ministers, since I had been drilled and practiced by my officials. We in *Domkrag* had concluded before self-rule that ministers should be fully informed about the details. First, this would ensure informed decisions. Second, when ministers were on their own without officials, they would be able to make the arguments. That was not a universal practice in all governments, and it was clearly not the case with the other three ministers of finance, who apparently had not been well briefed. When one is in a meeting with people who are not as knowledgeable, and one demonstrates one's knowledge, the others tend to keep quiet; they don't want to say something that would make them appear to be fools. The fact that I knew more about the subject than they did, and also appeared to know more than I was saying, helped me to carry the day in achieving substantial improvements in the agreement.

Because our arguments were sound, and perhaps as a kind of good neighbourliness, South Africa agreed to the particular aspects of the revenue-sharing formula we proposed. As a result, revenue would be determined by the level of our imports from all sources, including from South Africa. There would be a "compensation factor" to recognise polarisation effects and the price-raising effects of protective tariffs on goods we bought from South Africa. BLS also deserved compensation because we gave up our fiscal discretion in setting tariffs and excises to South Africa. In the end, the compensation factor increased the BLS revenue by a multiple of 1.42 times the rate of duty actually collected. For example, if the average rate of duty on all imports and excisable goods production was 15%, each BLS country would be entitled to receive revenue at a rate of 21.3% (15% times 1.42) of the value of its own imports from all sources. As our imports rose with economic development, so would our revenue—regardless of the size of the revenue pool. Later it really shocked the South Africans to realise how much we were taking. Our economies and our imports grew faster than South Africa's, so our share of the revenue pool kept rising.

Further Negotiations on the Revenue Sharing Formula

After the oil price shocks of 1973, the collections in the customs revenue pool fell rapidly as a percentage of imports in the whole CCA. The values of oil imports and of production of petroleum products both were a large share of the denominator in the mathematical equation that determined the rate of revenue. Oil duties, however, were based on the quantity, not the value, of oil products, so as prices rose, duty collections did not. As a result, the percentage rate of revenue in the formula fell, and BLS revenues started to decline, even though the value of our imports continued to rise. We made proposals through the Customs Union consultative mechanism to change the formula. We again based our proposals on studies of other countries' experience in collections of customs and excise revenues. South African officials were not in a position to dispute our positions, even though they did not like the result.

After several years of negotiations, South Africa agreed to a "stabilisation factor" in the rate of revenue. The rate of duty payable to the BLS countries on our imports would never drop below 17%, nor could it ever rise above 23%, regardless of what happened to the percentage rate of revenue for the whole Customs Union. This was a major benefit to the BLS countries. Once again the South African side did not realise how much our continued rapid economic growth would increase our share of the common revenue pool.

When we renegotiated in 1969, none of the BLS countries was in a position to provide accurate or timely data on the values of imports from and exports to South Africa. Therefore, the agreement provided for a complex formula of estimates of the revenue due the BLS from the revenue pool with adjustments after the actual values were known, creating a two-year lag before the receipt of adjusted payments. Everyone had expected adjustments in the payments would lead sometimes to increased payments to the BLS and sometimes repayments to South Africa. However, the rapid growth in the BLS economies caused the value of imports into BLS countries to grow very rapidly. As a result, revenue due to the BLS was underestimated in virtually every year, and South Africa was required to pay an adjustment to BLS. The sums involved were substantial—tens of millions of rand each year that were owed to BLS were not paid until two years after the goods had been imported and the duties paid. Interest was not paid, and the real value of the adjustment payment also depreciated due to inflation in prices.

During the 1970s, we argued strongly for a change in the revenue-sharing formula that would eliminate this lag in payments. In 1980, the four countries agreed to establish a study group to investigate the issues and propose a solution. Officials subsequently agreed to a change in the formula that would eliminate the lag in payments and substantially increase the payments to BLS. However, by this time the South African government's own finances had deteriorated, and their Finance Ministry was strongly opposed to any change that would increase payments to BLS.

The resistance to change was always at the political level. Logic was on our side, and the officials from South Africa were honest and competent civil servants who could see the arguments. We made use of this fact as we dealt with the next round of South African initiatives.

The Customs Union and the "Constellation of States"

In the 1950s, South Africa under the National Party had developed a grand design for how it would divide up southern Africa, including Namibia and the BLS countries as well as South Africa itself. Apartheid was about economics as well as politics, as Verwoerd's speech had made clear. There would be white-dominated areas called South Africa, and there would be economically dependent black areas that they called "Independent Homelands". They began creating these entities in the 1970s, beginning with Transkei, then extending "independence" to Bophuthatswana, Venda, and Ciskei before the strategy failed completely. The four became known in South African statements as the "TBVC States"—though they were recognised as independent only by South Africa and by one another. Several aspects of South Africa's approach to regional development, summarised in its vision of a "Constellation of States of Southern Africa", had a potential impact on Botswana; we had to respond to them.

South Africa extended the fiction of independence by applying the same terms to the TBVC states that the Customs Union provided the BLS countries. South Africa tried to create economically and politically viable homelands in the 1980s, and it increased spending on civil service and teacher salaries and on development projects. As a result, estimated imports in their revenue sharing formula increased—and so did the payments from South Africa to the TBVC treasuries. Each year South Africa paid out a larger and larger share of the revenue collected from tariffs and excise taxes to BLS, Namibia, and its own homelands. This ultimately created a major financial problem for South Africa.

To support their Constellation of States, a Development Bank of Southern Africa was established in the 1980s to make loans for development projects in the homelands. South Africa made it clear that it would be happy to extend such lending to the BLS countries. The South Africans apparently had decided on a strategy to reduce the Customs Union's revenue-sharing payments and substitute a programme of investments and aid from the Development Bank. In that way South Africa could both control its own expenditure level and also exert leverage over each recipient government. Projects under the aid programme would have to be approved by South

Africa, rather than individual governments deciding how to spend their own customs revenue.

As part of their strategy, South Africa commissioned a study of development in the region by Professor C. L. McCarthy of the University of Stellenbosch. For many months South Africa used the "forthcoming" report as an excuse for not responding to our arguments to deal with the lag in revenue sharing payments. They said they intended to bring proposals to the BLS for a reform of the entire Customs Union, and not only the revenue sharing formula, based on the McCarthy Report. Knowing their intentions, we were determined not to agree.

The McCarthy Report was issued in 1986. As we had anticipated, it made the case for treating BLS as if we were South African Bantustans, decreasing Customs Union revenue sharing, extending to the BLS the industrial policies of South Africa, and establishing an aid relationship. Our officials produced a lengthy and detailed critique that was delivered promptly to the South Africans and to Lesotho and Swaziland. We found fault with virtually every part of the report: its logic, its use of evidence, its review of the international studies of development strategy, and its conclusions. We pointed out where South African policies toward its homelands violated South African obligations to the BLS under the Customs Union Agreement. We reiterated all the arguments about the deficiencies of the revenue sharing formula. We said that the so-called TBVC States, which played a prominent role in McCarthy's report, were an internal South African issue, not one for the Customs Union members to consider. We suggested that, since South Africa was becoming even more protectionist, the BLS should have an increase in the compensation factor to recognise the higher prices we were paying for South African manufactures! The South African government never came back with a response. Later, when they asked for BLS proposals for reform of the Customs Union, we responded by saying we had made our proposals over many years; where were theirs? All we had seen was the report of a consultant.

I believe our strategy worked. We used our ability both to achieve consensus within government and to respond rapidly to any report or proposal from South Africa, or the result of any meeting, to maintain the initiative. We were able to keep the South African government from forcing the issues on its terms. By being strictly professional on the Botswana side, we encouraged it on the South African side. While the Customs Union Agreement was far from perfect, without it we would not only have lost substantial revenue, but perhaps more importantly we would have been without a very valuable tool in managing our relations with South Africa. For all these reasons, I kept a close eye on the discussions both while I was vice-president and as president.

Economic Interdependence and Sanctions

Starting in the early 1960s, South Africa was subject to increasing international economic pressures and sanctions that reached their peak in the 1980s. We always were subject to harassment by the South Africans, who wanted us to oppose sanctions and to say that sanctions against South Africa would hurt Botswana. We never yielded to their pressure. We stated that while we could not impose sanctions on our own, we could understand why other countries might wish to do so because of the South African government's actions against both its own people and its neighbours. Presidents Kaunda and Nyerere understood and supported our position, which made it possible for us to maintain our principles without losing the respect of other countries in Africa and beyond.

Our participation in the Customs Union made it easier for us to deal with South Africa on the issue of sanctions. In the late 1970s and early 1980s, both international sanctions and boycotts and its own internal policies helped create inflation in South Africa and led to balance-of-payments problems, and South Africa's rate of economic growth slowed as well. Concern about foreign exchange reserves and the international value of the rand became major political issues in South Africa.

Starting in the late 1970s, our economists began to study the impact of our growth, and that of Lesotho and Swaziland, on South Africa. Our rapid growth meant we were importing more and more South African manufactured goods. A study by one of our consultants in finance, Professor Earl McFarland of Williams College, demonstrated that a large share of the growth of South Africa's manufacturing was due to its exports to BLS and to Namibia. Our economists also calculated the importance of BLS and Namibia to South Africa's balance-of-payments. They showed that, without the favourable balance South Africa had with its Customs Union partners, it would be in even more serious trouble. We used these facts in our discussions with the South Africans.

For many years, South African political rhetoric emphasised that the entire southern African region was "dependent" on South Africa—economically, financially, and for transportation. It was part of their argument against international economic sanctions: If you hurt South Africa, you hurt millions of black people in the rest of southern Africa. The data our people developed raised an important rebuttal to that argument: We might have been "dependent" on South Africa for most of our imports, but we paid in hard dollars. In fact, South Africa was "dependent" on Botswana for a large share of its foreign exchange reserves!

In 1986, South Africa summoned the BLS countries to Pretoria for a meeting. Sanctions against the South Africans had again been increased, and they wanted to bully the BLS into publicly standing with them against sanctions. The senior South African official welcomed the group, and then he and others from their government and the Reserve Bank gave an extended assessment of the effects of increased sanctions on all members of the Customs Union. They even suggested that mandatory UN sanctions would release South Africa from such international legal obligations as the Customs Union Agreement.

After the South African officials had spoken, the heads of other delegations were asked to respond, as was customary. Baledzi Gaolathe, then our permanent secretary in finance, began with the usual courtesies. He thanked the South Africans for their hospitality and for their concern that increased sanctions could hurt the BLS countries. He went on to point out the economic importance of the BLS to South Africa (about which the South Africans did not seem well informed). He noted that if sanctions caused South Africa to be more protectionist, South African goods would become more expensive, and there would be a strong case for additional compensation to the BLS. He then observed that sanctions were the result of South African domestic policies, and he asked if the South African delegation would share with the BLS countries the steps their government proposed to take to resolve South Africa's domestic problems and thus remove the threat of sanctions.

John Stoneham, our director of financial affairs, followed by asking the South Africans when we were going to see the proposals they had promised based on the McCarthy Report, which had recently been issued. The South Africans suggested this was a good topic to discuss over lunch; the delegations adjourned. The aggressive message we had feared was never delivered.

Then in the late 1980s, the South Africans called a meeting of finance ministers. The South African finance minister led off with remarks about the state of their economy. As a consequence of economic sanctions and their deteriorating financial situation, he said it would be necessary to revise the Customs Union and other financial arrangements. Festus Mogae, then our minister of finance and development planning, responded with a detailed analysis of the importance of the BLS countries to South Africa's economy. He pointed out that South African exports to the BLS and Namibia were approaching the importance of South African gold exports! Without the Customs Union, he said, it was doubtful if the BLS would purchase such significant amounts from South Africa.

Mr Mogae was better prepared than anyone else, and that gave him an advantage. The South African minister was taken off guard, and his officials were very distressed that he had not been prepared for this information. At the tea break, they approached our people to inquire about the sources of the data and how they could check up on them. While one could never know their true intentions for that meeting, our people felt sure that the South Africans did not accomplish what they had hoped for; the meeting ended without any action.

The Customs Union Agreement was much more than it might have seemed. It obviously was a major source of revenue that led to our financial independence in 1972 and financed a great deal of our economic development. But it was also an important part of our live and let live approach to South Africa. It provided us with a legal framework for many aspects of our relationships with South Africa and a forum in which business could be transacted. We paid a great deal of attention to the Customs Union. We took initiatives and made proposals both because we felt they would benefit us and because they were a way to keep the South Africans off balance. We succeeded in maintaining the agreement, and we succeeded, too, in preventing the South Africans from finding a way of implementing their vision for regional dominance in the Constellation of States.

South Africa's "Independent Homelands"

When South Africa announced the "independence" of the Transkei in 1976, we were faced with a new set of problems. The next homeland scheduled for independence was Bophuthatswana, with which we shared many common border points as well as riparian rights and ethnicity. The South Africans began a campaign to pressure us into formally recognising these so-called states. We took as pragmatic a position as possible. For example, we decided not to make a fuss about travel documents and motor vehicle registrations issued by Bophuthatswana; we just accepted them. However, we made it clear in all our official dealings that we regarded the entire geographic area of South Africa as under the sovereignty of the South African government. It was a further aspect of live and let live, and in almost all areas it worked.

In dealing with riparian rights and with the railway, we faced awkward issues. As Gaborone grew, we needed to increase the capacity of the Gaborone dam. The World Bank refused to help us finance the dam until we had consulted with the other riparian users. This posed a problem, since the territory of Bophuthatswana included areas both upstream and downstream of the dam. When we went to the South Africans, they said: "Well, that area belongs to Bophuthatswana, not to South Africa, so you will have to talk with them." We initially refused to accept their position, but the World Bank insisted, so we eventually had to swallow our pride. Mr Mogwe did the groundwork with their so-called foreign minister. Without anyone knowing, I met Lucas Mangope, the leader of Bophuthatswana, at the Martins Drift border post, and we clinched the deal. However, the delays caused by the World Bank's insistence cost us close to P36 million.

My secret meeting with Mr Mangope over water rights had a precedent from the construction of the original dam at Gaborone. We then needed the agreement of Mozambique, since it was a downstream user of the waters of the Ngotwane River, and Mozambique was still legally a possession of Portugal. So in 1964 Alan Tilbury, David Morgan and I travelled to Lisbon for a clandestine meeting at which we obtained Portuguese agreement.

Another time when South Africa pressured us to recognise Bophuthatswana was when we were planning to take over Rhodesia Railways. The South Africans told us, through Mr Mangope, that we could not go into Mafeking; the trains would have to stop at the border at Ramatlabama. If we went into Mafeking, they said, we would need permits from Bophuthatswana, and we also would have to have people from Bophuthatswana stationed at Lobatse. We thought this was a Trojan Horse for formal recognition.

We knew the South African government, for all its faults, was very legalistic in its approach. In part, I think this was so they could demonstrate to the international community that they were honouring their legal obligations. Therefore, when Lucas Mangope told us we would have to come to him, I went directly to the South African foreign minister, Pik Botha. I sent him a letter pointing out that we had an agreement on railway access with South Africa, not with Bophuthatswana. Therefore, if our people and our goods could not enter South Africa, it would be a violation of the agreement. Fortunately, it also was in South Africa's interest to keep the railway in operation, so that legalistic approach worked. We were able to stick to our principles and avoid formal recognition.

The South African government was persistent in trying to persuade us to regularise our political relationships with both South Africa and the homelands. As they started to liberalise some of their policies in the late 1980s, they worked on our people to persuade me to take more formal diplomatic steps such as establishing a South African Consular office in Gaborone; I just had to put my foot down to say no.

Employment of Batswana in South Africa
Despite our rapid economic growth and increased employment opportunities, jobs in the South African mines continued to be a very important source of income to thousands of Batswana well into the 1980s. As South Africa's own problems grew, their government was under domestic political pressure to stop using foreign labour and to exclusively recruit South African blacks. Peter Mmusi and I worked with the recruitment agencies, who were acting on behalf of the mining companies, to slow down their reductions in Botswana. We argued that our people had for years helped make the South African mining industry what it was, and they should not simply cut off our people's employment there. We encouraged them to phase their reductions by not recruiting any new people but rather re-engaging those they had previously employed. Between 1977 and 1998, the numbers employed on the mines declined from 25,000 to 11,000. Those employed were largely men returning for another contract. These relationships were worked out independently of the South African government, though we were sure the recruiting agencies must have had discussions with their government.

Liberation Movements and Refugees
Our relationships with the South African government centred on their determination to maintain white supremacy in their country and in the whole region. To remain dominant, they needed to control and suppress all opposition to white supremacy, and they did so ruthlessly, both in their own country and in Namibia, which they governed. But opposition within South Africa became more intense and had turned to violent methods by the early 1960s. As a result, the National Party government made it clear they would take action against their opponents not only within South Africa but also in any neighbouring countries that harboured them.

The South African government's approach created a series of problems for us. We needed a policy on refugees—both those fleeing South Africa and those attempting to return. We needed to deal with the liberation movements who were in conflict with the South African authorities and wanted passage to and from South Africa. Our approach to the liberation movements affected our needs for intelligence gathering and for security and self defence forces, as well as our response to international calls for economic sanctions against South Africa.

The policy on refugees was first developed under Peter Fawcus, and it was in place before Legco was established; we continued the same policy after we became the government during self-rule. In 1963, Peter Fawcus had addressed Legco on the subject. He noted that our progress toward becoming a democratic, prosperous and non-racial country "can only be safeguarded by the strictest neutrality in our dealings with neighbouring counties who are so much stronger than ourselves and with whom we must trade if we are to live. [This policy] is a counsel of caution but not of timidity: Bechuanaland shall not become a mere pawn in international politics and shall certainly not be an instrument for any kind of action against other territories. At the same time Bechuanaland will continue to give asylum to persons who, if they return to South Africa, would face loss of liberty as a consequence of political opinions or acts expressed or performed before they left South Africa."

The colonial authorities practiced what they preached. There was a pipeline through which police and other colonial officials facilitated clandestine movement of ANC and other refugees to the north. Fish Keitsing, a former member of the ANC who had been in the Treason Trial with Nelson Mandela, wrote in his autobiography about the pipeline for refugees through his home in Lobatse. Once, when Nelson Mandela landed in Botswana, he was met by the police, who asked him if he was Mr Mandela. He said: "No, I am Mr Jaimeson," the alias by which he was travelling to the rest of Africa. The police, who were there to facilitate his movements said: "Well, we were sent here to meet Mr Mandela, but if you are Mr Jaimeson, then we must arrest you!" Of course, he then identified himself and was helped on his way. After independence, we took the same position as the colonial authorities had taken: We gave asylum to genuine refugees but did not permit the liberation movements to use Botswana as a base. We knew that if we did things too publicly, we would have been in trouble with the South African government.

The needs both for clear policies and for protection of our own security were evident before independence. During the August 1964 meeting of Legco, there were questions to the colonial government about South African government operations. These had included blowing up a Landrover belonging to Motsamai Mpho's Botswana Independence Party, the destruction of an airplane used to transport refugees, blowing up houses of refugees in Francistown, and the kidnapping of refugees within Bechuanaland. There also were allegations that some whites were involved. Arthur Douglas, government secretary, stated that it had been "partially but not wholly established" that some white residents who were non-citizens had been involved. We knew from the beginning we were on the front line of the struggle for liberation in all of southern Africa.

In his first speech to the National Assembly as president, Seretse Khama stated our policy clearly: "The foreign policy of my government will also be dictated by reason and common sense rather than by emotion and sentiment. Our first duty will always be toward the people of this country rather than to any world political ideologies, because the histrionics and fulminations of extremists outside this country will not help Botswana to achieve its destiny. In particular we will not permit Botswana to be used as a base for the organisation or direction of violent activities directed towards other states and we will expect reciprocal treatment from our neighbours. ...whilst we will continue to offer genuine political refugees a safe haven in our country, we will not permit such people to plan and attempt to achieve the violent overthrow of the government of any county from within the boundaries of Botswana. Any political refugees who behave in this manner will do so at their own peril and if they are detected, appropriate action will be taken against them." We followed this policy from that day forward.

After independence, we felt we needed to be certain our policies would be clearly defined in law. We passed a Bill on recognition and control of refugees, and we invited the United Nations high commissioner for refugees to review it. Their representatives made a series of recommendations to make the Bill conform to the UN's 1951 Convention on Refugees. We adopted their recommendations and brought the law into force in 1967.

Many Batswana had lived and worked and gone to school in South Africa, and some were heavily influenced by the liberation movements. Many of the changes that black people in South Africa wanted to see were the same changes that we wanted: removal of discrimination, improvement in the lot of blacks, economic opportunities, political equality, and the like. We in Botswana always welcomed members of the liberation movements because there were important interests in common, but we did not make a big song and dance about our relationship with them. If we had done so, it would have given our common enemy an excuse to take action against us, since the South African government operated on the principle that "whoever is not with us is against us". Also, we could not have refugees living here in large numbers on a permanent basis. The South African liberation movements wanted it the other way, and so did the Americans and some other African countries. Fortunately, people like Presidents Nyerere and Kaunda recognised our difficulties, and they helped us out by making the case both with the refugees and with the other countries.

President Nyerere was a very early convert to understanding our position. After we had established the Democratic Party, I went to Dar es Salaam to deliver a message to him from the late president. Instead of receiving me, he sent his assistant, which puzzled me. So, I snooped around and discovered that President Nyerere felt that we were just another Bantustan—not because we wanted to be, but because we couldn't help it. But once we became independent, and once President Kaunda had taken the issue of refugees to him, President Nyerere moved to the other extreme. He made it very clear to the liberation movements that they must not compromise our independence. I think it helped us that Nyerere not only had very good credentials with the rest of Africa but also developed a good and close personal relationship with both Seretse and me.

However, we were always in the middle. The South African government did not like us to receive refugees, and because we allowed them to pass through the country, South African authorities thought we were hobnobbing with the refugees. But, since we did not allow the refugees to stay in the country, some in the liberation movements thought we were hobnobbing with the South African government!

At the time we achieved self-rule, the Americans thought they would send all the South Africans they had been educating to Botswana. Their argument was that we did not have any educated people in Botswana, and therefore we could employ the South African refugees. They came and gave us pep talks about how we could bring South Africans closer to their homes, and at the same time they would help us develop our country. We felt otherwise; we knew many of them would work against South Africa from a base in Botswana. We also knew from past experience that the South African government would not hesitate to come after them and make us victims in the process.

By the end of self-rule in 1966, we had put the matter to bed, though not without some difficulty. Our Refugee Committee would identify who was a genuine refugee and who was not, and once we had done so, we made sure the refugees were told to move on to other countries to the north. Had they stayed, it would have clogged the pipeline. Some received military training and wanted to come back to stay in Botswana while they searched for how they could best infiltrate back into South Africa. In the past, they had been told in no uncertain terms: "That we don't allow."

Once I returned from a trip to find that Jimmy Allison, Seretse's permanent secretary, had almost convinced people in government that we should facilitate the refugees' return to their own countries. To Allison it seemed to be a simple matter: If they want to return, we should help them. I was incensed by that approach, and I thought it was completely wrongheaded and dangerous. But since I understood the matter to have been settled, I just left for my cattle post.

Seretse realised how unhappy I was about it, and he sent a policeman in the middle of the night to bring me back to Gaborone. Since I felt so strongly about the matter, he said I should go to Zambia to meet with the ANC leadership at their headquarters in Lusaka. So I went with Archie Mogwe, who was Allison's deputy, and we talked with President Kaunda, whom I had met on several occasions by that time. We asked him to arrange a meeting with Oliver Tambo, who was head of the ANC in exile. We spelled it out to Mr Tambo: It would serve neither their cause nor ours if the South African government were to think we were helping the ANC to infiltrate. If we were seen to be helping the ANC, it would give the South Africans a very good excuse to say: "If you fellows can't prevent these activities, we will move into your country to make sure you can keep them out." This was clearly understood by Oliver Tambo, who supported my position that we should not assist in sending refugees back to South Africa. We all knew that if the ANC folks could find a way to come back through Botswana, they would do so. For our part, we thought that would be okay, so long as we were not seen to be conniving with them or helping them to achieve their purpose.

When refugees came to Botswana, whether they were ANC, or PAC, or Black Consciousness Movement, we acknowledged the fact that they had run away from their country since they could not live there, and we treated them all as legitimate political refugees. Some stayed at my farm in Ghanzi, and my people there would remark: "You know, the ANC people are helpful and grateful, and they even make their own beds!" We did not have a major problem with the leadership of the movements who understood our predicament. Occasionally, however, uninformed individuals from other parts of Africa made statements critical of us for not providing bases of operation.

After the Soweto uprising in June 1976, we had a large influx of school children, some as young as twelve, who fled from South Africa. We were concerned they would saturate the schools in Gaborone, so we decided we should find some place where we could look after them. We settled on Dukwe, a camp north-west of Francistown. The youngsters were very unhappy with us as they had come from the large city of Johannesburg and did not want to be in an isolated rural area. We reasoned with them gently, but forcefully, to get their cooperation to move, and then we did all we could to facilitate their departure for schools in other countries. They went through a very difficult time, in part because they were young, and in part because they thought they were coming to "freedom" in Botswana. But once here they had to obey our laws, register with the police, and report their movements and whereabouts. Their experience with the law and with any government officials, especially police, had always been one of repression. They did not understand that a free society needed to have laws that its people obeyed.

While we were clear about providing refuge to those who were fleeing for political reasons, we were also clear that we were not a haven for just anyone. In 1978, for example, a South African named John Patrick Wall was arrested in Johannesburg and charged with financial fraud. While free on bail, he fled to Botswana and entered without a passport. Our police arrested him, and he was declared a prohibited immigrant and deported to South Africa to stand trial. Simon Hirschfeld, our commissioner of police, told the South African press: "Anyone else, whether from South Africa or elsewhere, trying to cross into Botswana the same way [to avoid prosecution] will be arrested immediately." *The Sunday Express* in Johannesburg headlined their story: "Wall's Simple Error: He Chose the Wrong Country!" We would receive genuine political refugees, but we were not in the business of harbouring common criminals.

Increased Pressure in the 1980s

As increasing numbers of refugees were returning and trying to use Botswana as a springboard for action against South Africa in the 1980s, we had all sorts of threats from Foreign Minister Pik Botha and his allies in the South African government. They tried to bully us, threatened to bomb our country, and sent people to tell us there were groups of refugees who had come into the country illegally. You could see they were looking for an excuse to say: "Since you can't control this situation, you should let us take over."

Sometimes the South Africans would send a mission to tell us that terrorists had crossed at Kazungula and to ask what we were doing about it. We responded that if they gave us the evidence, we would follow it up. If the

South African information was indeed right, we would ask the persons to leave, since we didn't want to give the South African government any pretext to come in and raid us. However, more often than not there would be no such refugees.

The South African government was very determined to stop infiltration of the ANC through Mozambique, and, in 1984, Mozambique was forced into signing what was known as the Nkomati Accord, which was billed as a "non-aggression" agreement. However, though it was couched in terms of mutual responsibilities, it effectively gave the South Africans license to stop things directly, and in practice they just marched in to Mozambique and did what they pleased. The lever they used on President Machel was the support South Africa had been giving to RENAMO, an armed anti-government group in Mozambique. The support was supposed to decrease after Nkomati, but in fact it continued.

I was invited to go to the signing at Nkomati, but I chose to go to the official opening of the Chobe Hotel that day instead. Much as I admired President Machel, I could not honestly be present at such a ceremony. Machel really had no choice but to sign, as Mozambique was under tremendous pressure from the South Africans, and he was trying to find a way of co-existing with them. He was somewhat unrealistic and seemed to believe that since he had struck a deal with the South Africans, the rest of us among the Front Line States would follow. He was certainly mistaken to believe we would do so.

In fact, there had been pressures on us from day one. South African journalists had come to interview us about joining South Africa. The South African government talked of how there could be a greater Tswana nation if we were to unite with Bophuthatswana. After it became clear we would not accept incorporation into South Africa, they would tell us how secure we could be if we were to tie our security to South Africa in an agreement of "non-aggression" such as the Nkomati Accord. Though it peaked like a heartbeat at times, the pressure to do their bidding was constantly on us.

South Africa ultimately made two vicious raids on Gaborone to send a message about the consequences of not cooperating. These overt attacks by the South African Defence Force took place on 14 June 1985 and 19 May 1986. They killed a number of people and destroyed alleged ANC houses in Gaborone. The latter raid even took place while the Eminent Persons Group from the Commonwealth was meeting with South African leaders. We were disgusted and outraged, and we did not hide it. We went to the United Nations and other forums to argue our case and explain how we were victimised. The international community supported us, and the United States even withdrew its ambassador to South Africa in 1985 partly in response to the raid.

Over the years Seretse and I, along with Foreign Ministers Mogwe and Chiepe, articulated our position on refugees as publicly and as clearly as we could. We felt that the more international support we could muster, the greater was the deterrent to South African government's inclinations to punish us. We tried to make sure there was an international uproar, so that

South Africa would know if they did worse to us the uproar would be much greater.

On occasion, the South African government would write us anonymous letters describing how miserable they would make our lives unless we submitted. Once I was approached through my brother Peter, who was given a message that my officials were doing nasty things behind my back. They didn't name the officials or the nasty things but just made the allegations. I called Lebang Mpotokwane, then secretary for external affairs, and Simon Hirschfeld, and one or two others, and I had my brother report the message to them. I did not think there was anything in it, but I thought my officials should know exactly what was done so they could see the attempt to divide and rule.

The last and most direct approach came when P. W. Botha was still president. He sent Mr Van Heerden, his director-general for foreign affairs, to tell me: "Toe the line or else." We met one on one, and Van Heerden told me they were prepared to translate my life into misery unless I cooperated. I simply listened and did not respond in any way, since I didn't want him to draw any conclusions from his visit. I also decided not to tell anyone about what he had said, since I did not want to cause any panic. If the South Africans really intended to take action, why didn't they do it? But if they wished to create panic by just threatening, then my telling people what he had said would give them what they wanted. As president, there were certain things I just swallowed, and I shared them only on the need to know basis.

Relations with the ANC

We dealt primarily with three people in the leadership of the liberation movements in South Africa: Oliver Tambo, Alfred Nzo, and Thabo Mbeki, all of the ANC. Mr Nzo wasn't a ball of fire, but he was secretary of the movement and was there whenever we met with either Mr Mbeki or Mr Tambo. Thabo Mbeki was their foreign affairs man, and he was very articulate and skilful. One time in Addis, we spent half the night talking about southern Africa. He said that it was not only South Africa itself that was being ruined by the policies of the National Party, but other countries in the region as well. When South Africa was liberated, it would be good not just for their people but for the whole region. Further, reconstruction and restitution for the effects of apartheid should be directed to all of southern Africa—all positions we had long espoused.

Oliver Tambo was a real statesman as the leader of the ANC. We had a problem only once, when he was overly aggressive at a 1975 meeting in Mauritius and threatened us with military retaliation unless we cooperated more fully. (I remember the meeting very well, since that was when the hijacked Israeli plane was being held at the Entebbe airport, and Idi Amin told us he had to rush back to help settle things. The next day the Israelis came to Entebbe and definitely settled them.) Mr Tambo said we were not allowing their people to go through Botswana because we were afraid of the South African government, and if we only were listening to those we feared, then the ANC, too, could instil fear in us. They could send people who could cause havoc in Botswana. But he settled down, and both before and after we had very good relations.

Later on, ANC sorties from Botswana into South Africa became frequent, and we would tell them they were putting us, as well as our usefulness to them, at great risk. The leaders would apologise profusely, blame it on "their boys", and stop for a while. They would say: "We are very sorry; these folks don't realise they are exposing you and risk losing another independent country." Sometimes Oliver Tambo would go so far in his praise of our role in helping with liberation that I'd have to say: "Now look, if Pik Botha heard you, he'd conclude we are providing you with bases and all kinds of other help, and then he would come after us!"

We had a difference with the ANC, as we did with SWAPO in Namibia. The ANC wanted to be recognised as the only legitimate movement in the liberation of the South African people. Since we took a public position against endorsing one particular party, we told each of them: "No, we are not going to subscribe to your view. We will give you all the help we can, but we must recognise there are other liberation movements inside South Africa. As to how well you rate, that will be decided when there are elections." While we believed the ANC was the major movement, and we may not have thought much of some of the other movements, we believed we should acknowledge the ANC without denying the existence of the others.

As our relationship with the ANC evolved in the 1980s, they started to have greater respect for us as a country and as a government that could be helpful to them. For example, there was to be a meeting in Lusaka at which they hashed out what they wanted to have in a resolution for the UN, and they decided they could benefit from some input from us. I had just torn a ligament in my knee and was in bed at State House, and they moved the meeting to Gaborone so I could talk with them. A short while later, Oliver Tambo took ill and went to hospital in the UK; I had been taken there for an operation as well, and we spent two weeks talking together. We gave them what help we could on their draft, and since we commented seriously and made substantive suggestions, they seemed to think that our input was important. They finished the resolution in Harare, and we sent a team headed by Louis Selepeng, then secretary of external affairs, to assist where needed. Our input became a part of the Harare Declaration, and perhaps we helped save them from painting themselves into a corner on a few points.

During South Africa's transition in the early 1990s, the ANC started to feel strongly about the Bantustan leaders and seemed to want to exclude them from the side of the liberation movements in any negotiations that might develop. We said to them: "Now look, the one mistake you should not make is to have the Bantustan leaders sitting on the same side as De Klerk. He will use them as black people who are opposed to what you are saying and suggest you are not representative of people's views." The ANC seemed to take our advice to heart.

In the end, the only Bantustan leader who did not behave sensibly was Lucas Mangope, the head of Bophuthatswana. We had planned that I should meet him at a farm in the Molopo to urge him to help in facilitating the transition to majority rule. But every time we were close to arranging a meeting, he would take some outrageous action, and we would have to put it off. He once referred to Nelson Mandela as a "bandit", for example, and we did not want to be associated with such behaviour. Mangope cut himself out of the post-apartheid order by claiming too much for his own abilities and popularity. If he had not behaved the way he did, he would have been in the fold with a position of responsibility.

Towards the end of apartheid, when De Klerk started to appear reasonable, Nelson Mandela had been released, and progress was being made, some of our people in foreign affairs felt we should begin to have normal diplomatic relationships. But my position was that we should do nothing to give the National Party government the impression we felt this was as far as they needed to go. I believed we should not do anything about normalising relationships until there was a new government.

During the transition in South Africa from 1990 to 1994, we were in almost constant contact with various parties there. The British had inquired whether our experience might be of use to the South Africans as they discussed their future. We did not want to push ourselves, but we said we would be willing to talk if they wished. There were some takers, and we contributed whenever the South Africans asked. A great many conferences, seminars and consultations were held among the various political, labour, and business groups in South Africa. During that time, there were substantial changes in the policies the ANC said it would pursue in a new South Africa; they became much more realistic and much less ideological in their approach. We tendered advice when we thought it was necessary, and we tendered advice when it was sought, and we responded to constitutional questions from their lawyers when we were asked. We always tried to be sure that we said: "This is what our experience has been, and this is what we did, but we recognise that your circumstances may be different, so the solutions we found here in Botswana may not necessarily work for South Africa."

Nelson Mandela was the most outstanding among the leaders in South Africa. For some reason, a very good rapport developed between him and me, so much so that one of his ministers wanted to know what there was between us! In our conversations, I made the case to him that we hoped the new South Africa would not think of a Constellation of States as the apartheid government had proposed, whereby we would become a dumping ground. I said I thought both countries would be better off as trading partners, whereby we would contribute to South Africa, and vice versa. I believe he recognised the importance of the point. We worked closely together on many regional issues after he became president of South Africa. And, most enjoyable for both of us was the occasion of my state visit to South Africa when we each bestowed our country's highest public honour on the other.

Chapter 18
Making Our Way in Southern Africa

When we achieved independence in 1966, whites ruled almost all of Africa south of the twelfth parallel. The Portuguese were the colonial power in Angola and Mozambique; Ian Smith's illegal regime in Southern Rhodesia had issued its Unilateral Declaration of Independence (UDI) in November 1965; and the National Party ruled both Namibia and South Africa. Malawi, under President Banda, was effectively a client of South Africa. Lesotho and Swaziland were "in the belly of the whale", as we used to say, so because of their extreme vulnerability they were of doubtful reliability in the struggle for liberation. Only Zambia, and to some extent Botswana, were truly independent of South Africa. Our only physical contact with independent Africa was with the Zambians at Kazungula.

Race relations in neighbouring countries have always influenced race relations in Botswana. In theory, we had nothing to do with South African apartheid; but in fact, it was practiced in Bechuanaland much as it was practiced in South Africa and the rest of the region. There were mutual suspicions even after independence, and some whites in Botswana behaved as if they were in South Africa. In the worst days of the Rhodesian war, for example, when Smith's people raided in the north-east of Botswana, black people's suspicions of whites were raised throughout the country. Tension would inevitably build up and people polarised. In the 1980s, when the South African government made threats and then undertook their raids on Gaborone, tensions again rose.

We knew our democracy in a non-racial, independent country would be at risk as long as there was an apartheid government in South Africa. We knew, too, that South Africa would try at all costs to keep the white monopoly of power both in their country and in their immediate neighbours. So from the very beginning, the future leaders of Botswana knew we would have to help promote change throughout southern Africa.

Matlo gosha mabapi is a Setswana proverb that literally means: "Two close huts cannot escape if one of them catches fire". Of course, what it really means is that you should try to prevent your neighbour's hut from catching fire, since if it burns, yours will also. This is one of the reasons why Botswana wanted to take the initiative in the region, first in the Front Line States and later in developing the Southern African Development Coordinating Conference (SADCC), which in 1992 became the Southern African Development Community (SADC). For the same reasons, we also helped other countries in the region deal with their internal problems wherever we felt we could.

The Front Line States
In the mid-1960s, Presidents Kaunda and Nyerere began meeting to exchange views and discuss strategy in the region. Both Zambia and Tanzania had huge pools of refugees—principally from South Africa, Rhodesia, Angola, Mozambique and Namibia. They needed to develop some harmonious way of

acting toward both the refugees and the governments that had forced them to take refuge. I think President Kaunda played a major role in involving Seretse Khama before 1970, and Seretse soon became an indispensable partner. President Kaunda seemed to not want to do things without involving Seretse, who in his quiet and jocular way would bring matters back into orbit when others became emotional. During the 1970s, I deputised for Seretse on many occasions when his health prevented him from going to the meetings. We would meet the liberation movements from the Portuguese colonies and from Zimbabwe, Namibia and South Africa to get reports on what they were up to and to discuss strategy and what we could do to help.

I've been told I was the one who coined the name "Front Line States" for the group, and it's possible that was the case. At meetings we dealt with the politics of the situation as well as security issues. We discussed how to assist the liberation movements with training camps, facilitate their transit through Botswana and Zambia, and so forth. Then as Angola, Mozambique and Zimbabwe achieved independence, their presidents joined the meetings.

We did not want to involve Lesotho and Swaziland in the Front Line States for two reasons. First, Presidents Kaunda and Nyerere did not trust their prime ministers. Second their geographic position made them vulnerable, so if the South Africans wanted to search their things on the way back from a meeting, they would do so. Malawi was excluded because of the way President Banda behaved—he had normal diplomatic relations with South Africa, exchanged state visits, and seemed to be willing to do their bidding in exchange for economic and other support.

President Nyerere was sceptical of whether there was any point in trying to engage the South African leadership in formal meetings. Most Front Line presidents were very sceptical of direct contacts when the South African government was engaged in military and economic destabilisation of the neighbouring states. President Kaunda had a different view from the others about the benefits of open dialogue, so he made approaches on his own. He met with John Vorster at Victoria Falls on one occasion. Then in 1981, he wanted to meet with P. W. Botha on the border between South Africa and Botswana, and we helped him with arrangements. He also invited Van Zyl Slabbert and a number of South Africans from different parties and viewpoints to meet in Zambia. He acted on his own in all these efforts, and they didn't seem to move things along.

There was always a difference, of course, between what one said in public and what one said in private. In the Front Line States, we tried to use both carrot and stick: One publicly, the other privately, whichever was appropriate at the time. That was true of communications with the liberation movements, as well as with the South African government and the Rhodesians.

The personal interactions of the presidents were important, of course, and the late president's humour would help to get us focused on the right things. One famous incident involving his sense of humour took place in 1979 at a meeting to discuss Namibia. South Africa was promoting Democratic Turnhalle Alliance (DTA) in Namibia as an alternative to SWAPO. At the same time, SWAPO was continuing to press its case as the "sole legitimate representative" of the Namibian people and was trying to get the Front Line States to endorse SWAPO over the DTA. Seretse was adamant that the Front Line States should not take sides and publicly favour one Namibian group over another. We in Botswana believed the matter of legitimacy should be settled by internal elections contested by all parties. Further, if the Front Line States endorsed SWAPO, it would give the South Africans a further excuse to delay independence for Namibia. Seretse said he wanted to be sure the South Africans should be seen as the principal stumbling block to democratic change and independence in Namibia—since in fact they were.

A few days after the meeting, a Sunday paper in Johannesburg carried the headline: "'I Want SA to be the Nigger in the Woodpile'—Seretse." The quotation was exactly what he had said, so we knew the South Africans had access to the meeting. How they got it, we did not know; perhaps some of the minutes had been picked up by pilots of a plane transporting one of the presidents. In any case, it was an accurate report.

Development Cooperation
The Southern African Development Coordinating Conference (SADCC) was formed in April 1980. During the early 1980s, Botswana provided the lion's share of the leadership and staff for SADCC, and many people wondered why Botswana would spend its resources in creating SADCC. It was easy to explain: Our participation was a case of enlightened self-interest. New countries had come into being—Angola, Mozambique, Zimbabwe—and we wanted to be sure that the arrival of new friends did not make them forget their old friends. We did not want to have one played off against another by South Africa or any other power. Therefore, we felt it would be a good thing if we formed an organisation that would coordinate development strategy for the whole region. The idea fit well with the OAU's desire to have economic blocks in five parts of the continent.

Some thought SADCC was a way of opposing South Africa, but it was more a case of protecting ourselves from South Africa. We could see a role for SADCC even beyond a new political dispensation in South Africa. At a meeting in Nairobi, I had pointed out to President Kaunda that we needed alternative ways out even if we had a friendly government in South Africa; if there were an insurrection or an economic collapse there, we would need alternative transport routes and trading partners. While we who would form SADCC were interdependent and on good terms bilaterally, we would have to seek ways for our survival collectively. It was not just a question of dealing with South Africa as a pariah; we also needed to coordinate development in the region even after apartheid. It was a matter often discussed by Seretse and Nyerere.

The first meeting to form SADCC was in Arusha, Tanzania, early in 1980, and I was sent to chair the meeting. We drafted the constitution at that meeting, and we received a lot of help from David Anderson and Tim Sheehy of the Commonwealth Secretariat. While Lesotho, Malawi and Swaziland were excluded from the Front Line States, they were invited into SADCC because we in Botswana said they could not be left out. We felt if we were to have regional cooperation for economic development, it was logical to include all the countries in the region. The late president sent me to Swaziland and Lesotho, and Mr Mogwe to Malawi, to invite them join SADCC, and they all accepted.

At that time, Zambia was getting into economic trouble, and in his search for solutions President Kaunda had been working with Professor Adebayo Adedeji of Nigeria, who was at the Economic Commission for Africa (ECA) in Addis. They hatched the idea for a Preferential Trade Area for Eastern and Southern Africa (PTA). President Kaunda wanted to merge the two efforts, his idea and SADCC, and have SADCC become a vehicle for implementing PTA. (PTA later became known as the Common Market for Eastern and Southern Africa, COMESA.) While we were preparing a draft for SADCC, so were Professor Adedeji and President Kaunda for PTA.

The meeting to formally launch SADCC was held in Lusaka in April 1980. Ministers were to meet first, and heads of state were to appear for the final signing of the agreements. President Kaunda's idea was that Professor Adedeji would produce the draft from which we would work, and that created a problem. Professor Adedeji's concept was for a grandiose trade area, while SADCC proposed pragmatic cooperation on economic development. I was to chair the meeting, and I was pressured by Zambian ministers to use Adedeji's draft as the basis for the agreement. I said to them: "Look, we met in Arusha, and we took decisions. In the light of those decisions, a draft has been produced. We cannot allow ourselves to be hijacked like this. We will use the SADCC draft as a basis, and, if there are good points from Professor Adedeji's draft, then by all means we should include them." Professor Balthazar, a very able gentleman and the first minister of finance in Mozambique, was on my side and he was most insistent too.

When I arrived at the meeting the next day I found Lebang Mpotokwane, our secretary of external affairs, and Tim Sheehy from the Commonwealth, surrounded by Zambian ministers who were pressuring them to convince me to start with Professor Adedeji's draft. I rescued them, and I began the meeting by saying that we had two drafts, and, since this was a SADCC meeting we would start with the SADCC draft and add whatever was appropriate from Professor Adedeji's draft. That was how we proceeded. We worked through the day and invited the heads of state to come in the following day to sign the agreement. It was the last official meeting Seretse would attend, but he came, weak as he was. Robert Mugabe was not yet sworn in as prime minister of Zimbabwe, but we persuaded him to come. He was initially inclined not to sign, but only to initial, but in the end he signed it, too.

I would say the difference between the approaches of SADCC and PTA/COMESA was the difference between reasoning and rationalising. In forming SADCC, we saw problems that could be addressed, and we tried to create a structure that would address the problems and that also had potential for further development if needed. COMESA had begun with a founding ideology, or point of view, about economic integration and then the organisation became a rationalisation for the ideology. We in SADCC wanted concrete results, and that was where we put our efforts.

Botswana was elected the first chairman of SADCC, and then was re-elected for 16 years. In one of the early years, President Banda suggested that the chair should rotate among countries. President Machel addressed Banda, wryly: "But Mr President-for-Life, the rotation would surely cause confusion." This was a phrase that Banda used to rationalise his monopoly on power in Malawi. President Banda retreated but then came with a proposal that there should at least be a vice-chairman. Again Machel tweaked him by saying: "But Mr President-for-Life, you yourself do not have a vice-president." Botswana was asked to remain chair because, I think, we were trusted both by other SADCC countries and by the donors as well.

In the early years, Botswana provided the secretariat for SADCC as well as the chair. The work fell most heavily on Lebang Mpotokwane and Ken Matambo, director of economic affairs. However, we felt there should be a permanent secretariat, even though we knew the dangers of creating a permanent bureaucracy. The first executive secretary could not handle the job, but we fortunately were then provided with Simba Makoni, a very bright young man from Zimbabwe.

In the course of regular meetings of SADCC, ministers and officials from Botswana often observed a lack of dedication of politicians and civil servants from some other countries. Some would neglect their duties, and when meetings were held in Gaborone, some would miss meetings to go shopping for personal things that were unavailable in their own countries. Botswana civil servants and politicians saw that this was not the way to behave if you were in the service of your country. It was a useful lesson.

SADCC changed its name in 1992 to the Southern African Development Community (SADC) to reflect the maturing of the organisation. We felt we had held the chairmanship for too long; after the first elections in South Africa, we engineered it so President Mandela would become the chairman. But, that was the beginning of trouble, because South Africa did not service the organisation the way we had done. We have seen over and over that smaller countries are likely to give greater attention to the details of international arrangements than do the larger countries, and that seems to have been the case with SADC, too.

A very good aspect of President Mandela's role as chairman of SADC was that he never threw his weight around in the group just because South Africa was the big brother. In SADCC, he always talked about "my presidents" when he was addressing other heads of state. When the going got tough, he was ready to take decisions and stick to them.

SADC and the Congo

After President Mandela became chairman, we got into problems over membership of the Congo and the Seychelles. During the time of Mobutu Sese-Seko, what was then called Zaire had applied to join SADCC. We were not happy about the idea of including them, largely because of Zaire's problems of governance. President Nyerere shared our concerns, and I remember in particular the first SADCC meeting in Gaborone at which he made his position quite clear. Over the years, when we had taken decisions about membership, we would first ask: Should we accept more states? Then, if we were to accept some, we would ask: What would be the conditions? We had already accepted Mauritius, and Seychelles had been knocking at our door.

Congo reapplied at a meeting in Malawi. It was the second meeting with President Mandela as chair, and he felt strongly that the Congo should be admitted. He did not say so in so many words, but I believe he felt SADC should not forego the resources that were present in the Congo. But, as the Seychelles had applied before the Congo, President Mandela felt that Seychelles, too, should be admitted if we were to accept the Congo. In fact, the Congo jumped the queue. Normally, they would have applied, and we would have stipulated the conditions; we would have considered them at the subsequent meeting and admitted them at the third meeting. But President Mandela was anxious that they become a part of SADC, and we found it very difficult to say no to him. Later events proved that membership of the Congo in SADC would lead us into real difficulties.

We divided the work within SADC on different areas of policy into sectors, such as transport or agriculture, and each sector was chaired by a different country. The issues in each sector would be discussed first by officials, then by the Council of Ministers, and then they would be passed on to the presidents. When the heads of state met, each country would report on its area of responsibility. The Organ for Security and Defence, as the sector concerned with security issues was called, was initially chaired by Zimbabwe. One of the things we had not anticipated was how the Organ for Security and Defence of SADC would work, and this led us into serious problems. Because of the sensitive nature of these subjects, we did not follow the sequence of moving from officials to ministers to presidents. In the Organ for Security and Defence, the matter would be reported directly by the president responsible to the heads of state.

SADC presidents were invited to Luanda to witness the signing of an agreement between President Dos Santos and Jonas Savimbi; at the time it was thought that UNITA and the Angolan government had reached a peace agreement. But Mr Savimbi did not show up, and President Mugabe took advantage of the gathering to hold the Organ's meeting and to report on its activities. But instead of reporting to a meeting chaired by President Mandela, the chairman of SADC, President Mugabe chaired it himself. Afterward, President Mandela's people felt this was wrong; as chairman of SADC, President Mandela should have chaired any summit meeting to receive a report, and they felt President Mugabe should be told this. President Mandela went to Zimbabwe to discuss the situation, and he came back by way of Botswana to tell me President Mugabe felt he had done nothing wrong, and that, in fact, he would do it again.

Despite efforts by President Chissano and myself to mediate, President Mugabe remained adamant that he should chair meetings to discuss activities of the Organ, and after that his relationship with President Mandela soured. Even though the chairmanship of the Organ was supposed to rotate yearly, Mugabe stuck to it in the Organ for Security and Defence.

In the Congo, Laurent Kabila's forces had defeated Mobutu's in 1997, but by 1998, Kabila himself was having trouble with his countrymen. Zimbabwe's minister of foreign affairs, called a meeting of SADC foreign ministers in Harare on one day's notice. In urgent situations presidents can get to meetings on short notice, since they can charter airplanes, but ministers cannot. Mugabe's minister took advantage of the fact that most of us were represented by ambassadors and high commissioners. Zimbabwe suggested that SADC should intervene in the Congo on the side of Kabila. The ministers and other representatives said: "We need to talk with our presidents." However, at the end of the meeting that day, Minister Mahashe announced that SADC had taken a decision to intervene in the Congo. Botswana and South Africa simultaneously made announcements that we were not party to the agreement. Then President Mugabe apparently stated that those who claimed a decision was not taken were hypocrites, since they were part of the decision. And, the rest is history: Zimbabwe moved into the Congo under the pretext of a SADC decision, and Namibia and Angola came in as well.

The situation in the Congo was a kind of cancer in the whole region that could easily spread. That was why it was so important for all of us in the region to promote a peaceful resolution, rather than intensifying the problems, as has happened with external intervention by parties choosing sides.

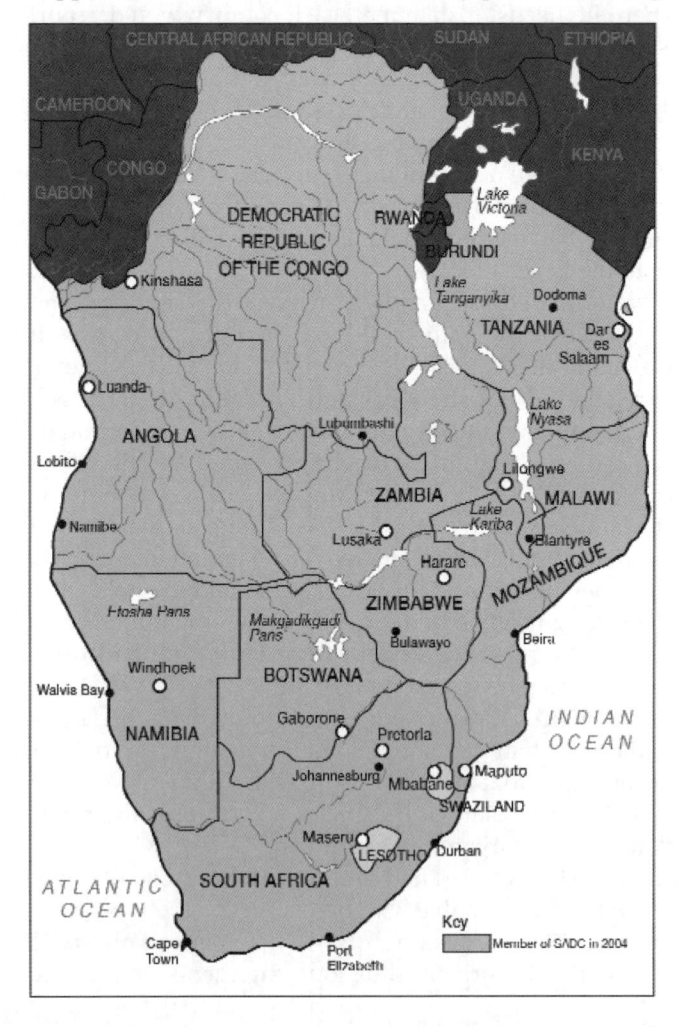

Map showing SADC members in 2004

Relations with Our Neighbours
In addition to our participation in the Front Line States and SADCC, there were a number of important developments in individual countries in the region that either affected Botswana or caused us to become involved with our neighbours. I dealt with the leaders of those countries on many issues and many occasions.

Zimbabwe
The behaviour of one's neighbours is important to one's own well being, and we have had difficult times with our neighbours in Zimbabwe, both before and after their independence in 1980. During the war in Zimbabwe from 1965 to 1980, the Smith government created constant problems for us. We had felt that UDI in Rhodesia would bring us difficulties, but we didn't have any idea how bad it would actually become. There had been rather liberal fellows in Rhodesia before UDI, but the Smith government turned very much to the right. During the bush war, Smith's people would follow Zimbabweans into Botswana, even into Francistown, to try to eliminate them. In the process, they killed our people as well. We became progressively more involved, and the Smith government's interest in Botswana intensified as the flow of refugees into our country increased.

One of their threats was that they would shoot down our planes if we flew refugees from Botswana into Zambia over the Kazungula border. The Kazungula ferry crossing to Zambia was our one common point with an independent African country. So, we were very glad to receive American assistance in building the road from Nata to Kazungula in the 1970s—a part of what we called the "lifeline project". Not only did the road itself provide us with another transportation link with the world, but American aid also showed the Smith government that we had the moral and financial support of the United States in our struggles.

By the beginning of 1979, there were over 20,000 Zimbabwean refugees in Botswana, mainly in Francistown and Selebi-Phikwe. We were constantly worried that Smith's people would come in and bomb the whole place as they had done in Mozambique. The war in Rhodesia was one of the reasons we formed the Botswana Defence Force (BDF) in 1977. We needed some way to reduce the raids in which both refugees and our own citizens were being killed. However, shortly after the BDF was formed, Smith's troops ambushed a BDF patrol inside Botswana at Lesoma, near Kazungula, and many of our boys were killed. It was one of the darkest hours of our first dozen years of independence, and the mass funeral in Gaborone was a very sad affair indeed.

In the late 1970s, Smith's foreign minister, Peter van der Byl, sought a clandestine meeting with Seretse. He said during the meeting: "You know, Seretse, if the Zimbabweans were like you, we would have no problem handing over to them." Seretse's retort was: "How would you know what they would be like without giving them the opportunity?" It was another example of how we in the BDP felt about determining legitimacy through elections. It was important that one be willing to risk elections if one believed in a democratic system, as some of the white Rhodesians professed to do.

We had long traded with Southern Rhodesia, with whom we had had a free trade agreement from colonial days. However, after UDI we assessed what position we should take on the international sanctions being imposed on the Smith regime. At the time we were still on British Grant-in-Aid to support our recurrent budget, and we were even more vulnerable economically than we became later. Nonetheless, we actively spoke against the illegal regime, and we undertook to restrict the importation of certain goods from Rhodesia. By the 1970s, about 10% of our imports came from there, and they took a much smaller share of our exports.

Our relationship with the Zimbabwean liberation movements was somewhat complicated. Our message to all liberation movements on their legitimacy was simple: What happened in free elections after handing-over was more important than what happened before the transition to an independent government. In Zimbabwe, the first movement we knew well politically was the Zimbabwe African People's Union (ZAPU). The movement was largely based in Matabeleland on our north-eastern border, and Joshua Nkomo, a former trade union leader and later the ZAPU leader, was almost worshipped in Matebeleland. While we came to know the ZAPU people first, we regarded ZAPU as we did other movements: They were important without being the only one. Over the years, Bishop Abel Muzerewa, Reverend Ndabaninge Sithole, and others came to Botswana, and we met with all of them, though each wanted us to regard them as the only legitimate movement. But because we had dealt with ZAPU first, Robert Mugabe and others in the Zimbabwe African National Union (ZANU) apparently concluded that we were recognising ZAPU as the one and only movement.

I first encountered President Mugabe when he was a freedom fighter, and I thought he was a hard working man. He was imprisoned for a long time, and after he was released, ZANU gained ground. We in the Front Line States tried to get ZANU and ZAPU to join together to form one liberation movement to oppose the Smith regime, but this proved very difficult. In part it was because of who would hold leadership positions as chairman and secretary-general. President Mugabe gave the impression that he was not keen to be chairman or secretary-general of the combined movements. Mr Nkomo was indecisive and saw virtue in both positions. Interestingly, at the time Mr Nkomo was clearly king of his group, but it was not as clear to us that Mugabe was the king of his.

We resolved at a Front Line States meeting in Lusaka that ZANU and ZAPU should propose a constitution that would bring their two movements together to more effectively oppose the Smith regime. They appeared to agree, but at a subsequent meeting ZANU and ZAPU reported to us that while they were travelling to the meeting, they had collided with a wildebeest, and their papers had been lost, so they could not give us their draft constitution! We said, all right, we didn't need to know chapter and verse, but could they please tell us the rough idea of what the papers contained. They said they couldn't remember! We saw that they did not want to merge and were really just playing for time. Further, those who knew more than we did told us that both movements were making secret contingency plans: ZAPU was preparing to see how they could overthrow ZANU if ZANU won elections, and ZANU was preparing to see how they would topple ZAPU if ZAPU won.

The two groups ultimately agreed to join in a Patriotic Front (PF), though they retained their original names and became ZANU-PF and ZAPU-PF. Archie Mogwe was our minister of foreign affairs, and he and Joe Legwaila, who was Seretse's senior private secretary, were actively involved in the final negotiations for Zimbabwe. It was a complex task. We first had the problem of getting ZANU and ZAPU to join together. Then we had to keep the PF together during the Lancaster House talks with the British and Smith's regime, and to get all parties to agree. The talks eventually led to a constitution, elections and independence in 1980.

The Lancaster House Agreement ended in a negotiated settlement instead of an outright and complete military victory for ZANU. President Mugabe was unhappy with the results, since he believed that if the war had continued, he would have been victorious over both the Smith regime and ZAPU. While he never said anything directly, his attitude was that we in Botswana were Nkomo's men. On the same principles as the South African government used, i.e. the friend of my enemy is my enemy, and he who is not for us is against us, he appeared to distrust us.

The 20,000 refugees at Francistown and Selebi-Phikwe were known to be mainly ZAPU supporters, and, after the Lancaster House agreements, there was an effort to keep them out of Zimbabwe until elections were over. We were told by the British there was no transport available for the refugees, and it was one time I found the British to be very unreasonable. We commandeered every government truck we could find to take the refugees to Zimbabwe so they could vote.

When the elections were over and ZANU had won, we received reports that several thousand ZAPU soldiers were training in Angola with Russian equipment. The reports further indicated they were planning to go into Zimbabwe through Botswana. Apparently ZAPU was going to implement its contingency plan. But the worst was yet to come. After the elections and the formation of a new government, the ZANU government moved its army into Matebeleland to suppress the ZAPU opposition. Mr Nkomo fled to Botswana, and we quickly brought him to Gaborone. We urged him to move on and bought him an airplane ticket, and eventually he went to England.

From the earliest days of Zimbabwe's independence, we had difficulty with their government. There were questions of trade and transportation, but security was the most serious issue. Defence Minister Nkala was particularly difficult, and he was reported to have wanted to shoot up the Dukwe refugee camp where many ZAPU refugees were living. Fortunately, President Mugabe prevented him.

In 1980, we had hoped that an independent Zimbabwe would help us reduce our dependence on South Africa and decrease our vulnerability, but that was not to be the case. To start with, Zimbabwe imposed duties on imports from Botswana in clear violation of our free trade agreement. We discussed this with President Mugabe, who blamed the problem on his minister for trade and said he would talk with him. Then the Zimbabwe officials claimed that Botswana's exports to Zimbabwe failed to meet the requirements for "local content" that would permit our duty-free exports. President Mugabe came to Gaborone to discuss it with me, and we thought we convinced him we were correct. When their government persisted in imposing the duties, Mr Kedikilwe, our minister of commerce, paid them back in their own coin by imposing duties on their exports to us. They came to us squealing! Since we imported more from them than they did from us, they suffered more from the reduced exports than we did. On another occasion, they began charging our trucks that hauled goods to Zimbabwe an entry fee of USD 80, while we charged their trucks P5; their charge was about 80 times more. When we complained, they did nothing, so we imposed a comparable charge, and again they objected loudly. The list went on.

Despite Zimbabwe's attitude, we persisted in trying to be cooperative neighbours and to find activities of mutual benefit. In the 1980s, at their request, we agreed to send them some of BCL's copper-nickel matte to be refined in Zimbabwe instead of in the US. This was a favour to Zimbabwe, since without our matte their smelter would have had to shut down, and their jobs would have been lost. At the Commonwealth meeting in Canada in 1986, I said to President Mugabe what I had told him earlier: "Our trade balance is in your favour so you should stop playing these games." But he said: "That is not so, I have been informed differently," and he went on to quote figures that included exports of copper-nickel matte from Botswana—exports we had agreed to as a favour to them and on which they were earning income from refining!

It was never clear how much of our problems with Zimbabwe was their bad management, and how much was intentional. President Mugabe himself was so reasonable in meetings that we thought for a while things might be happening without his knowledge. However, it was just not believable that he was ignorant of the long list of things that were done to the advantage of Zimbabwe and the disadvantage of Botswana.

President Mugabe can be very sweet. Whenever we would meet he would inquire in detail about my children and would remember specific things about them; he would ask why they never came over to see their uncle, and so forth. At the same time he can be a difficult customer. He is an orator and a good performer, and he has been a master at the game; he has played his political hand very skilfully.

With regard to Zimbabwe and its land problems since 2001, we in Botswana said: Yes, Zimbabwe had a land problem, and yes, it needed to be settled somehow. But we also asked: Could they not have done it differently? Interestingly, with the difficult situation in Zimbabwe—partly the takeover of white farms, but mainly persecution of many Africans and destruction of the capacity of the economy to function—we have not had a spill over in racial attitudes into Botswana. Batswana have truly been saddened by the political and economic destruction of Zimbabwe.

Namibia

We recognised the liberation movements in Namibia, and SWAPO in particular, since we did not think much of the Democratic Turnhalle Alliance (DTA), which was being promoted by the South African government. At one time, the OAU Liberation Committee was inclined to withdraw its financial support for SWAPO. However, Botswana argued at both official and ministerial level that the OAU should continue to support SWAPO financially. We felt that if the OAU was seen to withdraw its support, other countries might be inclined to do the same. Such a development would have been damaging to the whole effort to pressure South Africa on Namibian independence.

During the Namibian transition, Joe Legwaila, who was then our ambassador to the UN, served as deputy to the UN Special Representative in Namibia, Martti Ahtisaari. We sent people to Namibia to help and also to keep us up to date, and our high commissioner, Oteng Tebape, moved from Lusaka to Windhoek. We didn't want the Turnhalle Alliance or the National Party to win the elections, so we quietly tried to do some things to help SWAPO become the first elected government of an independent Namibia. We offered some vehicles, and we gave them advice on elections and on campaigning. I was the first president to pay a state visit to Namibia after their independence.

Our difficulties with an independent Namibia started with the descendants of the World War I refugees, primarily Hereros, but also Ovambos and others who had come to Botswana fleeing the Germans in 1914. They decided they wanted to go back to Namibia before independence. SWAPO was not keen on their return, since they thought those people would be in cahoots with the Turnhalle Alliance. We and SWAPO both talked with them; eventually we convinced them they should wait until Namibia became independent before they returned.

After independence, the Namibian government did not know where to settle the returning people, and they did not seem to want us to send them back immediately. However, they had difficulty putting it in such stark terms, so the refugees' descendants thought we were the ones who were keeping them from going back. Of course, all we were doing was trying to accommodate the Namibian government's wish. But, each side blamed Botswana.

If I ever became emotional at a *kgotla* meeting, it was at Xaudum, west of Tsodilo Hills, where I met with those wanting to return. One fellow first said nasty things about Batswana and accused us of being envious of their cattle. He then added that, if they decided they were unhappy after they had gone to Namibia, they would want to be able to come back to Botswana! I said: "*Le fatshe la rona gase koi!*" (Our country is not a skipping rope!) I was very angry that he felt he could be hopping over to Namibia and then hopping back to Botswana at his own whim.

The Namibian government had said to us: "Let people sell their cattle, and they can come over to Namibia. It is easier for us to settle people with money in their pockets than to settle their cattle." We said no, they could move with their cattle; but the Namibians would not allow it. Each side again blamed Botswana for the hard feelings. Eventually, some decided to go but others decided to stay, and those who left were allowed to take their cattle with them.

Our worst disagreement was when the Namibian government announced that Sedudu Island was part of Namibia, not Botswana. As I related in the previous chapter, we had consulted SWAPO about Sedudu Island during our boundary dispute with South Africa, and SWAPO had agreed with us. But after independence, the Namibian government tried to get control of it. We received a telegram from the DC at Kasane, Soblem Maeyane, saying he had been called to a meeting by an assistant minister from Namibia who was laying claim to Sedudu Island. We thought it was just politicking; we knew the Caprivi people wanted to be part of Botswana, and we had said we would not participate in the Balkanisation of any part of Africa.

We had long ago declared Sedudu Island a game area, and after the Namibians made their claims, we decided we needed to fly our flag there. President Nujoma tried to persuade us to take it down, since he said the area was in dispute. Of course, had we taken it down, we would have implicitly accepted the notion that it was in dispute. We took the issue lightly to start with, but it turned out to be serious. We had a BDF presence in the north, and that strengthened our hand, since the Namibians understood they could not simply walk over us. Eventually, we had to go to the International Court of Justice, a most unnecessary waste of time and resources, and the court confirmed our position. Once the issue of the island was settled, the Namibians have become good neighbours.

Zambia

Zambia was the only independent country in Africa with which we shared a border in 1966, and President Kenneth Kaunda was the first African leader to fully understand our situation and to take an interest in Botswana. We have had a special relationship with both the country and the man.

I had met President Kaunda before self-rule, when Seretse sent me to Zambia to brief him on what we were doing to prepare for independence. I was there for two days, but his people wouldn't give me an appointment to see him. I needed to leave Lusaka on a certain date because I had made arrangements to hitch a ride from Livingstone to the Chobe. (That I needed to hitch a ride is a reminder of how poor we were at that time.)

I finally managed to get in touch with President Kaunda, and he invited me to come see him that evening. We had a cup of coffee, and I told him about our objectives and how we were proceeding. He was very encouraging and said we had his support, which was very gratifying, given the stature he already had in the region. I later visited him to discuss the activities of the ANC and other liberation movements in Botswana, and Seretse visited on the occasion of Zambian independence. In return, President Kaunda was the first president to make a state visit to Botswana after our independence. He gave us 15 scholarships per year for our students to attend Zambian universities, and he also agreed to buy our beef. Over the years, he came to Botswana many times, and he attended the late president's funeral. He also was an important partner in the Front Line States in working for the liberation of southern Africa.

President Kaunda started out in Zambia with what was the strongest economy among the independent countries in the region, barring South Africa. The economy deteriorated substantially over time, in part due to the decline in the price of copper. However, there were two other factors. First, part of the problem was due to the economic management policies adopted by the Zambian government. Second, their decision to support the liberation struggle by closing the border with Southern Rhodesia after UDI in 1965 imposed very heavy costs, since they had been major trading partners.

Zambian trade with South Africa continued, since President Kaunda did not try to have the complete boycott he had with Rhodesia. However, trade with South Africa was done through Botswana, and, in order that Zambia would appear to have joined the boycott, it was not reported as Zambian trade with South Africa. Zambian statistics showed Botswana as the country of origin of goods that were actually manufactured in South Africa. Of course, the South Africans were happy to play along to get the Zambian business.

The restrictions of trade with Rhodesia and South Africa led to increased economic hardship and grumbling on the part of the Zambian population. It did not have a negative impact on President Kaunda's stature in the region. He took a leading role in the liberation struggle, and people felt that part of Zambia's suffering was the result of sacrifices it was making: Accepting refugees from Namibia, South Africa, Zimbabwe and other countries, and risking retaliation from both Ian Smith and the South African government.

President Kaunda was and is a very sincere man, and when he has embraced something, he has done so completely. He looked at socialism and concluded everything could be answered by the rules of socialism as he understood them. He saw benefits in a strict leadership code of behaviour for those in politics, and he pursued it vigorously. He and I talked about political matters, but we never talked about economic management, since our approaches were so different. He would tell me how he had visited Romania and had been given tractors, and how he was going to have state farms that would be ploughed by those tractors. However, though Zambia had so much more agricultural potential than Botswana, it was often not able to feed itself. I thought he was so committed to his beliefs that he would just listen politely if I tried to talk economics.

Near the end of his regime, I flew to Lusaka to meet with him. I pleaded with President Kaunda to let the democratic process take its course and to allow other people to contest free elections. He said he welcomed that advice, and he talked of why he was sometimes judged harshly. He argued that those who opposed him politically were good-for-nothing fellows, and that some were even involved in drug dealing. He then thanked me for coming to see him, and that was that. Later on, whether it had anything to do with what I said to him or was something he was going to do anyway, he liberalised politics and allowed other parties to exist, and he then was voted out of office.

President Chiluba took over in 1991, and he didn't miss an opportunity to say how undemocratic President Kaunda had been. We were the first country to which President Chiluba made a state visit, and at that time he said to me publicly at a state banquet: "You, Mr President, have nothing to fear, since your friend is in safe hands." But in fact, he translated President Kaunda's life into misery, persecuted him, and barred him from politics. I thought of going alone to see Chiluba to ask him to stop treating President Kaunda so badly. However, I learned that the British and the Americans were talking with him, and things eased for a while. Then the Zambian government denied him his citizenship, so Presidents Mandela and Mugabe and I decided to go to Lusaka to talk with President Chiluba. We wanted to point out that President Kaunda, having honoured the outcome of democratic processes, should be respected, Chiluba should not abuse the fact that the democratic processes had favoured him. But before we could approach President Chiluba, he had imprisoned President Kaunda.

We continued our efforts to meet with President Chiluba, but he had many excuses as to why he could not find a date that would work—he had to meet with the churches, who were calling him to account for his own behaviour, and so forth. In the meantime, some of his political allies, including Skota Wina, said unpleasant things about me, and accused me of interfering in Zambia's internal politics. In the end, of course, President Chiluba himself was called to account by his successor after he left the presidency in 2002. And President Kaunda's life has been much easier since Chiluba left office.

People seem to have forgotten that President Kaunda sacrificed personally to support the liberation of southern Africa, and so did his country. Since leaving office, he has not been given the kind of role he ought to have in the region. No single person did as much for the liberation of southern Africa as he did. I suppose he was neglected for a while because people felt that to ask him to do things would offend President Chiluba. That phase has now passed, and he should be called upon more often for his wisdom and experience.

Lesotho and Swaziland

Our relationships with Lesotho and Swaziland have been close and continuing in many ways. We shared a common heritage as former High Commission Territories, our membership in the Southern African Customs Union, common use of the rand currency for many years, and until 1976, the University of Botswana, Lesotho and Swaziland. Politically, however, we have always been poles apart. Lesotho as a constitutional monarchy has had chronic problems with representative democratic government, and Swaziland was and is a monarchy without representative government. Our position in the region, and our historic relationship, has permitted us to play a role that I believe was helpful to each country at different times, though never as helpful as we might have wished.

Lesotho

Chief Leabua Jonathan, the first prime minister of Lesotho, was a difficult man. In the elections in 1970, the counting of ballots went on until it became clear that he and his Basotho National Party were going to lose. At that point, he stopped the counting and just took power! He nullified the elections and suspended the constitution. After this coup, the late president sent an emissary to ask Chief Jonathan to allow a UN mission to come to Lesotho to examine the situation. Seretse argued that if the UN declared Chief Jonathan as the winner, it would put him in a stronger position. Seretse also pointed out that Jonathan would have the advantage of being in office, and that possession is nine-tenths of the law. But Chief Jonathan dismissed the idea.

Later one of the opposition, Ntsu Mokhehle came to Botswana as a refugee. We looked after him as we did so many others, and I think this displeased Chief Jonathan. However, we distinguished between Leabua Jonathan and Lesotho. Lesotho was a friendly state, and we arranged for Mr Mokhehle to pass through, as we later did for Joshua Nkomo as he fled from Zimbabwe. Some time after that, we thought we were getting Chief Jonathan to understand democratic processes, and we invited him to come to Botswana for a state visit. But then he threw some opposition politicians into jail, so we had to cancel the visit.

Lesotho, of course, was in a very difficult position. It was completely surrounded by South Africa, and most of its labour force was employed in South Africa, even many years after independence. Lesotho had a very high rate of literacy, much higher than most countries of similar income level. However, many of its talented and well-trained people worked abroad because of the political situation, and the country was deprived of what they could have contributed.

There were several times when there were serious conflicts within Lesotho, and the opposition parties, the king, the army and the government in Lesotho all expressed trust in Botswana, and we tried to be of help. There was a coup in 1994, and the army took power. The secretary-general of the Commonwealth asked Presidents Mugabe, Mandela and me to intervene. So President Mugabe and I went to Lesotho with the South African ambassador, and we talked with all the parties. The army had taken over twice before and it was again being naughty. We talked with everyone, including the churches and the king, and the outcome seemed very positive. However, a great deal of mutual suspicion remained, and it flared up again a year later.

President Mandela asked me and Mugabe to meet again with the various parties—the king and his men, the army, the opposition parties led by Mr Sekgonyane, and the government led by Ntsu Mokhehle. We came up with a memorandum of understanding among the parties, and we made it clear that whoever might break the agreement would have to answer to the outside parties. The army leaders agreed to come to Botswana to try to understand the relationship between our army and the political leadership.

If the problems are not in one's own country, one cannot really enforce an agreement unless one is prepared to intervene with military force. The parties inside the country ultimately must adopt the solutions; outsiders can be helpful only up to a point. After another coup in Lesotho in 1998, a subsequent memorandum of understanding among the internal parties agreed that South Africa and Botswana would go in with troops to keep the peace. For some reason, all parties were very appreciative of what Botswana did, but they thought the South Africans were a bit rough on them. Our troops were there for almost a full year, and we established good rapport with the army and the other parties. We have continued to be ready to help the Basutho whenever they might want to call on us.

Swaziland

At the time of Swaziland's independence in 1968, King Sobhuza II had reigned a long time, and by the time he passed away he had ruled for 65 years. He posed a good example of what happens when one does not separate traditional rule from the rule of a modern state. King Sobhuza was both the head of state and ruled all citizens, and the head of the Swazi Nation, which included only ethnic Swazis; there was often confusion as to which role he was playing. Before independence, Swaziland had the most diversified economy of the three High Commission Territories as well as the most diversified and viable agriculture. However, King Sobhuza had no interest in modern democratic institutions. The king suspended the constitution in 1973, and ruled the country himself. Swaziland has not developed either economically or politically in line with its potential.

When King Sobhuza died in 1986, he was succeeded by King Mswati III, who was then only 18 years old. Whereas his father had a long tradition of personal rule that pre-dated democratic institutions in other countries, Mswati became king after other monarchies had become constitutional monarchies, and after democratic institutions had taken hold throughout the world.

The situation in Swaziland was of concern to others in SADC. After Nelson Mandela became chairman of SADC, he went see King Mswati. He pointed out that the king in Lesotho had been overthrown because he wanted to be an executive monarch. If King Mswati wanted his role to last, he should hand over responsibility for governing to the people. However, the trade unions in South Africa had been talking with the trade unions in Swaziland, so the king was suspicious of President Mandela. President Mandela invited President Mugabe and me to also talk with the king at a second meeting in Pretoria. We said to him: "Your father was able to run Swaziland as he did only because South Africa, Mozambique, Zimbabwe, Botswana, and Lesotho were all under minority or colonial regimes. However, all of them are now democracies in one form or another. Today, your people cannot look at these neighbouring countries without thinking of demanding the same thing. The demand will be there, and it would be better if you pre-empt it and be seen to be willing, rather than being pushed."

King Mswati said he appreciated what we had said, but he would have to talk with his advisors. We told him to remember that his advisors had vested interests, and what they told him might not be because it was good for the country or good for him, but because it was good for them. We suggested that he let us talk with his advisors. He agreed, and a date was set. As I was flying to the meeting, I learned from Presidents Mugabe and Mandela that the king had postponed the meeting. I continued on and joined up with Alfred Nzo, South Africa's minister of foreign affairs. When we arrived in Swaziland, instead of finding the king's advisers, we found a big gathering of youth dancing around in a kraal. We were given a nice lunch and sent on our way. We found it very discouraging. But I have not given up. Since retiring as president, I have had the opportunity to talk with King Mswati on a number of occasions about the future in Swaziland. I still have hope that he will take the initiative and introduce the reforms that are needed to provide his country with a representative government responsive to the people.

Mozambique and Angola

The Portuguese were the last European power to relinquish colonial possessions in Africa. Liberation movements in both Mozambique and Angola began active military resistance in the 1960s, and the Portuguese fought back strongly. After Salazar died in 1974, however, there was a complete reversal of policy in Lisbon, and Angola and Mozambique were granted independence with great haste in 1975. There was no orderly transfer of power; the liberation movements were basically handed the countries, and the Portuguese took a great deal of property on their way out. Both of the eventual governments were Marxist in their orientation, and both were supported by the Soviet Union and Cuba. The Cuban troops in Angola greatly complicated things in the region.

The South African government had regarded Angola and Mozambique as a part of their buffer against independent countries in the rest of Africa. After 1975, not only were these countries ruled by blacks, but they also were friendly to the Soviet Union, which was supporting the ANC in its struggle against apartheid in South Africa. As a consequence, the National Party government in South Africa actively supported armed opposition to the governments of both Angola and Mozambique. This caused major loss of life, extensive human misery, and considerable economic destruction in both countries for many years.

Mozambique

In Mozambique, Frelimo was the dominant liberation movement, so there was little doubt about who would form the first government. Samora Machel was the first president, and when Mozambique became independent, he became a full member of the Front Line States. Whenever there was a Front Line States meeting, Machel would give a historical perspective and talk to other presidents with a tone of: "If only you knew about the liberation struggle." For some reason, he became quite attached to Botswana, even though, of course, our political and economic philosophies were very different. When we discussed Zimbabwe, he often would come up with examples of the way Frelimo had fought for independence in Mozambique. He allowed the liberation movements from Zimbabwe to operate from Mozambique, at a huge cost to his country. However, because he provided resources to ZANU, he was in a position to help get President Mugabe and ZANU to the negotiating table in Lancaster House for the discussions that ended the Zimbabwe war and led to independence.

During the war in Zimbabwe, the Smith government promoted the formation of a group called the Mozambique National Resistance (MNR). They armed the MNR, and encouraged them to oppose the Frelimo government, hoping that this would reduce Frelimo's ability to support ZANU's military actions. After Zimbabwe's independence in 1980, the South African government took over the support of MNR, and the group became known by its Lusophone acronym, RENAMO (Resistencia Nacional Mocambicana). It was part of South Africa's general destabilising policy in all of southern Africa, and there was slaughter and destruction in the countryside as RENAMO gained strength. At least 10% of the population was displaced from their homes, a quarter of the people were on emergency food aid for many years, the economy was destroyed, and tens of thousands were killed. Eventually the Frelimo government had to deal with RENAMO in political terms.

President Machel tried to get South Africa to act as a good neighbour, and in 1984 the two countries signed the Nkomati Accord, which was sold by the South Africans as a "mutual defence" treaty. But, of course, after Nkomati was signed, the South African government did not change its behaviour; it continued to support RENAMO and continued raids into Mozambique whenever it suited them. Another difficulty was that Malawi was giving cover to RENAMO and arresting people from Frelimo. Using an analogy of what South Africa had done to its neighbours, President Machel threatened Malawi and even said Mozambique's guns were trained on Malawi. That statement doubtless worried the South African government, and it may even have caused them to take action. The Front Line States gave Presidents Kaunda, Machel and Nyerere the task of trying to reduce the tensions with Malawi, and the three met in eastern Zambia in October 1986. It was on his way back from that meeting that Machel met his tragic death in an airplane crash. We in Botswana always suspected that the South African government was responsible.

President Machel's early death was a big loss, but his successor, Joachim Chissano, did an excellent job. President Machel was more of an ideologue, and while Chissano started that way, he moderated and was won over to a more pragmatic approach to economic policy.

Ultimately, it became clear that the government of President Chissano and RENAMO needed to come to terms. Fortunately, Alfonso Dhlakama, the RENAMO leader, was impressed by what was happening in Botswana. He apparently felt that if President Chissano could do what we had done in Botswana, there would be nothing to fear from Frelimo. After a good deal of preliminary work, the two parties from Mozambique along with President Mugabe, who was also assisting, decided they should come to meet in Gaborone, since all the parties trusted Botswana. They met here twice, with a pause that enabled them to return to Mozambique for consultations with their own people. The first time Dhlakama and Chissano embraced and called each other "brother" was at the Gaborone meetings. Those meetings paved the way for final meetings in Rome in 1992, to which President Mugabe, Dr Chiepe and I accompanied them.

At the meetings between the two sides, President Mugabe and I tried to ensure that each side would give way on some issues, so we could reduce the distance between them and make it possible to agree. We tried to point out when one or the other was being unreasonable. I believe our willingness to be patient, to be directly involved, and to do everything possible to keep the dialogue open was important in the parties reaching a successful conclusion.

The truce between Frelimo and RENAMO led to peace, and that peace was to be assured through elections. Our people went to help with that process, and the boys of the BDF were part of a peace-keeping force from the United Nations that remained through the transition to a multi-party state.

Angola

During the struggle for independence in Angola, there were three main groups: Holden Roberto's FNLA, Jonas Savimbi's UNITA, and Augustino Neto's MPLA. The Front Line States tried to help them to merge. We almost succeeded, but the three ultimately split apart and outside parties chose sides and supported their favourites economically and militarily. President Mobuto Sese-Seko in Zaire was a supporter of the FNLA; the Soviets took the side of Neto's MPLA; and UNITA hobnobbed with the South Africans.

A very bloody civil war raged in Angola almost continuously from 1975 to 2002, and there are still regional conflicts. The war destroyed the economy, and hundreds of thousands of people were killed or maimed. The struggle involved the Americans and the Soviets, as well as South Africa and Cuba. UNITA drew support from the South African and the US governments. Savimbi had visited Botswana to talk with us right after the Portuguese left, but we were worried by his South African connection. And, as time went on, it became clear that nothing other than becoming president would satisfy Savimbi. The MPLA was backed by the Soviets and the Cubans. The Soviets wanted us to support the MPLA, but we told them this was an African matter, and more importantly, as we said to all outsiders, it was an Angolan matter; they should settle it themselves. During the long civil war, we in Botswana tried to leave the matter to the Angolans. We did with them as we did with the Zimbabweans and the South Africans: We welcomed anyone to come and talk with us. But, as a small country, we had to be very careful not to involve ourselves in other people's affairs.

After the MPLA had established a government in Luanda and controlled a large part of the country, we recognised them as the government of Angola. Once President Neto and the MPLA had become the established government, we within the Front Line States supported them, and we tried to work with them. President Neto died in 1979, and his successor, Jose Eduardo Dos Santos, appeared to be prepared to see what the Front Line States could do for him. However, he didn't trust the other presidents enough to candidly discuss his problems. The MPLA government always viewed Botswana with suspicion, and President Dos Santos even said we were allowing Savimbi to acquire goods in Botswana and to operate there. I had to put the record straight with the other presidents at a Front Line meeting in Lusaka.

Angola was where I experienced my most serious brush with death. In 1988, just before I had left on a trip during which we would over fly Angola, Mma-Gaone and I had lunch with Mrs Lock, the widow of the former speaker of the National Assembly. I jokingly said to her: "Well, in an hour, I could be shot down over Angola," and we all laughed. We left Gaborone, passed over Maun, and started over Angola. As we were above Cuito Caanavale, human vanity led me to say: "Not so long ago this town below us was in the news about the hot fighting between the MPLA and UNITA." None of us knew that at that very time we were being fired on from the ground below. I was drinking a cup of tea when there was a shattering noise. I was traumatised, but I did not realise I was in real danger. The pilot skilfully brought the plane down, and we landed at the air strip at Cuito Bay. As we got out of the plane, I saw my blood streaming down my body, but I didn't know what had happened.

My people asked that I be taken to the hospital, and in order to make people act with speed, my officials told the Cubans running the airfield that I was the president. They thought that meant I wanted to be taken to the Presidential Villa, and that is where we went. Once there we made further entreaties, and they took us to the hospital. Fortunately, only Bashi Itketseng and I were injured, and I was the only serious one. The doctors bandaged us up, and late that night President Dos Santos sent his plane to fetch me to Luanda. At Luanda, they took me to the hospital where the doctors did not ask any questions or even ask my permission. They just put me out and operated to remove some metal and patch me up. I later learned that a splinter from the engine had struck me, just missing my spinal column, and it had stopped just short of entering the thoracic cavity.

President Dos Santos came to see me the following day. He is a man who seldom smiles, but he gave one of his rare smiles and said: "You know, I don't believe in God, but if this is not a miracle, I don't know what else it is." The Angolan forces had aimed four ground-to-air missiles at us while we were passing over Cuito Caanavale. They all missed, so they detailed two MIGs after us. One MIG fired a heat-seeking missile that hit the right engine. Our pilot later told me the missile had sheared off the engine, and he could see the engine flying alone ahead of the plane for a few seconds! If it had hit between the two engines, we would have all died peacefully, without knowing anything.

At that time there was no direct communication between Luanda and Gaborone, so we had to be in touch via Brussels. People in Botswana heard that our plane had been shot down, and they were convinced I had been killed and they were being told lies. After a couple of days, I came back to Gaborone to show I was still alive and functioning. I then went to London for further medical treatment. I lived with the residual pain for a year or two, and for a long time I could feel it when the weather changed. Fortunately the pain has completely disappeared, and there were no psychological after effects.

Tanzania

Julius Nyerere was a father figure to the liberation movements, and he was committed to the liberation of all peoples of Africa. There did not seem to be any economic or strategic reason why he and Tanzania should have been so involved in the movement; it seemed to be a matter of principle. Tanzania took on a very large burden of hosting the ANC and other liberation movements, and it provided education and training and other support. Before our independence, President Nyerere had just taken Botswana to be a Bantustan, since in his view there was very little we could do or say against South Africa. But as he came to realise what we were prepared to say and do, he swung to the other extreme and became one of our biggest defenders.

President Nyerere was close to both Seretse and me as we worked with him in the Front Line States, and he and Seretse were the force behind the establishment of SADCC. Within the region, Tanzania was wedded to SADCC, but not to the PTA/COMESA. SADCC was more pragmatic, and COMESA was more based on ideology. People might have expected Tanzania to have been drawn more to the ideology, but in fact that was not the case. The Tanzanians were practical and pragmatic and sought arrangements that were committed to results.

While President Nyerere was a Pan-Africanist, he believed in achieving it in stages. For example, he thought if we were successful in SADCC, we would be better able to move beyond the region. In the late 1970s, I represented Seretse at an OAU Summit meeting on the Lagos Plan of Action at which Nyerere argued that the five separate African regional groupings should do their homework and become successful in cooperation. Their success would then make it easier for a larger merger over time. Meanwhile, people like the Ghanaians were arguing for a leap into a grand design such as Kwame Nkrumah would have promoted.

President Nyerere spoke at my retirement dinner. Among other things, he said: "Mr President, you might find in retirement you are even more busy than you have been as president!" When I went to say good-bye to him the next day, he was already planning to have me take over from him in the Rwanda genocide investigation, or take on the Congo negotiations. I eventually undertook both of those tasks, as I relate in the next chapter.

Our Role in the Region

One reason we Batswana have been so committed to democratic principles is that we have seen first hand the tragic consequences when those principles are ignored. As I have told young colleagues thinking of going into politics: "If you want to be a politician, you must be prepared to lose an election." That is one of the bases of democracy. A theme of these regional stories, however, is that many leaders of other countries were democratic only as long as they were favoured by the outcome of a democratic process.

In the beginning, the OAU was wedded to the principle of non-interference in the affairs of other countries, but it has progressively abandoned that position. Now the principle in the OAU's successor, the African Union (AU), is that no leader should be accepted into the AU unless he or she has been democratically elected. Existing leaders were given an exception.

People are often puzzled by why some African presidents are so reluctant to make critical public statements about other presidents who are misbehaving. We usually try to work with other countries and their leaders through private conversations. In such conversations, we have tried to make clear the interconnections of countries and the consequences of bad behaviour by one country for that country's neighbours. There have been many cases where leaders have tried to be privately helpful to another president, or have worked with some of that president's own ministers to try to get their president to see reason. The African approach is to try to be diplomatic, while a European or American approach is to attack problems head-on and often publicly. We believe if you want to influence someone, you have to first make the person understand you are a friend. An enemy or adversary cannot use persuasion; one has a better chance of influencing someone as a friend. So, the SADC presidents have tried to avoid putting up a show that would make a fellow president think they were pressuring him as his enemies.

After all, a president is a president, and he has a country. He has a following, and he was chosen by those people. Even if there is dispute about the election, when you challenge the president you are not just doing it to him as a person, you are challenging his supporters as well. You are in effect saying you don't have trust in the people who have chosen him. At that point, reason flies away, and Dame Emotion moves in, and you can end up with a worse situation than when you started.

For almost all our history, there has been a pattern in our international relations. People have trusted Botswana—the donors have trusted us, the other countries in the region have trusted us. The reason, I suppose, is a question of character, and character is a composite outcome of an interplay of factors. The trust we have been accorded must have emerged from what people, rightly or wrongly, thought Botswana was. I think a trust has evolved through the experience of working relationships and a realisation that we have not exploited situations. We have tried to play a modest role in helping others in the region as well as protecting the interests of our own people.

The trust we have been shown is a wonderful compliment, but it is something of a burden, since we are often called upon to take on responsibilities. When I was chairman of SADC for 16 years, people knew I was doing it only because it had to be done, not because I craved to be chairman. People can count on Batswana to say things honestly, not because we think we are going to benefit from them. And we are ready to stand back when there is no need for us to continue to be involved. We have stuck to our principles, taken initiatives where we thought that others, not just ourselves, would benefit, and tried to do all that is necessary to make the initiatives successful.

Chapter 19

Diplomacy, the Great Powers, and the United Nations

At independence, we were starting *de novo* in international affairs, and fellows like me were naïve in many respects. We tried to analyse the situation, set priorities, and use our resources carefully. We had major external threats from the Smith regime in Rhodesia and the Nationalists in South Africa, so one priority was to gain allies from the rest of the world to attempt to reduce those two threats. We also needed aid, both financial and technical, so the other priority was to expand our friendly relations with countries and international organisations that might assist us. As time went on, and we became known as a trustworthy country, we began to play other roles, primarily in the region, as I related in the previous chapter. Since my retirement, I have been asked to undertake a number of diplomatic missions in Africa, principally to lead the inquiry into the Rwanda genocide and to serve as Facilitator for the dialogue in the Democratic Republic of the Congo that led to agreement on a coalition government in April 2003 and a new constitution in 2006.

Our approach to international diplomacy was guided by the same principles that we used at home: consultation, persuasion, the importance of democratic elections in selecting a country's leaders, and non-interference in the affairs of other countries. As a people who had long depended on diplomacy rather than force, we knew that good allies could help us deal with troublesome neighbours. We also knew it was important to keep our friends well informed. We wanted the support of the democratic countries, so we emphasised our role in the region with them. As a non-racial democratic country, we hoped to demonstrate that such a government could be successful even in southern Africa.

Because of our scarcity of both personnel and financial resources, in establishing diplomatic missions we concentrated our resources where we thought they would best help meet our objectives. In the beginning, our only embassy in Africa was in Lusaka, since Lusaka served for many years as a contact point with the liberation movements from Zimbabwe, Namibia and South Africa. Our London high commissioner at first represented us on a non-resident basis with other European countries as well as with Nigeria. After it became clear we would need good relationships with the European Community (now the European Union) to ensure both aid and favourable treatment for our beef exports to Europe, we established a resident mission in Brussels. For 20 years, our only other resident diplomatic missions were embassies in Washington and at the United Nations in New York, which provided non-resident representation to a number of other countries in the Americas.

In organising ourselves for international diplomacy, we did not start with a substantive minister of foreign affairs but instead had a minister of state in the Office of the President. Mr Nwako and later Mr Masisi served in that role. The idea was that the president would be the only one who could speak authoritatively on diplomatic matters. Therefore, if the minister of state made a tentative commitment that we later realised was unwise, he could be rescued by the president without having Botswana go back on its word. After we had become a bit more sure of ourselves, we created a minister of foreign affairs who could make binding commitments to others.

It was many years before we permitted anyone other than the president to travel by first class on official business. This was not only because we were poor, but also because we did not wish to be seen squandering money. This led to some interesting experiences. On one occasion, I was representing the late president at a heads of state meeting in Addis. Emperor Haile Selassie was at the airport with a guard of honour to meet me, expecting that the vice-president of Botswana would come out the first class door. Not only was I in economy, but I had also neglected to bring my yellow fever card. I was declared not fit to be admitted to Ethiopia; the Emperor left, and I was locked up in quarantine. Eventually, the Ethiopian official who was supposed to be looking after me discovered who and where I was. The guard of honour was reassembled, and the Emperor was recalled to welcome me. I tried to explain I was to blame for the mix-up, but the poor fellow looking after me was in trouble!

On a later trip, I was on a flight that touched down in Kinshasa. The speaker of the National Assembly in Zaire was regarded as the equivalent of a vice-president, so he stood at the first class exit to greet me, while I, of course, came out of economy. I later tried to make an apology, explaining that our resources were very limited. The speaker scolded me and said: "You must take into account the embarrassment you cause others"—because we did not travel by first class!

Diplomatic Relations

The UK was our colonial ruler and, at the beginning, our only source of financial and technical assistance. Therefore, our relationships with the British government were extremely important. Over the years our relationship with the Commonwealth was also valuable for the associations it gave us internationally, the role it played in southern Africa, and the technical assistance we received. We received hundreds of technical assistance personnel from the UK, from bright young university graduates to seasoned technicians and administrators in many fields. The British stood by our side during problems with the South African government, and this was very valuable to us. We agreed to a BBC transmitter being located at Francistown, which was not popular with our neighbours, but having a British installation was something of a deterrent to military actions by the South African or the Rhodesian governments in that area. The British were also the suppliers of the first aircraft for the BDF.

The Americans were helpful from the outset. I went there on several occasions to talk with them about aid and about the situation in southern Africa, and I would visit the World Bank, one of our important donors. In our relations with South Africa, the US said the right sorts of things when we were in trouble, such as when the South African Defence Force raided us in the 1980s. The Americans were careful with their dollars, but they helped where they could.

Both as a great power and by temperament, the Americans are somewhat impatient to get things done, and they are also inclined to think they know best. We saw this tendency in a number of situations in the region, and I had to contend with it when I was Facilitator in the Congo. Of course, they had many different interests in the region and throughout the world, particularly during the Cold War, and these sometimes complicated our diplomatic relationships with them.

We allowed the Americans to install a Voice of America transmitter in the north-east. This was a risk, since our neighbours Rhodesia and South Africa were not in favour of us doing so, for much the same reason we wanted it there. Much later, the US was helpful in the training of BDF personnel and in selling us military equipment. They even undertook joint exercises with the BDF during the 1980s. While some Batswana were quite nervous about such exercises, Mr Mogwe and I thought it was a jolly good thing to do. At the time, the hard-liners in South Africa were threatening to upset the apple cart in Botswana. If they thought the Americans were likely to be in Botswana, it was a helpful deterrent. When we later built the BDF airport west of Molepolole, Namibia, Zimbabwe and South Africa all seemed to think it was built with American help and for their use. It was useful to us, as a minor military power, to have our neighbours think we had powerful friends who would be prepared to take our side. In fact, the Americans had nothing to do with the airport.

The fondness of some anti-communists in the US for Jonas Savimbi and his UNITA organisation in Angola created difficulties in the region. Several times we in the Front Line States thought things were moving toward resolution in Angola, and then Mr Savimbi would get encouragement from his friends in the United States and become difficult. Chester Crocker, who headed African affairs in the Reagan administration, explained in his book on southern Africa how he and others in the administration had problems with the American right wing, which supported Savimbi. Had not Jonas Savimbi received so much help and encouragement from the South African government and the US, the long and destructive civil war in Angola might have ended much sooner.

We were careful with the Soviets, since we knew their interest in establishing an embassy in Gaborone did not reflect interest in us, but rather in South Africa and the rest of the subcontinent—and the South African government thought so, too. The Soviets wanted to push us into choices we did not want to make. For example, when the MPLA and UNITA were battling it out in Angola, we felt they should settle things between themselves at the ballot box. But Soviet Ambassador Belegolos would come to give us long lectures on why we should support the MPLA instead of remaining neutral. We thought it was clear the Russians were just using us; it certainly was not in Botswana's interest at that time to choose sides in what we viewed as an internal dispute. The Soviets offered us scholarships, and though we were desperately in need of trained manpower, we felt our people should study in English, and studying in Russian would increase their training time. The Soviets felt that we were turning them down because we disliked them, but that was not the main reason. However, before independence the opposition did send some students.

The Soviets had a large number of people in their embassy, and we had to throw some of them out on several occasions for meddling in our internal affairs and acting against our interest. The presence of a Soviet Embassy intensely displeased South Africa, but we felt we had a sovereign right to have it in Botswana. In addition, one of our basic principles was that we would not do things for simple ideological reasons. Therefore, it was appropriate for us to recognise and cooperate with any country whenever we thought we might benefit from our relations with it.

Our relations with China were initially complicated by the fact that there were two Chinas. I led us into establishing diplomatic relations with Taiwan after independence because I was naïve in international affairs. We were not ideologists, so we embraced whoever wanted to do business with us, provided they appeared to have clean hands. Then the Chinese from the People's Republic of China (PRC) quietly let us know they wanted to have an embassy here, and they made it clear they could not do so unless we threw out the Taiwanese. Over time, we realised the better thing to do was to go with the PRC. The great powers sometimes meddled in things they should not, and since the opposition had embraced the PRC, we were concerned that the Chinese might be disruptive. However, President Nyerere, in particular, told us the Chinese were a good bunch of people, and that they did not interfere in internal affairs.

So, we eventually told the Taiwanese they had to leave, and we invited the mainland government to come in. The Nixon administration told us they had a problem with this, even though at the very time they themselves were preparing to make an opening to China. A year or so after we had established diplomatic relations with the PRC, the Americans did as well. On the late president's first visit we received a loan of 14 million yuan toward rehabilitation of the railway, and we have had very good diplomatic and economic relations with the Chinese ever since.

Our international relationships with other industrial countries have been largely associated with their aid programmes, as I have mentioned earlier. The Scandinavians helped us in part, I suppose, because they were hopeful that a working, non-racial democracy next door to South Africa would be a good thing, though they never really announced it in that way. Whatever their initial motives, they found we were people with whom they could do business. They and others discovered that we in Botswana could use their aid properly and effectively, and we became a good demonstration site for other countries. The donors could point to us and say that aid can and does work if used properly, and it can produce beneficial results.

The United Nations
We looked to the United Nations as an important forum, as did many newly independent countries in Asia and Africa. We knew that because of our

location and small size, many people would regard Botswana as a South African Bantustan. If we were to be taken seriously and be accorded the respect of an independent country, we would have to establish our credentials in Africa and then with other nations, including the great powers. The UN provided a useful forum in which we could demonstrate our principles and our approach. The late president's first address to the UN General Assembly in 1969 clearly defined our foreign policy and our position on South African liberation.

Seretse appointed Professor Z. K. Matthews as our first permanent representative to the United Nations. He was a very distinguished black South African of Botswana origin who had been at the forefront of the movement for racial justice in South Africa. A lawyer by training, Professor Matthews had been a professor of Law and Anthropology at Fort Hare University; the late president and Nelson Mandela were students during his time there. As an active leader in the ANC, Professor Matthews nurtured the development of its Youth Wing in the 1940s and proposed the adoption of the Freedom Charter in the early 1950s. In 1961, he was the final witness for the defence in the infamous South African Treason Trial. His appointment as our ambassador was a way of signalling to the world that our credentials in the struggle for freedom were in proper order. Mr Matante, of course, criticised the appointment in Parliament, on the basis that Professor Matthews was not a Motswana!

As time went on, we saw the important role our mission at the United Nations could play. Our ambassadors there kept us informed of opinion in different parts of the world, and they worked to establish good relations, including with countries where we had no resident diplomatic representation. Because the UN played an important role in a number of regional developments, including the independence of Namibia, our successive ambassadors, especially Joe Legwaila, took an active part.

The UN and the Great Powers in Africa

Over the past 40 years, Africa has been plagued by civil wars and violent ethnic and political conflicts. These have cost the lives of millions of innocent people and have disrupted societies and economies. In many areas, such as Rwanda, Burundi, Sudan, Congo, Liberia, and southern Africa, these conflicts spilled across borders and threatened neighbouring countries and international peace. In such instances, there was a strong case for action by outsiders, and the UN is the one body, through the Security Council, where one could act under international law and back it up with enforcement. However, little that is significant by way of enforcement or restoration of peace can happen unless the major powers agree to make it happen. Therefore, in dealing with difficult situations, the permanent members of the Security Council must agree what action will be taken, and they must be joined by other countries in carrying it out.

I believe the best thing for the UN to do in crisis situations is to get the people on opposing sides to talk and to help them to reach a decision as to what should be done. Then, the United Nations should monitor and enforce implementation of the resolutions that were adopted by the parties to the conflict. As part of the resolution, whether it involves the Liberians, or the Israelis and the Palestinians, or the Congolese, there must be an agreement as to what is to be done, and parties should be made to honour the agreement that has been reached. Of course, that then leads to the questions of what is sufficient force to make them do so, and what the appropriate rules of engagement are, in order for a military mission to be effective in enforcing agreements.

When an agreement is reached in an internal conflict, some external group must be in a position to adjudicate later differences and ensure compliance. External forces could be provided by the African Union or by the United Nations, or some other agreed group from outside the country. In Lesotho, for example, South African and Batswana troops were part of the solution to enforce an agreement that we had helped to broker among the internal parties. Since each situation would be different, each would require a specific solution. For example, dealing with Cote D'Ivoire has been more complicated than Liberia, since the former was a more complex economy and there were also racial overtones. There was a legitimate government in Cote D'Ivoire, and one that only had purported to be legitimate in Liberia. But, at the end of the day, I would treat each situation the same when enforcing an agreement. If an agreement is violated, it is not a matter of who started shooting first; it is a matter of all parties honouring the agreement they have reached.

While I was president, we were asked several times to provide troops for UN missions, and in some cases we agreed, but in some we did not. In Somalia, the first President Bush took the initiative, and the matter was taken to the Security Council. The Americans and others appealed to Africans, saying this was really an African matter. We looked at it and said yes, it would be a pity if only Americans, Europeans and Indians went to Somalia, so we subscribed to the UN mission, as did Nigeria. When we agreed to send troops to Somalia, it was, in part, because we were assured of the logistical support, and we also had an evacuation strategy if there were an emergency. So, we thought it would be worth the risk.

Somalia was the first time that soldiers of the BDF wore the blue helmets of a United Nations force. And, our soldiers came out tops; both their fellow soldiers and the people of Somalia felt our troops were fellows who had come with a sense of mission and knew what to do to bring peace to their country. The Somali involvement was a clearer case than some others have been, since those in authority had been thrown out, and the other parties needed help in settling their differences.

In Mozambique, we had been involved in reaching a settlement on a political level. Ultimately, there was a truce between Frelimo and RENAMO that led to peace, but that peace had to be assured through an election process to select a new government. At the request of the UN, our people went to help with that process, so again the BDF wore the blue helmets, and our senior officer served as second in command to a Brazilian. I visited our soldiers a few times in Somalia and in Mozambique, and I was very proud of what they were doing and how they behaved.

When the UN becomes involved, and a country is asked to contribute to the process, a number of important issues must be resolved. First there is the question of the rules under Chapters VI and VII of the UN Charter. Under Chapter VI, when the men in blue helmets are there as peacekeepers, or just as observers, they have sometimes been unable to even protect themselves. Under Chapter VII, the rules of engagement approved by the UN Security Council must also be appropriate to the task the troops are given and the situation they will face.

To make the United Nations more effective, one has to start with definable objectives: For exactly what purpose are we sending troops? To what dangers are we exposing them? How do we make sure they are not sitting ducks? What are the logistical arrangements, and are the resources and supplies adequate to the task? And, in the event of a catastrophe, are there adequate arrangements for evacuation? It may be appropriate to say that the UN troops should not enter the fighting. But under no circumstances, whether under Chapter VI or Chapter VII, should people be put in a situation where they could be shot at and not be able to shoot back. I saw what had happened in Rwanda; and in Sierra Leone a whole UN contingent was taken by a bunch of street boys; the troops had not been given authorisation to use force even to defend themselves. That was, in my view, simply wrong.

While the BDF participated in some missions with the UN, there were some instances where we respectfully declined. People must understand that a president is not going to send his troops if they can't defend themselves and might be slaughtered like chickens. There was an instance in the Congo Brazzaville when we were asked to send troops, and I refused since there were inadequate provisions for their support. Another time there was a debacle on the Rwanda-Congo border: The *Interahamwe* and the former Rwandan army joined the refugees who had settled on the border, and they were threatening the peace. We were approached to assist, and we said no; we could not send our people there, since we could not see how we would even supply them with their requirements. We were asked to go to Haiti and we agreed; but we were ultimately not needed.

I have mentioned that President Nyerere had told me I would be busier in retirement than as president, and he was correct! I have been asked to undertake a number of missions in Africa; several were done on a confidential basis, and leading observer missions to elections in various countries were public but short-lived assignments. Two were very public and involved actions of the United Nations and a number of the major powers as well. From 1998 to 2000 I chaired the International Panel of Eminent Personalities to investigate the 1994 Genocide in Rwanda and Surrounding Events. As soon as that assignment was completed, I accepted the invitation of the Congolese, who used the good offices of the OAU, to serve as the Facilitator for the Inter-Congolese dialogue in the Democratic Republic of the Congo, an assignment that extended from January 2000 to April 2003. Some officials who have worked with me for a long time have said I have a taste for hopeless causes; perhaps they are correct.

The Rwanda Genocide

The Genocide in Rwanda involved the slaughter of 800,000 people in 100 days between April and July 1994. The International Panel to investigate it was appointed by the OAU, and I was asked to chair it. My six colleagues were a distinguished and experienced group of individuals from Africa, Asia, North America, and Europe: General Ahmadou Toumani Toure, former head of state in Mali; Lisbet Palme, Chairperson of the Swedish Committee for UNICEF; Ellen Johnson-Sirleaf, then a former minister in Liberia and in 2005 elected president of Liberia; P. N. Bhagwati, former chief justice of the Supreme Court of India; Hocine Djoudi, former ambassador of Algeria; and Stephen Lewis, former ambassador of Canada. We were provided with adequate budget, a good staff and necessary logistical support for our mission; we had transport when we needed it, whether internationally or within Rwanda; and we received good cooperation from the governments of the major powers when we visited them during the course of our inquiry. We interviewed hundreds of individuals from Rwanda, Burundi, the Democratic Republic of the Congo, Uganda, Tanzania, the OAU, the UN and several of its agencies, representatives of governments in the United States, France, Belgium, and NGOs from many countries. In Rwanda, we toured the buildings, including churches and schools, which held thousands of human skulls, the remains of some of the 800,000 who were murdered.

We titled our report *Rwanda, the Preventable Genocide*, since we concluded that "the world that mattered to Rwanda—its Great Lakes Region neighbours, the UN, all the major Western powers—knew exactly what was happening and that it was being masterminded at the highest levels of the Rwandan government. ... The Rwandan genocide could have been prevented by those in the international community who had the position and the means to do so. But though they had the means, they lacked the will. The world failed Rwanda."

Our 300-page report and a number of books and articles tell the tragic story. I mention here some of the factors that are relevant to some of the civil wars, genocides and massacres that continue to plague the world.

The responsibility for the tragedy can be pinned on both the Rwandans and also the rest of the international community. But the Rwanda of 1994 was the result of history, including colonisation by the Germans and the Belgians. For hundreds of years, Rwandans had lived as Tutsis and Hutus, defined partly by ethnicity and partly by class. The classes had been sorted according to wealth rather than ethnic origin. If you had more than 30 head of cattle, you were regarded as a Tutsi. The fewer cattle you had, the more you were forced to till the land, and the more you became thought of as a Hutu. There did not seem to be much problem until the colonialists came—or at least, this is how the Rwandans would like to see it.

The colonialists came with the concept of indirect rule, and they thought they would use the upper classes, the Tutsis, to manage the other 80% of the population. While that was bad enough, the social mobility that had existed before the colonialists arrived was also arrested. People were registered and classified, and so they permanently became Tutsis and Hutus, with a defined hierarchy. It was similar to the racial classifications established in South Africa. The Tutsis were groomed for higher responsibility, so they were the ones who were given access to education and received a greater share of available scholarships. However, in certain fields that were not seen to improve their social or economic status, such as the religious ministries, the Hutus were allowed access.

The stratification was bad enough with the Germans, but then the Belgians came, and the Roman Catholic Church took over. They behaved as if the Good Lord had made the Tutsis a higher class; and what God had made, no man should tamper with. However, when the colonial era neared its end and democratisation came on the horizon, both the Belgians and the church started to realise the country soon would be ruled by the majority. So they switched over to the other extreme and hobnobbed with the Hutus against the Tutsis.

The increased emphasis on ethnic division as an instrument of colonial rule in Rwanda had parallels in many other parts of Africa. But as we said in our report: "different identities, ethnic or otherwise, do not in themselves cause division or conflict. It is the behaviour of unscrupulous governing elites that transform differences into divisions...and choose to manipulate such differences for their own self-interest." The complexity increased with the diaspora of refugees into neighbouring countries, especially Uganda, as a result of attacks on Tutsis by the new Hutu ruling elites. For example, in 1986 the victorious 14,000-man National Resistance Army of Yoweri Museveni (now president of Uganda) contained some 3,000 Tutsi refugees from Rwanda, including Paul Kagame who became head of military intelligence. Kagame was commander of the Tutsi forces that invaded Rwanda in 1994 at the time of the genocide, and he later became president of Rwanda.

While there was a great deal of complexity, some things became clear to us in the Panel. First, in the early 1990s, the government of Rwanda under President Habyarimana had been working in concert with a group of young militia, the *Interahamwe* (those who attack together). The *Interahamwe* preached and carried out ethnic violence against Tutsis, and also against politically moderate Hutus. Second, a radio station RTLM (*Radio Television Libre des Mille Collines*) associated with extremist Hutus both inside and outside government put out a constant message of racial hatred toward Tutsis and preached the need for their elimination. Third, arms were cached throughout the country to be available to the militias at the appropriate time. Fourth, there were lists of the names and addresses of Tutsis and moderate Hutus targeted for assassination. All the relevant persons in Kigali, including diplomatic representatives of the major powers, knew about the existence of the lists, and their existence had been reported to the UN headquarters in New York. These facts were all well known.

The rest of the facts are also clear. On 6 April 1994, President Habyarimana's plane crashed on landing at Kigali airport for reasons still unknown. The genocide began then and lasted until July. During that time, the international community failed to take any meaningful action to stop it.

A small United Nations peacekeeping force was already in Rwanda by 6 April. It had been sent in late 1993 as an Article VI mission to assist in implementing the Arusha peace accord among the warring parties in Rwanda, including Kagame's troops in Uganda and Habyarimana's government. Lt. General Romeo Dallaire, a Canadian, was in command of the UN mission; he was fully aware of the situation. As events developed, he appealed to New York—for permission to protect innocent people from slaughter, for a modification of the mandate and rules of engagement, and for more troops to prevent the genocide from continuing. Every request was refused. By General Dalliare's own account, he eventually became deranged by the impossible position in which he and his troops were placed and their resulting inability to help prevent the loss of hundreds of thousands of lives.

We in the Panel concluded that an effective force of as few as 5,000 trained troops, properly deployed and supported, could have either prevented the genocide completely or stopped it before it had taken such a terrible toll. Our conviction was based in part on the fact that, in some instances, the UN forces faced down the *Interahamwe* without even firing a shot. The blue helmets were clearly well-trained troops who seemed prepared to use deadly force, and they bluffed the extremist militia into withdrawing. The slaughter was carried out primarily by ill-trained and undisciplined militia, or by people's neighbours, and it even took place in churches.

In some cases, it was as if the church people had agreed to support whatever the extremist Hutus and *Interahamwe* did. When people came to the churches for asylum, the cleric would be there and would give them assurances they would be protected; at a convenient time, he would disappear, and the Hutus would come in and slaughter them. Not only did this happen in place A or B or C, but it happened all over, with the same pattern. We didn't find a single community that said: "But for the help of the church we would not be alive." We only found people who said: "Had we not been betrayed by the belief that we would be protected by the church, perhaps not so many would have died. We would not have all congregated in one place where it was easy for those people to come and do their devilish work."

We also placed blame on the Tutsis, including Mr Kagame, for committing their own atrocities. For instance, after Kagame's forces had taken over Rwanda, he wanted the UN to separate the *Interahamwe* and the Rwandan army from the genuine refugees, all of whom had fled to refugee camps in eastern Congo. The agencies running the Congo camps thought that if innocent people were in the camps, then Kagame would not attack. So, they left the soldiers and *Interahamwe* among the refugees. Kagame and the Rwandans kept saying: "Remove the people, remove the people, separate the genuine refugees, or we will hit them all." The refugees were not separated, and when Kagame released his venom on the camps, the casualties were terrible, and hundreds of innocent people died.

As we read the cables and faxes and interviewed people, we on the Panel concluded that we were seeing and hearing the truth; and, for the most part, people were candid. By tracing the communications and interviewing the people involved, the Panel established clearly that the United Nations in New York, the Americans, the French and the Belgians all knew what was about to happen before the genocide, and they also knew what was happening during it. As we said, the world failed Rwanda.

The major powers can move quickly when they wish to, but in this case they did nothing. And, nothing short of moving quickly in those 100 days would have worked. The silence and lack of action of the Americans was particularly significant. Our conclusion was that, since the Americans had just been humiliated in Somalia, they felt politically they could not act. This was, perhaps, understandable. But as the leader of the international community, if they were not willing to act, who would? The Americans did not seem to object to other countries going to Rwanda, but those countries naturally expected leadership to come from the US. The American officials whom we interviewed were very defensive, of course; but their role could not be denied.

The French and the Belgians were nearly criminally culpable. The French seemed to be in cahoots with Habyarimana, and evidence showed the Belgians certainly were. Then when seven Belgian soldiers were killed in April, instead of bringing in reinforcements, the Belgians simply flew out the rest of their people, and the French did the same. Later, the French arranged a corridor for the retreating Hutu army to leave Rwanda, and this, of course, incensed the Tutsis and Kagame. The French thought we were too hard on them in our report; but the surprising thing was that they did not say they had been judged unfairly. We thought we were inviting trouble by criticising the Americans, but there was no rebuttal to our report from them, either. Nor did the Belgians deny what had been done and not done. Kofi Annan was the man on the spot, since he was responsible for the UN Peacekeeping office in New York. Other Africans did the bit they could, but the situation was beyond their capacity to deal with. However, some Africans we talked to simply absolved themselves of any blame.

NGOs can play an important role in helping mitigate disasters, but they can have their own faults at such times, and we encountered them in our investigation. Once the media took an interest, some NGOs took advantage of the worldwide television coverage and made the case for their own organisations. They sometimes exaggerated both the extent and nature of the crisis and their own role in trying to solve the problems. Sometimes they presented themselves as experts on the causes of the problems or the actions of the various parties, when they simply may have been trying to promote their own interests. Sad to say it, but it is true.

The media played a role in showing how ghastly the whole episode was, but if they had taken an interest beforehand, they could have shown what could have been done to prevent it. The genocide was not a spontaneous explosion; it was planned, and its existence was known. The Belgian media published pieces of news that showed clearly what was going on before the genocide began. Other international media were aware of the developments, but they took no notice of them until they could show the bodies flowing down the rivers into Lake Victoria. Although the media, especially the Belgian media, did report on the extremist radio station in Rwanda, they did not do so in a manner that discouraged its activities. We have seen again and again that the media do not become interested until there is a disaster that will show up well on television. By then, it is often too late.

The Rwanda genocide was preventable, up to and even after 6 April 1994. As we in the Panel looked at the tragedy—and the roles played by Rwandans, international organisations and especially the UN, the leaders of the major powers, and the media—we concluded it could have been stopped.

Individuals and governments were culpable. People don't do such things because they don't know better; they have choices, and they make them.

The Inter-Congolese Dialogue, 2000-2003
The Democratic Republic of Congo (DRC) has had a tragic history. It was pillaged under Belgian colonial rule and rushed to independence in 1960 with few trained people and little sense of national identity. Its minerals, size and location made it a pawn in the Cold War. Its first president, Patrice Lumumba, was murdered by the troops of Mobutu Sese-Seko, apparently with the cooperation of Western intelligence services. Mobutu ruled as a corrupt dictator for over three decades, supported until the end of the Cold War as an anti-communist by the Americans and other Western countries. In 1994, refugees, armed militia and soldiers from Rwanda flooded into the eastern Congo, and soon there was a full-scale civil war. Laurent Kabila's armed insurgents finally toppled Mobutu Sese-Seko, and Kabila became president in 1997. By 1998, Laurent Kabila himself was facing a rebellion supported by the governments of Rwanda and Uganda in the eastern Congo. That was when President Mugabe took the initiative to involve troops from Zimbabwe, Angola and Namibia on the side of Kabila's government, which also received armed support from Chad and Sudan. Millions of people lost their lives in the civil war.

By 1999, the principal combatants within the DRC—Kabila's government, the Rally for Democracy in the Congo (RDC) and the Movement for the Liberation of the Congo (MLC)—realised none of them could win a war, despite the military involvement of other countries. They seemed to conclude that they were destroying the whole country to no avail. Sanity finally prevailed, and in July and August 1999 those three parties in the DRC and the governments of Angola, Namibia, Rwanda, Uganda and Zimbabwe signed a cease-fire agreement. The parties from the DRC also adopted what was known as the Lusaka Agreement, in which they committed themselves to undertake a "National Dialogue and Reconciliation" to be conducted "under the aegis of a neutral facilitator chosen by the Parties". The dialogue was to lead to a new political dispensation in the DRC. The agreement provided for a total of just over three months to select a facilitator, conduct the dialogue, and establish new institutions. The schedule lagged from the very beginning, and the parties signed the final Act on 2 April 2003, rather than in November 1999.

My involvement began when I was finalising the Rwanda report in Addis. Salim Salim, the secretary-general of the OAU, told me the Congolese parties had been talking with him about possible candidates to be Facilitator. The three principal belligerents had to agree, and they had already rejected eleven other individuals; but they thought I might do! I told him I would not accept; but the next day he came to tell me the Congolese belligerents had agreed on my name. I told him if he needed a quick answer, it would be no. In any case I would have to discuss the assignment with the government of Botswana. I rang President Mogae, and I said "I told Salim Salim that I could not answer without talking first with you. If he does call, I hope that you are not going to say yea. You and I must discuss it first." The following day, Kofi Annan rang to say: "We know how difficult this job is, and we will do everything possible to help." President Mogae and I talked again, and on 28 December I wrote to say I could accept the appointment.

I thought the proper thing to do would be to touch base with President Kabila first, so I initiated a call but was unsuccessful in arranging a visit. I was invited to meet with the Security Council, and, since President Kabila was also going to be in New York, I tried to see him there. Finally Richard Holbrooke, the American ambassador to the UN, went to President Kabila's apartment and phoned me to say: "I am with President Kabila; would you like to say hello to him?" I then met with Kabila, and he was quite cold toward me and my mission. He asked if my intention was to give his government the ability to lead the country into a new dispensation. I told him I thought answering that question was what the dialogue was all about; it would be up to the Congolese to decide which way to go. So, we parted; but his desire and that of his son and of their advisors to be assured of the top position, before we even started, influenced the next three years.

Inadequate resources were a major factor that delayed the dialogue. When we started it was just Quett Masire—no piece of paper, no pen, no room to sit in. For much of the next three years, we struggled to get cooperation from all the parties, both within the DRC and outside, and to find the funds and supporting staff to make the dialogue possible. Gradually we put resources together. The British provided Philip Winter to be *chef du cabinet*; Archie Mogwe, my long-time colleague, was available and became a senior political advisor. Professor Hacen Labatt from Mauritania was a godsend, since his facility with French helped us understand the nuances. He served for much of the time in Kinshasa as our additional senior political advisor. Bo Heinebäck was seconded by Sweden, and he worked with donors. When, two years after I had begun, we finally reached the point of meeting in the dialogue, I was able to bring in a number of experienced people, such as Ellen Johnson-Sirleaf of Liberia, who had been a member of the Rwanda Commission with me, Moustapha Niasse, former prime minister of Senegal, and General Abubakar of Nigeria.

I was banking on help from the international community, since I had been assured of assistance by Kofi Annan and others. But to get started, I raised a loan from the Botswana government to be repaid whenever we received a budget. I called a donor's conference in New York to report on the bits and pieces that had been pledged and the restrictions that had been attached by the donors. I told the conference it was most unreasonable for them to give me this assignment and then tie my hands. To assure accountability, I arranged for the accountant general of the Botswana government to be responsible for the funds and Price Waterhouse Coopers to be the accountants. We appointed auditors, invited donors also to appoint auditors, and said we would provide monthly reports.

Transport was also an issue. It would be very time consuming, if not impossible, to do the necessary travel by commercial plane; further, flying from Nairobi to the borders of the Congo in small planes was very uncomfortable for people the age of Mr Mogwe and me. Richard Holbrooke suggested that the South Africans might put a plane at my disposal, but I knew the Congolese saw red whenever they saw the South Africans. The Americans said they would make arrangements for me to be flown as and when necessary, but only once did they provide a plane.

In thinking of how to organise the dialogue, I considered a number of issues. We would have combatant parties in the room, both major forces and smaller regional ones, as well as unarmed political parties not associated with the combatants and civil society, or *forces vives*. However, the Congolese had never experienced representative government or consensus decision making at a national level. To produce something like a national consensus, we would have to devise ways of engaging all the parties. Each one would need to feel it had not only participated but had approved of the final result. Everyone would have to learn to compromise; otherwise the exercise would go nowhere. And, the dialogue would have to be comprehensive. We would need to address not only high-level political and security issues but also the social, educational, economic and financial questions that would face a government under a new political dispensation.

As the Facilitator, I would have to be, and be perceived to be, fair to all sides, and absolutely discreet in my opinions; otherwise I would become irrelevant and be written off. I knew from experience I would need to understand all the issues, so each party would feel its concerns were being addressed. A great deal of patience would be required, and I was sure that from time to time I would have to be very stubborn and to take risks—to rule decisively on issues, or to insist on my rights as Facilitator to seek information or to meet various parties.

Further, the DRC had suffered not only from internal disputes but also from the intervention of other countries, both neighbours and the great powers in Europe and America. I would have to keep those other parties informed. I anticipated difficulty with some of them from time to time, and unfortunately I was correct to do so. The whole puzzle had many moving parts.

I came home from New York in January 2000, and I worked up a questionnaire that I could use in going around the Congo—what did they think was the cause of the war, what did they think should be done, and so forth. Then I spent a week in Kinshasa talking with people. I wanted to visit other regions, but the Congolese authorities didn't seem keen for me to make the visits, and I got nowhere. So, I went to Kenya and chartered a plane, and we went to Goma and to Gbadolite to talk with the major rebel forces.

For the whole of that year our efforts were constantly frustrated, primarily by Laurent Kabila. For example, in May 2000, I thought we should visit a few towns in the Congo in addition to the three held by the rebels (Goma, Bunia, and Gbadolite). Mr Mogwe and I boarded a Congolese airline for Kinshasa at Johannesburg, but after we had been seated, we were asked to get off. I asked by whose authority, and they said by the authorities in Kinshasa, but I told them those authorities knew of our plans. They wanted to remove Mr Mogwe and me from the plane, and I said: "If the Congolese want to throw me into their prisons in Kinshasa, so be it, but I will not get off." They asked for my passport, and I said I would surrender mine only if all other passengers did so. Finally they gave up and we flew off to Kinshasa.

In Kinshasa, we again explained to a liaison officer from the president's office our need to visit some of the areas in the Congo. We waited overnight for an answer, and two hours after we were to have left I was invited to meet the minister of the interior. He started asking questions: "Why do you want to visit every town in the Congo?" "Are you just a tourist or are you a facilitator?" "Are you going to meet with the churches?" I took up the issue of attempting to remove us from the plane in Johannesburg; I said I had been treated like a drug dealer. They eventually left me alone, but they never gave us permission to travel, and we ended up coming back to Gaborone by way of Nairobi. If I were not so stubborn, I might well have given up the whole project.

Later that month, I managed to meet President Kabila. I told him I wanted to hold a preparatory meeting in Cotonou, Benin, on 5 June, and a substantive meeting of the dialogue on 3 July. Kabila said he couldn't respond, because he would like to hear what other parties said about the issues before reacting. He again said he did not want me to visit any places where other participants were located. So, I went through Nairobi again and this time flew back to the towns in the eastern Congo.

After my trips to visit the internal parties, I made it a point to go to the signatory states to be sure they were fully informed. While briefing Museveni in eastern Uganda, I learned that the Congolese government were hinting they would not go to Cotonou, because they could not sit at a table with people whose hands were covered with blood—as if there were any parties whose hands were not! I came back to Gaborone, and as I was boarding a chartered plane to Benin, I learned that Kabila's government had publicly announced that it was not going to Cotonou. We went anyway, and on the 3rd we heard nothing, and on the 4th we began to worry. Then we received word that, just as the representatives from civil society and from the political parties were going to board the plane to Cotonou, Kabila's security people seized their travel documents.

I phoned everybody I could think of: Chiluba, Mogae, Annan, Obasanjo, everyone. They did their best. President Chiluba went to Lumumbashi where Kabila was; President Obasanjo even sent a minister to ask that he be allowed to fly the participants to Cotonou, but they were refused. And, even if the others had been allowed to travel, the fact that the government people had not come would have prevented us from doing anything.

Despite repeated efforts by OAU, SADC and UN leaders, nothing happened to further the dialogue during 2000. All year long, Kofi Annan and President Obasanjo continued to call me to say: "Please don't back out."

Laurent Kabila was assassinated on 16 January 2001, and his son, Joseph Kabila, became the new president of the DRC ten days later. In February, the younger Kabila announced he would resuscitate the Inter-Congolese dialogue. A month later, he invited me to meet with him in Kinshasa, and we had a very good meeting. He seemed keen to change the situation, so I agreed to start from where we had left off. About that time, someone asked me if the young Kabila was different from his father, and I said I thought he was better. The fellow replied: "It doesn't take much to be better than the old Kabila." But as time passed, I think Joseph Kabila came to like power, and he was no longer the Kabila I had seen on 18 March 2001. I don't know if his nature changed, or if the change was due to those who put him in power.

In the Lusaka Agreement of August 1999, the three combatants had agreed that political parties and civil society would be included on an equal footing, so there would be five "components" in the dialogue. Because almost two years had passed, I thought they should recommit themselves to those basic principles, and so I visited the three combatants. I was surprised but pleased to find that they thought it was a jolly good idea. As we showed each party what others had said, they would say: "Why not add this point as well." They finally all agreed on 14 principles. When we met on 3 May 2001 to sign, one would say: "There's no comma here," and the other would say: "This article is wrong," and so forth, but at least we were making progress.

Eventually, at midnight we reached agreement, but then the leaders of the two main rebel groups said: "We will not sign if Kabila is not here." After further objections over this and that, my patience ran out, and I said: "Gentlemen, for a year and five months I have been working with you. I will let those who care to sign the principles sign them; that's it." Finally, they all signed.

The sixth of the 14 principles said each of the five components would appoint its own representatives without interference. So, I detailed Mr Mogwe and Professor Labatt to supervise the elections to see that those in authority did not impose their will on civil society or political parties in their areas. They went by air to 19 cities in the Congo during June and July 2001, and were sometimes marooned without transport to the next place.

We had the 14 agreed principles, and we had representatives selected for each of the five components. As it was necessary for people to come to know one another, I suggested a pre-meeting as the next step. We also needed to agree where to meet, to draft rules of procedure and an agenda for the dialogue, and so forth. In August 2001, 75 people representing each of the five components of the dialogue came to Gaborone. Never had Congolese from all parts of the country come together, and they were very pleased with the results. They made the necessary decisions and left with "the spirit of Gaborone", after agreeing to meet in Ethiopia on 15 October. I then went to brief the principals, the SADC heads of state, the signatory states, the big powers, and the UN. On my way back, I went to see Kabila, Bemba, and Onusumba, and they agreed to implement the agreements, though President Kabila again asked why they could not be given more time.

The agreement called for the dialogue to include about 300 people and last for 45 days. Such a meeting would cost about $4.5 million. We only had

$250,000 in our coffers, and a few promises here and there, and the hotels in Addis were asking for a $2 million down payment. I said to the participants: "Let's honour the undertaking and meet on the 15th; we'll plan what to do about the shortage of funds, and take any other steps we can." However, after we had arrived in Addis, President Kabila said we should not make any decisions, and then his government walked out. The only thing we agreed upon was that the follow-up meeting should be in South Africa. I continued to work on finances, and the Dutch, the British, the Americans, the Norwegians and the Swedes came up with additional funds. But the real breakthrough came when President Mbeki said the South African government would pick up any deficit that might remain from the meetings in South Africa.

Eventually, we met in Sun City on 25 February 2002, two years behind schedule. Even then, the main combatant parties dragged their feet. Jean-Pierre Bemba objected that political parties had composed their team without involving him. Government said they couldn't proceed until it was agreed that President Kabila would lead the interim government—like father like son. And so it went. Finally, the pressure from external parties was needed. The UN Security Council passed a resolution saying all should go back to the table, and foreign ministers of the signatories to the Lusaka agreement did the same, and we were able to resume.

We had divided the dialogue into five commissions—defence and security, political and constitutional, economic and finance, social and cultural, peace and reconciliation. The latter three commissions did very well, and each of them arrived at its resolutions. The facilitators chairing the meetings would meet with me each evening so we could see what was coming up and where we might assist. In spite of the odds, the dialogue came up with 36 resolutions addressing every aspect of a new political arrangement.

However, two issues bedevilled the process. One was President Kabila's role, and the other was the army. During the transition, should Joseph Kabila be head of state? Some said yes, some no, some not necessarily, and there was lots of argument. I believe the others would easily have agreed on Kabila if his delegation had not made it a precondition; once again I saw that if one need not force an issue, one should not try to do so. On the second issue, President Kabila's proposal was that the other belligerents should join his army. The others said: "The legal army in the DRC is that of Mobutu Sese-Seku; Kabila's army is a rebel movement just like ours. We should throw all the groups together and start afresh." So it dragged on.

On 19 March I called people together and said we were going to put the two contentious issues into a new ad hoc committee. At that meeting, I told the delegates: "In my experience as a former president, I am aware that most wars have ended at the negotiation table. The only difference is in the number of people who lose their lives before the leaders come to the conclusion that they have to negotiate and compromise. In most cases, people fail to compromise not because they are strong and brave, but because they are uncertain and fearful for their future. To postpone dealing with your fears is simply to place yourself in greater danger and a weaker position."

Five days before the end of the conference, we tackled the interim government issue. As Facilitator I could not make suggestions, since they would inevitably be in favour of one side or another. So, I invited Thabo Mbeki to join us, and he came with a proposal of how each of the five components should be represented. Various objections were raised. This was a Friday, and I said: "Why don't you study the proposal tonight, and let's meet tomorrow." They said: "That's too short a time, let's meet on Monday." So I said: "I will compromise. You bring us the suggestions on Sunday noon, and we will produce a synthesis and discuss it on Monday." But by Tuesday afternoon, I had to call the three parties who had sent their submissions to say: "You have brought your reactions to Mbeki's proposals, but two components have not." I did not say which ones, but they all knew it was the government and MLC.

On Wednesday, while President Mbeki and I were meeting with the five components, Kabila's and Bemba's lieutenants announced that they had agreed that Kabila would be president and Bemba would be vice-president in a new interim government. The next day we all met, and I said: "This agreement is not acceptable, since the results must come at the conference table, not at a bilateral level." We tried again to reach agreement but failed, so I closed the meeting, and said each component should leave three representatives to talk about how the interim government should be formed. There was a great hue and cry, and some said: "But we have been here 52 days." (Of course forgetting 20 days when nothing was done, and of the 32 that remained the weekends were not used, so there were very few days of actual meetings). It was very discouraging.

The major powers had encouraged Kabila and Bemba to do their separate deal; they took a simplistic view that if those two agreed, the rest would follow. Our office in Kinshasa was continually blasted with the message: "What are you doing with this dialogue? These people have already made up their minds." Some of my people working on the dialogue were totally demoralised. I addressed the UN Security Council at a special meeting in Luanda, and I told them what was happening and why a bilateral solution was futile: Three armies were fighting, two of these were joining to fight the third, but the third was the strongest of the three, based on land controlled and army size, and a bilateral solution would just polarise the situation. And, within a month Kabila and Bemba were accusing one another of cheating. So, on it went.

We appealed to Kofi Annan to talk to the Americans, the French and the Belgians. In May 2002, Annan appointed Moustapha Niasse as a special emissary, and he worked from June of 2002 through March 2003, visiting all the internal parties to come up with a proposal that would give something to everybody. He visited all the external forces and urged them to encourage the three main belligerents to be flexible and constructive. Part of the problem all along, of course, was that within each belligerent group there were hard-liners as well as those who felt excluded, so agreements were very difficult to reach. Moustapha Niasse kept insisting, as I had throughout the dialogue, that an "all inclusive agreement" was needed.

Ultimately, these efforts were successful, and the two who had signed the side deal at Sun City agreed to withdraw it. In January 2003, I made another trip to brief the major powers and the UN to be sure they were on board. We resumed the dialogue in Sun City on 1 April 2003, and the closing ceremony and the signing of the final Act by the parties took place on 2 April. We had tried to do our best to give the Congolese a chance to start over. We knew the implementation would be difficult, and it has proven to be so. Periodic fighting continued, and a constitution was not adopted until early in 2006.

Throughout my three years and three months working on the Inter-Congolese dialogue, my colleagues and I tried to keep everyone involved and informed—whether they were inside or outside. We wanted to be sure that those outside exercised influence for good where they could, and also that they did not give the wrong signals that would encourage the belligerents or other parties to be too stubborn.

The great powers played various roles. The British supported me to the hilt. Even after the Sun City talks failed to reach agreement in 2002, Jack Straw wrote me to say: "You have done a marvellous job; we are behind you." My interaction with the French consisted largely of answering a series of pessimistic questions. The Belgians seemed enthusiastic about helping but did not seem to know how. They were also critical of my approach—for instance they would ask: "Why do you have these commissions on different subjects?" And: "If people discuss things without their bosses, their bosses could reverse the decisions in the evening." I held my ground, since I felt people needed a chance to get some practice in playing a governing role before they were given the full responsibility. I told them: "Those people must learn to clear things with their principals. If they think they are going beyond their mandates, they should ask for an adjournment and go and consult." The Belgians gave in on the use of commissions; but then they said finance and economics should be done by the Europeans, not by the Congolese! I told them that would be a recipe for disaster; how can one not expect a country to take responsibility for its own finances if they are to be independent in all other ways? Belgian officials remained adamant, but their Minster, Louis Michel, saw my point, and they gave in.

The EU sent as observers a bunch of youngsters who were very cynical. Wherever we met, whether it was Addis Ababa, or Gaborone or Sun City, they apparently sent back very adverse reports on the progress. However, among the EU ministers, I was supported to the hilt by Poul Nielson from Denmark and Chris Patton from the UK.

The Americans were helpful in getting the elder Kabila to start the process, and they made encouraging noises after the Gaborone meeting. But, then it transpired that the American ambassador to the Congo was encouraging Bemba and Kabila to go it alone, so I called him and asked if it was so, and if it was, didn't he see the danger? He assured me that he wouldn't do a thing like that! I told the American ambassador that I thought his behaviour showed that the international community was not really serious about genuine reform in the Congo. The Americans had a worldwide agenda, and they tried to find short cuts. They do not always have the patience needed to deal with complicated situations, especially when they are not of strategic importance to them.

The dialogue gave the Congolese their first opportunity to come together to frame a future for their country. They had never been through a democratic process of consultation, and we had to start at the very beginning. We pressed them to achieve what we believed they could. The Kabilas and their people did not want to participate without a guarantee of the result, and they used every trick in the bag, but they were not able to discourage us from keeping on. At one stage one of the participants asked me how I could be certain that if they agreed to the proposals, the other sides would also agree. I told them what I have always told aspiring politicians in Botswana: There is always a risk in politics in a democratic setup. If you are afraid to take a risk, you cannot be a politician. I said it was reasonable to assume that if others saw one party was accommodating, as was true of some of the participants, then those others would also begin to be accommodating.

I hope the practice the Congolese gained in seeking consensus, negotiating their differences, and learning to settle their disagreements through dialogue instead of force, will benefit their country in the long run. I have devoted so much space in this memoir to the dialogue in the hope that our experience might prove useful to those dealing with other post-conflict situations.

Chapter 20
Family Man, Farmer and President

A politician has a private life and a public one, and balancing the two was not always easy. Mma-Gaone and I were married before I ever thought about joining politics, and four of our six children were born after I had become a political leader, two after I became vice-president. I continued to farm while I was in politics, and the competing demands for time created difficulties on occasion. And since retiring from office my life has been full of new ventures and new assignments.

A Family Life

Very early on, Mma-Gaone and I decided to separate our family from my life in politics. Shortly after I had entered politics, a man whom we did not know came to see me about some matter. After he had left, Mma-Gaone innocently asked me what the man wanted. I had thought about how we should handle such situations, so I said to her: "This time I will tell you, but from now on I will not share the subject of these meetings with you, and here is why. I know that you will want to protect me. But people may try to trick you into saying things, especially if you are questioned about allegations that might be made against me. What you say in trying to defend me could be damaging to me, and even to you and to our family. So, it is better if you know absolutely nothing about these matters; that way you cannot be put in a compromising position." From then on, I did not follow the practice of some politicians who told their spouses everything of the day's events. I think Mma-Gaone understood why I was doing it that way. We have had a cruise that was very smooth sailing, largely because we separated the different parts of our lives.

Having said that, while I was in politics Mma-Gaone was always accommodating, understanding and very supportive of what I was doing. She was the one who took care of the children and our home, looked after my needs and even packed my suitcase for travel. In the early days, before I became a minister and drew a salary, we depended on her salary as a teacher to make ends meet, and even to help meet the party's expenses during 1962. Many times when I was meeting with someone from out of town, we would meet through lunchtime, and I would invite the person to come for some food. Or a group of constituents, even 10 or 20 at a time, would arrive and expect to be given tea or a meal as part of their meeting with me, and Mma-Gaone would take care of them. As secretary of the party, our home was for all practical purposes the office of the party headquarters, and people came and went and stayed if they needed to. I have been very grateful for her support and assistance.

When I became vice-president and we moved to Gaborone, it was to a new official house for the vice-president. We suddenly had a house much larger than our own modest home, and it fell to Mma-Gaone to furnish it from scratch, and to make it ready for the official and unofficial entertaining we would be called upon to do. And, of course, there were even more visitors who came and expected tea or a meal or a place to stay. She looked after them as well as our children.

While vice-president, I was often visited by people seeking help in solving their problems or wanting to present their case, but it was nothing compared to what I experienced when I became president, and we moved to State House. Shortly after I became president, I said to a friend: "Now I understand why Seretse had that big wall constructed around the State House grounds!" There was always someone wanting something. Mma-Gaone was the hostess on many occasions, and she learned to deal with protocol for visitors, some of whom could be quite insistent on such matters.

After I became president, Mma-Gaone took on the role of Mother of the Nation. She initiated the First Lady's Charity Fund, for which she raised funds and distributed monies to organisations and individuals who did charitable work. It became something very close to her heart, and it was quite exciting for both of us to have her undertake this. It was good for her, and it was good for the whole country as well. She saw needs and became involved before many of the women's organisations we know today had been established. Mma-Gaone and I travelled together on many occasions after she became First Lady, and she also made many visits on her own to international conferences, especially on women's issues. She has been a strong proponent of the Special Olympics for the disabled, and she has travelled to support Botswana participants in international competitions.

We have been blessed with six children: three daughters, Gaone (1958), Mmasekgoa (1960), and Matshidiso (1969), and three sons, Mpho (1961), Mmetla (1963) and Moabi (1968). Mma-Gaone and I agreed we would keep our children out of my life in politics. I didn't want them to have trouble or difficulties with other children over political arguments. I tried to be a good father despite the many demands of politics and farming. I remember once coming back from a party conference and arriving at about suppertime. Moabi shouted "Daddy, Daddy, what have you brought me from Molepolole?" I said: "Love, my son," to which he replied: "Where is it?" One of them asked me another time why their mother was always the one to buy presents for them, and never their father. I told them my job was to earn the money, and then "I turn it over to your mother and she manages everything else." It has indeed been up to her to see that everyone's needs have been met, including mine.

All six of our children went to Thornhill in Gaborone for primary school, and five went to Maru a Pula, while Matshidiso went to Waterford in Swaziland. They all went on to higher qualifications as well, and each had some education in the US or the UK. One has a diploma, two have bachelor's degree and three have master's degrees. Mma-Gaone and I believed that the best gift we could provide for our children was a sound education. That was our luxury, instead of cars or clothes or vacations.

Gaone took her O-levels at Maru a Pula, and then she earned some money to put herself through a typing course at Kiyanda College in Kenya and then another course in the UK. Partly through the good offices of Professor Tom Tlou, she secured a place at Luther College in Iowa, where he had studied.

After one or two semesters with our support, she earned her way through by typing papers for other students and working for the school. She knew that five brothers and sisters also needed education, so she should not take more than her share. She motivated and set an excellent example for her brothers and sisters. Later she received her MA in Administration in Illinois.

Mmasekgoa did her BSc in Electronics in London and received an MBA at the University of Pittsburgh in the US. She worked for telecoms in Botswana, and, after her marriage to the Reverend Trevor Mwamba (now Bishop of Botswana) she moved to Oxford where he was studying. They had three children, and she commuted every day to London for her telecoms job there. She returned home and applied for the job of chief executive of the Botswana Export Development and Investment Agency, to which she was appointed. She is the mother of a son, Eno, and twin daughters Seneo and Lukwesa.

Mpho was always mechanically inclined, and after Form V he went to the UK for a three-year course in motor engineering and then courses in fabrication and fleet management. He now has a business in Gaborone, servicing and repairing cars, which he also collects. His wife Setshego teaches in Jwaneng, and his daughter Sego lives with us in Gaborone.

Mmetla studied electrical engineering at the University of Cardiff and then joined Debswana. He first worked at Orapa, and then was part of an exchange and worked on the diamond mines in Namibia for a couple of years. His wife, Doreen, is a medical doctor who studied in London and then did a four year gynaecological course in Cape Town, and Mmetla was able to work for the Anglo-De Beers group there. Now he is quite senior in the management at Debswana, Doreen practices medicine in Jwaneng, and they have twin sons, Ame and Tumo. Mmetla has also decided to take an interest in managing our farming operations.

Moabi did his degree in Animal Health at the University of Illinois. I tried to persuade him to join the BMC to gain some management experience, but he said he preferred to manage my farming affairs. He worked for me for a while, but as fathers and sons often do, we had our differences, and so he moved to the building industry. He now has a company that does telecoms installations all over Botswana. His daughter Keletso attends school in South Africa, and he and his wife Mother, a University of Botswana graduate working in the private sector, are also parents of a new son, Amir.

Matshidiso, whom we call Tshidi, has always had an independent mind. We had planned to send her to Maru a Pula, but, while she was visiting friends in Swaziland, she decided to take the entrance exams to Waterford. Then she sent us a letter to say that she'd been accepted, and would we please send the fees! So, we obliged. She finished secondary school in the UK and did her degree at Pepperdine University in California. After she did an MSc in Public Sector Management, she worked in the US and the UK. She now has a job with the AIDS Vaccine Institute in New York, though we wish she would come back to Botswana, or at least to southern Africa, as we think she's been away for too long!

I know it was difficult for the six of them to grow up as the children of a politician, especially as the children of a vice-president and a president.

Mma-Gaone and I tried to make sure they lived their own lives, and we kept them out of the public eye. I tried to be sure they were never put in a position where it appeared that their accomplishments in school or in jobs were because their father was the vice-president or the president. However, anyone wanting to be a detractor could make any kind of accusation, and that sometimes happened. I am sure they are all greatly relieved I am out of politics. There can no longer be an implication that their successes are due to their father's position. And, they have told me they want to read this memoir so they will know what I was doing all those years!

Farmer and Politician
I am a farmer at heart, and never did I think I would be in politics for 37 years, or a president for 18. Therefore, I had decided early on I should retain my rights on the land as much as possible, so that when I retired from politics, I could start where I left off.

When I became vice-president, I wanted to maintain my lands in Kanye and the cattle posts I had established in Ngwaketse. But, as a country, we wanted to encourage African farmers to acquire some of the freehold farms that had formerly been restricted to whites. This led to my decision to farm in Ghanzi. After I became president, I had little control over my own time, and I eventually had to give up active management of my cattle. I retained the farms and leased them out until I retired. Since retirement, I've returned to cattle farming, and I have also tried my hand at some other new ventures.

Farming in Ngwaketse
Before independence, I had established two boreholes for cattle posts, one at Makgakabe, and the other at Sethulo. However, they were both in the blue tick area, so I couldn't hold cattle there when I brought them from Ghanzi to the abattoir in Lobatse. I offered to turn the two boreholes back to the Land Board, provided they would allocate me two sites outside the blue tick areas. I left the developments I had made—boreholes, houses, and so forth—at the original places to help make the exchange acceptable to the Land Board, and those farms were then taken up by syndicates of farmers. I acquired two areas near Sekoma through the exchange. Of course, when I received permission for the exchange, the new sites at Sekoma were not farms but just raw land that required complete development. I drilled 13 boreholes, but all were blank. I asked the Land Board if I could look for water outside my farms and pipe it to them, and they gave me permission. I did get good water at Kwakwala that yielded ten cubic meters per hour, but I had to lay a pipeline 16 kilometres to the centre of the first farm and an additional seven kilometres to the second.

When TGLP was introduced, those who had boreholes in a TGLP area where there was no other disputed land could make an application and would be granted first option on the new lease rights. Ray Molomo and Kgosi Linchwe also applied for the two farms I had developed near Sekoma, but since I had already made considerable investment, the Land Board leased the TGLP ranches to me. In 1987, I started fencing them as two independent farms. By then, I had cattle farms in Ghanzi, so I decided to introduce game farming on one of the Sekoma farms. It needed to be properly fenced and then stocked with game.

I remember the first time I saw a lion as a child. It had been killed only twelve kilometres west of Kanye; that lion, of course, wouldn't have been there without game to live on. Today, one can travel 200 kilometres west from Kanye without seeing a single lion and hardly any other game. On my farms at Sekoma 30 years ago, there would have been eland, gemsbok, hartebeest, springbok, impala, and zebra, among others. Of all of these, only springbok were found on the farm in the late 1980s. Our policies toward game and how we implemented them have led to the depletion of game. We need to start game farming if we want to bring back the game; hence my venture.

My attitude toward game is the same as it is toward land: We will save the game, as we will save the land, only if we decide to manage it on a commercial basis. The view of the Game Department on how to save the game is quite different. They believe in trying to control, rather than to manage. They think they can protect the game by charging high fees to either kill or capture animals to stock a farm. I think that it is very short sighted. Even though I was going to conserve and manage the game on my farm, I had to pay for permits as if I was going to kill the animals. As president, by law I did not need a permit to shoot game; but I felt I should apply for capture permits. Being president did not confer any preferential treatment in such permits. When Mr Nwako was minister he had given me permits to capture giraffe, but when Mr Kedikilwe became minister he denied me giraffe permits!

There are now a number of game farms in Botswana that might show the way for others. In Ngwaketse, my brother and I have game farms, and one or two others are under development. White farmers in Ghanzi like Gavin Richard, Braam DeGraff, and the Vickermans, who command more resources than we do, have a number of game farms with chalets for tourists. They look after game as part of their tourist business, which is where I think the future of game conservation must lie. I hope to develop my farm for photographic safaris, and for some hunting as well. However, the Game Department controls these animals as if they were still on state land instead of on my farm. If a client comes to shoot game as a part of the necessary culling, the Department will charge them as if they were shooting game in the wild. If the government encouraged game farmers, we farmers would conserve game as a resource, promote our tourism industry, and protect the veld as well. For that to happen, our officials will have to begin thinking of promotion, rather than control.

Farming in Ghanzi

At independence, we inherited a system in which white farmers owned all the farms in the Tuli Block and the Ghanzi Farms. There were two schools of thought as to what should be done. One was that we should just take them over, as President Mugabe recently has done in Zimbabwe. Our response as a party and as a government was to say that we needed development in Botswana; those who have already been successful should not be discouraged from further developments or told to go away. The other alternative for us was to farm like the white farmers, and we in Botswana had plenty of unused land. It was clear from the results on experimental farms that by using improved management, as many whites were doing, we would be able to improve cattle production substantially.

We tried to encourage African citizens to buy freehold farms, since we thought it would be good not only economically but also politically to have black farmers in those previously all white areas. Seretse and others bought land in the Tuli Block, but I bought in Ghanzi. Seretse always asked me why I went so far. My answer was that if you have money, you can buy a farm wherever you want it, but if you don't have enough money, which was my circumstance, you have to go to a place you can afford.

At self-rule, some white farmers in Ghanzi thought we were another Congo in the making, and they left their farms. We in government became very concerned about these deserted farms. To put the farmers' fears at bay, some of us would lease and run some of the farms. They were open to anyone and were being offered on long-term lease with an option to buy, and their availability was advertised in the *Government Gazette*. We in government wanted to avoid having people just speculate on land, and farmers had their own interests to be looked after (such as ensuring they were paid for developments they had effected on farms if they left them). A committee of three farmers, along with someone from the Ministry of Agriculture, was responsible for allocation. The farms at Ghanzi were available on very easy terms, though development conditions had to be met every year—fencing, boreholes, kraals, a cattle crush, and so forth. One could only hold those farms as long as one continued to develop them, and the process was monitored by the livestock officer in Ghanzi. Israel Kgosi and David Maganu were two who forfeited their rights after they had been allocated farms because they did not meet the development requirements.

Gaerolwe Kwerepe, Ntwakgolo Sekgua and I were the first black citizens to buy in Ghanzi. We selected three adjacent farms, and we divided the responsibilities for managing them amongst ourselves. We were given permission by Jack Falconer, the director of veterinary services, to stock them with cattle from Maun. He required us to quarantine the cattle at Kuke for six months—which to us meant six months free grazing at the government quarantine camp! But shortly afterward, like the invitees to the wedding in the Bible, the other two said they had other things to do with their time. So I had to re-think the plan, and I went to my two brothers. David said no, but Peter said he would join me. We became the first blacks to hold lands in Ghanzi, and a few others have followed.

I needed to farm in the south, close to Ghanzi, so I could get there from Gaborone by taking the plane that flew to Ghanzi on Wednesdays and came back on Thursdays. I worked out an arrangement with Reg Vize, a shopkeeper who had been in Legco with me. He agreed to fill up his lorry with petrol and leave it at his shop. I'd arrive in Ghanzi, jump in the lorry and go to the farm. I'd return it when I came back, and he would send me the bill for mileage.

After Peter and I each took a farm, we found they were too small for our purposes, so when some others became available, we exchanged them. We took possession in 1969 and moved in during 1970. At the time, they actually were nothing but raw land, and we spent days just hunting for the survey beacons that defined the boundaries.

Farming is often something of an adventure. One day we were surveying to make a cut line in order to square off the farm. We had a high tripod that we located over the corner fence post. Someone needed to be raised up by a block and tackle to the top of the tripod; from there, the person could visibly establish points over the tree line. My fellows were all reluctant, so I went up. As I neared the top, friction had heated the rope; when I grabbed for it coming off the pulley, I burned my hand and let go, so I fell. However, the hook at the end of the rope just caught the crotch of the new Levi jeans Quill Hermans had brought me from a trip to the US. I hung face down over the fence post—and my men were frozen! I had to issue instructions on how they should let me down, and finally I reached the ground safely.

The farms Peter and I had acquired were 5,000 hectare farms, which in Ghanzi is quite small for a good farm, since the carrying rate is at best ten and more likely 15 to 20 hectares per beast. Later, I hired two farms from N. K. Grobler for five years, with the option to buy. At the end of the five years, I exercised my options, and the National Development Bank lent me the funds to buy them.

After I had acquired these farms, I became the largest black landowner in Ghanzi. Many holdings in Ghanzi were much larger; whites like Thomas Hardbattle had eleven farms, and Ghanzi Ranches had 18, and others had many more. But by 1977, it had become a political issue that I was "grabbing" land. When the farms were owned by whites, nobody made any fuss about it; but when they became my farms, I was suspect. Some people assumed I was able to do things because I was vice-president or later president. However, I had worked very hard, and I had saved my money, and I had also borrowed to buy and develop those farms.

The original Ghanzi farms were in the water-bearing limestone area. Tsheko Tsheko as minister of agriculture proposed developing additional farms for black citizens in the adjacent sandveld area. Government drilled 20 boreholes, but only one yielded sweet water, and the plan was nearly abandoned. However, Seretse and I proposed that we establish new 10,000-hectare farms on the periphery and encourage cooperative arrangements; black farmers on the new farms and white farmers on the established farms could share both water and grazing land. While I exercised my option on the new farms, others who were allocated them failed to do so. When the new farms were not developed, the claims fell away, and over time the white farmers have picked up those 10,000 hectare farms. This was another case where we tried to provide opportunities for indigenous citizens to develop economically, but they were never taken up.

Farming in Lobatse

When I became president, I had been on the eve of going into milk production at Maradu Farm near Lobatse. I had not wanted to start a dairy with expensive cattle; so in 1979 I had worked out a plan to build up a herd by using semen from pure Jerseys to progressively breed good milkers from local cows. But that plan was frustrated by my becoming president, since I had no time to ensure the management of such a venture. So, in 1987 I started an ostrich farm on the site where I had previously planned to raise dairy cows, or *maradu*; and the place became Maradu Ostrich Farm!

I decided to go into ostrich farming because I believe in the diversification of our agriculture. The way our fathers farmed was not the most rewarding way, and I believed, as I still do, that we must try different ways. Places such as Upington in South Africa are far worse than much of our land and climate, but they produce more than we do. They do so by farming in a diversified fashion, focusing on high value products. If I were a young man, I would venture into many more areas. We need leaders in all sectors of our economy who will demonstrate that these things do work. I believe if they do, the followers will be as many as blackberries in summer.

To stock the ostrich farm, it was necessary to apply for permits for ostriches from the Wildlife Department. The permits were allocated separately for eggs, chicks and adults, and I learned by trial and error. I started with adult birds, but that was not viable, as they are very difficult to domesticate. Also, baboons would come early in the morning and climb the fence, and the ostriches would panic and break their legs or their necks. So, we decided to try chicks, and later we discovered it was better to collect eggs and hatch them in an incubator. The new chicks bonded to their human keepers and were quite manageable. When we finally worked it out, and it became successful, I thought it was something for which in the old days the colonial government would have given me a decoration. However, some of our local people felt it was scandalous. Mr Dabuta of the BNF even asked in Parliament whether I thought I was God, since ostriches were God's creatures and were meant to be raised in the wild!

By 1995, there were about 56 ostrich farmers in Botswana, and some farms like those of Peter Kirby and Tim London were very large. We all felt we would be better off if we could raise the birds to maturity, slaughter them locally, and market them in East Asia, where Korea and Japan are the biggest buyers. We approached government with a proposal that they build the abattoir and lease it to the farmers. But, it took five years of to-ing and fro-ing. When government doesn't want to do something, it wants someone else to say no. After two feasibility studies (by Price Waterhouse Coopers and a French firm) had said: Go ahead, government said these were really pre-feasibility studies. The French team did a further study and said: Now is the time to go ahead. But, no one in government was ready to say yes. We formed the Botswana Ostrich Company to take over and run the abattoir after it had been built. Selecting a location took time, but eventually the area adjacent to the airport in Gaborone was chosen. Then objections from the meat people delayed the decision. Implementation was slow: Should electrical service be underground or overhead? Should it share the water supply with the airport? After construction, there were delays in training staff, and in the veterinary inspections.

Meanwhile, we farmers suffered. Before 2000, I had been selling to South Africa. Since the abattoir was supposed to open in 2001, I made my plans accordingly. But, it did not open, and while cattle will graze while you are waiting for the market, the ostriches we should have sold were eating out of my own pocket! And, beyond a certain stage the value of the bird declines because the quality of the skin deteriorates. The delays were so long that farmers fell by the wayside, and the 56 aspirants had dwindled to only a few in the Tuli Block, Molopo, Ghanzi, and Lobatse.

In ten months, two ostriches can bring 20 offspring to the market, so once the abattoir was running at capacity, throughput could increase rapidly. Of course, quick multiplication leads to a short and wide swing in ostrich prices over the cycle. For many years, only farmers in the Klein Karoo in South Africa grew ostriches, and they managed the supply to keep up the price in much the same way as De Beers managed the supply of diamonds. But now the whole world raises ostriches, so the prices will vary. Nonetheless, I believe ostriches are a good business for Botswana.

Problems of Part-time Farming
Through all these ventures, I was incurring development costs financed in large part by loans from the NDB and the commercial banks. All was well while I bred cattle and could service my loans from cattle sales. But after I became president, I could not devote enough time to farming, and the management of my farms declined. Once when I was abroad, for example, 1,000 cattle were brought to Lobatse. The cattle arrived too late, we had lost our quota at the BMC, and so they were not accepted for slaughter. The veterinary officer at Lobatse decided I was taking advantage of the fact that I was president, and that I assumed I would get the quota anyway, which was not the case. So, the cattle were not properly cared for, and they died like flies from Heartwater, as they were now in a blue tick area. I did what I could when I came back to the country, but I suffered a big financial loss.

Due to recurring problems of management, my ability to service my loans became compromised. Eventually, people started talking about it, and I thought it was doing neither me nor the country any good. Therefore, in the late 1980s and early 1990s I sold my cattle, paid off the debts so I could keep the farms, and leased them out. Now that I am retired, I am re-stocking, and I hope that before I pass on the farms will be fully stocked.

A friend once remarked that since Botswana is such a small country, and everyone knows everyone else: "There is no such thing as an arm's length transaction." When a civil servant or a politician is involved in a business transaction and knows the person on the other side, it is easy for people to conclude that favours were exchanged. It is precisely for this reason that we established clear procedures and such institutions as the Land Boards. Over the years, when we have had violations of these procedures, some people have lost their jobs and have even gone to jail as a result. Part of the price one pays for being in politics is that people are free to make their accusations, whether or not there is anything to the story.

Projects in Retirement

One of the benefits of no longer being in politics is that now my businesses are just my businesses. Since I retired in 1998, I have tried some ventures that have provided employment for people in Kanye, and that I hope will be good investments as well.

In the early 1970s, Oxfam had given Botswana money for small dams that could be used for horticulture in areas near villages where people could grow fruits and vegetables. We'd preached the gospel of horticulture to people, but we had few converts, and I'd long been peeved by the fact that the dams had not been used. One of these dams near Kanye had been idle for 15 years. When it was first built, 80 groups were formed to farm there. When I returned to Kanye in 1998, there were only 13 women doing a small bit of farming, mostly by watering can, on a fraction of one hectare. So, I asked if I could also have a place. They told me that if the agricultural demonstrator had no objection, then they would allocate me some land. I applied, and there was no objection from the local agricultural officer. So, I started de-bushing, and digging out stones. Then I was told I really needed permission from the regional agricultural officer. When I asked, he responded that I would get a lease eventually, but he was so pleased someone was taking up this project that I should start immediately, and I did. Vegetables properly done are a lucrative venture, especially since it is possible to get more than two crops, and with good management, three full crops per year. My vegetables now are being sold in Kanye and through wholesalers elsewhere as well. I found one could make as much income in a year from a couple of hectares of cabbages as one could earn as the president of the country!

Once we had cleaned out the land for vegetables, we had a stony barren area, and I got the idea to produce chickens. We constructed a few houses, and chickens have been added to the business as well. Our statistics show that it had taken decades for us to produce most of our fresh vegetables, eggs, chickens and a number of other agricultural products instead of importing them. Few people took advantage of these opportunities. If more people had exploited them, Botswana would have developed and diversified farther than it has.

I've also become a sorghum miller since retiring. While sorghum is ideally suited for the climate in Botswana, it is very labour intensive. It has been a good subsistence crop, but it is difficult to produce sorghum and sorghum meal commercially. In addition to the costs of ploughing and planting and weeding, someone must scare the birds, thrash the grain, and then stamp and polish it before turning it into flour. While our traditional culture was to eat sorghum meal from the sorghum we produced ourselves, mealie-meal (maize meal) took root instead when it became readily available in the shops.

In the mid-1960s, the Rural Industries Innovation Centre (RIIC) in Kanye came up with a new design for a sorghum mill that made sorghum meal more competitive with the cost of mealie-meal. Two mills were established, one at each end of the village. Since RIIC wanted to empower locals, they gave one to a co-op, and sold another to one of their workers and helped him finance his purchase. He was an enterprising local mechanic, and after he had purchased 51% and thought he was prosperous, he started drinking beer; eventually the mill, then known as Boriic, went bankrupt. The cooperative started well, but they didn't know the difference between cash flow and profit-and-loss, so they, too, got into trouble and went heavily into debt. Within the space of a year, a village that had two mills had none. After I retired, I was approached to see if I would pay the debts and take over the co-op mill. I was reluctant but was persuaded to do it. An Asian trader had bought the other for speculative purposes, and I bought that one from him as well. In 2001, I began operating them both, and I would say they have been so-so as commercial ventures.

After I acquired the mills, I increased the area I was ploughing and planting in sorghum. Both farming and milling involve a risk for costs and final sale prices, but by combining the two stages one can reduce the overall risk. For example, in the 2002-03 season, BAMB was paying a farmer P52 per bag, while they would sell that bag to a mill for P77. By selling my sorghum to my own mill, I would have an added P25 per bag to help cover the cost of milling, and the viability of both the farming and the milling would increase. What is even more important is that the mills bought sorghum from local farmers at a price of P60 to P66 per bag in the year it started under new management.

I have always enjoyed experimenting with new techniques of farming and ranching, and learning about ostriches, game farming, vegetables and poultry. I was frustrated during my years in politics because I saw so many opportunities that I could not pursue. I have always felt that Botswana could achieve much more in agriculture than we have managed to do so far. I think the absence of successful black farmers as role models in newer areas such as horticulture or dairy, have kept us from achieving our potential. Perhaps what I have been doing in my retirement will provide an example of what could be accomplished by other Batswana in farming.

Other Activities in Retirement

President Nyerere was correct in saying I would find myself busier in retirement than as president. Since I retired, I have undertaken a number of assignments or projects, mainly in Africa. I have done these because I have felt the service might accomplish something worthwhile. I have not charged any fee, though sometimes people have paid out-of-pocket expenses, sometimes that plus per diem. When I did the Rwanda inquiry for three years, they paid me a sitting allowance when we met, and as Facilitator in the Congo I was given an honorarium for the work. By and large, these have been tokens. When I went to South Africa to talk about the election process, they gave me a Kruger coin plus a ballpoint pen wrapped in beads; and when I talked about museums they gave me another pen. I have sometimes taken the initiative to address a problem or to offer advice, and in those cases I have received nothing by way of compensation or expenses. The Botswana government has provided me with transport costs for these volunteer operations when they have agreed they were beneficial for the country or the region. The Commonwealth has asked me to do a few things, and they pay my hotel bill and laundry and meals. I went to Brunei to talk with the African finance and planning ministers; they said I would get an honorarium, but it has yet to come into my bank account, though of course they sent me the ticket to get there and back and paid my hotel bill.

I am grateful that the Botswana government provided me with a pension, a house in Gaborone, and office facilities and staff. These things have enabled me to continue to contribute in whatever way I can to Africa's progress. These activities included serving as an observer of elections in a number of countries for SADC, or the Commonwealth, and once at the request of President Jimmy Carter. I think we in Botswana learned a great deal about how to encourage democracy, good government, and economic development, and if I can be of use to others, and to share the benefits of our experience, I am glad to do so.

Postscript

The process of writing these memoirs has reminded me of some basic themes or principles that guided us as we built Botswana and established its democratic traditions. I shared a commitment to these principles with Seretse Khama and with many other colleagues. Some were not spelled out but simply developed organically, and they became accepted as ways of proceeding. Looking back, one can see that they often reinforced one another. They are not listed in any particular order.

1. Most important choices involve taking calculated risks. Whether contesting an election, choosing a person to lead a ministry, investing in a project, or planting a crop, the outcome is uncertain. One must take risks if one is to lead, and one must assess those risks carefully before deciding.
2. The nation does not reside in any one individual. Individuals must look after the nation, and a sound nation can then create opportunities for each individual to develop to the greatest extent he or she can.
3. The essence of democracy is an informed electorate. Whether one is an ordinary voter, a member of Parliament, a minister or the president, one must understand the basis on which he or she is making a decision.
4. Consultation leads to better decisions and to decisions that are more likely to stand up to criticism. In traditional Tswana culture, a chief would not opine until he had heard others do so at the *kgotla*. Once everyone has had a say, then the leadership can take a decision.
5. An effective opposition is good both for the nation and the government of the day. A good opposition sharpens the debate and ensures that all relevant arguments are heard before a decision is taken. It brings to light issues of concern to the general public.
6. Thorough analysis and good staff work are important in reaching sound decisions. The need to be well informed and the benefits of broad consultation are both served by good analysis. Ideologies or "isms" are not a substitute for analysis of the facts.
7. Better decisions will be made when civil servants and technical experts talk directly with political leaders. Politicians come to understand the reasoning and civil servants learn to address the concerns politicians believe are important.
8. Teamwork and collective responsibility for decisions are terribly important if government is to work effectively. People should be completely candid in airing their views before a decision is made so that all sides of a question are fully understood. Once a decision is taken, a government should speak with one voice.
9. Respect must be earned. One must demonstrate that one is worthy of respect if one expects to be held in esteem, whether as an individual, a politician, a political party, or a nation.
10. Small nations must rely on principles. If they have sound principles and stick to them, then they can appeal to the conscience of friendly countries and international institutions. However, small nations also

need to rely on their wits and their diplomatic skills, since inevitably they face larger countries—neighbours or not—or other parties who have conflicting interests or objectives.
11. By anticipating developments and planning how to address crises before they arise, one can minimise the costs of bad fortune such as droughts or the malevolence of others. Simply put, the way to get out of trouble is to stay out of trouble. Once one is in severe difficulty, it is usually too late to do anything but mitigate the problem. It is more costly to take action later than if one had acted sooner.
12. If one does not need to force an issue in order to achieve an objective, it is best not to push too hard. There is no point picking a fight if one does not have to do so.
13. When dealing with complex conflicts and differences, patience is a major virtue. Pushing parties to agree before they have worked through all their differences may result in an agreement, but it will not be stable or lasting.
14. Anyone can make a contribution to the nation's development, regardless of age, race, gender, nationality, tribe or religion. Openness to good ideas and a willingness to learn from the experience of others are important attributes of an effective government.
15. The freedom to express one's ideas and opinions and to challenge the ideas and opinions of others is fundamental for both democracy and development. Most of the above principles cannot be followed unless there is such freedom.

Abbreviations

ALDEP	Arable Lands Development Programme
AMAX	(formerly) American Metal Climax
ANC	African National Congress
ARAP	Accelerated Rainfed Arable Programme
ARDP	Accelerated Rural Development Programme
AU	African Union
BAMB	Botswana Agricultural Marketing Board
BCL	Bamangwato Concessions Limited
BCSA	Botswana Civil Service Association
BDC	Botswana Development Corporation
BDF	Botswana Defence Force
BDP	Botswana (formerly Bechuanaland) Democratic Party
BDVC	Botswana Diamond Valuing Company
BEDU	Botswana Enterprise Development Unit
BHC	Botswana Housing Corporation
BIP	Botswana Independence Party
BLS	Botswana, Lesotho and Swaziland
BMC	Botswana Meat Commission
BNF	Botswana National Front
BPC	Botswana Power Corporation
BPP	Botswana (formerly Bechuanaland) People's Party
BSAC	British South Africa Company
BUCA	Botswana University Campus Appeal
CCA	Common Customs Area
CDC	Commonwealth (formerly Colonial) Development Corporation
COMESA	Common Market for Eastern and Southern Africa
CSO	Central Selling Organisation
DC	District Commissioner
DRC	Democratic Republic of Congo
DTA	Democratic Turnhalle Alliance
ECA	Economic Commission for Africa
ECC	Economic Committee of Cabinet
EU	European Union
Exco	Executive Council

FAP	Financial Assistance Policy
FMD	Foot and Mouth Disease
GPT	Graduated Personal Tax
IMF	International Monetary Fund
JAC	Joint Advisory Committee
JC	Junior Certificate
Legco	Legislative Council
LMS	London Missionary Society
MFDP	Ministry of Finance and Development Planning
MLC	Movement for the Liberation of the Congo
MNR	Mozambique National Resistance
MP	Member of Parliament
MPC	Mineral Policy Committee
NDB	National Development Bank
NEMIC	National Employment, Manpower and Incomes Council
NGO	Non-governmental Organisation
OAU	Organisation for African Unity
PAC	Pan Africanist Congress of South Africa
PDSF	Public Debt Service Fund
PRC	People's Republic of China
PS	Permanent Secretary
PSP	Permanent Secretary to the President
PTA	Preferential Trade Agreement for Eastern and Southern Africa
RDC	Rally for Democracy in the Congo
RENAMO	Resistencia Nacional Mocambicana
RIIC	Rural Industrial Innovation Centre
RSF	Revenue Stabilisation Fund
RST	Roan Selection Trust
SADC	Southern African Development Community
SADCC	Southern African Development Coordinating Conference

SHHA	Self-Help Housing Agency
SWAPO	South West African People's Organisation
TBVC	Transkei-Bophuthatswana-Venda-Ciskei Bantustans
TGLP	Tribal Grazing Lands Programme
UBLS	University of Botswana, Lesotho and Swaziland
UDI	Unilateral Declaration of Independence
WUC	Water Utilities Corporation
ZANU	Zimbabwe African National Union
ZAPU	Zimbabwe African People's Union

Select Bibliography

—, Legislative Council, *Hansard*, Mafeking, 1961-64.

—, Legislative Assembly, *Hansard*, Gaborone, 1965-66.

Bechuanaland Protectorate, *African Council Procedures and Minutes*, Mafeking, 1961-64.

Botswana Democratic Party, *Raising a Nation: Botswana Democratic Party, 1962-2002*. Gaborone: Front Page Publications, 2002.

Colclough, C. & McCarthy, S. *The Political Economy of Botswana: A Study of Growth and Distribution*. London: Oxford University Press, 1980.

Dutfield, M. *A Marriage of Inconvenience: The Persecution of Ruth and Seretse Khama*. London: Unwin Hyman, 1980.

Edge, W. A. & Lekorwe, M. H. (eds.) *Botswana: Politics and Society*. Johannesburg: J. L. van Schaik, 1998.

Fawcus, P. *Botswana: The Road to Independence*. Gaborone: Pula Press and The Botswana Society, 2000.

Government of Botswana, National Assembly, *Hansard*, Gaborone, 1966-98.

Harvey, C. (ed.) *Papers on the Economy of Botswana*. London: Heinemann, 1981.

Harvey, C. & Lewis, S.R., Jr. *Policy Choice and Development Performance in Botswana*. London: Macmillan, 1997.

Head, B. *When Rain Clouds Gather*. London: Heinemann, 1972.

Holm, J. & Molutsi, P. (eds.) *Democracy in Botswana*. Athens: Ohio University Press, 1989.

Leith, J.C. *Why Botswana Prospered*. Quebec City: McGill-Queens University Press, 2005.

Lewis, S. R., Jr. "Explaining Botswana's Success" in Harrison, L.E. & Berger, P.L. (eds.) *Developing Cultures: Case Studies*. New York: Routledge, 2006.

Ministry of Overseas Development, *The Development of the Bechuanaland Economy*. London: H. M. Printers, 1965.

Morton, F. & Ramsay, J. (eds.) *The Birth of Botswana: A History of the Bechuanaland Protectorate from 1910 to 1966*. Gaborone: Longman Botswana, 1987.

Morton, B. & Ramsay, J. *The Making of a President: Sir Ketumile Masire's Early Years*. Pula Press: Gaborone, 1994.

Parson, J. *Botswana, Liberal Democracy and the Labor Reserve in Southern Africa*. Boulder, Colorado: Westview Press, 1984.

Parson, N., Henderson, W. & Tlou, T. *Seretse Khama, 1921-80*. Gaborone: Macmillan, 1995.

Ramsay, J., Morton, B. & Mgadla, T. *Building a Nation: a History of Botswana from 1800 to 1910*. Gaborone: Longman Botswana, 1995.

Schapera, I. *Tribal Innovators: Tswana Chiefs and Social Change, 1795-1940*. Cape Town: Athlone Press, 1970.

Sillery, A. *Botswana: A Short Political History*. London: Methuen, 1974.

Tlou, T. & Campbell, A. *History of Botswana*. Gaborone: Macmillan, 1997.

Transparency International, *Corruption Perception Index*. Berlin: Transparency International, various years.

World Bank, *World Development Indicators*. Washington, D.C.: World Bank, various years.

Index

abattoir (*see also* Botswana Meat Commission) 23, 26, 40, 163, 196, 320, 325
    ostrich abattoir 324, 325
Abubakar, General 309
Accelerated Rainfed Arable Programme (ARAP) 175-6, 218
Accelerated Rural Development Programme (ARDP) 160, 217
Adams, Bertie 14-15, 36, 249
Addis Ababa 112, 298, 308, 313, 315
Adedeji, Adebayo 277
Africa Confidential 139
African Advisory Council 30, 44, 73
African Council 31-2, 61, 64, 65, 73, 76, 98, 185, 199
African Development Bank 137, 154
African Echo 19, 36
African National Congress, *see* ANC
African Union (AU, *formerly* Organisation for African Unity, OAU) 112, 276, 285, 295,
    302, 303, 304, 308, 311
Afrikaans 9, 11, 252
agricultural development 14-19, 26, 37, 175-77, 187-90, 194-8, 218, 246
agriculture 7, 14-19, 112, 164, 172, 175-7, 218, 231, 244, 257, 263-7, 290, 321-27
Ahtisaari, Martti 285
airlines 175
Algeria 162
Allison, Jimmy 75, 268
all-party caucus meetings 115, 117, 158, 159, 161, 165
AMAX, *formerly* American Metal Climax 202-3, 212, 213
Amin, Idi 105, 271
ANC (African National Congress) 75, 104, 110, 111, 112, 116, 253, 266, 268, 270-3,
    286, 291, 295
Anderson, David 276
Anderson, Joseph 52
Anglo-American Corporation of South Africa/Anglo 202-4, 206, 208, 210-14
Angola 119, 162, 250, 274, 275, 276, 279-80, 283, 291, 293-4, 299, 308
Annan, Kofi 307, 309, 311, 314
anti-corruption unit 240
Arable Lands Development Programme (ALDEP) 175, 218
artificial insemination 18
Assails, Sammy 107-8
Atkins, Dennis 11
attorney-general 72, 94

Babirwa 72, 184
back-benchers 70, 83, 88, 115
Bagwasi, Botshabelo 144
Bahurutshe 1, 72
Bakaa 72
Bakalaka 72
Bakalanga 62, 72, 184
Bakgatla 48, 72, 239, 252
Bakwena 1, 72

balance of payments 158, 159, 262
Balete 72, 184
Balopi, Patrick 55, 127
Balthazar, Professor 277
Bamangwato Concessions Limited, see BCL
Banda, Hastings 275, 277-8
Bank of Botswana 94, 97, 147-8, 157-8, 161, 165, 214, 254, 255
Bangwaketse 1, 8, 14, 72
Bangwato 1, 4, 12, 31, 72, 89, 129-30, 143, 185, 199, 247
Bantustans (see also homelands) 123-4, 232, 261, 267, 295, 301
    leaders 76, 272
Barclays Bank 243
Barlas, Richard 34
Barolong 72
Basarwa 73, 234-6
Batawana 1, 72, 143, 174, 184
Bathoen II, Chief (also B2) 66, 198
    after 1965 elections 123-125
    and constitutional reforms 31, 64, 67, 73-5, 77, 200
    approaches to South Africa 123-5, 250
    elections in 1969 53, 125
    relationship with Masire 4-5, 7, 8, 12, 13-4, 22, 24-9, 53, 77, 123-6, 130, 200
    resignation from chieftainship 124-5
    role in Exco 32, 73, 220
    role in politics and BNF 53, 116, 119, 125-7, 130, 143
Batlokwa 76, 184
Batsile, Calvin 54
Batswapong 72
Batten, James 36
Baylor University 238
BBC transmitter 298
BCL (Bamangwato Concessions Limited) 165, 172, 173, 199, 202-4, 212-3, 231, 233, 284
BDF, see Botswana Defence Force
BDP, see Botswana Democratic Party
Bechuanaland/Bechuanaland Protectorate 2, 7, 11, 13, 14, 19-20, 29, 30-1, 33, 35, 37-9, 43, 45, 60, 72-3, 74, 83, 148, 183, 184, 187, 219, 225, 246-9, 266
Bechuanaland Democratic Party, see Botswana Democratic Party
Bechuanaland Training Centre 225
Beeby, Alf 107-8, 148
Belegolos, Ambassador 299
Belgium/Belgians ix, 304-8, 314-5
Bemba, Jean-Pierre 158, 312, 313, 314
Bent, Alan 187
Berlin Conference (1885) 253
Bhagwati, PN 304
"Big Five" 134
Bill of Rights 68
BLS (Botswana, Lesotho and Swaziland) 255, 258-63
Black Consciousness Movement 268
Blackbeard, Colin 54, 133
Blackbeard, Roy 133, 134, 197
Blacknote 241

BNF, *see* Botswana National Front
Bobonong 185, 186
Boers 27, 184, 246, 253
Bokaa 72
Bophuthatswana 124-5, 260, 264, 270, 272
borders, *see* boundaries
borehole(s) 183, 188-9, 236, 320-21
Boro River 174
Botha, Pik 88, 257, 264, 269, 272
Botha, PW 271, 275
Botsadi 6
Botswana Agricultural Marketing Board 171, 176, 327
Botswana Building Society 171
Botswana Civil Service Association (BCSA) 229, 231
Botswana Defence Force (BDF) 97, 129-30, 132, 134, 143, 281, 286, 293, 298, 299, 302, 303
Botswana Democratic Party (BDP)/*Domkrag* ix, 33, 41, 46, 48-60, 70, 80, 91, 111, 138, 154, 160, 198, 199
   Aims and Objectives 48, 60, 146
   and chieftainship 49-50, 74-6
   attitude toward "isms" 69, 113, 227
   creation of 48
   elections 1965-99 56-60, 123-36
   factions *ix*, 90, 133-5
   financing 55-6
   national principles 49, 61, 144, 146
   newspaper 21, 52
   overall development record 102, 182, 243-5
   party office 52-6, 241
   policy on economic opportunities and disparities 216-45
   policies toward South Africa under *apartheid* 46, 246-73
   recruiting 51, 53, 127, 131-3
   relations with opposition parties 110-22, 140-3
   symbols 51-2
   Tsholetsa House 53
   working with Seretse Khama in the leadership 48-50, 52-3, 67-8, 103-5
Botswana Development Corporation (BDC) 168, 171, 172, 175, 212
Botswana Diamond Valuing Company 207-8
Botswana Enterprise Development Unit 177
Botswana Housing Corporation (BHC) 167, 169-71, 231, 240, 241
Botswana Independence Party (BIP) 127, 266
Botswana Meat Commission (BMC) 40, 168, 243, 325
Botswana National Front (BNF) 58, 110, 116-17, 119, 120, 121, 124, 125, 127, 130, 131, 133, 135, 141
Botswana Ostrich Company 324
Botswana People's Party (BPP) *ix*, 33, 41, 44, 46, 48, 49, 50, 51, 52, 58, 67, 98, 110, 111, 116, 118, 115, 127, 133, 135, 198
Botswana Polytechnic 226
Botswana Power Corporation (BPC) 172, 173, 174, 204, 212
Botswana Progressive Union 118
Botswana Railways 163
Botswana RST 202
Botswana Training Centre 226

Botswana University Campus Appeal (BUCA) 224
boundaries 252-3, 286
BPP, *see* Botswana People's Party
brigades 226, 227
Britain/British/UK/United Kingdom 25, 30, 31, 33, 72-3, 75, 78, 89, 103, 105, 106, 148, 149, 153-4, 162, 218, 229, 246, 247, 248-9, 250, 253, 283, 297, 298, 309, 313, 315
British Labour Party 53
British legacy 30-1, 48, 78-9, 82, 239
British Overseas Development Institute 100
British South Africa Company 30, 184, 246
Brown, Roland 200
Buckley, William 113
budgetary independence 156-7, 164, 168, 182, 217-8
Bunia 311
bureaucracy 101-2, 129, 217, 218, 278
Burundi 301, 304
Bush, George HW 193, 302
Bushmen, *see* Basarwa
Butale 134
Buthelezi, Mangosuthu 179, 180

cabinet 83
    changes 88-9
    collective responsibility 70, 87, 102, 128
    decisions 84-5
    selecting people for 85-8
    workings 83-4, 87, 210, 212
Cambridge Overseas Exam 220, 223
Canada 154, 162, 209, 225, 284
capital, selection of Gaborone as 37-8
Capital Continuation Classes 82, 228
Caprivi Strip 252-3, 286
Carter, Jimmy 328
Cattle/*moraka*/livestock 5, 18, 26-7, 37, 40, 66, 187-90, 194-8, 320-3, 325
    lung disease 117, 197
    owners 190, 195, 198
    post 2, 3, 190
Census 2, 70, 131, 135, 138, 171, 216
Central Selling Organisation (CSO) 204, 207, 208, 210
Certificate of Rights 192
Chad 308
Chambers, Robert 217
Chand, Abas 32, 36, 43, 67
chief justice 94
chiefs/*dikgosi*/chieftainship/*kgosi* 4-5, 30, 31, 49-50, 59, 61, 68, 72-6, 130, 143-4, 183, 184
    development of Masire's views on 4, 24-9
Chiepe, Gaositwe *vii*, 12, 88, 89, 102, 127, 132, 213, 214, 270, 293
Chiluba, Frederick 288, 311
China 84, 103, 119, 247, 300
Chissano, Joachim 279, 292
Chobe 20, 73, 173, 184, 270, 286
Christie Commission 241

churches 2, 13, 21, 219, 222, 238, 247, 305-6, 311
Ciskei 260
Citizen Entrepreneurship Development Agency 182
Citizenship Act 142
civil service/civil servants 79, 95, 98-102, 197, 240, 245
civil war(s) 293, 301, 304, 308
Clinton, Bill 193
coal 214-5
Colclough, Chris 230
Cold War 118, 247, 299, 308
Colonial Development Corporation (CDC) 40, 185, 227
colonial government 13, 25, 30, 61, 98-9, 148, 183, 266, 304, 305
Commission on Review of the Incomes Policy 232
commissioner of labour 233-4
commissions, *see* presidential commissions
committee on local government 64, 99
Common Customs Area (CCA) 178, 255, 259
Common Market for Eastern and Southern Africa (COMESA) 277, 295
Commonwealth 36, 38, 140, 154, 248, 270, 276, 284, 289, 298, 327, 328
communal ownership of land, *see* land, tribal
community secondary schools 222-3
Congo, *see* Democratic Republic of Congo
Congo Brazzaville 303
consensus 31, 102, 186, 310, 316
Constellation of States 260, 263, 273
constitution 31, 59, 61, 68, 69, 71, 72, 74
constitutional conference of 1963 41, 61, 67-76, 105, 111
consultation 25, 31, 62, 86, 96-8, 102, 185-6, 188, 199, 200, 240, 329
contingency planning 161-3
copper/nickel 146, 163, 165, 172, 199, 202, 206, 212, 213, 284, 287
cordon fences 155, 196-7
corruption 167, 202, 239-42, 245
Cote D'Ivoire 302
Cotonou 311
Crocker, Chester 299
Crown/State land 38, 72, 73, 184, 199
Cuba/Cubans 119, 291, 293-4
Cuito Caanavale 294
currency *see* pula, rand
customary law and courts 65-7, 74, 141-2
customs revenue 156, 203, 213, 256, 259-60, 263
Customs Union 86, 147, 156, 178, 179, 203, 246, 251, 253, 255-63, 288

Dabutha 120, 324
Dada, Satar 133, 242
Daily News 128, 137, 139
Dallaire, Romeo 306
Dambe, Amos 48, 51, 53, 68, 187
dams 38, 174, 264, 326
De Beers 84, 91, 134, 136, 147, 165, 167, 202, 204, 204-13
DeGraff, Braam 321
De Klerk, FW 272-3

Debswana 84, 91, 134, 136, 147, 165, 167, 205-11, 231, 243
Deitrichs, Dr 258
Delimitation Commission 61, 70, 71, 131, 135
Democratic Party, *see* Botswana Democratic Party
Democratic Republic of Congo 158, 278-80, 295, 301, 303, 304
    Inter-Congolese Dialogue 303, 308-16
Democratic Turnhalle Alliance 275-6, 285
Department of Labour office 251
Development Bank of Southern Africa 260
Dhlakama, Alfonso 292
diamond(s) 198, 204-13
    cutting 84-5, 134, 211
    discovery 204
    exports 160, 165, 204, 206, 210, 211
    marketing 207-8
    revenues 161, 204, 206, 210, 211
    strategies 204-5
diplomacy 297-301
diplomatic
    missions 297
    relations 251-2, 298-301
discrimination 37, 39, 45, 58, 64, 141, 142, 163, 267
diseases
    animal 196-7
    human 219, 237-9
Disele, Kebatshabile 126
District Commissioner (DC) 15, 21, 25, 30, 42, 47, 50, 61,72-3, 75, 98
diversification 37, 164, 180, 244
Djoudi, Hocine 304
Domkrag see Botswana Democratic Party
donors 79, 149, 153-6, 300, 309-10
Dos Santos, Jose Eduardo 279, 293-4
Douglas, Arthur 45, 61, 67, 78, 266
Dow, Unity 142
drought 79, 218, 252
    relief programmes 79-80, 176
Dukwe 269, 283
Dumbrell, Henry 19
dyslexia 10

Eaton, Dick 133
ecologists 174
Economic Committee of Cabinet (ECC) 97, 101, 151-2, 159, 181
economics
    economic management and planning 146-67
    economic opportunities and disparities 216-45
    economic strategies and programmes 168-82
    mineral development policies 199-215
    policies on land and cattle 183-98
Economic Opportunities Commission 180-1, 232
education 39, 219-28
    of electorate 56-7, 113-14

primary 220-22
  secondary 39, 222-4
  technical and vocational 225-6
  tertiary 39, 224-5
Edwards, Bob 34, 107, 173, 187
Egypt 162
Election Manifesto (1974) 216
elections in Bechuanaland/Botswana
  1965 61, 56-60, 123-5
  1969 125
  1974 126, 216
  1979 127
  1984 130, 192
  1989 133
  1994 135
  1999 135
elections in
  Lesotho 289
  Mozambique 293
  Zambia 287
  Zimbabwe 281
employment 168, 175, 177, 180, 231, 244, 265, 326
Employment Policy Unit 177
England, Russell 15, 27, 31, 32, 36, 37, 42, 105
England, Sheila 81
Entebbe 271
equality/inequality 216, 232, 243, 244, 247, 267
Ethiopia 312
European Advisory Council 30, 44
European Union (EU) *formerly* European Community 154, 155, 177, 196, 297, 315
evaluating overall record 102, 182, 243-6
exchange rate 147, 158, 159, 254
Exco (Executive Council) 31, 32, 35-6, 73, 220
expatriates 39, 100, 154, 231
Export Canning Company 40

factions, within BDP 90, 133-5
Falconer, Jack 322
famine 79-80
Fawcus, Isabel 32-4, 81
Fawcus, Peter 21, 31-3, 35, 37, 40, 44, 61, 62, 67, 75, 76, 78, 92, 107, 148, 164, 204, 265-6
Federal Party 33, 110
fencing 25-6, 187, 189, 190, 196, 320, 322
Financial Assistance Policy (FAP) 177, 181-2, 205
Financial Times 206
Finlay, David 33, 98
First Lady's Charity Fund 318
flag 81-2
flats for members of Parliament 243
FNLA 293
food for work 80
foot and mouth disease 196

Ford Foundation 34, 154
foreign exchange reserves 158, 161, 163, 164, 165
Fort Hare University 7
Fouche, Jim 252
Four National Principles 49, 61, 144-5, 146
France/French *ix*, 154, 304, 306, 307, 314, 315
Francistown 38, 47, 150, 155, 174, 219, 221, 228, 281, 283, 298
free trade agreement 178
freedom (of expression) 330
Freedom Square 77, 120, 122
Freehold 184, 192, 246
Frelimo 291-3, 302
Front Line States 270, 274-6, 281, 282, 287, 291-3, 295, 299

Gabane 1, 38, 71
Gaborone 135, 136, 150, 167, 171, 181, 203, 208, 209, 219, 222, 228, 255, 268, 270, 281, 283, 284, 294, 299, 311, 315, 317
  freehold land (Gaborone block) 38, 184, 192-4, 246
  venue for international meetings 272, 278, 292, 312
Gaborone dam 38, 264
game 155, 176, 189, 190, 193, 321, 324
Game/Wildlife Department 321, 324
Gaolathe, Baledzi 86, 99, 147, 206, 215, 262, 262-3
Gare, Aaron 19
Gaseitsiwe, Bathoen (*see also* Bathoen II, Chief) 125
Gaseitsiwe, Mookami 27-8, 63
Gaseitsiwe, Seepapitso 22, 187
Gates Foundation, Bill and Melinda 238
Gbadolite 310, 311
gender discrimination 141-2
Germany/Germans 154, 155, 203, 213, 226, 246, 250, 304, 305
Germond, Jerry 28
Ghai, Dharam 230
Ghanzi 20, 43, 47, 72-3, 133, 150, 169, 184, 221-2, 234, 236, 246, 321-3
Going, Hubo 11, 15
Goma 310, 311
Graduated Personal Tax 66
Grant-in-Aid 148, 149, 157, 218, 229, 282
Great Powers/Major Powers 301-3, 304, 307, 310, 314, 315
Grobler, NK 323
Gugushe, Joe 32

Habyarimana, President 305, 306, 307
Haile, AJ 11
Haiti 303
Harare Declaration 272
Hardbattle, John 236
Hardbattle, Thomas 236, 323
Harrison, DS 19
Harvard University 238
Haskins, Jimmy 32, 36, 38, 67, 92, 131, 133
Hay, Doctor 22

headman 1, 8
health care 219, 237-9
Heinebäck, Bo 309
Hereros 285
Hermans, Janet *vii-viii*
Hermans, Quill 34, 97, 99, 100, 107, 108, 148, 157, 170, 172, 203-4, 227, 255, 323
High Commission Territories 246, 247, 248-50, 255, 288, 290
High Court 34, 66
Hirschfield, Simon 149, 240, 269, 271
HIV/AIDS x, 219, 237-9, 244
Holbrooke, Richard 309, 310
homelands (*see also* Bantustans) 260, 264-5
Hong Kong 240, 249
hospitals 219
House of Chiefs 74-6, 83, 144, 200
housing 169-71
Hurvitz, Cyril 40
Hutu 304-7
Hyundai 179-80

identity card, *see Omang*
IMF 94, 99, 154, 159, 166, 254
Incomes Policy 164, 170, 216, 229-33, 244
Independent Electoral Commission 140
indirect rule 25, 30, 73, 304
industrial court 233
inflation 149, 150, 158, 159, 165, 167, 262
Information Department 137
infrastructure 149, 168-9
Interahamwe 303, 305, 306
Inter-Congolese Dialogue 308-16
International Court of Justice 286
International Monetary Fund, *see* IMF
International Panel of Eminent Personalities 303
Ireland 155
Isaksen, Jan 159
Itketseng, Bashi 294

Jameson Raid 30
Jansen, Doctor/"artificial cows" 18
Japan/Japanese 154, 226
Japie, Rre 217
Johannesburg 6, 19, 20, 22, 32, 255, 311
Johnson-Sirleaf, Ellen 304, 309
Joint Advisory Council (JAC) 30-31, 44, 73
Jonathan, Leabua 224, 289
journalists 137-9
Jwaneng 161, 166, 205, 208-11, 236, 242

Kabila, Joseph 312-16
Kabila, Laurent 179, 279, 280, 308-12, 316
Kagame, Paul 305, 306, 307

344

INDEX

Kalabeng, Rapontsheng 121, 123, 187
Kalulu, Minister 122
Kamaga, Ruben 122
Kanagasi 73
Kang 57, 150
Kanye 1, 2, 6, 10, 11, 12, 13, 21, 22, 26, 27, 76, 125, 126, 128, 134, 171, 186, 211, 218, 326, 327
Kanye Junior Secondary School 13
Karakubisi 73
Kaunda, Kenneth 112, 262, 267, 268, 274-7, 286-8, 292
Kazungula 156, 162, 274, 281
Keaiketse, Bennett 52
Kedakubile, Pitso 27
Kedikilwe Commission 223
Kedikilwe, Ponatshego 22, 132, 133-4, 139, 161, 284, 321
Keitseng, Fish 111, 266
Kenya 194, 310
Ketlokgetswe, Serara 228
Kgabo Commission 191, 241
Kgabo, Englishman 51, 53, 57, 68, 96, 188, 191, 200, 222, 241
Kgalakgadi 5, 73, 126, 169, 214, 236
Kgari 127
Kgasa, MLA 19, 24, 27
Kgaswe 214
Kgopo family 1, 2, 4, 5, 6
Kgopo, Kgopo 6, 128
Kgosana, Philip 112
kgosi, see chiefs/chieftainship
Kgosi, Israel 322
kgotla 4, 8, 20, 24, 25, 26, 27, 67, 125, 129, 130, 143, 144, 183, 185, 186, 188, 198
    role of 62-3, 65, 77
Khama III, Chief, *also* Khama the Great 72, 184
Khama, Ian 129-30, 143
Khama, Ruth (née Williams) 12, 31, 38, 52, 106-8, 247
Khama, Seretse 4, 7, 22, 40, 112, 204, 228, 244, 283, 286, 318, 322, 329
    and Chief Bathoen II 53, 73, 123-5
    and chiefs/chieftainship 31, 36, 48-50, 73, 74-6, 123-5, 130, 199-200, 216
    death and funeral 108-9, 127-9
    health 105-6, 127, 255, 275, 277
    leadership of BDP and government 33, 37, 39, 40-1, 48-50, 52-3, 56, 58, 61, 67-8, 74-6, 78, 80, 83, 85, 97, 99, 103-5, 111, 113, 123, 136, 163, 199-200, 216, 255
    marriage 12, 31, 38, 106-8, 247
    and race relations 45, 49, 60, 104
    official portrait controversy 129
    prohibited immigrant in South Africa 38
    relations with South Africa during apartheid 38, 114, 118-9, 247, 248-51, 266-9, 270, 275-6
    relationship with Masire ix, 32, 40, 53, 71, 83, 84, 85, 86, 90, 99, 103-9, 111, 125-6, 147, 157, 193, 323
    role in regional affairs 274-77, 281, 287, 289, 295, 301
    sense of humour 55, 105, 110, 113, 275-6
    son, *see* Khama, Ian

Khama, Tshekedi 4, 31, 199, 202, 222, 247
Khan, Sham 56, 133
Kigali 305
Kinshasa 298, 309, 310, 311, 312, 314
Kirby, Ian 193
Kirby, Peter 324
Kokong 5
Koma, Gaolese 189
Koma, Kenneth 90, 93, 116-18, 122, 124-5, 130, 131, 198
Kreditanstalt für Wiederafbau 202
Kule 73
Kuwait 154, 162
Kwelagobe, Daniel 96, 131, 132, 133-4, 136, 139, 169, 241
Kwele, Daniel 117-18
Kweneng 15, 188, 209, 211
Kwerepe, Gaerolwe 322

Labatt, Hacen 309, 312
Lake Victoria 307
Lancaster House Agreement 283, 292
land
    allocation 16, 27-8, 183, 184-5, 190-5
    boards 184-6, 190-1, 194, 211, 320, 325
    Crown/State 38, 72-3, 184, 199
    freehold, grants by chiefs 184
    leasehold 191
    tenure, types 183-4
    tribal 73, 169-70, 183-91
    urban 192-4
    utilisation 186, 187, 189
Landell-Mills, Peter 96, 97, 100, 107-8, 148, 172, 227
law *see* customary law
Leader of the House 91
Legco (Legislative Council) 30-41, 43-7, 57, 59, 61, 67, 73, 74, 76, 92, 111, 141, 164, 195, 216, 220, 248-50, 265-6
Legislative Assembly 61, 67, 78, 79, 111, 113
Legwaila, Elijah *vii*, 94, 100
Legwaila, Joseph 89, 283, 285, 301
Lesotho (*previously* Basutoland) 157, 172, 224, 246, 248, 254, 255, 261, 262, 274-5, 276-7, 288-90
Letlhakane 205, 210
Letlhaku, William 12
Lewis, Ambassador Stephen 304
Lewis, Aubrey 13
Lewis, Judith Frost *viii*
Lewis, Stephen R., Jr. *viii*
liberation movements *see* ANC, Black Consciousness Movement, PAC, SWAPO, ZANU, ZAPU
Liberia 112, 301-2
Libya 162
lifeline projects 162, 281
Linchwe II, Chief 64, 67, 75, 116, 252, 320

INDEX

Lipton, Michael 177, 180
livestock (*see* cattle)
Livingstone, David 111
Lobatse *ix*, 14, 15, 26, 34, 38, 48, 150, 184, 221-2, 228, 246, 264, 266, 323-5
Lobatse Crescent School 222
Lobengula, Chief 184
local government 29, 61, 62, 63-7, 78, 105, 218
    elections 58, 64, 126
localisation 38-40, 154
Lock, Albert 92, 294
London, Tim 324
London Missionary Society (LMS) 2, 7, 13, 123
Lotshwao, Motsalore 26
Luanda 294
Lumumba, Patrice 308
Lumumbashi 311
Lusaka 268, 272, 277, 282, 285, 286, 287, 294, 297
Lusaka Agreement 308, 312, 313

Machel, Samora 270, 278, 291, 292
Macmillan, Harold 31
Maeyane, Soblem 286
Mahalapye 14, 15, 38, 48, 110, 171
Mahalelo, Pheranyane 18
Mafeking *ix*, 21, 22, 30, 34, 37, 59, 82, 221, 247, 251, 264
mafisa 195
Magang, David 89, 128, 134, 169, 193-4
Maganu, David 322
Mahashe, Minister 280
Maina, David 134
Makaba II/Makaba the Great, Chief 1, 5, 25
Makgalemela, Rre 55
Makgekgenene, Lemme 242
Makoni, Simba 278
Makunda 73
Makwa, John 63
Malan, DF 12
Malawi 246, 274, 275, 276, 292
Maruping, Peter 125
Manchwe, George O 13
Mandela, Nelson 76, 116, 179, 180, 250, 266, 273, 278, 279, 288, 289, 290, 291, 301
Mangope, Lucas 264, 272-3
Mannathoko, Richard 47
manpower budget 160
Mantanzima, Kaiser 123
Manthe, Tau 15
manufacturing 177, 181
Maradu Ostrich Farm 324
Maribe, MA 48
Marina, HRH Princess 82
Maru a Pula Secondary School 81, 228, 318
masimo 2, 4, 9

Masire, Quett Ketumile Joni (*also* RraGaone/Sir Ketumile)
   ancestors 1
   and Botswana as an open society 121-2
   and matters affecting Botswana's security 118-21
   and SADCC/ SADC 276-80
   aunts 7
   becomes president 128-9
   brothers (Basimane/David, Basimanyana/Peter, Bontlohile) 2, 3, 5, 6, 8-9, 20, 241, 271, 321, 322, 323
   brushes with death 3, 22, 58, 294, 323
   children (*see also individual names*) 6, 318-20
   developing Vision 2016 144-5
   early influences 3-6
   economic development policies
      and HIV/AIDS 237-9
      cattle and other agriculture 175-7, 187-90, 194-8,
      diamond policies 204-12
      education policies 219-28
      infrastructure development 168-71, 219
      land policies 183-94
      macroeconomic policies 159-61, 163-7, 229-34
      mineral development 199-215
      overall record *ix, x*, 102, 146, 167, 182, 243-5
      planning 146-53, 161-3
      rural development 216-8
   education 6-7, 9-12, 147
   Facilitator of Inter-Congolese Dialogue 297, 299, 303, 308-16, 327
   family life 2-9, 21-3, 317-20
   farmer 14-19, 42-3, 320-7
   father, *see* Masire, Joni
   grandchildren 319
   grandfather, Masire-a-Sealetsa 4-5
   grandmother 2, 5-6, 9
   guiding principles 250-1, 329-30
   house in Gaborone 193, 328
   journalist 19-21
   leadership in BDP 48-60
   marriage 21-23
   minister of finance and development planning 147
   mother, *see* Masire, Gabaipone
   names 1
   policies toward South Africa 246-73
   regrets and disappointments 100-2, 125-6, 129-30, 133-5, 167, 174, 177, 190, 235, 237, 238, 244, 283-4, 291, 324-5
   relations with opposition parties and their leaders 110-22
   relations with the press 137-9
   relations with whites 10-12, 42-7
   relationship with Chief Bathoen II 4-5, 7, 8, 12, 13-4, 24-9, 53, 77, 124-6, 130, 200
   relationship with Seretse Khama *vii, ix*, 32, 53, 71, 80, 83-6, 90, 99, 103-9, 111, 123-6, 147, 157, 193
   relationship with South Africa (*see also* South Africa under *apartheid*) 11-2, 123-5, 246-73

INDEX

responsibilities after parents' deaths 7-9
retirement *ix*, 303, 326-8
role in political developments before independence 30-41, 42-7, 61-82
role in political developments 1965-98 123-45
Rwanda genocide inquiry 304-8
leadership in government 83-102
sisters (Gabalengwe, Morufhi) 2, 6, 8-9, 21, 122
teaching 13-14, 24, 228
uncles 5, 7, 8, 16, 21, 110, 121
views on chieftainship 24-9, 49-50, 74-7, 143-4
views on corruption and politics 137, 239-42
wife, *see* Masire, Mma-Gaone
Masire, Gabaipone 1, 4, 7
Masire, Gaone 6, 22, 318-19
Masire, Gladys Olebile, *see* Masire, Mma-Gaone
Masire, Joni 1-4, 5, 7, 8
Masire, Matshidiso 318, 319
Masire, Mma-Gaone 6, 21-3, 55, 70, 294, 317, 318, 320
Masire, Mmetla (wife, Doreen) 222, 318, 319
Masire, Moabi (wife, Mother) 318, 319
Masire, Mpho (wife, Setshego) 10, 222, 318, 319
Masire-Mwamba, Mmasekgoa (husband, Trevor Mwamba) *vii*, 318, 319
Masisi, Edison 50, 92, 187, 242, 298
Maswikiti, Mudongo 128
Matambo, Ken 278
Matante, Philip 37, 44, 46, 51, 52, 58, 67, 68, 71, 77, 110, 111, 113, 115, 116, 122, 127, 176, 301
Matebeleland 282
matimela (stray cattle) 36, 66-7
Matthews, Norman 15
Matthews, ZK 301
Matsitama 202
Maud, John 31
Maun 65, 106, 174, 186, 294, 322
Mauritius 278
Mayer, Dr 250
Mbaiwa, Sam 120
Mbeki, Thabo 179-80, 271, 313, 314
McCarthy Report 261, 263
McClaren, CC 42, 43
McFarland, Earl 262
media 121, 137, 138, 236, 307-8
mephato (regimental labour) 28, 29, 55, 66-7, 228-9,
Merafhe, Mompati 132, 133-4, 143
Merriweather, Dr Alfred 36, 92, 134
Michanek, Ernst 189
Michel, Louis 315
migrant labour 246
Mineral Policy Committee (MPC) 201, 206, 212, 213, 214
Mineral Rights in Tribal Territories Bill 200
minerals 146, 160, 164, 199, 200, 206, 244
mines 2, 6, 161, 204-8, 210, 211, 218, 236, 242, 246, 265

Mines and Minerals Act 201, 240
Ministry of Education 226
Ministry of Health 237, 239
Ministry of Finance and Development Planning (MFDP) 147, 149, 152, 158, 159, 160, 253
Ministry of Local Government and Lands 241
Mmadirelang 120
Mmakgongwana, Rre 63
Mmankgodi 1
Mmegi 138, 227
Mmusi, Gabriel 233
Mmusi, Peter 87, 89, 90, 131, 132, 133, 136, 137, 161, 165, 166, 180, 183, 233, 234
Moapare, Boy 128
Mochudi 48, 67, 76, 87, 120-1, 127, 129, 171, 252
Modisi, Luke 110
Modisi, Mogolori *vii*
Moditswane, Nketsang 121
Mogae, Festus G *x*, 20, 87, 88, 89, 94, 135, 147, 161, 239, 242, 263, 309, 311
    becomes president *ix, x*
    PSP 93-4
    selecting Ian Khama as vice-president 89, 143-4
    vice-presidency 90-91, 135
Mogobe, Ntau 26
Mogoditshane 15, 71
    land affair 191, 193, 241
Mogomotsi, Segametse 120-1
Mogwe, Archie *vii*, 11, 12, 13, 54. 81, 88, 89, 108, 126, 127, 132, 162, 228, 264, 268, 277, 283, 299, 309, 310, 311
Mohumagadi, Mmafane (MmaSeepapitso) 24
Mokaila, DM 22
Mokama, Moleleki 46, 47, 94, 128, 130
Mokgosi III, Chief 64, 67, 75
Mokhehle, Ntsu 289
Mokolodi Trust 193
Molefhane, Mike 99
Molema, Modiri 32
Molepolole 84, 85, 106, 134, 171, 212, 218, 299
Moleta, Chief 1, 5
Molefe, Ralph 18
Molomo, Ray 320
Molopo Farms 133, 246
Molosi, Peter 194
Molwakapelo, Rre 28
Mookodi, Bias 7, 10, 12, 13, 14, 22, 79, 116
Moore, Thomas 25
Montshiwagae, Rre 13
Monwela, Dikgothi 128
Morake, Joel 11
Morake, KP 53, 55
Morgan, David 32, 36, 44, 46, 67, 264
Morgan Grenfell 210
Morupule 202, 204, 214
Moses, Kgosi Thebe 52

Mosielele, Letlhole 32, 68
Mosinyi, Goareng 32, 36, 48, 51, 126, 128
Mosinyi, Luke 187
Motebejana ward 1, 8
Motlogelwa, Bantu 18
Motsemme, Gilbert *vii*
Motsete, KT 50, 67, 80, 81, 99, 110, 111, 198
Motshidisi, Klaas 99, 233-4
Mozambique 250, 264, 270, 274, 276, 290, 291-3, 302
Mozambique National Resistance 292
Mpho, Motsamai 7, 67, 111, 114, 116, 118, 122, 127, 128. 228, 266
MPLA 293, 294, 299
Mpotokwane, Lebang 99, 271, 277, 278
Mpuchane, Sam 99
Mswati III, King 290-1
Mugabe, Robert 277, 279, 280, 282, 283, 284, 288, 289, 290, 291, 292, 293, 308, 321
Murray-Hudson, Hugh 81, 203, 227, 228
Museveni, Yoweri 305, 311
Mutsumi 128
Muzerewa, Abel 282
Mynhardt, CJ 67

Nairobi 27, 310,311
Naledi ya Botswana ix, 19-21, 30, 36, 53, 93, 137
Namibia 158, 169, 207, 246, 250, 252-3, 260, 262, 263, 265, 272, 274, 275, 276, 280, 285-6, 287, 297, 299, 308
Naro 234
national anthem 81
National Assembly, *see* Parliament
National Development Bank (NDB) 168, 171, 172, 175, 325
National Development Plans 151, 159, 168, 232, 235
National Employment, Manpower and Incomes Council (NEMIC) 165, 230, 233
National Party of South Africa 11-13, 247, 248, 260, 271, 273, 274, 285, 291, 297
National Policy on AIDS 238
National Policy on Incomes, Employment, Prices and Profits 230-2
National Resistance Army 305
Nchindo, Louis 20
Ndebele 184
negotiations 147, 178, 257-9
neighbours 247, 281-96
Nethering, "Jambo" 46
Neto, Augustino 293
newspaper(s) 19, 20, 21, 52, 59, 137, 138, 139, 227, 247
Ngamiland 20, 117, 197
Nganunu, Julian 94, 95, 99, 209, 213
NGOs 81, 154, 238, 304, 307
Ngwaketse 1, 15, 30, 63, 70, 135, 143, 186, 218, 250, 320
Niasse, Moustapha 309, 314
nickel, *see* copper/nickel
Nielson, Poul 315
Nigeria 73, 297, 309
Nkala, Minister 283

Nkomati Accord 270, 292
Nkomo, Joshua 282, 283, 289
Nkrumah, Kwame 19, 110, 112, 295
Nojane 73
non-racialism 47, 104, 133, 250
Norland, Donald 156
Norman-Walker, Hugh 78, 200
Norway/Norwegians 162, 225, 313
Notwane Club 81
Nujoma, Sam 286
Nwako, Moutlakgola 7, 20, 41, 48, 49, 50, 56, 61, 68, 86, 88, 89, 90, 92-3, 128, 130, 131, 189, 193, 230, 298
Nyerere, Julius 112, 262, 267, 274, 275, 276, 278, 292, 295, 300, 303, 327
Nzo, Alfred 271, 291

OAU, Organisation for African Unity, *see* African Union
Obasanjo, Olusegun 311
oil crisis 162, 256
Okavango 20, 113, 127, 154, 173-4, 191
old age pensions 234
Old Naledi 170
Olsen, Clara 55, 136
Omang 118, 142, 143, 234
"one man, one beast" 224
Onusumba 312
Oppenheimer, Harry 202, 204, 208-9, 213
opposition 93, 120, 136, 160, 198, 233, 243, 251, 329
    leaders 115-18
    parties 110-15
Orapa 150, 156, 174, 204, 205, 208, 209, 210, 211, 212, 236, 242
Organ for Security and Defence of SADC 279
ostrich farming 324
Ovambo 285

PAC (Pan Africanist Congress) 46, 110, 111, 112, 116, 268
Palme, Lisbet 304
Pan-African movement 112, 295
Pandamatenga 101, 176
paramount chiefs 72, 74
parastatals 167, 168, 171, 175, 231
Parliament (*also* National Assembly) 67, 69, 71, 73, 78, 83, 84, 116, 128, 133, 135, 141, 143-4, 151, 158, 159, 160, 164, 165, 176, 187, 243, 251, 266-7
Patriotic Front (PF) 89, 283
Patton, Chris 315
Peace Corps volunteers 155
Penal Code 64-5, 67
People's Party, *see* Botswana People's Party
People's Republic of China (PRC) 84, 300
permanent secretaries 93-4, 95-6, 98
Phakalane 193-4
Pilane, Mmusi 48
Pitso, RC 16

planning 148-50, 151-3
Podbrey, Joe 116
Portugal 264, 274, 275, 291
post-independence financial arrangements 105
Preferential Trade Area for Eastern and Southern Africa (PTA) 277, 295
Presidential Commission on Economic Opportunities 180-81, 183, 232
presidential commissions 97-8, 116, 180-1, 183, 191, 222-3, 230, 232, 241
press, *see also* media 138-9
principles 41, 47, 54, 242, 244-5, 250-51, 265-7, 273, 281-2, 295, 329-30
Prinz Brau 128, 179
Productive Employment Development Fund 181, 205
Public Debt Service Fund (PDSF) 157, 164, 166, 171, 205
Public Service Commission 240
pula 81, 157-9, 163, 173, 166, 253-5
Pula Fund 161, 163, 167, 205
Puso ya naalano 59, 78

race relations 42-7, 70, 274
Race Relations Act 46
Rachele Primary School 6
racial discrimination, *see* discrimination
Radio Botswana 128, 138
Radio Television Libre des Mille Collines 305
radio(s) 138, 188, 305
radio learning campaign 188
Raditladi, Leetile 32, 48, 110
railway 163, 264
Ramotswa 15, 38, 211
rand/Rand Monetary Area 157, 158, 166, 173, 246, 254
Rantshado, Sedumedi 12
Refugee Committee 268
refugees 247, 265-71, 274, 275, 283, 305
relief programmes 79
RENAMO 270, 292, 293, 302
respect 6, 124, 262, 272, 301, 329
Revenue Sharing Formula 258-60
Revenue Stabilisation Fund (RSF) 157, 164, 165, 166, 205
Rey, Charles 4-5
Rhodes, Cecil John 30, 184, 246
Rhodesia, *see* Zimbabwe
Rhodesia Railways 163, 264
Richard, Gavin 321
riots 120-21
riparian rights 264
Roan Selection Trust (RST) 199, 202
Roberto, Holden 293
Roberts, Simon 65
Roman Catholic Church 305, 306
Rome 293
Rowland, Richard 2
royalties 203, 204
Ruele, Greek 127, 134

Rural development 216-8
Rural Industries Innovation Centre 326
Russia, *see* Soviet Union
Rwanda genocide 295, 297, 301, 303, 304-8, 327

Saane, Andrew 21
SADCC, *see* Southern African Development Coordinating Conference
sales tax 166
Salim, Salim 308, 309
San, *see* Basarwa
sanctions, *see* South Africa, sanctions against
Sandford, Stephen 176
Saudi Arabia 154
Savimbi, Jonas 279, 293, 294, 299
Scandinavians 154, 162, 300
Schmidt, Helmut 203
school feeding programme 14, 79
school fees 221
Seame, Dihatlho 67, 129
Sebego, Ronald 197, 198
Sebeso, Gaefalale 128
Sechele, Gagoumakwe 134
Sechele, Philip 111
security 114, 118-21, 162, 253-4, 266
Security Council, *see* United Nations Security Council
Sedudu Island 252, 286
Segokgo, Motlatsi 50, 53, 64, 66, 68, 240
Segkoma, Chief 184
Sekgonyane 289
Sekgua, Ntwakgolo 322
Sekoma 320-1
Selassie, Haile 298
Selebi-Phikwe 156, 163, 165, 172, 173, 202, 212, 233, 236, 281, 283
Select Committee on Racial Discrimination 45, 98
Selepeng, Louis 272
Self-help Housing Agency (SHHA) 170-71, 174, 231
self-help projects 80, 81
self-liquidating project 160
self-rule 30, 36, 49, 61, 68, 78-9, 182, 268, 322
Senegal 309
Senghor, Leopold 112
Seralanyane, Kesupile 17
Seretse, Lenyeletse 89, 233
Serowe 48, 73, 84, 85, 129-30, 134, 143, 150, 171, 186, 211-2, 218, 221, 226
Sese-Seko, Mobutu 278, 279, 293, 308, 313
Setlhatlhane, Segolobe 29
Seychelles 278, 279
Shannon, Joe 241
Sharpeville massacre 248, 250
Shashe project 172-3, 202-4, 212-13
Shashe River School 227
Shaw, John 13

Sheehy, Tim 276
Shell Coal 214-5
Sierra Leone 303
Sim, George 44
Sithole, Ndabaninge 282
Skelemani, Phandu 94
Slabbert, Van Zyl 275
Smith, Ian 47, 114, 120, 155, 246, 253, 274, 281, 282, 287, 292, 297
Sobhuza II, King 290
soda ash 204, 213-14
Solomon, Morewagole 27
Somalia 302
sorghum 326-7
South Africa
    in SADC 276, 278-80
    support during Inter-Congolese Dialogue 310, 313-4
    transition to democracy 272-3
South Africa before 1994, *see also* Bantustans, Front Line States, homelands, SADCC,
    SADC 1, 7, 11, 12, 13, 19, 31, 38, 58, 75, 84, 86, 177, 210, 219, 227, 295, 301
    incorporation of Bechuanaland or Botswana into 123-5, 248-50
    security/defense/intelligence issues 62, 84, 114-5, 161-3, 172-4, 253-4, 265-7,
        269-71, 298, 299
    Botswana citizens working in 2, 6, 11, 265
    raids on Gaborone 251, 270, 274, 299
    liberation movements, *see* ANC, PAC
    economic relations, *see also* pula, rand, Customs Union 157-9, 160, 172-4, 178-80,
        202-3, 213, 231, 261-3
    relations with Botswana during *apartheid* 246-73
    sanctions against 261-3, 287
South African Breweries 179
South African Maize Board 252
South African Reserve Bank 254-5, 262
Southern African Customs Union, *see* Customs Union
Southern African Development Community (SADC) 155, 278-80, 290, 296, 311, 312, 328
Southern African Development Coordinating Conference (SADCC) 274, 276-8, 295
Soviet Union/Soviets/Russia 119, 210, 247, 283, 291, 293, 299-300
Sowa Pan 213-14
Soweto uprising 269
Speaker, choosing 91-3
Special Branch 118, 123-4, 253-4
Special Olympics 318
Steenkamp, Phil 93-4, 255
Steinberg, Ben 27, 48, 50, 56
Stevens, Mike 162
Stockwell 240
Stoneham, John 263
Straw, Jack 315
Sudan 301, 308
Sun City 313, 315
surplus liquidity 161
Swaneng Hill School 227
SWAPO 104, 272, 275-6, 285, 286

Swaziland 157, 179, 224, 246, 254, 255, 261, 262, 274-7, 288, 290-91
Sweden 155, 189, 309, 313

Taiwan 300
Tambo, Oliver 268, 271-2
Tanzania 162, 274, 276, 295
Tati Company 184, 200
Tati Concession 73, 184, 200, 246
TB (tuberculosis) 239
TBVC States 260, 261
teachers 7, 9, 13-14, 156, 220, 221, 228
teamwork 87, 102, 329
Tebape, JJ 99
Tebape, Oteng 285
television 138
Telli, Dialo 112
Temane, BK 134
Templesman, Maurice 212
Tennant, Julian 75, 124
Thema Commission 222, 223
Thema, Ben 12, 20, 76, 111, 127, 128, 131, 228
Therisanyo/Consultation 21, 52, 131
Tibone, Charles 99, 162, 211, 214
Tiger Kloof 4, 7, 9-14, 110, 116
Tilbury, Alan 31, 33, 61, 62, 65, 67, 75, 79, 91, 94, 108, 124, 214
Tirelo Setshaba 228-9
Tjamzashe, William 7
Tlokweng 38, 85, 171, 179
Tlou, Thomas 318
Tonota 1, 87
Toure, Ahmadou Toumani 304
trade unions 233
Transitional Plan for Economic and Social Development 113, 148, 151
Transkei 260, 264
Trans-Kgalakgadi Highway 269
Trans-Kgalakgadi Railway 214
transparency 99, 202, 239
Transparency International 241
Treurnicht, Andries 257
tribal
    land 26, 73, 169-70, 184, 185, 190, 191
    reserves 72, 184
Tribal Grazing Land Programme (TGLP) 134, 185, 187-90, 195, 218, 236, 241, 320
Tribal Land Act 185, 187
tribalism 47, 117, 144, 238
tribes 1, 70, 72, 74
Tsatsi, Paul 11
Tshegofatso, Mma 16
Tsheko, Tsheko 20, 32, 45, 48, 50, 68, 75, 122, 127, 187, 230, 323
Tshipinare 130
Tsholetsa House 56, 128
Tshweu, Tshwene 27

INDEX

Tsodilo Hills 295
Tsoebebe, Archelaus 32, 45, 48, 50, 64, 110, 111, 131
Tswaipe 119-20
Tswana culture and customs 6, 31, 62, 63, 141
Tubman, William 112
Tuli Block 44, 119, 133, 184, 200, 246, 248, 250, 321, 322
Tunisia 162
Tutsi 304-7

UDI (Unilateral Declaration of Independence) 253, 274, 281, 287
Uganda 304, 305, 308, 311
UN, *see* United Nations
Unified Teaching Service 221
Union Agreements 246
unions 233-4
UNITA 119, 279, 293, 294, 299
United Nations 154, 262, 285, 289, 293, 297, 300-8, 311-2
    Security Council 301, 302, 303, 309, 313
United Nations High Commissioner for Refugees 267
United States/America/Americans/US 95, 119, 141, 209, 250, 267, 284, 300, 302
    assistance to Botswana 154-6, 162, 226, 252, 270, 281, 298-9
    role during Inter-Congolese Dialogue 310, 313, 314, 315
    role during Rwanda Genocide 304, 306-7
    role in Angola 293, 299
universities 76, 140, 229, 287
University of Basutoland, Bechuanaland and Swaziland (UBLS), *see also* University of Botswana 220, 224, 288
University of Botswana 120, 224-5, 229
urban land 192-4
USAID 156, 202

Van der Byl, Peter 281
Van Gass, Hendrik 44, 248-9
Van Heerden 271
Van Rensburg, Patrick 226, 227
Venda 260
Venson, Pelonomi 142
Verwoerd, HF 114, 248-9, 250, 260
veterinary restrictions 155
vice-presidents 84, 135, 143
    selecting 89-90
Vickerman, Hendry 133, 321
Vision 2016 144-5
Vize, Reg 322
Voice of America transmitter 299
Vorster, John 275
voting age 140

wages and salaries 39, 229-32
Wall, John Patrick 269
Wallace, Stationmaster 42-3

Wandi, Agricultural Officer 15
Wapoloko, Rre 16
water 173-4, 209, 216, 219, 264
Water Utilities Corporation 172, 173, 174, 175, 204, 212, 219
West, Geoff 159
Wharren, Mr 66, 216
White Paper, Local Government in the Bechuanaland Protectorate 64
Williams, Mike 98
Wina, Skota 288
Winstanley, Bridget 81
Winstanley, George 81
Winter, Philip 309
witchcraft 16, 120
World Bank 146, 153, 154, 172, 202, 264, 298
World Food Programme 79, 154
World War II 11, 28, 247

Xandum 285

Yates, Deane 228

Zaire, *see also* Democratic Republic of Congo 179, 278, 293, 298
Zambia 146, 206, 253, 268, 274, 277, 281, 286-8, 292
Zimbabwe, *formerly* Southern Rhodesia, *see also* UDI 194, 199, 253, 275, 278, 297
    liberation movements, *see* ZANU and ZAPU
    security/intelligence/defence issues under Ian Smith and UDI 114, 155, 156, 281, 291, 298
    refugees 281, 283
    racial attitudes in 47, 58, 62, 250
    relations with Zimbabwe after independence, *see also* Mugabe, Robert 232, 276, 279, 283-4
    trade with 178, 231, 287
    intervention in Congo 279-80, 308
    war in 47, 120, 274, 281-3, 292
Zimbabwe African National Union (ZANU) 89, 112, 282, 283, 292
Zimbabwe African People's Union (ZAPU) 89, 110, 112, 282, 283